Learning and memory
An introduction

Learning and memory
An introduction

JACK A. ADAMS

Professor of Psychology
University of Illinois
at Urbana-Champaign

 1976

THE DORSEY PRESS   *Homewood, Illinois   60430*
Irwin-Dorsey International   Arundel, Sussex   BN18 9AB
Irwin-Dorsey Limited   Georgetown, Ontario   L7G 4B3

First Printing, January 1976
Second Printing, July 1976

ISBN 0-256-01783-2
Library of Congress Catalog Card No. 75–22680
Printed in the United States of America

Preface

THIS BOOK was written for the college and university student primarily, although anyone who is fascinated with how we learn and remember should find it interesting. All of us are curious about the workings of learning and memory processes. There are various kinds of understanding about how such things work; and this book is about one kind of understanding—the scientific kind. Psychology is the science of behavior, and the study of learning and memory has been one of its concerns for a long time. In the beginning the concern consisted of introspective curiosities about one's own mind and informal observation of the behavior of men and animals as they learned and remembered. Later, when psychology became an organized scientific discipline, it took to the laboratory and set up systematic learning and memory situations for men and animals so that the determining factors for learning and memory processes could be isolated and known, and it is these data that are the focus of this book.

Part I of the book is about learning, and Part II is about memory. In Part I you will encounter learning by reward (positive reinforcement), classical conditioning, punishment and the learning of fear based on it, and verbal and motor learning. Our knowledge of learning has become so considerable that it now has many practical applications, and these have not been slighted. In prescientific times our knowledge about learning and memory was haphazard and application of the little knowledge that we had was correspondingly haphazard; but as our knowledge matured our applications of it became increasingly precise, and today we are using it to improve our lot in this life. In the realm of learning applications you will find accounts of behavior modification and behavior therapy that are used in the school and the clinic to regulate behavior that is inappropriate, programmed learning that has become a part of many instructional situations, and biofeedback which holds promise of becoming a therapeutic tool by controlling, through learning mechanisms, such biological functions as blood pressure.

Part II begins with a survey of man's search for understanding of human memory. It continues with accounts of how the various ways that we can learn verbal material affect recall, and this includes mnemonic devices, those aids which increase our powers of recollection. From ancient times man has known about mnemonic devices, but it is only in our time that their worth has been tested. Theories of why we forget are then presented. In the final chapter, we meet an interest in memory for sentences and prose. Much of psychology's research on human memory has been done with simple verbal units on the assumption that they are a better analytical device, but developments in linguistics and psycholinguistics, as well as practical thrusts, have turned some psychologists toward the study of language with sentences and prose as the units of analysis.

All of these laboratory findings and applications are interleaved with the theories that psychologists have developed about the processes that underlie them. Scientists cannot resist attempts to organize their findings conceptually. But with or without theory, the experiment reigns in experimental psychology, as it should, and this book is rooted firmly in experiments on the variables and processes of learning and memory. It is hoped that the reader will acquire an understanding of these variables and processes insofar as we know them, and will appreciate the methods which experimental psychologists use to reveal them.

The manuscript was given critical readings by Howard F. Hunt, Consulting Editor in Psychology for The Dorsey Press, James F. Juola of the University of Kansas, and Alexander Pollatsek of the University of Massachusetts. The editorial advice which these reviewers gave me improved the book, and I am grateful for it.

JACK A. ADAMS

Contents

part ONE | Learning

chapter 1

Introduction to learning

WHY BOTHER with the scientific study of learning when we seem to know so much about it already? From the beginning, humans have seen the benefits of learning for the transmission of cultural knowledge and the teaching of useful skills. That schools have existed for thousands of years is evidence of some understanding of the principles of learning and of our application of them, as is less formalized learning in the parent teaching skills to the child. Why bother with the scientific study of learning if societies have been accomplishing all of these complex kinds of learning for so long?

The answer is that folk wisdom cannot be discounted, but neither can it be canonized. Through trial and error people "luck onto" many relationships in their world that are useful and which are later elevated to principles when the phenomena come under the icy scrutiny of scientific investigators. That a primitive physician might rub dirt on a wound and prevent infection is understandable in terms of our modern knowledge about penicillin mold. The difference between the primitive physician and a modern physician lies in the identification of cause and effect and the added sophistication that it brings. The primitive physician probably believed that the dirt had curative powers in its own right or, more remotely, that a god of healing worked through the physician and the dirt to accomplish the cure. But those cures were fortuitous cures because the primitive physician did not really understand the responsible agent in the dirt and why it worked as it did, and so was as likely to use the dirt treatment for a headache. The modern physician knows the specific relationship between the penicillin mold and infection and knows when and when not to apply it. Through systematic observation, usually in laboratory experiments, scientists have determined the specific relationship between penicillin mold and infection, and have ruled out alternative explanations that were plausible in the beginning. Once having established a reliable relationship between penicillin mold and infection, the investigators can pursue related lines of investigation and can devise new strains of mold for even more effective cures. Except by accident, the primitive physician had no way of discovering a different kind of dirt with greater healing power.

The same is true of the common sense knowledge of learning that people have distilled from centuries of everyday experiences. People learn—but it is never clear why the teaching operations that are performed achieve the behavioral results that they do. One teacher might assume that reading while standing is important for a young child first learning to read because she has always had her students read while standing and they have always learned to read. But the more fundamental operation in the situation is practice repetitions of the reading material, with standing irrelevant. By knowing through research that practice is a fundamental variable for reading, and standing an indifferent variable, more systematic and effective training can be accomplished and lines of research can be suggested to make even more effective uses of practice.

But suppose prescientific people did not misidentify the variables in a cause and effect relationship as our primitive physician did. They are then in a position to have a measure of control over aspects of their world, but only a small measure. Power is limited without the more comprehensive knowledge that systematic science can bring. Someone may have learned enough mechanics to build a footbridge, but lack the technical power to build the Golden Gate Bridge. Similarly, in the field of learning, we have known for thousands of years that a wide variety of animals can be taught various behavioral acts with food as reward. Granting that the lay person has some understanding of rewards and their power to effect behavior, that knowledge is crude and probably no greater than the primitive person's knowledge of physics when building the footbridge. The science of physics can lead to the Golden Gate Bridge, and so can the pursuit of rewards and their mechanisms by psychologists lead to detailed knowledge and scientific power in the control of behavior. Today, our knowledge of rewards and how they work is being used routinely in regulating behavior in the home, the classroom, and the clinic. It takes the institutionalized agencies of science, doggedly pursuing knowledge century after century, to eventually give us an impressive power to control our world.

THE NATURE OF SCIENTIFIC LAWS

The fundamental goal of a science is the uncovering of scientific laws for its subject matter and, for the psychology of learning as an arm of the science of psychology, the goal is finding the laws that relate the behavior we call learned to the events that determine it. A field becomes worthy of the name "science" to the extent that it has its phenomena described by scientific laws.

What is a scientific law? A *scientific law* is a generalization about characteristics of events that we observe. A scientific law has an event which is predicted, called the *dependent variable,* and one or more events which do the predicting, called *independent variables.* Any reliable relationship between dependent and independent variables can be a scientific law. The law can be qualitative, of a simple "if–then" form, such as: If a response is rewarded then it will be learned. Or the law can be quantitative: The probability of a response occurring is an exponential function of the number of rewarded trials.

What does a scientific law do for us, apart from giving a careful statement of a relationship in the world? There are two consequences of a scientific law, and they usually go together: *prediction* and *control.* All scientific laws allow prediction. The position of the moon tomorrow can be predicted from the position of the moon today, and a dog will perform the trick of rolling over more reliably after it has been rewarded for it 20 times than twice. Most scientific laws allow control, in addition to prediction, because manipulation of the independent variables determines what happens to the dependent variable and so puts us in control of the dependent variable. In this sense of control, the position of the moon cannot be controlled, although the behavior of a dog can be controlled by rewarding it or not. We like to have the sciences arm us with power to control the physical world, although we are less sure about psychology and the control of human behavior. Humans have a strong subjective sense of free will, and find it morally repugnant that someone can control them. Yet a moment's reflection should dispel the distaste because our behavior is being manipulated in countless ways, all the time. Any parent, for example, is a massive controller of her or his child's behavior even though it is cloaked in such euphemisms as love, concern, and parental responsibility.

An important property of scientific laws is that they be as general as possible. If the law of gravity was specific it might predict only the fall of 10-lb. bodies, and it would be a good law within its narrow domain. But the law of gravity which physics has found for us is a general law for all objects of our world. This single expression gives us enormous power in predicting and controlling the trajectories of bodies, and it is a great scientific achievement.

What do specific and general laws look like in psychology? Most of our laws in psychology are rather specific, which is typical of a young science. We find the correlation between reading performance and a test of vocabulary, or the relationship between the rate of learning a list of words and length of the list; laws such as these are low-order.

They can be good laws but their domain of operation is narrow, like predicting the fall of 10-pound objects. In time we will integrate these specific laws into more masterful relationships, but now we have little of it. Integration has been tried, however, and the psychology of learning has been one of the arenas where attempts have been made.

From the turn of the century until about 1950 there was a strong urge to put the specific laws of learning together into a comprehensive principle of learning. It failed, but not for want of effort. Prominent learning scientists like E. L. Thorndike, C. L. Hull, and E. R. Guthrie each expressed a general law of learning which they believed would explain all animal and human learning. All of these people made admirable attempts, with the loftiest of scientific goals in mind, but they traveled a rocky road, and none of their laws have acceptance today. No one today is attempting a general law on learning; time has given us a feeling of caution that those who went before us lacked. Now, when we consider what we know about the different types of learning for a wide variety of response classes, we are awed by the prospect of a general law that can embrace them all. Indeed, the prospect may be illusory. Psychology may not be able to follow the model of the physical sciences with their general laws.

Is the finding of laws the end of scientific activity in psychology? Certainly it is a major goal, but it is not the end. Beyond laws is theory, where we specify a few abstract principles that organize the laws and transcend them. Theory will often contain hypothetical, unobservable states. Atoms and electrons are examples from physics, and they have been eminently useful theoretical constructions. In the psychology of learning such unobservables as "habit" and "image" have been used in theoretical attempts.

HOW WE DEFINE AND STUDY LEARNING

That we have no general law of learning means that we have a number of specific laws. If learning has so many different manifestations, how do we define and study it?

The different laws of learning, which we will encounter in the chapters that follow, all represent different definitions of learning. What is it they have in common that causes us to call them all the laws of learning? The answer is that they all deal with a relatively enduring change in behavior. *Learning* is a relatively stable tendency to react, and the storage and retrieval of this persistent internal state is the topic of *memory*. Learning and memory are two sides of the same behavioral coin. Learning is acquisition of the persistent disposition, and memory is its fate over time and its activation when recollection takes place.

One would think that learning would be difficult to study because it is rather generally defined as a stable tendency to react, and yet it is meaningfully studied in many experiments each year. Here is how to collect data on learning, and it is not as difficult as it might seem:

1. Define a response that can be reliably observed. This is the dependent variable.
2. Define one or more operations that you can reliably manipulate and believe to be learning operations. These are the independent variables.
3. Create learning opportunities where the response is performed under the conditions defined by the independent variables.
4. Observe changes in the response.
5. Rule out changes in the response as a function of nonlearning states like motivation and fatigue.
6. If the response shows improvement over the training series and some persistence with time is observed, then learning has occurred.

Following these six steps gives learning data, and starts you down the road to law-finding. Consider how we would teach a dog to lift its paw and use the situation to observe learning. First we would objectively define lifting of the paw, and reliably distinguish it from any other movements of the foot that might occur. Next, we would choose an independent variable that would induce learning—e.g., a food reward every time the dog lifted its paw. A series of learning trials would then be administered, where the dog is given a piece of food every time it raises its paw, and the occurrence or nonoccurrence of paw-lifting is recorded on each trial. On the first block of ten trials only one instance of paw-lifting behavior may be observed, but nine instances might well be observed on the last ten trials. This change in behavior would be identified as learning, and reasonably so.

Not all performance is as revealing of learning as this example, and it has caused psychologists to distinguish between *learning* and *performance*. The problem is that nonlearning states can enter to cloud the learning that is present (this is point 5 in the six points listed above). Motivation is frequently one of the variables that obscures learning. Consider the student who knows the material very well (learning) but is lacking in academic motivation and flunks out (performance). An animal may not give a learned response if it is fully satiated after a meal because its hunger motivation is gone and there is no interest in a food reward. Fatigue is a nonlearning state that can operate to obscure learning also. A skilled athlete who is too tired cannot reveal the high skill learned. The point is that we cannot always accept observed performance as an undistorted mirror of learning. We must be sensitive to nonlearning processes when we study learning, and, as necessary, control them.

SUMMARY

Our concern with science had its beginning in the knowledge and skill that were important for accomplishing the tasks of everyday life. As science became formalized and institutionalized, its concerns became systematic as it sought the laws of natural phenomena. A scientific law is a generalization about observable events, is a relationship between events called independent and dependent variables, and gives the power of prediction and usually the power of control over the dependent variable.

A law of learning is a relationship between measures of behavior that are the dependent variables, and determinants of the measures, called independent variables. A law of learning must have nonlearning effects eliminated, and when this is done the law of learning will reflect a relatively stable tendency to react under the conditions specified by the law. Learning operations produce a state that has some persistence over time, and the persistent state is called memory. Thus, learning and memory are closely related.

chapter 2

Instrumental learning and positive reinforcement

THIS CHAPTER is about reinforcement, one of the most powerful determiners of behavior that psychologists know. We have always known that behavior can be changed by rewarding some responses and not others, and have used this knowledge in ways we saw as advantageous. Hard work earns more pay than idleness, the boy who does his chores receives his weekly allowance, otherwise not, and the college student hitchhiking home has a long wait rewarded with a ride direct to her home town and learns that patience has a payoff. By experimentally studying reinforcement, psychologists have extended our knowledge about it and have increased the range of situations where it can be applied. In recent years reinforcement has been used for changing the aggressive behavior of delinquent boys in a reformatory and the sloppy eating behavior of patients in a mental hospital.

Psychologists prefer the term "reinforcement" to "reward," although some use the two terms interchangeably, and they distinguish between positive and negative reinforcement. *Positive reinforcement is any event that follows a response and increases the performance level of the response;* It is a reward sought by the subject. *Negative reinforcement* increases performance also, but as a consequence of its removal, not its application. A child will learn to withdraw a hand when burned on a hot stove, but could also learn to avoid the hot stove for candy (positive reinforcement). This chapter is about positive reinforcement. Chapter 5 will discuss negative reinforcement.

DEFINITIONS, DISTINCTIONS, AND PROCEDURES

Reinforced learning comes under the classification of *instrumental learning.* The subject is an active agent in instrumental learning because

9

the subject's response is instrumental in producing the reinforcement. Reinforced learning can have a stimulus which becomes the cue for occurrence of the response. An example is saying "Roll over" to your dog, and every time that it obeys you reward it with meat. Soon it will roll over reliably to your command. Or reinforced learning can occur without a specific stimulus. In this latter case you give your dog a piece of meat every time that it rolls over, and here also it will roll over regularly although you will not have it under the control of a command. Skinner (1938) called the instrumentally learned response without a specific stimulus an *operant,* and its instrumental learning is often called *operant learning.* When the response is with an identifiable stimulus, called the *discriminative stimulus,* it is called a *discriminated operant.* The command "Roll over" is the discriminative stimulus for the discriminated operant that you teach your dog.

The five essentials of reinforced learning

Here is what it takes to demonstrate learning through positive reinforcement:

1. A defined response class. Behavior is complex, continuous, and multidimensional, and out of it all we must choose the response class that we want to have learned and which we will reinforce. The response class chosen does not matter just as long as it can be objectively and reliably observed. The response can be big, like rewarding a speech, or it can be small, like rewarding the lift of a finger. And we can reward a response of any precision. A dog can be rewarded for rolling over in a precise way, like rolling to the left in 1.5 seconds, or we can ignore the precision of the roll just so long as the dog rolls over.

2. Reinforcement. Like response class, the definition of reinforcement is generous providing it meets certain criteria. Most fundamental is that the reinforcer must be an event whose occurrence increases the level of the defined response. Reinforcement can be a piece of food to the dog when it rolls over, or it can be a pat on the dog's head. Anything is accepted as a reinforcer if it works by increasing the level of the designated response.

3. Motivation. A response has to occur before it can be reinforced, and this means an organism motivated enough to behave. Laboratory animals customarily are made hungry or thirsty before they are put in a learning situation for food or water reward.

4. The reinforcement must be correlated with occurrence of the response class. The response and the reinforcement do not always have to occur together, although often they do. More important is that the relationship between response and reinforcement be reliable and predictable in some sense. The reinforcement can occur after every response, every 10th response, or after responding has been in progress for 30 seconds, but whatever the relationship it must be a predictable one.

   5. The reinforcement must follow the response.   There is little evidence that learning can occur when the reinforcement precedes the response.

Performance measures and laboratory tasks

   The heart of reinforced learning is that the level of the response is at an indifferent level before reinforcement, and with reinforcement the performance level increases. Psychologists mostly use standard measures and laboratory tasks for the systematic manipulation of reinforcement variables so that the transition from the indifferent state to the learned state can be charted and controlled.

   The frequency of response measure.   Frequency of response is a fundamental measure for instrumental learning. Before learning the response occurs infrequently, and after the learning process has begun the number of responses increases.

FIGURE 2–1
The T-maze—a device which often has been used in research on animal learning. The animal is rewarded when it chooses the correct goal box.

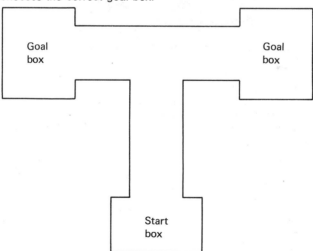

   Figure 2–1 shows a simple kind of apparatus where response frequency is the measure. It is a T-maze, and it is a choice discrimination task. The early history of maze learning is filled with various kinds of complex mazes with many turns and blinds, but the complexity of these mazes made the control of relevant variables difficult. By the 1940s

psychologists were turning to the T-maze as a simple choice learning situation better suited to their experimental purposes. Rats are usually the experimental subjects in T-mazes, and the task might be learning to turn left on each trial. Every time the animal turns left it is rewarded in the goal box at the end of the run, otherwise not, and soon it is turning left on more and more of the trials until eventually it does it 100 percent of the time.

FIGURE 2–2
A bar-press apparatus, often called the *Skinner box,* that is commonly used in research on animal learning. Pressing of the bar produces a reward.

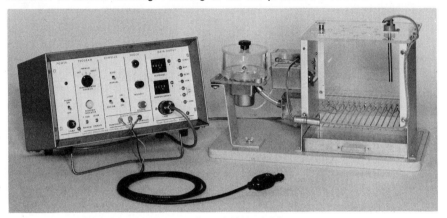

Source: Ralph Gerbrands Company, Inc., Arlington, Mass.

FIGURE 2–3
Learning often produces an increase in the number of responses. The curve of learning can be plotted in terms of the number of responses made per unit of time.

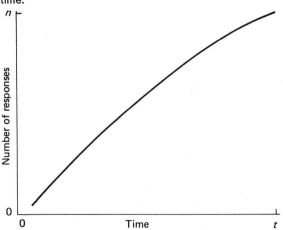

The most common device to produce the frequency of response measure is the "Skinner box," named after B. F. Skinner who invented it, where an animal subject learns to press a bar or a key for food or water reward. Usually the animal is a rat or a pigeon. Figure 2–2 has a picture of the Skinner box. The Skinner box is often used in the study of operant learning. The response occurs at the discretion of the animal, so the number of responses per unit of time, or the rate of response, is a primary index of learning. The frequency of responses that occurs per unit of time can be plotted, and this is shown in Figure 2–3, but it is also common to cumulate response frequencies over time. The latter produces a cumulative frequency curve (Figure 2–4), and

FIGURE 2–4

A cumulative frequency curve, derived from the data shown in Figure 2–3. The number of responses for successive units of time in Figure 2–3 are added to produce the function shown here. The more responses per unit of time the steeper the slope of a cumulative frequency curve.

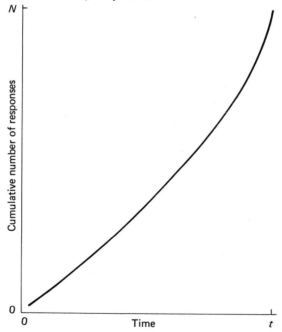

the rate of responding is revealed in the slope of the curve (steep slope-fast responding). Standard recording apparatus to produce a cumulative curve is commercially available for connecting to Skinner boxes. Other apparatus that is attached to Skinner boxes is called programming apparatus, and it is used mainly to control the delivery of reinforcement. The experimenter may want reinforcement of every response, every other response, or the first response that occurs after each 30-second interval. Programming and recording equipment for Skinner boxes has become quite sophisticated. Some laboratories have fully automated arrays of Skinner boxes.

The latency of response measure.   Latency, or the time to make a response, is another measure that is used, and a "straight runway," or "straight alley," which is shown in Figure 2–5, is a learning apparatus

FIGURE 2–5
A device that is commonly used in research on animal learning, called the *straight runway.* The animal is rewarded for running from the start box to the goal box, and the time to make the run is recorded.

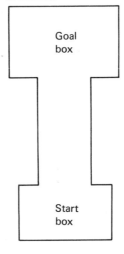

where latency is the measure of performance. The animal is put in one end and has the assignment of running to the other end for reinforcement, and the duration of the act is the measure. Slowness of response can be deliberately rewarded and trained, but in many skills an increase in learning and an increase in speed of responding go together. The straight runway is such a situation. Figure 2–6 shows a learning curve

FIGURE 2–6

A learning curve in terms of the time to make the responses, or response latency, as it is usually called.

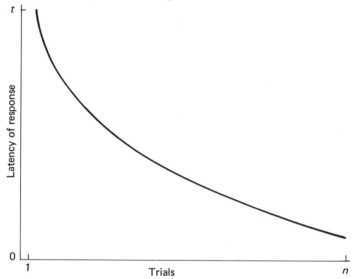

in terms of latency. Sometimes investigators will plot the reciprocal of latency, which is called speed. A speed curve increases with learning, and this is intuitively appealing to some, although it contains no more information than the latency curve.

SCHEDULES OF REINFORCEMENT

For a long time psychologists studied continuous reinforcement, where every response of the specified kind was reinforced. Why continuous reinforcement was codified in the procedures of learning is a mystery. Perhaps an unverbalized reason was that the study of learning required the development of a learned response, and continuous reinforcement was a reliable way of doing it. Maybe another reason was that the withdrawal of reinforcement is the defining operations of extinction and the lowering of responsiveness (to be discussed later in this chapter), and so an investigator might have reasoned that intermittent reinforcement with its occasionally reinforced responses is, in part, the condition of extinction. Why should we risk weakening a response when learning is the study of its strengthening? Whatever the reasons, they were not enough to constrain B. F. Skinner who challenged this orthodoxy in the 1930s. Skinner (1956), in discussing his curiosities as a young scientist, questioned the conventional wisdom of continuous reinforcement and tried reinforcing only some of a rat's responses. Instead of the response becoming intermittent like the reinforcement, it carried on at a steady rate. Since then, Skinner and his followers have been forerunners in research on reinforcement, and have investigated many kinds of programs, or schedules, of delivery for reinforcement. Today continuous reinforcement is considered only a special case, of minor interest in its own right.

The reasons for studying intermittent reinforcement have become compelling since the 1930s. Research has demonstrated that schedules of reinforcement are powerful determiners of behavior. No less important is that behavior in our everyday world is seldom reinforced continuously. The reward of publication comes to a striving young writer only for some articles, and a child in the classroom has only some efforts praised by the teacher. Our understanding of such behavior depends on understanding the effects of intermittent reinforcement.

The four basic schedules

The two main kinds of schedules are the *ratio schedule* and the *interval schedule*. The *fixed schedule* and the *variable schedule* are principal subtypes of the two main ones. A ratio schedule has reinforcement delivered after a fixed number of responses, which means that a fixed number of nonreinforced responses can occur before the reinforcement. Time is an irrelevant variable for a ratio schedule; number of responses is the factor that determines the delivery of reinforcement. An interval schedule requires that a given amount of time go by before a response is reinforced, and number of responses is irrelevant. Whether a schedule is fixed or variable depends upon the constancy of the ratio or the time factor.

First, let us consider each of the four basic schedules and its effect on response acquisition, or the original learning of the response, and on response maintenance.

The fixed-ratio schedule. When a specified number of responses must occur before a reinforcement is delivered, and this number is a constant throughout learning, we have a fixed-ratio or *FR* schedule. If the subject is reinforced after every 50th response the schedule is designated *FR* 50. The schedule *FR* 1 is reinforcement after every response, which is continuous reinforcement, and it is a special case of the fixed-ratio schedule. In cases of infrequent reinforcement it is necessary to start the subject on a low ratio and gradually increase it until performance under the high ratio is attained.

Figure 2–7 shows the four basic schedules plotted in terms of cumulative frequency of response, so the steeper the slope of the curve the faster the response. These curves are for the steady state responding after the initial acquisition period has passed. The hash marks on the

FIGURE 2–7
The four basic schedules of reinforcement.

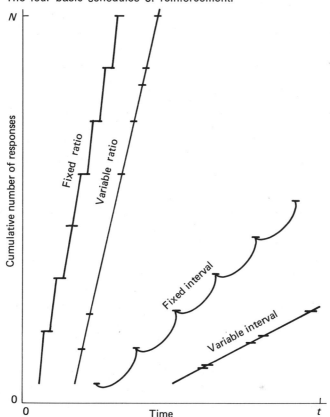

curves are points of reinforcement. Characteristically, as shown, the fixed-ratio schedule produces a high rate of responding. Pigeons may peck hundreds of times per minute for grain reinforcement under a fixed-ratio schedule, and intuitively one can understand the high rate because the faster the subject responds the more reward it gets.

The world is full of examples of reinforcement under fixed-ratio schedules. A frequently cited example is the piece-rate system in a factory, where the production of n units produces a payment. Historically, trade unions have opposed the piece-rate system because it extracts high production levels from workers to the point, it is contended, of being inhumane. Management undoubtedly is less discontented with the high production than are the unions.

The variable-ratio schedule. As the name implies, reinforcement comes after a variable number of responses rather than after a fixed number, as in the fixed-ratio schedule. This does not mean that the reinforcement is random but rather that it has a statistical definition and occurs after a specified number of responses *on the average.* Consider a variable-ratio schedule of 50, which is called *VR* 50. Reinforcement may be after 2 responses or 200, but over a long series of responses the subject will be rewarded for every 50 responses on the average. Figure 2–7 shows that the response rate for the variable-ratio schedule is high.

The best example of the variable-ratio schedule is gambling with a slot machine. A slot machine will average a certain level of payoff, with the occurrence of payoff unsystematic and variable. You can win 3 plays in a row, or lose 50 in a row. Some psychologists would say that the gambler has a need for gambling which is being satisfied by frequent playing, but learning psychologists are more inclined to say that a high response rate is being sustained by a variable-ratio schedule.

The fixed-interval schedule.   A fixed-interval schedule is periodic. The first response that occurs after the specified period of time has passed is reinforced. A subject might be reinforced after every two minutes (*FI* 2) or every five minutes (*FI* 5). No matter how few or how many responses made within the interval, reinforcement is not forthcoming until the time interval has passed.

Figure 2–7 shows the performance function for the fixed-interval schedule, and it is characterized by a moderate rate of responding and a distinct scallop effect. The moderate rate is intuitively understandable because a high response rate has no payoff in reinforcement. Only responses at specified points in time have payoff. Subjects could perform perfectly under a fixed-interval schedule if they were perfect time-keepers and had within them physiological clocks that would tick off the exact interval between reinforcements. A subject would need to respond only at the times designated by the inner clock. The curve for the fixed-interval schedule in Figure 2–7 does suggest that some kind of rudimentary timekeeping is going on. After reinforcement, the response rate drops off because the subject knows that some time must pass before reinforcement is available again. As the interval continues the subject seems to develop a feeling that the time of reinforcement is approaching because the response rate picks up and guarantees a reinforcement shortly after it becomes available.

An example of a fixed-interval schedule is feeding a child at regular times, ignoring pleas for food between meals. No matter how much the child might cry for food, feeding would occur only when he or she cries the first time after feeding time arrives. Crying would increase as the time of feeding approaches, and decrease after feeding, as the scallop effect in Figure 2–7 implies.

The variable-interval schedule.   A variable-interval schedule is aperiodic. Responses are reinforced after varying time intervals, whose length averages out to the time value that defines the schedule. The subject might, for example, be rewarded for the first response after Minute 1, Minute 3, Minute 6, Minute 11, etc., with a reinforcement occurring every 5 minutes on the average (*VI 5*). As with the fixed-interval schedule, the number of responses within the interval is irrelevant; only the first response after the interval receives the reinforcement. Figure 2–7 shows that the variable-interval schedule has the lowest rate of all the four schedules, and the performance curve is smooth. As with the fixed-interval schedule the subject gets nothing for high rates of responding, so response rate tends to be low.

An example of a variable-interval schedule is fishing. On the average you catch a fish every hour, but you could catch two of them in a five-minute period and then have a three-hour wait for the next one.

Superstitious behavior

Schedules of reinforcement are various kinds of intermittent reinforcement, and they can explain different kinds of everyday behavior, as we have seen. A major kind of everyday behavior which intermittent reinforcement can explain, and which has not been discussed, is superstitious behavior.

Why does the dice player blow on the dice each time before throwing? Why does the football coach wear a "lucky hat" to the game? According to a learning interpretation these "meaningless" pieces of behavior first occurred in accidental association with reinforcement (winning the roll of the dice, winning the football game), and this increased their probability of occurrence in the future. The superstitious act may not have been rewarded regularly, but reward occurred often enough to insure the act's frequent occurrence. Skinner (1948) was the first to demonstrate the learning of superstitious behavior. He found that pigeons who received a pellet of food irrespective of their behavior came to perform bizarre acts, like turning around two or three times in a ritualistic dance, or repeatedly pecking the upper corner of the cage. These eccentric elements of behavior accidentally came to be paired with reinforcements from time to time, and eventually they occurred with some regularity. The reason for superstitious acts being strange is that they are uncontrolled and accidental at the time of reinforcement, and so they have a bizarre character. We think there is nothing eccentric about kinds of behavior that we deliberately choose for learning. Thus, we choose key pecking as the response which we reinforce for a pigeon, and we think it a perfectly normal unit of behavior, but when we play no role in the choosing we see the behavior as bizarre. Normal or eccentric, the behavior is covered by the same laws of reinforcement.

STIMULUS GENERALIZATION

Not all reinforced responses are correlated with a discriminative stimulus, but often they are, and when this happens it is said that the response is under *stimulus control*. This section is about *stimulus generalization,* which is an aspect of the topic of stimulus control.

The interest in stimulus generalization derives from the fact that stimulus control is imperfect—a subject will respond to values of the stimulus other than those used in training. Your dog will approach you whether your whistle is loud or soft even though all of its training was with a loud whistle. Some have seen stimulus generalization as biologically adaptive, and Ivan Pavlov, the great Russian physiologist, was among them (Pavlov, 1927, p. 113). Our behavior would be hopelessly ineffective if we responded only to stimulus values that were present in learning. A jungle animal would not survive very long if its defensive reactions were not sensitive to some variation of cues that signified a threat.

Laboratory procedures for studying stimulus generalization

The laboratory method for the study of stimulus generalization is to reinforce a response in the presence of a stimulus, called the training stimulus, and then shift to a different stimulus that has never been reinforced before and test without reinforcement for level of responding. A well-known experiment by Guttman and Kalish (1956) illustrates the standard method. Pigeons in a Skinner box learned to peck a key whose color as the training stimulus was either a wave length of 530, 550, 580, or 600 millimicrons. (To the human eye, but not necessarily the pigeon eye, these wave lengths represent, approximately, green, yellow-green, yellow-orange, and orange.) At the generalization test the same color or a different one was presented, and the pecking rate determined. Figure 2–8 has the findings, and curves like these are called *generalization gradients.* Notice that the best performance on the test is the training stimulus, that responses occur for a range of stimuli around the training stimulus, and that performance falls off rapidly when the color of the stimulus is changed.

Generalization gradients and discrimination training

The steepness of the slope of the generalization gradient is the degree to which a stimulus has the response under control. Very steep slopes indicate that the stimulus controls the response quite explicitly, and gradual slopes imply sloppy control where a considerable range of stimulus values will elicit the response. The slope of the generalization gradient is not a naturally endowed property of the sensory system, although

FIGURE 2–8

Generalization gradients for four training stimuli.

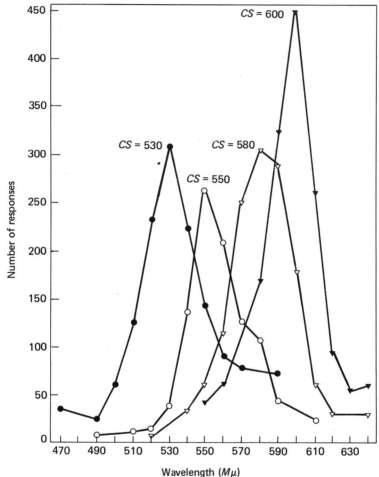

Guttman, N., & Kalish, H. I. Discriminability and stimulus generalization. *Journal of Experimental Psychology,* 1956, *51,* 79–88. Reprinted by permission of the American Psychological Association.

there might be an element of this, but rather it is capable of being shaped by the training methods that are used to place the response under control in the first place. Discrimination training is a good way to control the slope of the generalization gradient.

In discrimination training, the training stimulus is reinforced according to a prescribed schedule, and one or more other stimuli that are similar to the training stimulus are presented also but never reinforced. In nondiscriminative training, the training stimulus is always present throughout responding whether reinforcement is occurring or not, and other similar stimuli are never presented (except at the generalization test). An experiment by Jenkins and Harrison (1960) illustrates the effect of type of training on the generalization gradient. They compared discriminative and nondiscriminative training. A tone was used as the stimulus, and pigeons were the subjects. Key pecking was the response. In nondiscriminative training the birds were reinforced in the presence of a continuously sounding 1,000-cycle per second tone. In discriminative training, the tone sometimes sounded and sometimes not, and only responses in the presence of the tone were reinforced. The test for generalization evaluated response level where the stimuli were no tone, 300, 450, 670, 1,500, 2,250, 2,500, and 1,000 cycles per second. The results for nondiscriminative training are shown in Figure 2–9, and the tone

FIGURE 2–9

The generalization gradients of three pigeons who had nondiscriminative training.

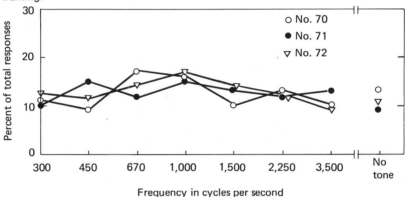

Jenkins, H. M., & Harrison, R. H. Effect of discrimination training on auditory generalization. *Journal of Experimental Psychology,* 1960, *59,* 246–253. Reprinted by permission of the American Psychological Association.

acquired no stimulus control over the response—the gradient is completely flat. But discriminative training was quite different, as Figure 2–10 shows. The 1,000-cycle tone had strong control over the response, with much reduced responding to adjacent stimulus values.

How is it that discrimination training increases stimulus control? It was once thought that guaranteeing the sensory reception of a stimulus during learning would guarantee that the response would become associated with it, but today this belief is hardly held at all. In recent years the old topic of attention has been awakened (e.g., Mostofsky, 1970), and now we are trying to better understand how some stimuli, or dimensions of stimuli, out of the massive stimulus complex that impinges on

FIGURE 2–10

The generalization gradients of five pigeons who had discriminative training.

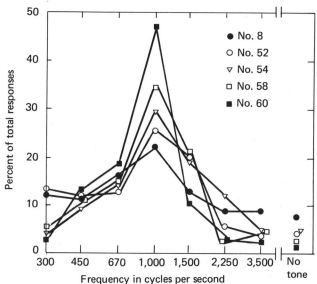

Jenkins, H. M., & Harrison, R. H. Effect of discrimination training on auditory generalization. *Journal of Experimental Psychology*, 1960, *59*, 246–253. Reprinted by permission of the American Psychological Association.

a subject during learning, are selected for association with a response. In the context of attention, a flat generalization gradient and the lack of stimulus control it represents, can be seen as a failure of attention to the training stimulus during learning. Discrimination training, on the other hand, creates good stimulus control because it forces attention.

EXTINCTION

So far in this chapter we have been discussing positive reinforcement and how its occurrence increases the probability of a response. No discussion of positive reinforcement would be complete, however, without examining the effects of withdrawing reinforcement after the response has been learned. This is the topic of *extinction*. Here is the definition of extinction when the response has been put into the system by positive reinforcement: *Extinction is reduction in the performance level of a response by the withdrawal of reinforcement.*

Figure 2–11 shows extinction data from a rat in a Skinner box, reported by Skinner (1938). Food reinforcement was withdrawn and the part of the cumulative response curve before the intersecting line is the classic

FIGURE 2–11
A cumulative response curve which shows extinction, a 48-hour rest at the point
of the intersecting line, and spontaneous recovery.

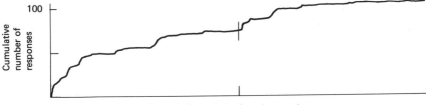

Skinner, B. F. *The Behavior of Organisms.* Englewood Cliffs, N.J.: Prentice-Hall, 1965.
Adapted by permission of Prentice-Hall, Inc.

extinction effect, where the animal's responsiveness steadily declines until
it stops responding altogether. The intersecting line is a 48-hour rest
period where the animal was returned to the home cage and, upon
return to the experimental task, another established effect for extinction
appears—*spontaneous recovery,* or the regaining of some responsiveness
with time after extinction. At the end of the first session the animal
had ceased responding and was extinguished, but on return to the box
it temporarily had a rapid rate of responding and then eventually
stopped responding again. Ellson (1938) showed that spontaneous recovery is a gradually increasing function of time, rising to a maximum
of about 50 percent of the strength that was held before the rest interval.

Number of reinforcements and resistance to extinction

The more times that the response is reinforced the higher the probability of the response, and some have thought of this effect in terms of
the response getting stronger and stronger as reinforcements are gained.
And, the stronger the response the more resistance to extinction it will
have and the longer the response will persist in the absence of reinforcement. This reasonable expectation is borne out in fact because the more
reinforcements that a response has been given the longer it takes to
extinguish it.

A study by Williams (1938) demonstrated the positive relationship
between number of reinforcements in acquisition and resistance to extinction. He used rats and a Skinner box with bar press as the response.
Different groups of animals received either 5, 10, 30, or 90 continuous
food reinforcements in the acquisition trials. An extinction session followed, and the animal was considered extinguished when it went five
minutes without pressing the bar. In a situation like this a criterion
of extinction must be specified because it is never clear when the animal
has lost all potentiality for responding. The time between responses

gets longer and longer in extinction, and a time duration without a response, usually a rather long time, is specified as reasonable evidence of response potentiality being absent, or nearly so. Figure 2–12 has Williams's findings, and it shows that the greater the response strength,

FIGURE 2–12

The number of responses in extinction as a function of number of reinforcements in acquisition.

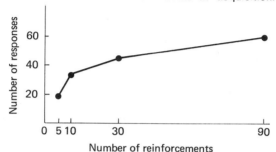

Williams, S. B. Resistance to extinction as a function of the number of reinforcements. *Journal of Experimental Psychology,* 1938, *23,* 506–522. Reprinted by permission of the American Psychological Association.

as defined by the number of reinforcements, the greater the resistance to extinction. Williams's findings are considered reliable because they have been obtained by others (Perin, 1942; Harris and Nygaard, 1961; Dyal and Holland, 1963).

Williams used continuous reinforcement, and there is the same outcome when intermittent reinforcement is used. Wilson (1954) gave rats training in the conventional bar-pressing task, and different groups of animals received either 15, 50, 85, 120, 240, and 500 food reinforcements under a 2-minute fixed interval schedule. After training, five daily extinction sessions were given. The results are shown in Figure 2–13. Williams's data in Figure 2–12 are for one extinction session. Notice that they correspond in general with the Day 1 findings of Wilson in Figure 2–13. When Wilson's extinction data are pooled over five days they show a strong and linear relationship between resistance to extinction and number of reinforcements.

Schedules of reinforcement and extinction

In the late 1930s Humphreys (1939a, 1939b) discovered that extinction rate was retarded when reinforcement during acquisition was intermittent, and since then this phenomenon has been repeatedly verified and explored. The issue can be posed this way: With number of rein-

FIGURE 2–13
The number of responses in one or five daily extinction sessions as a function of number of reinforcements in acquisition.

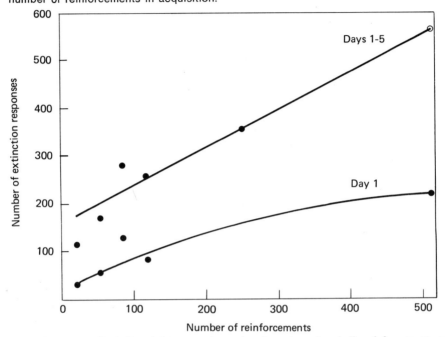

Wilson, M. P. Periodic reinforcement interval and number of periodic reinforcements as parameters of response strength. *Journal of Comparative and Physiological Psychology,* 1954, *47,* 51–56. Reprinted by permission of the American Psychological Association.

forcements in training held constant, what is the effect of schedules of reinforcement on extinction? Mowrer and Jones (1945) showed that with number of reinforcements in training held constant the less frequently the responses were rewarded the greater their resistance to extinction. Boren (1961) repeated and extended the earlier work of Mowrer and Jones, again using rats and bar pressing. All animals received 560 food reinforcements, and different groups of them had fixed-ratio training schedules from continuous reinforcement to 20:1 (1 reinforcement for every 20 responses). The extinction results are shown in Figure 2–14. The less frequently a response is reinforced the harder it is to extinguish.

Theories of partial reinforcement effects on extinction

The effects of partial reinforcement on extinction have been theoretically stimulating for the psychology of learning. When Humphreys first brought the effects to our attention in the 1930s the psychology of learn-

FIGURE 2–14

The number of responses in extinction as a function of several values for the fixed-ratio schedule of reinforcement in acquisition.

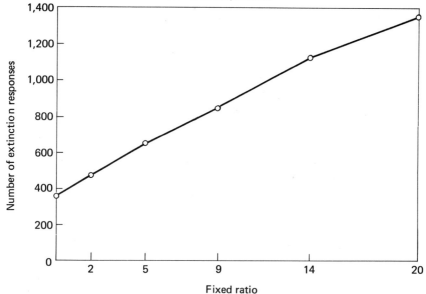

Boren, J. J. Resistance to extinction as a function of the fixed ratio. *Journal of Experimental Psychology*, 1961, *61*, 304–308. Reprinted by permission of the American Psychological Association.

ing was firmly entrenched in the concept of habit, with habit strength positively related to number of reinforcements. One of the measures of habit strength commonly used was resistance to extinction, with the rationale that stronger responses required more extinction trials to eliminate than weaker ones. The studies by Williams (1938) and Wilson (1954) that were just discussed are consistent with such thinking. The relationship between habit strength and extinction was a deeply entrenched idea when Humphreys (1939a) assailed it with data which showed that half the number of reinforcements presented intermittently produced greater resistance to extinction than 100 percent, continuous reinforcement. This finding created difficulty for the prevailing view of habit strength because, somehow, fewer reinforcements were producing greater resistance to extinction. There might have been a shortage of theoretical explanations for partial reinforcement and extinction in the beginning, but time has taken care of that problem. Today we have several theories of partial reinforcement and how it affects extinction.

The expectancy hypothesis. Humphreys (1939a, 1939b) not only opened this topic with his data but also with the *expectancy hypothesis* that he offered in explanation of his data. Rather than have reinforce-

ment related to habit strength, and nonreinforcement in extinction offsetting that strength, Humphreys held that a learned response occurred
because the subject developed an expectancy of reinforcement, and that
it extinguished because the expectancy had faded. Intermittent reinforcement is a condition of uncertainty about reinforcement. When the
extinction trials begin, and all of the trials are nonreinforced, the subject
cannot tell the nonreinforced extinction trials from the intermittent
sequences of nonreinforced trials that it had been receiving during the
learning trials, and so it expects reinforcement to occur soon and it
maintains its responding. As the extinction trials go on and on, and
no reinforcement is forthcoming, the expectancy of reinforcement dis-
solves and responding finally stops.

The discrimination hypothesis.   Mowrer and Jones (1945) conducted
one of the early studies of intermittent reinforcement and extinction,
and they offered the *discrimination hypothesis*. Mowrer and Jones used
a Skinner box with food reinforcement for their rat subjects, and they
hypothesized that pressing the bar and turning to the trough and eating
food establishes distinctive patterns of stimulation. In extinction, after
100 percent reinforcement, there is no more eating of food, the patterns
of stimulation change, the animal discriminates the change, and soon
stops its bar pressing as a result. When reinforcement is intermittent,
the stimulus patterns in acquisition are ambiguous because the bar press
is sometimes followed by eating responses and sometimes not, and so
noneating trials are similar to extinction trials. The animal has trouble
distinguishing acquisition trials from extinction as a result, and so its
responding persists longer. This discrimination hypothesis is not unlike
Humphreys' expectancy hypothesis which has the persistence of responding in extinction dependent upon the expectancy of reinforcement which
in turn depends upon a subject's perception of the similarity of extinction
and acquisition trials. The discrimination hypothesis, and the stimulus
generalization hypothesis (see below) which is its direct descendant,
received more attention than the expectancy hypothesis, probably because the phrasing in terms of stimulus properties and discrimination
had more objectivity and testability for some.

Explicit tests of the discrimination hypothesis failed to support it.
A consistent finding in the psychological literature is that partial reinforcement increases resistance to extinction even though trials of continuous reinforcement occur between the partial reinforcement trials and
the extinction trials. The trials of continuous reinforcement occurring
just before extinction should make the discrimination between reinforced
trials and nonreinforced extinction trials easy, thus upsetting the usual
effects of partial reinforcement on extinction, but this is not so. Theios
(1962), Quarterman and Vaughan (1961), Rashotte and Surridge
(1969), and Leung and Jensen (1968) report data which show the

standard effects of partial reinforcement on extinction even though considerable amounts of continuous reinforcement intervened.

The stimulus generalization hypothesis. *The stimulus generalization hypothesis* is a close relative of the discrimination hypothesis, and it was defined by Sheffield (1949). Reinforcement after a response on a trial produces characteristic stimuli, like taste or food particles in the mouth when the rat makes a response for food reward, and these stimulus patterns are part of the stimulus complex to which the response on the next trial becomes conditioned. Similarly, nonreinforcement produces its own characteristic pattern of stimuli. Nonreinforcement on extinction trials represents a change from the stimulus patterns that prevailed in acquisition, whether reinforcement had been intermittent or 100 percent, and the change in responsiveness that occurs depends upon the degree of stimulus change (stimulus generalization). Partial reinforcement, having both reinforced and nonreinforced trials, has stimuli patterns more similar to extinction than continuous reinforcement, and so there is more resistance to extinction. Sheffield made the further assumption that the stimulus aftereffects of reinforcement and nonreinforcement dissipate with time.

A straightforward prediction from the hypothesis is that partial reinforcement effects will appear in extinction when trials are massed but will be absent when trials are widely distributed in time. Sheffield (1949) reported data consistent with the hypothesis but there were several experiments in the immediately following years that contradicted it, causing it to decline in status. The most telling experiment was performed by Weinstock (1954). A strong test of the Sheffield hypothesis would be to use very widely distributed trials to guarantee the fading of the stimulus consequences of reinforcement and nonreinforcement, and Weinstock met the requirement with a 24-hour intertrial interval throughout. Rats were the subjects, and the apparatus was an L-shaped runway with food as reinforcement. Running speed was the measure of performance. Four groups of animals were given 75 acquisition trials with either 30, 50, 80, or 100 percent reinforcement. Twenty extinction trials followed, and the expectation from the Sheffield hypothesis was no differences in extinction. The results appear in Figure 2–15. As usual, intermittent reinforcement increased resistance to extinction, but the long intertrial interval had no effect on it. Other experiments manipulated the intertrial interval also, and sought the effects predicted by the Sheffield hypothesis, but the outcomes were negative (Surridge and Amsel, 1964; Grant, Schipper and Ross, 1952; Wilson, Weiss, and Amsel, 1955; Lewis, 1956).

The sequential hypothesis. We saw in the study by Weinstock (1954) that resistance to extinction increases as the percentage of reinforced trials decreases. Is percent of reinforcement the basic determiner of

FIGURE 2–15
Negative results for the stimulus generalization hypothesis. A 24-hour intertrial interval was supposed to have eliminated the partial reinforcement effect in extinction, but the standard effect was obtained.

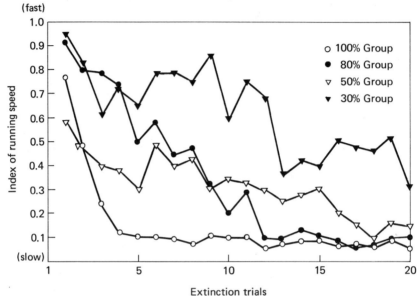

Extinction trials

Weinstock, S. Resistance to extinction of a running response following partial reinforcement under widely spaced trials. *Journal of Comparative and Physiological Psychology,* 1954, *47,* 318–322. Reprinted by permission of the American Psychological Association.

resistance to extinction? Is that all there is to it? There are two other ways of viewing this matter.

The first way is that *number* of nonreinforced trials in acquisition, not percent of reinforcements, is the fundamental determiner of resistance to extinction. As percent of reinforcement decreases, the number of nonreinforced trials increases, and so perhaps number of nonreinforced trials is the most basic variable of all. With total number of trials held constant in acquisition, percent reinforcement and number of nonreinforced trials are reciprocally related, but if total number of acquisition trials is allowed to vary, then the two measures can be disassociated. An experiment by Lawrence and Festinger (1962, Experiment 5) established that number of nonreinforced trials was a robust variable for resistance to extinction. An S-shaped runway was the task, with rats as subjects and food as the reward. Their groups had either 33, 50, 67, or 100 percent reinforcement, with subgroups having different numbers of trials to disassociate percent reinforcement and number of nonreinforced trials. Extinction to a criterion followed, and trials to criterion was the measure. The partial reinforcement groups had more trials to extinction than the continuous reinforcement group, which is the standard finding. But, when the trials to extinction measure was examined as a joint function of percent reinforcement and number of nonreinforced trials, the nonreinforced trials were found to be the most important determiner of behavior. Trials to extinction increased linearly with number of nonreinforced trials. Uhl and Young (1967) conducted a similar experiment, using bar-pressing as the response for rats to learn. Their results were the same—the number of nonreinforced trials, not percent reinforcement, was the strong determiner of resistance to extinction.

The second way is that number of nonreinforced trials *in a sequence* between reinforced trials is the primary variable rather than percent reinforcement or the total number of nonreinforced trials in acquisition. It is true that the total number of nonreinforced trials will increase as percent reinforcement decreases, but it is also true that the length of the run of nonreinforced trials between reinforcements will increase. Which is the more fundamental variable for extinction? Gonzalez and Bitterman (1964) probed this possibility with rats as the experimental subjects, bar pressing as the task, and food as the reinforcement. One group had 100 percent reinforcement in training, 2 had 60 percent, and 2 had 30 percent. The 60 percent groups had either short or long runs of nonreinforced trials between reinforcements, as did the 30 percent groups, where a short run was as many as 5 nonreinforced trials and a long run was as many as 16 nonreinforced trials. After extensive training, extinction to a criterion followed. As expected, the partial reinforcement groups had greater resistance to extinction than the 100 percent reinforcement group but, more importantly, the long-run groups had greater resistance to extinction than the short-run groups. Capaldi (1964, 1966, 1967) has used findings such as these as the foundation of his *sequential hypothesis*.

The sequential hypothesis is grounded in the concepts of habit and stimulus generalization. The essential features of the hypothesis are that a length of a nonreinforced run of trials is a stimulus to which the response becomes conditioned, and that the various lengths generalize to each other in accord with the principles of stimulus generalization. Extinction, being a series of nonreinforced trials, is a stimulus to which generalization from the nonreinforced runs in acquisition will occur. A primary implication is that longer runs of nonreinforced trials will produce greater resistance to extinction than shorter runs, which was the finding of Gonzalez and Bitterman (1964). Capaldi (1964) found the same thing when he varied the length of the run of nonreinforced trials before a reinforcement in a straight runway situation with rats, with percent reinforcement constant. Greater resistance to extinction was obtained with the longer run. Capaldi and Kassover (1970) obtained similar findings with their experiment.

A merit of a worthy scientific hypothesis is that it will generate a number of provable assertions, sometimes counter-intuitive ones. As we have seen, resistance to extinction increases as the percent of reinforcement decreases (Weinstock, 1954). The sequential hypothesis squares with this well-known finding because the lower percentages of reinforcement will have the longer sequences of nonreinforced runs. However, if a training situation with a higher percent reinforcement was designed to have some longer sequences of nonreinforced trials than a lower percent reinforcement situation, then greater resistance to extinction should be found for the higher percent reinforcement, which reverses the standard finding. This was the good idea of Capaldi and Stanley (1965), and they tested it with rats, a straight runway, food reinforcement, and running speed as the measure. Their results are shown in Figure 2–16 for extinction days, and it deserves to be compared with Weinstock's finding in Figure 2–15. As the sequential hypothesis predicts,

FIGURE 2–16
Evidence for the sequential hypothesis. Shown is a reversal of the standard effect of partial reinforcement on extinction, which was predicted by the hypothesis.

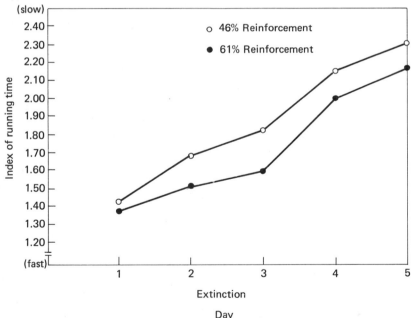

Capaldi, E. J., & Stanley, L. R. Percentage of reward versus *N*-length in the runway. *Psychonomic Science*, 1965, *3*, 263–264. Reprinted by permission of The Psychonomic Society, Inc.

the highest percent reinforcement has the greatest resistance to extinction (fastest running time in this case).

The frustration hypothesis. Amsel (1958, 1962, 1967) has been the chief architect of a frustration theory which includes partial reinforcement effects on extinction. Frustration is determined by such variables as the blocking of an ongoing response, the delay of reinforcement, or the reduction in size of an anticipated reinforcement, but Amsel's focus for partial reinforcement is frustration through the omission of anticipated reinforcement.

Here are the basic elements of Amsel's frustration theory for instrumental responses:

1. The response has received positive reinforcement and has appreciable strength.
2. The reinforcement of an instrumental response sequence produces a learned anticipation of the reinforcement.
3. Nonreinforcement of the response thwarts anticipation of the reinforcement and frustration results.
4. Frustration is a primary drive. (A primary drive does not depend on the learning history of the organism. Hunger and thirst are examples.)
5. Aspects of the primary frustration drive can be conditioned to stimuli and aroused as anticipatory frustration early in the response sequence. Anticipatory frustration is a learned, or secondary drive, and it complements the component of frustration that is a primary drive. (Secondary motivation is treated more completely in Chapter 5 where fear is discussed.)
6. As a drive, frustration has an energizing effect on behavior.

These theoretical assertions account for partial reinforcement effects on extinction in two ways. First, when reinforcement is partial, frustration as a primary drive is aroused on the nonreinforced acquisition trials and energizes behavior beyond that contributed by the nonreinforced extinction trials themselves. One hundred percent reinforcement has only arousal of the primary frustration drive in the nonreinforced extinction trials, and so response rate in extinction should be lower as a result. Second, the energizing effect of frustration as a secondary drive contributes to slowing the extinction rate after partial reinforcement. Once this secondary drive has been learned under partial reinforcement, it is regularly aroused by stimuli in the situation and the result is a higher drive level in extinction and a higher response rate.

A fundamental line of proof for the frustration hypothesis is showing that omitted reinforcements have an energizing effect on behavior. The experiment which made this point was by Amsel and Roussel (1952).

They trained rats in preliminary trials to run two straight runways for food reinforcement. After training, the animals were given test trials. Half of the test trials on Runway A were reinforced and half were not. Runway B was reinforced on every trial. Each trial on Runway A was followed immediately by a trial on Runway B. The measure of performance was running time. The results are presented in Figure 2–17. Running times on the left-hand side of the figure are for the pre-

FIGURE 2–17
Evidence that frustration has an energizing effect on behavior. Running time in a straight runway is faster after reward omission than after reward.

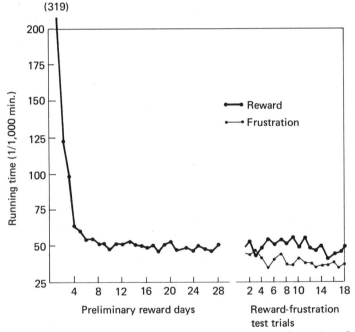

Amsel, A., & Roussel, J. Motivational properties of frustration: I. Effect on a running response of the addition of frustration to the motivational complex. *Journal of Experimental Psychology*, 1952, *43*, 363–368. Reprinted by permission of the American Psychological Association.

liminary trials where all runs were reinforced. Running times on the right-hand side are the times for runs in Runway B which were preceded by runs in Runway A that were reinforced on only half the trials. A run in Runway B following nonreinforcement in Runway A was a frustration test and, according to Amsel's theory, should be faster than after a reinforcement in Runway A. The empirical outcome confirmed the theory. Running times in Runway B were faster on the frustration tests.

The Amsel and Roussel experiment is an appropriate test of frustration theory because the theory says that an instrumental response first must be established in some strength, and the subsequent nonreinforcement of the response is a frustrating state of affairs. Partial reinforcement was a part of their study as a way of defining the frustration test trials, but an experiment by Amsel and Hancock (1957) dealt with partial reinforcement more explicitly. They followed the same procedure as Amsel and Roussel, except that throughout the experiment the trials on Runway A were reinforced half the time. A test trial on Runway B was given after each trial on Runway A, and the running times are shown in Figure 2–18. Notice, again, that the trials with omitted rein-

FIGURE 2–18

Further evidence that frustration is energizing for behavior. The effect, as revealed in faster running times, increases with number of trials.

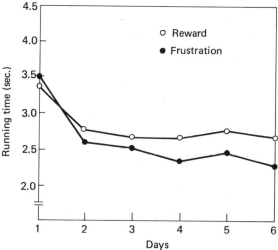

Amsel, A., & Hancock, W. Motivational properties of frustration: III. Relation of frustration effect to antedating goal factors. *Journal of Experimental Psychology*, 1957, *53*, 126–131. Reprinted by permission of the American Psychological Association.

forcement have faster running times, as theory predicts. Notice, too, that the frustration effect does not appear in the early trials. This makes theoretical sense because the running response in Runway A does not have much strength in the beginning and so nonreinforcement of it is not frustrating.

A potential difficulty. There is mounting experimental data (Robbins, 1971) in test of these competing hypotheses which we have just reviewed, but there is no resolution of them. Ordinarily, the scientific

course is a steady production of experiments until the weight of evidence
tilts toward one of the hypotheses and the scientific community comes
to accept it. Eventually this will happen, but in the meantime investigators must turn their attention to a variable that has been uncontrolled
in studies of partial reinforcement, and until its influence is known there
can be no careful assessment of the various hypotheses.

It is always assumed in psychological experiments that the behavior
of one animal in the experimental environment leaves the behavior of
another unaffected. Apparently this is not so. The evidence is mounting
that there are distinctive odors associated with nonreinforcement, and
possibly reinforcement, and that these odors are influential stimuli for
behavior. These odors are of a class of stimuli called *pheromones* which
an animal emits and which arouses a reaction in another animal (Gleason
and Reynierse, 1969; Birch, 1974). Because the pattern of reinforcements
and nonreinforcements is the essential stuff of partial reinforcement,
it is clear that any pheromones associated with them is a variable to
be reckoned with. All of the hypotheses on partial reinforcement that
have been reviewed count on memory of past stimuli associated with
reinforcements and nonreinforcements, not current chemical stimuli resulting from past reinforcements and nonreinforcements, to determine
behavior. No hypotheses about such behavior have ever considered odors
as an influential variable, nor have any controls for them ever been
used. The accumulating evidence is that an animal can be influenced
by the odors from its own previous nonreinforced behavior or the nonreinforced behavior of another animal.

An experiment by Wasserman and Jensen (1969) is an example of
how odor can effect the running behavior of rats in a straight runway.
After preliminary training, their experimental animals were given test
runs where the floor of the runway was covered with paper which was
either new, had been traversed by an animal on nonreinforced extinction
trials, or traversed by an animal on reinforced trials. They found that
runs down the alley on papers that had been used by animals during
extinction were substantially slower than runs when new or reinforcement paper was used.

Morrison and Ludvigson (1970), using rats in a T-maze, made choice
contingent upon discrimination of an odor of reinforcement or nonreinforcement at the choice point. The "odor of reward" was created by
allowing a hungry rat to eat at the choice point. The "odor of nonreward"
was created by allowing a hungry rat to spend the same amount of
time at the choice point without eating. These odors, if they exist, were
to be cues for a turn in the maze. If odor can be a discriminative
stimulus the animal should be able to choose a particular arm of the
maze when the odor is present and receive reinforcement for it. One
group received odor of reward as a cue for turning into one arm of the

maze and odor of nonreward for turning into the other arm. A second group received odor of reward as a cue for one arm and clean floor paper (intended as a minimum odor condition) as a cue for the other arm. A third group had odor of nonreward and clean paper as cues, and a fourth group had clean paper on all trials. The results were that only the groups which had the odor of nonreward as a cue showed any learning of the discrimination.

The general tenor of the research literature on this topic is that nonreinforcement definitely has a distinctive odor associated with it and that reinforcement probably does not. Moreover, there is the definite sentiment in the literature that the odor of nonreinforcement is aversive (e.g., Mellgren, Fouts, and Martin, 1973) and that animals will avoid areas where nonreinforcement has occurred. What is the source of the odor? If we knew the source of the odor we would be in a position to control it in experiments where it is unwanted (e.g., studies of partial reinforcement), but as yet the source is unknown. There is no observable urination or defecation associated with nonreinforcement, although urine is implicated in one study (Jones and Nowell, 1973). Morrison and Ludvigson (1970) suggest that the odor comes from the emotionality created by the frustration of nonreinforcement, and they cite the experiment of Valenta and Rigby (1968) in direct support of their hypothesis. Valenta and Rigby affected the bar-pressing behavior of rats by using as cues the air that had been drawn from the cages of rats that had been recently shocked or not. The animals could discriminate the two kinds of air, which means that the emotionality associated with shock produces a distinctive odor. If frustration is an emotional state also, then frustration could conceivably produce a discriminable odor. And, if frustration is an important consequence of nonreinforcement, as Amsel has argued, then we have odor as a consequence of nonreinforcement. It is clear that investigators of partial reinforcement and extinction have pheromones as a puzzle to solve before they can get on with their theorizing.

PRACTICAL APPLICATIONS

The more mature a science becomes the more useful it is. When we have good scientific laws and use them in practical situations we can change events in behalf of human goals. In recent years, extensive applications have been made of our knowledge of learning, and it is a sign of our growing understanding of variables that influence the learning process. Most of the understanding has come from research on animals, as the studies reviewed in this chapter indicate. The reader with an interest in human behavior might have been impatient with the coverage of animal learning that was given, but it is justifiable because this is where so much of the knowledge that is applied to human behavior comes from.

The positive reinforcement that has been the topic of this chapter has been a domain of extensive application in the home, school, and clinic, and it should not be surprising because learned behavior is so widespread in these situations. Nevertheless it has been surprising to many because they were reared in other schools of psychological explanation. A follower of an older school might, for example, say that a kindergarden child cries regularly because its needs are unfilled, but a contemporary psychologist who knows the laws of learning might say that the crying behavior is being sustained at a high rate by intermittent reinforcement, and if we could identify the reinforcer we could withdraw it and extinguish the response. The application of the laws of learning to human affairs is called *behavior modification,* and typically it is used to eliminate unwanted behavior. The principles of positive reinforcement are also used in the classroom to build desirable academic skills, and this approach has come to be known as *programmed learning* because the elements of a topic are systematically programmed to elicit the responses of an academic skill, which are reinforced when they occur. Let us consider examples of behavior modification first before turning to the essentials of programmed learning. The examples are based on positive reinforcement, which is the topic of this chapter, although behavior modification often steps outside the laws of positive reinforcement. Many human behavioral disorders involve emotional learning and its extinction, which is a somewhat different case that will be discussed in Chapter 5.

Behavior modification

Getting rid of undesirable behavior is primarily a matter of defining the response class to be manipulated, in finding the reinforcer that is sustaining it, and in withdrawing the reinforcer to extinguish the unwanted behavior. In some cases the elimination of undesirable behavior is not enough; it may be necessary to reinforce a new, more suitable response to replace the old one that has been eliminated. Most often behavior modification methods are used to change the behavior of individuals, although increasingly it is used to redirect the behavior of entire groups, like a classroom or a ward of patients in a mental hospital.

The modification of individual behavior. An example of behavior modification (Hart et al., 1964) was a four-year old boy who cried excessively in preschool, although he was otherwise normal and healthy, and the investigators hypothesized that the crying was being sustained by adult attention. An episode of crying behavior was defined as a cry loud enough to be heard 50 feet away which persisted for 5 seconds or more, and it was this response class that was manipulated, using teacher attention as the reinforcer. The sequence of events and the results are shown in Figure 2–19. To determine a baseline of the crying behavior so that change in it could be known, the teacher kept track

FIGURE 2–19

Number of crying episodes of a child extinguished on two occasions by the withdrawal of adult attention, which was serving as a reinforcer.

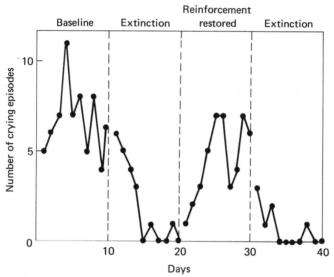

Hart, B. M., Allen, E., Buell, J. S., Harris, F. R., & Wolf, M. M. Effects of social reinforcement on operant crying. *Journal of Experimental Child Psychology,* 1964, *1,* 145–153. Reprinted by permission of Academic Press, Inc.

of the number of crying episodes with a pocket counter for the first ten days. During this time the boy was treated in the normal manner, receiving the usual attention from the teachers whenever he cried spontaneously. For the next ten days the teachers completely withdrew their attention when he cried (this did not apply if the crying was caused by injury, like from a playground fall). Notice in Figure 2–19 how the offensive behavior extinguishes. Then, for the next ten days, to show how crying was under the control of reinforcement, the teachers reinstated their old attentive behavior and the crying was readily reestablished. A second extinction series followed for the next ten days, and once again the crying stopped.

Visual attending is particularly critical for the deaf because circum-

stance has denied them a primary sense channel, and Craig and Holland
(1970) report an interesting experiment on increasing the frequency
of visual attentive behavior among young deaf children in a classroom
situation. As in the case of the boy's crying behavior that was discussed
above, attentive behavior had to be defined, and primarily it was a
matter of looking at the picture or object that the teacher was using
in the instructional task of the moment. In front of each child on the
desk was a small box with a light, and if the child was visually attentive
for ten seconds the light flashed. At the end of the session the child
received a piece of candy for each light flash received. Figure 2–20

FIGURE 2–20

The acquisition and extinction of visual attentiveness in deaf children.

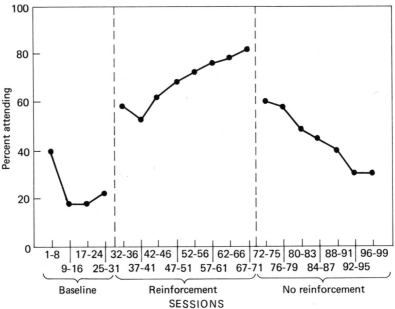

Craig, H. B., & Holland, A. L. Reinforcement of visual attending in classrooms
for deaf children. *Journal of Applied Behavior Analysis*, 1970, *3*, 97–109. Reprinted
by permission of Editor, *Journal of Applied Behavior Analysis*.

shows the sequence of procedures and the results that were obtained.
A baseline first was established in the initial classroom sessions, and
reinforcement was then introduced. The result of reinforcement was
an impressive increase in visual attention. The reinforcement was then
withdrawn in the final sessions, and the attentive behavior extinguished.

Self-imposed starvation is a disorder called *anorexia nervosa,* and
it is not to be confused with weight reduction through a rational dieting
plan. Patients with this disorder can die, and tube feeding has been

among the treatments that have been used to forestall such a grim consequence. Garfinkel, Kline, and Stancer (1973) assumed that the disorder was primarily behavioral, not physiological, and they used positive reinforcement to bring weight gains in five young women patients who had been hospitalized for the ailment. The 5 patients had lost 24–40 percent of their original weight at the time of hospitalization. The plan was to reward the patients with privileges like weekend passes and off-ward socializing with friends if they gained 0.15 kg (.34 lb) per day or 1 kg (2.2 lb) per week. The results for the five are shown in Figure 2–21. By the end of the treatment they had regained 87–95 percent of their original weight.

FIGURE 2–21
Gains in weight for five patients suffering from anorexia nervosa, a drastic loss of weight imposed by self-starvation. The cure was reward for gains in weight.

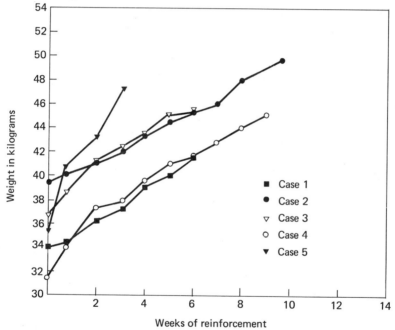

Garfinkel, P. E., Kline, S. A., & Stancer, H. C. Treatment of anorexia nervosa using operant conditioning techniques. *Journal of Nervous and Mental Disease,* 1973, *157,* 428–433. Reprinted by permission of The Williams & Wilkins Co., Baltimore.

Token economy. Tokens are symbolic rewards, like poker chips or "points," which are dispensed whenever the desired behavior occurs. Having received a token, the subject can exchange it for "backup reinforcers" of value to the subject. The type of backup reinforcer that will work depends on the subject population. Tokens will have value for children in a primary school classroom if they can be exchanged for toys but, in a mental hospital with adult patients, cigarettes, toilet articles, or extra food serve better as backup reinforcers.

The term "economy" in "token economy" derives from tokens being used as payment when the members of a group behave in a defined way, just as members of our society receive money when they perform acts that are valued, and so tokens become a medium of exchange in an "economy." There is no reason why tokens cannot be used for modifying the behavior of a single individual, but it seems that they are most often used as a reward that can be efficiently administered when members of a group perform acceptably. Later, and leisurely, the tokens can be exchanged for backup reinforcers.

Consider this study by Mann and Moss (1973), who were concerned with the socially maladaptive behavior of a group of young veterans in an acute treatment facility of a Veterans Administration hospital. The men were under the age of 30, with police and drug records common among them. Half of the patients had a record of violent assault, both before hospitalization and during it. As a group, their behavior was socially maladaptive, and they lacked vocational and social skills to find a job and to get along with people. Mostly they preferred to sit around the hospital—eating, sleeping, and watching television. With aluminum discs as tokens, the patients were placed on a very extensive token regime in an effort to socialize them. Tokens were earned for socially desirable behavior like cleaning the ward, bed-making, attendance at a daily business meeting, and attendance at group therapy sessions. In particular, token rewards for job-seeking or employment were generous. Payment with tokens was required for many of the amenities of everyday life. Snacks, coffee, game room privileges, and weekend passes required tokens. Even sleeping and eating required tokens. A bed was provided but tokens were required for the purchase of a mattress, and tokens were required to buy a pass for entry into the main dining hall.

Figure 2–22 has an example of the Mann and Moss data, and it shows how the token reward affected attendance at daily business meetings. The baseline period, before the token economy program began, shows that about half of the patients bothered to attend the meeting on time, but after token reward was introduced the attendance jumped to 85–100 percent. The reversal condition is a disassociation of response and reward, where the tokens were given regardless of whether the meeting was attended or not. We would not expect the behavior to be affected by reward when the reward is not contingent on the response, and this expectation was fulfilled in the reversal period because the attendance returned to baseline level. When tokens were reinstated in the second treatment period the attendance jumped to a high level again.

FIGURE 2–22

Token rewards were administered during the treatment periods, and the effect on attendance at daily business meetings by patients of a hospital ward is shown.

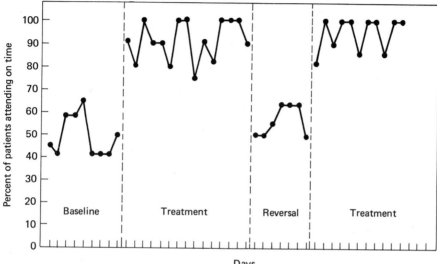

Days

Mann, R. A., & Moss, G. R. The therapeutic use of a token economy to manage a young and assaultive inpatient population. *Journal of Nervous and Mental Disease*, 1973, *157*, 1–9. Reprinted by permission of The Williams & Wilkins Co., Baltimore.

Mann and Moss had about the same success in controlling bed-making and ward-cleaning.

The most fundamental question of all is whether the new, desired behavior generalizes to other, nonreinforced situations. Will the patients of the Mann and Moss study continue to be concerned with neatness, punctuality, and productive employment after their release from the hospital and when they operate in a totally different environment? Mann and Moss did not conduct a follow-up and test for "generalization," as it is called, (not to be confused with stimulus generalization), but when tests of generalization have been made they have not been encouraging. A review of research on token economy classrooms (O'Leary and Drabman, 1971) found little evidence for generalization of the improved behavior to other times and situations. Levine and Fasnacht (1974) wrote an article with the title "Token Rewards May Lead to Token Learning," and they were pessimistic about generalization although they believed that token systems had value for the regulation of behavior in a restricted environment like a hospital ward where the subjects are under close supervision.

How behavior can be maintained indefinitely in new situations after positive reinforcement has been withdrawn is a difficult problem. The withdrawal of reinforcement is an extinction situation, and so we are asking for an elimination of extinction. Intermittent reinforcement is a way to slow the rate of extinction, but it would not eliminate it. At present the only known way to offset extinction is to continue the reward, but this would not be possible outside the training situation unless the subject was self-reinforced. This is not as far-fetched as it might seem. After external reinforcers have been delivered for a time, and the subjects are informed about the behavior that is desired, they can be aware of the desired response whenever they make it and reward themselves. In the realm of behavior modification, Kanfer and Karoly (1972) and Karoly and Kanfer (1974) have extended positive reinforcement along these lines. The principles of self-reinforcement are still in the developmental stage, but they show promise for maintaining behavior once external reinforcement has been withdrawn.

Programmed learning

If we can shape behavior of the pigeon in the laboratory and the untidy patient in the hospital with positive reinforcement, why can we not use it to mold academic skills in our schools? Skinner (1961, 1968) contends that any academic subject matter is an elaborate set of responses, usually verbal, and can be shaped with positive reinforcement like any other elaborate set of responses of any organism. Skinner, who has orchestrated so much of the modern research on positive reinforcement, sees five difficulties with our present classroom practices:

1. They are based on punishment, where the pupil must give the correct response to avoid punishment. That learning can occur this way is established in the history of education and elsewhere (see Chapter 5), but Skinner regards it as a poor way. The student might indeed learn under threatening circumstances but the punishment also might cause a chronic absentee who avoids the fearful classroom.

2. Reinforcement is usually delayed. A student will hand in a set of arithmetic problems and have them returned three days later.

3. Positive reinforcement is unstructured and infrequent, when it is used at all. Some teachers are conscientous in commenting with something like "Right" and "Wrong" about the student's efforts, but some hardly bother.

4. The members of a class are expected to learn at the same pace, which is an unrealistic expectation because it fails to consider individual differences in learning rates. Some students learn rapidly and spend a good portion of their time in boredom, and other students learn slowly and struggle to keep abreast of the class pace.

5. The structure of a course of study is often inefficient, considering the complex kinds of behavior to be learned. Of course the organization

of a course depends on the skill of the instructor, and many courses are well organized. A realist must admit, however, that some courses lie on that colorless plain between chaos and distinction.

The result of our present-day instructional methods is inefficient learning, and a system that excites neither teacher nor pupil. However it need not be, Skinner contends. Why cannot a course be laid out in progressive steps, with positive reinforcement contingent on the accomplishment of each step? The organization of these steps could be structured by experts, and then this ideal program of study could be put on a machine for use by students everywhere. And why could not a student study independently with a pace adjusted to personal learning capabilities? Exactly this kind of thing has been done, and the devices to conduct programmed learning are called *teaching machines*. The unit of the program is a question or a problem, and the student who responds correctly to it is immediately informed of the correctness and is moved on to the next step. Skinner recommends that the steps be small so the chance of error is small and the chance of success and reward correspondingly high. And, all of this proceeds at the student's own pace.

The first teaching machine was invented by E. L. Pressey of Ohio State University (Pressey, 1926). Pressey's original interest was the automatic administration of a test, like an intelligence test, and he invented a device with four keys for response and a window for presenting multiple choice test items. The pressing of a key turned up a new question, and the correct responses were tallied on a counter at the back of the machine. Pressey made the perceptive observation that the machine could teach as well as test if the subject was allowed to continue responding to an item until the correct answer was found, and he designed his machine for this mode also. Pressey's original teaching machine is shown in Figure 2–23.

After about 50 years the modern teaching machine has come to use a digital computer for the storage and control of the information, and the largest developmental effort underway is the PLATO system at the

FIGURE 2–23
The first teaching machine, invented by S. L. Pressey.

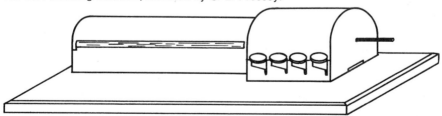

Pressey, S. L. A machine for automatic teaching of drill material. *School and Society,* 1927, *25,* 549–552. Reprinted by permission of the Society for the Advancement of Education, Inc.

University of Illinois (Bitzer and Skaperdas, 1970). PLATO is an acronym for Programmed Logic for Automated Teaching Operations. Figure 2–24 shows a student at a PLATO station. In 1974 there were 650 terminals in operation, and more to come. At present, PLATO is

FIGURE 2–24
A student using PLATO, a computer-based teaching machine developed by the University of Illinois.

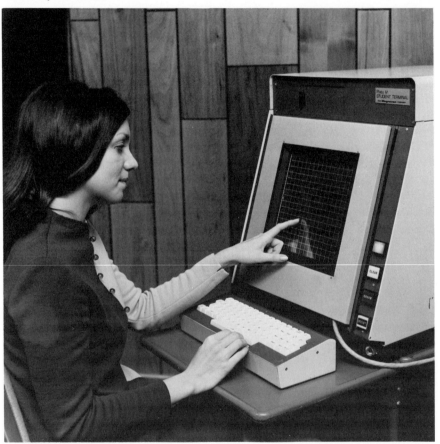

Reproduced by permission of the Computer-Based Education Research Laboratory, University of Illinois at Urbana-Champaign.

teaching courses that range from psychology and chemistry to exotic languages. Audio units produce sound that is synchronized with the visual presentation for foreign language instruction. Pictorial presentations are a part of the system also. Computer graphic techniques can draw anything on the display from a map to a cartoon-like rat pressing a bar for a vivid point about reinforcement, and slides are used to present photographs.

SUMMARY

This chapter was concerned with positive reinforcement, which is often called reward. Positive reinforcement is defined as any event that follows a response and increases the probability of occurrence of the response. Positive reinforcement is sought by the subject (e.g., food), in contrast to negative reinforcement which is unpleasant and causes learning by virtue of its removal (e.g., electric shock).

Reinforcement is not always delivered after every response but is sometimes delivered intermittently according to a schedule. The two basic schedules of reinforcement are ratio schedules, where reinforcement occurs after a specified number of responses irrespective of time, and interval schedules, where reinforcement is delivered on a time schedule irrespective of number of responses. Each of these two basic schedules are further classified into fixed and variable schedules, depending whether number of responses or time between reinforcements is fixed or is variable with a statistical definition.

Sometimes a reinforced response is associated with a stimulus, although it need not be, but when it is the response is said to be under stimulus control. Stimulus control is imperfect because the response can be elicited by stimuli which are similar to the one used in training, and this is an effect called stimulus generalization. The tendency to respond is greatest for the training stimulus and less for the similar stimuli which have not been reinforced.

The withdrawal of positive reinforcement produces a decrease in the probability of responding, and this effect is called extinction. The most powerful determiner of extinction is schedules of reinforcement. Extinction of a response that has been learned under continuous reinforcement is fast relative to one that has received intermittent reinforcement.

Our knowledge of positive reinforcement has increased greatly in recent years, and today it is being used in the school, the clinic, and the home to modify behavior along desired lines. The use of positive reinforcement to produce behavioral change in practical situations is called behavior modification. The use of positive reinforcement for step-wise, structured learning of academic skills in the classroom is called programmed learning.

REFERENCES

Amsel, A. The role of frustrative nonreward in noncontinuous reward situations. *Psychological Bulletin*, 1958, 55, 102–119.

Amsel, A. Frustrative nonreward in partial reinforcement and discrimination learning: Some recent history and a theoretical extension. *Psychological Review*, 1962, *69*, 306–328.

Amsel, A.   Partial reinforcement effects on vigor and persistence: Advances in frustration theory derived from a variety of within-subjects experiments. In K. W. Spence and J. T. Spence (Eds.), *The psychology of learning and motivation* (Vol. 1). New York: Academic Press, 1967, pp. 1–65.

Amsel, A., & Hancock, W.   Motivational properties of frustration: III. Relation of frustration effect to antedating goal factors. *Journal of Experimental Psychology*, 1957, *53*, 126–131.

Amsel, A., & Roussel, J.   Motivational properties of frustration: I. Effect on a running response of the addition of frustration to the motivational complex. *Journal of Experimental Psychology*, 1952, *43*, 363–368.

Birch, M. C. (Ed.),   *Pheromones*. North-Holland Research Monographs: Frontiers of Biology (Vol. 32). Amsterdam: North-Holland, 1974.

Bitzer, D., & Skaperdas, D.   The economics of a large-scale computer-based education system: PLATO IV. In W. H. Holtzman (Ed.), *Computer-assisted instruction, testing, and guidance*. New York: Harper & Row, 1970, pp. 17–29.

Boren, J. J.   Resistance to extinction as a function of the fixed ratio. *Journal of Experimental Psychology*, 1961, *61*, 304–308.

Capaldi, E. J.   Effect of N-length, number of different N-lengths, and number of reinforcements on resistance to extinction. *Journal of Experimental Psychology*, 1964, *68*, 230–239.

Capaldi, E. J.   Partial reinforcement: An hypothesis of sequential effects. *Psychological Review*, 1966, *73*, 459–477.

Capaldi, E. J.   A sequential hypothesis of instrumental learning. In K. W. Spence and J. T. Spence (Eds.), *The psychology of learning and motivation* (Vol. 1). New York: Academic Press, 1967, pp. 67–156.

Capaldi, E. J., & Kassover, K.   Sequence, number of nonrewards, anticipation, and intertrial interval in extinction. *Journal of Experimental Psychology*, 1970, *84*, 470–476.

Capaldi, E. J., & Stanley, L. R.   Percentage of reward vs. N-length in the runway. *Psychonomic Science*, 1965, *3*, 263–264.

Craig, H. B., & Holland, A. L.   Reinforcement of visual attending in classrooms for deaf children. *Journal of Applied Behavior Analysis*, 1970, *3*, 97–109.

Dyal, J. A., & Holland, T. A.   Resistance to extinction as a function of number of reinforcements. *American Journal of Psychology*, 1963, *76*, 332–333.

Ellson, D. G.   Quantitative studies of the interaction of simple habits: I. Recovery from the specific and generalized effects of extinction. *Journal of Experimental Psychology*, 1938, *23*, 339–358.

Garfinkel, P. E., Kline, S. A., & Stancer, H. C.   Treatment of anorexia nervosa using operant conditioning techniques. *Journal of Nervous and Mental Disease*, 1973, *157*, 428–433.

Gleason, K. K., & Reynierse, J. H. The behavioral significance of pheromones in vertebrates. *Psychological Bulletin*, 1969, *71*, 58–73.

Gonzalez, R. C., & Bitterman, M. E. Resistance to extinction in the rat as a function of percentage and distribution of reinforcement. *Journal of Comparative and Physiological Psychology*, 1964, *58*, 258–263.

Grant, D. A., Schipper, L. M., & Ross, B. M. Effect of intertrial interval during acquisition on extinction of the conditioned eyelid response following partial reinforcement. *Journal of Experimental Psychology*, 1952, *44*, 203–210.

Guttman, N., & Kalish, H. I. Discriminability and stimulus generalization. *Journal of Experimental Psychology*, 1956, *51*, 79–88.

Harris, P., & Nygaard, J. E. Resistance to extinction and number of reinforcements. *Psychological Reports*, 1961, *8*, 233–234.

Hart, B. M., Allen, E., Buell, J. S., Harris, F. R., & Wolf, M. M. Effects of social reinforcement on operant crying. *Journal of Experimental Child Psychology*, 1964, *1*, 145–153.

Humphreys, L. G. The effect of random alternation of reinforcement on the acquisition and extinction of conditioned eyelid reactions. *Journal of Experimental Psychology*, 1939, *25*, 141–158. (a)

Humphreys, L. G. Acquisition and extinction of verbal expectations in a situation analogous to conditioning. *Journal of Experimental Psychology*, 1939, *25*, 294–301. (b)

Jenkins, H. M., & Harrison, R. H. Effect of discrimination training on auditory generalization. *Journal of Experimental Psychology*, 1960, *59*, 246–253.

Jones, R. B., & Nowell, N. W. Aversive and aggression-promoting properties of urine from dominant and subordinate male mice. *Animal Learning and Behavior*, 1973, *1*, 207–210.

Kanfer, F. H., & Karoly, P. Self-control: A behavioristic excursion into the lion's den. *Behavior Therapy*, 1972, *3*, 398–416.

Karoly, P., & Kanfer, F. H. Situational and historical determinants of self-reinforcement. *Behavior Therapy*, 1974, *5*, 381–390.

Lawrence, D. H., & Festinger, L. *Deterrents and reinforcement.* Stanford: Stanford University Press, 1962.

Leung, C. M., & Jensen, G. D. Shifts in percentage of reinforcement viewed as changes in incentive. *Journal of Experimental Psychology*, 1968, *76*, 291–296.

Levine, F. M., & Fasnacht, G. Token rewards may lead to token learning. *American Psychologist*, 1974, *29*, 816–820.

Lewis, D. J. Acquisition, extinction, and spontaneous recovery as a function of percentage of reinforcement and intertrial intervals. *Journal of Experimental Psychology*, 1956, *51*, 45–53.

Mann, R. A., & Moss, G. R. The therapeutic use of a token economy to manage a young and assaultive inpatient population. *Journal of Nervous and Mental Disease*, 1973, *157*, 1–9.

Mellgren, R. L., Fouts, R. S., & Martin, J. W. Approach and escape to conspecific odors of reward and nonreward in rats. *Animal Learning and Behavior,* 1973, *1,* 129–132.

Morrison, R. R., & Ludvigson, H. W. Discrimination by rats of conspecific odors of reward and nonreward. *Science,* 1970, *167,* 904–905.

Mostofsky, D. I. (Ed.). *Attention: Contemporary theory and analysis.* New York: Appleton-Century-Crofts, 1970.

Mowrer, O. H., & Jones, H. Habit strength as a function of the pattern of reinforcement. *Journal of Experimental Psychology,* 1945, *35,* 293–311.

O'Leary, K. D., & Drabman, R. Token reinforcement programs in the classroom: A review. *Psychological Bulletin,* 1971, *75,* 379–398.

Pavlov, I. P. *Conditioned reflexes.* (G. V. Anrep, trans.). Oxford: Oxford University Press, 1927.

Perin, C. T. Behavior potentiality as a joint function of the amount of training and the degree of hunger at the time of extinction. *Journal of Experimental Psychology,* 1942, *30,* 93–113.

Pressey, S. L. A simple device which gives tests and scores—and teaches. *School and Society,* 1926, *23,* 373–376.

Pressey, S. L. A machine for automatic teaching of drill material. *School and Society,* 1927, *25,* 549–552.

Quartermain, D., & Vaughan, G. M. Effect of interpolating continuous reinforcement between partial training and extinction. *Psychological Reports,* 1961, *8,* 235–237.

Rashotte, M. E., & Surridge, C. T. Partial reinforcement and partial delay of reinforcement effects with 72-hour intertrial intervals and interpolated continuous reinforcement. *Quarterly Journal of Experimental Psychology,* 1969, *21,* 156–161.

Robbins, D. Partial reinforcement: A selective review of the alleyway literature since 1960. *Psychological Bulletin,* 1971, *76,* 415–431.

Sheffield, V. F. Extinction as a function of partial reinforcement and distribution of practice. *Journal of Experimental Psychology,* 1949, *39,* 511–526.

Skinner, B. F. *The behavior of organisms.* New York: Appleton-Century, 1938.

Skinner, B. F. Superstition in the pigeon. *Journal of Experimental Psychology,* 1948, *38,* 168–172.

Skinner, B. F. A case history in scientific method. *American Psychologist,* 1956, *11,* 221–233.

Skinner, B. F. *Cumulative record.* New York: Appleton-Century-Crofts, 1961.

Skinner, B. F. *The technology of teaching.* New York: Appleton-Century-Crofts, 1968.

Surridge, C. T., & Amsel, A. Acquisition and extinction under single alternation and random partial-reinforcement conditions with a 24-hour intertrial interval. *Journal of Experimental Psychology,* 1966, *72,* 361–368.

Theios, J. The partial reinforcement effect sustained through blocks of continuous reinforcement. *Journal of Experimental Psychology,* 1962, *64,* 1–6.

Uhl, C. N., & Young, A. G.   Resistance to extinction as a function of incentive, percentage of reinforcement, and number of nonreinforced trials. *Journal of Experimental Psychology,* 1967, *73,* 556–564.

Valenta, J. G., & Rigby, M. K.   Discrimination of the odor of stressed rats, *Science,* 1968, *161,* 599–601.

Wasserman, E. A., & Jensen, D. D.   Olfactory stimuli and the "pseudo-extinction" effect. *Science,* 1969, *166,* 1307–1309.

Weinstock, S.   Resistance to extinction of a running response following partial reinforcement under widely spaced trials. *Journal of Comparative and Physiological Psychology,* 1954, *47,* 318–322.

Williams, S. B.   Resistance to extinction as a function of the number of reinforcements. *Journal of Experimental Psychology,* 1938, *23,* 506–522.

Wilson, M. P.   Periodic reinforcement interval and number of periodic reinforcements as parameters of response strength. *Journal of Comparative and Physiological Psychology,* 1954, *47,* 51–56.

Wilson, W., Weiss, E. J., & Amsel, A.   Two tests of the Sheffield hypothesis concerning resistance to extinction, partial reinforcement, and distribution of practice. *Journal of Experimental Psychology,* 1955, *50,* 51–60.

chapter 3

Mechanisms and theories of positive reinforcement

THE LAST chapter held that there are a wide variety of events that can serve as positive reinforcers in instrumental learning, and no attempt was made to specify what they are or how they might work. A nonanalytical position like this is called *empirical reinforcement*, which asserts the reality of reinforcement but has no explanation for it. Psychologists interested in theory are discontented with the empirical reinforcement view and they hope that someday a masterful theorist will come along and link all reinforcers together with a single theory. This day has not yet arrived. In the meantime, this chapter discusses the various kinds of reinforcers and the prominent theoretical attempts to explain why they work as they do.

SECONDARY REINFORCEMENT

Learning psychologists make the distinction between primary reinforcement and secondary reinforcement. *Primary reinforcement* does not depend on the learning history of the organism; it is closely identified with reinforcers that aid biological survival. Responses that are learned for food reward or water reward are examples. *Secondary reinforcement,* however, depends upon a history of learning; experience determines whether or not a stimulus will be a reinforcer. There is no satisfying explanation of secondary reinforcement, as we shall see.

There is an intuitive reasonableness about a hungry organism learning a response for food reinforcement, and the intuition is not without its scientific justification. A response that is learned through primary reinforcement becomes a reliable way of obtaining something that contributes to biological survival. It is not surprising that the processes of evolution have given us learning through primary reinforcement, and if that was all there is to reinforced learning we would have a tidy biological explanation. A difficulty arises in the fact that most of the positive reinforcers that influence the learning of human behavior do not have much to do with biological needs. An adult works for paper (money), and a child studies hard in school in exchange for words of praise from the teacher. How can these seemingly neutral stimuli serve as reinforcement?

The psychologist's answer is that a neutral stimulus gains reinforcing power by association with the response being learned, the primary reinforcement, or both. Neutral stimuli that have gone through this associative process will develop the power to maintain behavior and reward new learning, just as primary reinforcers do, and they are called *secondary reinforcers* or *conditioned reinforcers*. If this generalization is true, it means that any neutral stimulus can be a reinforcer with the proper associative history and, so, we come to have an explanation of why we will learn for money or a smile. With the different learning histories that each of us have, it is not surprising that what is reinforcing for one does nothing for another. The problem with the secondary reinforcement generalization is that it has had an indecisive theoretical history, and we lack a convincing explanation of why so many different neutral stimuli reinforce so many so well.

It should be clear that the emphasis throughout will be with positive secondary reinforcement, based on primary reinforcement like food and water for the appetitional drives of hunger and thirst. The association of neutral stimuli with aversive events will be covered in Chapter 5 on punishment and fear.

Background: Early studies that defined the topic

The first demonstration of secondary reinforcement was by Frolov in Pavlov's laboratory (Pavlov, 1927, pp. 33–34), using classical conditioning procedures (see Chapter 4). Using the Frolov experiment as point of departure, Williams (1929) conceived the idea of using a neutral stimulus that had been paired with primary reinforcement as reinforcement for the learning of a new response in an instrumental learning situation. Rats were Williams's subjects, and she first imbued a white goal box with secondary reinforcing power by regularly rewarding the response to it in a simple discrimination situation. These animals were then shifted to a complex, multiple maze with a neutral goal box and were allowed to wander around, one trial a day, for eight days. On Day 9 the white goal box from the discrimination training was introduced as the goal box for the multiple maze, and at this point the animals had a substantial drop in errors, relative to control groups that had no prior secondary reinforcement training. The white goal box, however, gradually began to lose its secondary reinforcing powers because errors began to increase as test trials continued in the multiple maze. Williams asked if the white goal box had taken on the rewarding power of food, and she concluded that it had.

Skinner (1938, pp. 82–83) obtained the same kind of results with rats in the bar press Skinner box situation. A click of the food magazine was first associated with eating out of the food tray, and then click of the food magazine (now empty) was used to reinforce bar pressing. Definite learning of bar pressing occurred but the rate of bar pressing decreased after a while as the click began to lose its secondary reinforcing powers, which is the same phenomenon observed by Williams. Perhaps the most widely cited of the early studies on secondary reinforcement were by Wolfe (1936) and Cowles (1937). Chimpanzees were taught to insert poker chips in a vending machine for raisins and peanuts. Cowles taught his animals to learn a new choice response, where poker chips with their newly acquired secondary reinforcing power served as the reward.

The early studies that we have reviewed so far have all used a secondary reinforcer for the learning of a new response, but another line of evidence emerged in an experiment by Bugelski (1938). He used rats as subjects, and bar press in the Skinner box as the response. The animals were first trained to eat food pellets delivered from a food magazine that had a distinctive click, with the bar absent. The bar was then introduced, and the animal had to learn to press it to receive the food from the magazine with the click. The test for secondary reinforcement came in the extinction trials that followed, where food no longer followed the bar press. Half of the animals had the click accompanying the bar press and half did not. The animals who received the click in extinction gave 30 percent more responses than those who did not have it. C. L. Hull published an influential book on learning in 1943 entitled *Principles of Behavior* with a provocative chapter on secondary reinforcement that featured the Bugelski experiment. From then on the Bugelski work was regularly cited as a basic study in the domain of secondary reinforcement.

Secondary reinforcement as reinforcement

The foregoing section discussed the viewpoint that a neutral stimulus can develop the power of reward and can be used for the learning of new responses. Investigators continued to generate research in support of this reinforcement interpretation, but they were not without their debates about the mechanisms of secondary reinforcement as time went on.

The discriminative stimulus hypothesis. A notable debate centered on the conditions of pairing the neutral stimulus and the response being learned with primary reinforcement. Is it necessary to have a response learned with primary reinforcement for the neutral stimulus to become a secondary reinforcer? Or is the response merely the device for producing the primary reinforcement, whose pairing with the neutral stimulus is the defining condition for secondary reinforcement? Skinner (1938, p. 82) believed that the association of the neutral stimulus and primary reinforcement was sufficient. Hull (1943, pp. 97–98) accepted this but went even further and said it was necessary that a response be made to the neutral stimulus and that it be strengthened with primary reinforcement. Keller and Schoenfeld (1950) took the same position when they said it was necessary for the neutral stimulus to control the response by having a response learned to it. Such stimuli are called discriminative stimuli, and this view of secondary reinforcement has been called the *discriminative stimulus hypothesis.*

The discriminative stimulus hypothesis was put to test in an experiment by Schoenfeld, Antonitis, and Bersh (1950). Two groups of rats were trained in bar pressing. One group had a light turned on for one second after the bar press had delivered the food and the food was being eaten, which is a pairing of the stimulus and the reinforcer. The other group was not administered the light. The tests were extinction trials, where food was withdrawn and both groups received the one-second light for each bar press. If only pairing with primary reinforcement is required for secondary reinforcement, the group that received the light in training should enjoy secondary reinforcement benefits in extinction and emit more responses than the other group. The extinction performances of the two groups did not differ, as it turned out, and it can be concluded that more than the pairing of the neutral stimulus and the primary reinforcer was involved, which is what the discriminative stimulus hypothesis implies. Using an entirely different technique, Stein (1958) came up with evidence that contradicted this experiment by Schoenfeld and his colleagues. Stein's study was based on the knowledge that direct electrical stimulation of the brain can have positive reinforcing effects. His approach, which was ingenious, was to repeatedly pair a tone as a neutral stimulus with electrical brain stimulation of the rat. The animal made no response to get the positive reinforcer, so if the tone worked as a secondary reinforcer in the learning of a new response it might be taken as evidence against the discriminative stimulus hypothesis. In the tests that followed the pairings, the tone was available as a secondary reinforcer for bar pressing, and the result was a significantly higher rate of responses than for control conditions.

The short life of secondary reinforcers. Another debate concerned the temporariness of secondary reinforcing effects in laboratory experiments. From the first experiment by Frolov it was noticed that the secondary reinforcing stimulus loses its power after a few trials, in an extinction-like fashion, and from time to time it must be re-paired with the response and its primary reinforcer for a restoration of potency. The short life of secondary reinforcers has been observed repeatedly by investigators, and they find it troublesome in explaining the durability of reinforcers like money in the everyday world. Secondary reinforcement as conceived and studied in the laboratory could be on the wrong track for explaining reinforcers like money, but conversely it could be on the right track with only more understanding and elaboration needed. Maybe the secret of durable secondary reinforcement lies in grasping the role of intermittent reinforcement. Consider money, once again. The pairing of money with primary reinforcers is not a continuous reinforcement schedule because often money is received for an act without an accompanying primary reinforcement; the act, the money and primary reinforcement are paired only occasionally. Saltzman (1949), in a well-known experiment on the learning of a new response with secondary reinforcement, first taught his rats to run down a straight runway to a distinctive goal box for food, and then used the goal box as the reward to learn the choice response in a T-maze. Klein (1959) used the same procedure as Saltzman except that he used several schedules of intermittent primary reinforcement in the straight runway, and he found that the rate of learning the T-maze increased as the percentage of primary reinforcements in the runway decreased from 100 to 20 percent. But the most notable work on intermittency and secondary reinforcement was by Zimmerman (1957, 1959).

Zimmerman (1959) used rats as his experimental subjects and sought to imbue a buzzer with secondary reinforcing powers in a straight runway situation. The animal was placed in the start box, the buzzer was sounded, and then the door of the start box was raised and the animal ran down the runway for a food reward, sometimes, at the other end. The food reward was on a variable ratio schedule. The buzzer, however, occurred on every training trial. The test was the learning of a new response in the same runway apparatus. The start box now had a bar present, and the rat had to press the bar one or more times, depending on the schedule, to sound the buzzer and open the door for an opportunity to run to an empty goal box. The buzzer–door event first occurred for every bar press, then was changed to a variable ratio schedule, and finally to a fixed ratio schedule. The animals were run on the test until they stopped bar pressing. The interesting thing about this experiment is its contrast with earlier experiments that found secondary reinforcement effects so temporary. Zimmerman's animals pressed the bar for thousands of responses over 10–14 days. Wike and Platt (1962) also obtained impressively high levels of responding with a task and procedures about the same as Zimmerman's. Apparently durable secondary reinforcement is related to intermittent rewarding and, if so, we are moved much closer to understanding the high effectiveness of secondary rewards in everyday life.

A standard scientific tactic is to look at an investigator's procedures and data and ask if they are a result of entirely different variables than the investigator believed. Looking at this tactic in action provides good insight into how scientists think and work, and the reaction to Zimmerman's experiment is a good example of it. There were others who looked at Zimmerman's findings and concluded that they were a consequence of frustration as an aversive state of affairs. As with fear, an organism will learn responses which give freedom from frustration. Experiments by Daly (1969) and Daly and McCroskery (1973) have shown that rats will learn bar pressing and hurdle jumping to escape the frustration produced by denying them anticipated rewards. In the Zimmerman experiment the animal is confined in the start box in the periods between buzzer–door events, and it is reasonable to suggest that the bar pressing was sustained by escape from the frustration of confinement.

Consider the experiment by McNamara and Paige (1962) on escape as the reward, not the secondary reinforcing stimulus, as in the Zimmerman experiment. Their experiment was procedurally very similar to Zimmerman's. In training, the rat was placed in a start box and when the experimenter sounded the cue (a buzzer or a light), the animal was allowed to go to the goal box for food. Fifty percent reinforcement was used in training, with one half of the animals receiving buzzer on reinforced trials and light on nonreinforced trials (or vice versa). On the test sessions the rats were divided into two groups, where a bar press as the new response being learned now allowed escape to an empty goal box. One group had the reinforced cue come on with the bar press, and the other the nonreinforced cue, with both being on a continuous reinforcement schedule. The results were consistent with Zimmerman's, where hundreds of bar presses occurred on the test sessions. But of most interest was that the latency of the bar-press response became *faster* with trials. *Learning* was taking place, rather than the waning of secondary reinforcing powers for a stimulus that is customarily found on test trials where a new response is learned. And, bar pressing occurred just as efficiently for the nonreinforced cue as the reinforced cue. If secondary reinforcement had been the determiner of the behavior the reinforced cue should have produced the most bar presses.

A similar experiment with a similar outcome was by Wike, Platt, and Knowles (1962). Rats were used, and they followed Zimmerman's procedures closely. An experimental group and four control groups were used. The experimental group was treated the same as Zimmerman's animals. Training to impart secondary reinforcing powers to a new stimulus (buzzer) preceded the test where a bar press, which allowed escape from the box and sounded the buzzer for every five presses of the bar, was the new response to be learned. The control groups had no secondary reinforcement training, only the test with the bar pressing. The four control groups were:

Control Group I: Receive the buzzer and escape from the box for every fifth press of the bar.
Control Group II: Escape from the box on every press of the bar but no buzzer.
Control Group III: Receive a buzzer for every fifth press of the bar but no escape permitted.
Control Group IV: Pressing of the bar produced no buzzer and no escape.

If the buzzer is a secondary reinforcing stimulus as Zimmerman said, then the experimental group should do better than all of the control groups which had no secondary reinforcement training. But, if escape is the fundamental variable operating, the experiment group and Control Groups I and II should be the same and perform at a higher level than Control Groups III and IV which were denied escape. The latter was the case, and the investigators concluded that escape from frustration, not secondary reinforcement, was the key factor operating in Zimmerman's data. Apparently, confinement in the box is itself frustrating, which is easy to believe for an animal that explores as much as the rat.

In an experimental counterattack, Zimmerman (1963) produced evidence that some genuine secondary reinforcement effects beyond frustration might exist in the kind of situations that have entered this controversy. In this study with rats, Zimmerman paired a light–tone combination with drinking on an intermittent reinforcement schedule, and then used the light–tone combination on an intermittent reinforcement schedule as a secondary reinforcer to train a bar-press response. No escape was permitted from the box. The result was success in training bar pressing in the absence of escape, with a considerable number of bar-press responses emitted over five test sessions. But the number of bar presses was considerably less than Zimmerman (1959) had obtained before, suggesting that escape from the box in the earlier study was a contributing factor, as Zimmerman's critics had implied and documented. Nevertheless, the message of Zimmerman's 1963 experiment is that frustration and escape from it is not the whole story. Zimmerman is supported by a similar experiment (Fox and King, 1961) which compared continuous and intermittent reinforcement in both training and test, and without the possibility of escape. The highest level of performance for the new response acquired with secondary reinforcement occurred when both training and test were under intermittent reinforcement schedules.

Secondary reinforcement as the information value of a stimulus

Another way of looking at secondary reinforcement is that a stimulus with secondary reinforcing powers has a reliable capability for informing about the occurrence of primary reinforcement. A stimulus is effective as a secondary reinforcer to the extent that it reliably predicts primary reinforcement. Egger and Miller (1962, 1963) have done interesting work on this idea, and their 1962 experiment illustrates the approach. Two stimuli were presented to rats in association with food, where Stimulus 1 was a light and Stimulus 2 was a tone (or vice versa). For Group A, Stimulus 1 came on 2 seconds before the delivery of a food pellet, and Stimulus 2 came on 1.5 seconds before the pellet. Both stimuli terminated together when the pellet was delivered. Group B had the same stimulus sequence preceding food delivery as Group A but, in addition, received aperiodic presentations of Stimulus 1 alone without food. A bar-press response that had been previously learned was then extinguished, and the secondary reinforcing strengths of Stimulus 1 and Stimulus 2 were tested in relearning after extinction. Bar pressing now delivered either Stimulus 1 or Stimulus 2 on a fixed ratio schedule. The information hypothesis makes two main predictions. First, Stimulus 1 should produce more responses for Group A than Group B because it was associated with food 100 percent of the time for Group A and only part of the time for Group B. Second, Stimulus 2 should produce more responses for Group B than Group A. Stimulus 2 had 100 percent association with food for both groups, but it is totally redundant with Stimulus 1 in the case of Group A and predicted nothing new whereas it was not fully redundant with Stimulus 1 in the case of Group B and was the best predictor of food. The results supported these expectations. Group A had more responses to Stimulus 1 than Group B, and Group B had more responses to Stimulus 2 than Group A. Egger and Miller see their data as consistent with the discriminative stimulus hypothesis, which requires a response to be made to the stimulus, but one can legitimately wonder if the response is necessary at all. Could the secondary reinforcement mechanism be one of getting the organism to comprehend the relationship between stimulus and food and come to "know" that the stimulus "means" food? An interpretation like this is a cognitive one which implies a power of the organism to relate events in its environment and later use these acquired relationships to guide responding; there is no requirement of a response to be associated with a stimulus. If a rat has been running down a straight alley for food in a white goal box, and later learns to choose the arm of a T-maze that has the white goal box, is it because it knows that the white box predicts food? Continuing this reasoning, it can be assumed that a stimulus loses its secondary reinforcement power in a new learning situation because it becomes a promise unfilled. The stimulus no longer predicts primary reinforcement, and responding declines as a result. As we shall see in our discussion of cognitive theory later on in this chapter, the occurrence of the response as a requirement for learning is an item of controversy.

Secondary reinforcement as the elicitation of an established response

Earlier an experiment on secondary reinforcement by Bugelski (1938) was reviewed. During training his rats produced a click every time the bar was pressed for food reward, and the subsequent presence of the click in extinction served to produce more responses than for a control condition that was denied the click. In a similar experiment, Miles (1956) had a light come on in training every time his rats pressed the bar in the Skinner box for a food pellet. His experimental variable was the number of light–food pairings. The test was extinction, where half the animals had the light come on with the bar press and half did not. Like Bugelski, more responses were emitted in extinction with the light than without. Moreover, the greater the number of light–food pairings in training the greater the number of responses in extinction. A legitimate way to view experiments like these is in terms of the stimulus as secondary reinforcement which imparts strength to the response just as primary reinforcement does. When the stimulus is present in extinction its positive influences somewhat offset the weakening effects of the extinction process. But it was Bugelski himself (1938, pp. 91–94) who emphasized that data such as these are congenial to another, and simpler, interpretation. Why cannot one assume that the click is part of the stimulus complex to which the approach to the bar and the bar press are learned and its presence in extinction increases the probability of these responses?

Speaking of the click, Bugelski (1956, p. 93) says:

> . . . It is rather a part of a pattern that evokes a particular response. Every part of the bar press is controlled by stimuli of a direct or unconditioned nature or by conditioned stimuli. The click is such a conditioned stimulus.

Bugelski (1956, p. 271) goes on to say:

> . . . To select out the click and glamorize it into a "secondary reinforcer" is totally unnecessary, gratuitous, and theoretically harmful.

Bugelski said that the click might just as well be considered a motivator, which is a hypothesis that has had an occasional advocate (see review by Wike, 1971).

One should keep in mind that Bugelski's *elicitation hypothesis* applies to only certain kinds of experiments where the response is the same from training to test. The hypothesis is inappropriate for the kind of secondary reinforcement experiment where a previously neutral stimulus is used to develop a new response.

Conclusion on secondary reinforcement

Secondary reinforcement flowered quickly on the scientific scene as the hope for explaining all of our social rewards, like money and praise, but hope has wilted. Not only do we lack a laboratory analogue of money as a reinforcer, but we find the field in a state of theoretical confusion and no clear ideas about where to go next. Bolles (1967, p. 368) said, "There is probably no concept in all of psychology that is in such a state of theoretical disarray as the concept of secondary reinforcement." When untidy theoretical conditions like this prevail, the data become of minor concern until a new theorist comes along and gives us cause to be excited about them once again.

THEORIES OF REINFORCEMENT

Drive reduction theory

Clark L. Hull (1884–1952) was a prominent learning theorist whose ideas about the mechanisms of the learning process were rooted in the theory of biological evolution. The drive reduction theory of reinforcement, which was a prominent part of Hull's theorizing, holds that biological survival requires optimum conditions of food, water, air, temperature, intactness of body tissue, etc., and when there is a deviation from an optimum a state of primary need exists. The organism then responds to regain its physiological balance and achieves what is called homeostasis, and the response sequence which reduces the need and optimizes survival is the one that is reinforced and learned. Thus, the hungry animal learns responses that lead to food, and the thirsty animal learns responses that take it to water. Hull said that the organism had a hierarchy of responses available to it in any instrumental learning situation, with one leading to reinforcement and the others not. Initially, responses that fail to produce reinforcement can dominate in the response hierarchy and cause the animal to make inappropriate responses (errors). These inappropriate responses are not reinforced, however, and they extinguish, while the reward-producing response gets stronger and stronger with each reinforcement and eventually dominates the response hierarchy and occurs all the time.

Hull had a highly formalized theory of behavior, much of it stated mathematically (Hull, 1943, 1952). Hull's 1943 book *Principles of Behavior* is an important book in the psychology of learning, and in it Hull defines an increment of habit strength for a response whenever the response produces an event which reduces a need (a reinforcement). For learning to occur, there must be a concurrent drive or motivational state that impels the organism to action, and an increment of habit strength for a response accrues each time the drive is reduced and the organism's need state is moved closer to homeostasis.

The drive reduction theory of reinforcement makes a measure of biological sense, and there is still some credibility for it in the domain of punishment and fear (see Chapter 5), but it has fallen from favor as an explanation for positive reinforcement. There are several reasons for the theory's decline.

One reason is that the time between a primary reinforcement and the reduction of a biological need can often be relatively long as positive reinforcers like food and water are gradually absorbed into the tissues. The result is a long delay of reinforcement—too long for effective learning. The argument has been made that a biological need state is accompanied by internal stimuli, which Hull called drive stimuli, and it is the reduction in their intensity that produces the learning, not the reduction of need. Effects on performance have been found before any nutritive value possibly could be extracted from food (Kohn, 1951), suggesting a usefulness of the distinction between drive and its stimuli, and biological need. A related line of research is concerned with the effect of saccharin as reinforcement in animal learning. Saccharin is a sweet-tasting substance of no nutritive value which is often used as a sugar substitute in diets. Saccharin passes through the body chemically unchanged. Sheffield and Roby (1950) used a T-maze with saccharin solution in the goal box of one of the arms of the maze and water in the other. Hungry, but not thirsty, rats came to choose the saccharin side almost 100 percent of the time. The performance of these animals was almost as good as for rats who received food reinforcement. Whatever the mechanism of saccharin reinforcement, it seems unlikely that it is biological need reduction. A final argument against drive reduction is secondary reinforcement, where events have the power of reinforcement but obviously have no power for reducing biological need. A child will learn the multiplication tables solely for the rewarding praise of the teacher. What biological drives are reduced by praise?

Contiguity theory

The theoretical issue raised by contiguity theory is this: Is more than occurrence of a response to a stimulus necessary for learning? The drive reduction theory of reinforcement says, "Yes, the physiological effect of the reward is necessary," and contiguity theory says, "No, only the response is necessary." Edwin R. Guthrie (1886–1959) was the champion of contiguity theory, and his principle of learning is: *A combination of stimuli which has accompanied a movement will on its recurrence tend to be followed by that movement* (Guthrie, 1952, p. 23). On the surface this principle would seem a denial of the power of reinforcement, but that would be folly because the efficacy of reinforcement is as solidly established as any of our laws in psychology, and Guthrie was not given to folly. Rather, Guthrie said that the function of a reward was to remove the animal from the stimuli acting just before reward. Reward prevents the animal from making other, competing responses to the stimuli, and so when the stimuli occur again the response occurs again. Guthrie studied the escape of animals from a puzzle box by latch manipulation which was followed by the receipt of a reward on the outside. The obtaining of the food when the animal steps outside the box keeps it from making other responses to the stimuli of the box's interior. On the next trial the animal tends to repeat the latch-manipulating escape response because no other responses have been learned to the surrounding stimuli. One would think that learning would occur in one trial, and indeed it is a theoretical possibility with Guthrie's theory, but stimuli ordinarily will change from trial to trial. Sources of the change might be attentional mechanisms or shifts in internal bodily stimuli which are just as much a part of the stimulus complex as environmental stimuli. The result is that only some of the stimuli associated with the response on the last trial will occur on the next trial, and so the response has less than a perfect chance of occurring. Over a number of trials most of the stimulus elements eventually become connected to the response, and it is then that the response is learned.

What do psychologists think about Guthrie's theory? Unlike Hull's theory, Guthrie's theory was simple in its structure and difficult to test. His almost anecdotal style suggests a lack of rigor but it is also possible that his relaxed style obscures solid principles of learning. Estes (e.g., 1950) attempted a mathematical theory of learning that was fundamentally based on Guthrie's thinking, and with some success. All in all, it seems fair to say that today Guthrie's theoretical thinking is not seriously influencing present-day thought about mechanisms of reinforcement. No one has proved it wrong, but not enough psychologists are convinced of its correctness either.

Cognitive theory

The learning of sign-significate expectations. If contiguity theory asks: "Is only a response to a stimulus necessary for learning?" than it might be said that cognitive theory asks if even the response is necessary. Cognitive viewpoints in learning flowered under the stewardship of Edward C. Tolman (1886–1959) in the 1930s and 1940s, declined in the 1950s, and found renewed interest in the 1960s and 1970s in the realm of verbal learning and memory, as later chapters of this book will testify. Mainly, our concern here will be with Tolman's conceptualization of positive reinforcement (Tolman, 1932, 1948).

Tolman believed that the laws of behavior must be expressed as relationships between environmental variables and measures of observable behavior. However, his cognitive theorizing used terms with a strong subjective tone that caused some to see a thinly veiled mentalism with little solid scientific substance. Such critics were misled by the subjective terminology, and they often failed to grasp the thrust of Tolman's thinking. The essence of Tolman's theorizing is that an organism does not learn a goal response to stimuli but rather develops a cognitive grasp of what goes with what, or what leads to what. On learning trials an organism encounters stimuli, or *signs*, on the way to the goal or reward, and these stimuli become cognitive events in the mind of the organism that signify the goal and reward, or *significates*, as Tolman called them. The significate is not always a reward event; it can be a later stimulus event in the sequence that the signs, as immediate stimuli, imply. Through learning the organism comes to have the signs bonded by an *expectation*, so that when the signs are encountered in the environment they give an expectation of the significates to come. When the significates confirm the expectation, there is a *belief* in the signs. A cognitive map of what leads to what is developed as the organism purposefully moves toward the attainment of a goal. Depending upon the state of the organism (e.g., motivation), *demand* will vary for different kinds of goal objects, and demand level is a determiner of performance. In learning a task with problem-solving features, like a maze, the organism will entertain *hypotheses* about signs and significates, and part of learning is the testing of hypotheses and coming up with signs that arouse expectations which reliably signify the goal. Positive reinforcement in Tolman's system plays a confirmatory role for expectations. The rat turns left in the T-maze because it has an expectation of the reward and the goal box, and it is confirmed when the goal is attained.

In exasperation over psychologists often using different labels for the same variable or phenomenon, you might reasonably ask if there is any real difference, when adjustments are made for terminology, between Tolman's formulation and Hull's. Does it make any conceptual difference whether a reward confirms an expectation or reduces a drive? The answer is "no," if that was all there is to it, but the issue has more dimensions than terminology. Unquestionably, Tolman implied that perceptual experience affects cognitive events, and it is these cognitive events that determine observable performance. The implication is that almost any stimulus could signify the successful completion of an act, and it hardly has to be the food or water that is ordinarily used. A light coming on after a bar press might do as much for rat learning as a food pellet. Pure perceptual learning can occur. How stimuli are organized and follow one another as the organism moves through the environment is a fundamental part of the learning process. Put a rat in an empty T-maze without reward and it will learn that the stimuli of the start box are followed by those of the choice point and both maze arms radiating from the choice point have end compartments. The rat should benefit from this knowledge if later asked to learn the maze with reward. Hull and Guthrie had no implications like these.

The latter example was not chosen frivolously because it is the essentials of a famous experiment by Blodgett (1929) on latent learning. Hungry rats were subjects, and the task was learning a complex maze that had several blind alleys as response possibilities between the start box and the goal box. Three groups of animals were used. One trial a day was administered for seven or nine days. Group I, which was a control group, was given conventional reinforced training, where food reward was found in the goal box after each run. Experimental Group III had the same procedures as the control group except that reward was not introduced until Day 3. Experimental Group II was treated the same as Experimental Group III except that the reward did not begin until Day 7. The results are shown in Figure 3–1. If the animals of the experimental groups had learned nothing on their unrewarded trials we would expect their learning to begin at the point of the first rewarded trial and be gradual. But such was not the case. Learning rate was precipitous once the reward was introduced, and the performance curves quickly moved to the level of the control group that was rewarded throughout. The Tolmanian explanation of these data is that the animals benefitted from perceptual learning of the maze in the prereward trials. The food reward was in demand for the hungry animals, and when it was introduced they put their knowledge to work and readily solved the maze. The Blodgett findings have been challenged numerous times and in various ways, and the majority of the studies sustain Blodgett and a cognitive interpretation (MacCorquodale and Meehl, 1954, pp. 199–213). Theories that place a necessity on reward strain to explain how wandering around a maze without reward can produce learning.

McNamara, Long, and Wike (1956) conducted closely related experiments. In their first experiment they used a T-maze and two groups

FIGURE 3–1

Unreinforced exploration of the maze by Groups II and III produced benefits for the rat in subsequent reward learning. The *x* is the point where the reward was first introduced. These data have been used to argue against the necessity of reward for learning.

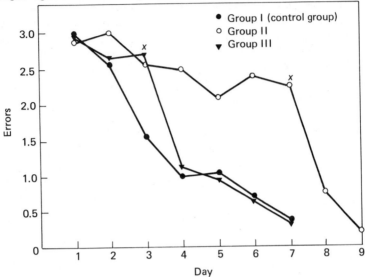

Blodgett, H. C. The effect of the introduction of reward upon the maze performance of rats. *University of California Publications in Psychology,* 1929, *4,* 113–134. Reprinted by permission of the University of California Press.

of rats. The control group learned the maze in a standard fashion, with reward after each trial. Training continued until the animals chose the correct side of the maze 95 percent of the time. The experimental group had identical experiences *except* each rat was dragged through the maze in a little basket; each rat was given the same experiences of right and wrong choices as a matched rat in the control group. Both groups were then given the same 16 extinction trials as a test, where they both ran the maze under standard running conditions. The results were no difference between groups on the test, which is supporting for cognitive theory. A theory that requires a reinforced response for instrumental learning would expect no learning at all by the experimental group. The critical responses in a maze are running movements and, most importantly, choice behavior at the choice point. The animals in the experimental group were required to do neither, yet they learned. Cognitive theory would say that being dragged through the maze in a basket provides an opportunity for perceptual learning about the route to food. In their second experiment, McNamara and his colleagues dramatically reduced extra-maze cues by painting the experimental room black, surrounding the maze with black cloth, and reducing the illumination. Otherwise procedures were about the same as the first experiment. One might expect, theoretically, that the experimental group which must rely on perceptual learning would have some trouble because the visual environment was so degraded. The control group, however, would be expected to fare better. They have the same poor visual environment as the experimental group but they have information from the internal, kinesthetic cues from movement and the experimental group in the basket is denied it entirely. As expected from a cognitive learning position, the control group learned and the experimental group did not.

Hypothesis behavior, awareness, and operant verbal learning. Tolman's theory raised two questions which continue to divide learning psychologists: To what extent is conscious hypothesis behavior part of the learning process? To what extent is conscious knowledge of the situation, the response, and the reinforcement required for learning? These questions seem innocent enough, but they gain in substance when we look at the position of E. L. Thorndike in the psychology of learning and contrast it to Tolman's.

There was systematic laboratory work being done on animal learning by the end of the 19th century, and a major figure to step forward was E. L. Thorndike. He was the strong beginning of research on reinforced learning in the United States, and his approaches and ideas are still with us, both in the laboratory and out. If Thorndike had been a highly specialized psychologist who worked on a narrow class of problems the significance of his ideas might have been lost or at least delayed for a time, but he was a man of wide interests. He started out as an animal psychologist (as a Harvard student he was ordered out of his rooming house because he was raising chickens in his room for research), and he came to work extensively on human learning. In his lifetime he saw his ideas taught in every department of psychology and every college of education in the country.

Thorndike's doctoral dissertation (Thorndike, 1898) was about reward learning. We have come to have a good understanding of reward learning, so Thorndike's work might seem trite from our mature stance, but in historical context it was not trite but emerged as a stand against the prevailing psychology of the day. The human psychology of the time introspectively analyzed one's own consciousness to determine its elements and structure, and it was called *structuralism*. The animal psychology of that period was under the influence of Darwinism, and its literature had accounts of animal behavior in terms of intelligence and reasoning as adaptive mechanisms, speculations about consciousness in animals and where it emerged on the phylogenetic scale, and the kinds of animal behavior that did or did not require consciousness. Thorndike's interpretation of reward learning was a strong stand against these prevailing mentalistic conceptions of animal behavior, as well as running counter to structuralism.

Thorndike said that an animal did not use conscious reasoning and active thought processes in learning. Instead, learning is a trial and error process. The animal makes many random movements in the situation and one of them leads to reward. The reward causes the successful movement to receive an increment in strength, and it is boosted in relation to all of the other movements that can occur in the situation. These other movements, by not being reinforced, are extinguished. Rewarding of the correct movement on subsequent trials steadily increases its likelihood of occurrence, and when its dominance is complete the learning is complete. Later, Thorndike used his conception of animal learning to explain human learning. A child learning to solve an arithmetic problem will make various wrong answers but when the correct response does occur the teacher will reward it by saying "Right." As in animal learning, rewards for the correct responses eventually cause them to occur with good regularity. Thorndike had no more use for conscious, active mental processes in human learning than in animal learning. For Thorndike, the reward acts to strengthen the response in a wholly automatic fashion, whether the person (or animal) is consciously aware of it or not. Thorndike (1935, p. 62) said that "a person may increase the probability that certain situations will evoke certain responses without knowing at the time that he is doing so or afterward that he has done so." Similarly, Thorndike (1935, p. 63) said that reward will strengthen the connection "regardless of the learner's knowledge about the tendency or ability to identify, describe, or control it." This position is known as the *behaviorist* viewpoint, and is to be contrasted to the cognitive viewpoint. Behaviorism was a movement in psychology that began in 1913 (Watson, 1913), and its rejection of consciousness and its emphasis on laws that relate observable stimuli and responses complemented Thorndike's position. Behaviorism has had a full life and is still a robust movement in the United States. Many behaviorists today are followers of B. F. Skinner, who is the undisputed ruler of modern-day behaviorism.

Tolman's cognitive psychology has an organism who is mentally active during the learning process and who is not a passive recipient of reinforcement. Hypotheses are entertained during learning about what leads to what and about the implications of the reward for behavioral options. Tolman (1958, pp. 109–112) believed that conscious awareness can accompany human hypothesis behavior, although he saw no necessity for it.

The cognitive descendants of Tolman in the 1960s and 70s took a stronger position than Tolman's and held that hypothesis behavior is a conscious aware process, and that learning does not occur until the subject has become aware of the stimulus-response-reinforcement relationship. Reinforcement does not automatically inflict an increment of habit. Instead it is but a signal which informs the subject of the expected response, and the subject proceeds to test various hypotheses until learning what the reinforcement means for his behavior. Learning is a problem-solving situation, and when the problem is solved the subject produces the response with high reliability and regularly earns the reward. Behaviorists, of course, deny all of this in debate and experiment, and a main arena for the confrontation is *operant verbal learning*. Theoretical and experimental papers on this topic now number in the hundreds, and it is instructive to examine it and see how the two theoretical forces operate in defense of their positions. It is not surprising that human verbal learning is the arena because conscious awareness can be given a definition at the human level as we shall see. What awareness might mean for animals is not clear. Expectedly, cognitive psychologists are interested mostly in human behavior and have only passing interest in animal behavior. Behaviorists operate freely in both provinces.

In the context of operant verbal learning "awareness" means a grasp of the principle of reinforcement where the subject knows the kind of responses that will produce reinforcement. Thorndike and Rock (1934) were the first to do an experiment on operant verbal learning. A subject was presented with a list of words and for each one was required to give the first association that came to mind as quickly as possible. If the response was sequentially related to the stimulus word as in speaking or writing, the experimenter rewarded the subject by saying "Right." Otherwise the experimenter said nothing or "Wrong." For example, YOURS–TRULY was rewarded but YOURS–MINE was not. Learning definitely occurred, with the average number of responses correct going from about 3 to 6 from the first to the 30th block of 10 responses. But what about awareness? And how do we know an aware subject? There are two methods that have been used to define an aware subject. One is to ask the subject to verbalize the principle of reinforcement. The other is to examine individual learning curves for "insightful" jumps to near 100 percent correct. This latter method assumes that after becoming aware of the principle of reinforcement, a subject should be able to respond almost perfectly all of the time. Thorndike and Rock used this second method. They examined their data for insightful leaps in performance and found none, and they concluded that learning can occur without awareness. This study is the pioneering one for the field, and investigators have been reacting to it ever since.

An experiment of the kind that is commonly done today is by Cohen et al. (1954, Experiment 1), and it also supports the behavioristic position by finding evidence for learning without awareness. They used the Sentence Construction Task, developed by Taffel (1955). The stimulus for eliciting a response was a card with a verb and six pronouns printed on it: *I, we, he, they, she,* and *you.* The subject's task was to make up a sentence using the verb and one of the pronouns. There were 80 such cards, each with a different verb and with the order of the pronouns randomized on each one. The rewarded response class was sentences that used *I* and *we,* and subjects of the experimental group had them rewarded with "Good" from the experimenter. Nothing was said to a control group. The results appear in Figure 3–2. The

FIGURE 3–2

The effect of rewarding subjects with "Good" every time they composed a sentence that began with *I* or *we.*

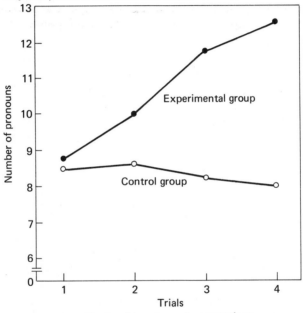

Trials

Blocks of twenty card presentations

Cohen, B. D., Kalish, H. I., Thurston, J. R., & Cohen, E. Experimental manipulation of verbal behavior. *Journal of Experimental Psychology,* 1954, *47,* 106–110. Reprinted by permission of the American Psychological Association.

rewarded subjects learned and, for our theoretical concerns here, none were found aware of the principle of reinforcement in a postexperimental interview.

A tilt toward the behaviorist's position in this experiment by Cohen et al. should not be taken as decisive because there are other experiments which support the cognitive view and shift the balance back again. Consider an experiment by Levin (1961). Cohen et al. used four questions in the post-experimental interview, and it was Levin's thesis that the four questions insufficiently probed for awareness. Perhaps the learning without awareness which Cohen et al. found was because of aware subjects who were misclassified as unaware. Levin repeated the Cohen et al. experiment but used instead an extended interview of 16 questions, the first 4 being the same as Cohen et al. Learning without awareness was found when the subjects were classified with the first four questions, which is the same as Cohen et al. found. But, when the probing for awareness was deeper with the extended interview, some of the subjects classified as unaware by the first four questions were now classified as aware. Looking at the data again with this new classification of subjects, only aware subjects now learned. Levin's experiment highlights the continuing problem of how awareness should be determined.

A well-known experiment by DeNike (1964) also supports the cognitive view of operant verbal learning. DeNike had his subjects say any words whatsoever that came to mind, and from this verbal outpouring he selected human nouns for reinforcement. The reinforcement might look like this:

Subject: "Is girl happily do architect," etc.
Experimenter: "Mmm-hmm Mmm-hmm," etc.

Each subject was required to say 300 words. After every 25 words there was a pause and the subject was required to write thoughts about the experiment, which was the source of information about awareness. DeNike's study had two groups of subjects, an experimental group and a control group. The experimental group first had 50 words without reinforcement to determine the baseline for human nouns without reinforcement, followed by 250 words where human nouns were reinforced. Learning would be shown by an increase in the number of human nouns from the baseline. The control group also had the first 50 words without reinforcement, and random reinforcement of the remaining words 10 percent of the time. The procedure for the control group is considered a good one because it received "Mmm-hmm" events from the experimenter just as the other group, but since they were not response contingent they could not contribute to learning.

DeNike's results are shown in Figure 3–3. Using the verbal reports, DeNike classified the subjects of his experimental group as aware or unaware, depending on whether a subject was able to verbalize the principle of reinforcement when writing thoughts about the experiment after every 25 trials. These data are on the left-hand side of Figure 3–3; notice that they handily fit the cognitive conception of learning. Only a subject aware of the principle of reinforcement learns. The right-hand side of Figure 3–3 is another plot of DeNike's data, and it is also in keeping with the assumptions of cognitive psychology. Here the

FIGURE 3–3

Effects of reinforcing human nouns as the subjects spoke any words that came to mind. The curves on the left show that the only subjects who learn are those aware that human nouns are being reinforced. The data on the right show the sharp increment in performance that results at the point of awareness.

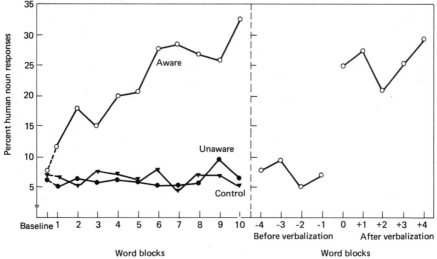

Spielberger, C. D., & DeNike, L. D. Descriptive behaviorism versus cognitive theory in verbal operant conditioning. *Psychological Review,* 1966, *73,* 306–326. Reprinted by permission of the American Psychological Association.

data of the aware subjects of the experimental group are plotted with respect to the block of trials where the principle of reinforcement was first reported. Cognitive theorists contend that there should be a dramatic leap in performance level at the point of discovering the principle of reinforcement, and indeed so. Probably the reason that Thorndike and Rock (1934) did not find an insightful jump in performance was that their subjects were required to respond as fast as possible, and so did not have time to use the principle of reinforcement even though they might have known it. Weiss (1955) presents evidence in support of this possibility.

Investigators of operant verbal learning who have concerned themselves with these theoretical issues have almost always studied acquisition and have not appreciated the implications of extinction. The typical behaviorist today accepts the empirical facts of extinction without a theory to explain them. Cognitive psychologists have not particularly bothered to theorize about extinction either, but nevertheless their position has implications for extinction. One implication is that the decline in performance that is extinction occurs because the subject entertains new hypotheses about the changed conditions of reinforcement, and these cause her or him to try other responses in an attempt to acquire reinforcement again. The outcome is a decline in occurrence of the criterion response that had been receiving reinforcement. But notice that the criterion response is not weakened—the subject is only electing not to give it as he or she tries other response possibilities. If asked, the subject should be able to give the response fully again. Another implication is that extinction need not occur if subjects perceive the continued occurrence of the criterion response as a requirement of them. An example of failure to extinguish is found in Cohen et al. (1954, Experiment II). Patty and Page (1973, p. 312) report a subject who failed to extinguish because he thought that the experimenter was testing persistence. When the trade is in voluntary thought processes a subject's perception of the situational demands becomes important.

Patty and Page (1973) tested the implication that the extinguished response could be reinstated in full strength if the subject were asked. They used the Sentence Construction Task, with "Good" being the reinforcement for sentences beginning with *They*. Reinforced training continued until a performance criterion of 13 correct out of 15 was met. Withdrawal of reinforcement followed for 45 trials, and then the experimenter stopped and gave these instructions before giving 15 trials more:

> OK. Let's pause for a moment. I'm going to give some further instructions; it's important that you don't answer me or talk back in any way, just listen. You remember that for a long time I said "Good" after some of your sentences. Now for a long time I haven't said anything. This next part is a test to see if you knew, and can still remember, what it was that you did that made me say "Good" before. I'm going to show several more cards and won't be saying anything, but I want you to make your sentences in such a way that I would have said "Good" before. This way you will demonstrate by your actions that you knew why I said "Good." Let's start again.[1]

The results are shown in Figure 3–4. The decline in performance that is extinction readily occurred, but notice that it does not represent a permanent weakening of response tendency. The subjects fully reinstated the criterion response when asked, as cognitive psychology implies.

DeNike's experiment (DeNike, 1964) is representative of a number which show a strong correlation between learning and reports of awareness, and one would think that the behaviorists would collapse under the onslaught of such convincing evidence. Never. That awareness is a mediating event on which learning depends is the cognitive position, and the behaviorists acknowledge it as one possibility. There are two other main possibilities, however, and the behaviorists are attracted to both of them (Greenspoon and Brownstein, 1967; Kanfer, 1968). One

---

[1] *Journal of Experimental Research in Personality,* 1973, Vol. 6, pp. 308–309. Reprinted by permission of Academic Press, Inc.

FIGURE 3–4

The extinction of a verbal operant response in Trial Blocks 7–9 after reaching the criterion of acquisition in Block 6. Block 10 shows response reinstatement on request.

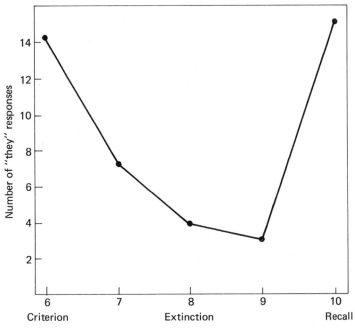

Blocks of 15 trials

Patty, R. A., & Page, M. M. Manipulations of a verbal conditioning situation based upon demand characteristics theory. *Journal of Experimental Research in Personality,* 1973, *6,* 307–313. Reprinted by permission of Academic Press, Inc.

is that the cognitive psychologists have it backwards. Awareness does not mediate learning. Rather, it is learning that mediates awareness, and so awareness is incidental and after the fact. Reinforcement produces a change in response probability, the subject notices the change, and becomes aware of the principle of reinforcement as a byproduct. The other possibility is that awareness is a verbal report in its own right, and it is wrong to conceptualize it as consciousness. Given that the verbal report is a function of the same variables as the criterion response, they will be correlated, but correlation is not causality, as generations of students in statistics courses have heard their instructors say (a correlation between barrooms and churches in cities does not mean that drinking causes religion or vice versa). In truth, all three of these possibilities are plausible and, in sad truth, there is no incisive experimental data that allows us to choose among them. However a new threat to the behaviorist's position is the extinction data of Patty and Page (1973) in

Figure 3–4. From a behavioristic stance it is hard to see how extinction can be reversed on request. Perhaps extinction will be the skirmish ground of the future.

Prepotent response theory

The prepotent response theory of reinforcement belongs to David Premack. As are all learning theorists, he is fascinated with the classic issue of why some events are reinforcers and others are not. The theory is refreshing because it bypasses standard positions like the strengthening of stimulus-response associations and drive reduction. Premack states a theory of reinforcement entirely in terms of responses and their probabilities.

It is always good strategy for a theorist to outline the position that he is reacting against, and Premack (1965, pp. 129–133) discusses the three basic assumptions about reinforcement which all learning psychologists accept:

1. A reinforcer is a stimulus which, if delivered in a certain relation to the response, will produce a change in frequency of that response. Some stimuli have the property of reinforcers and some do not.

2. Reinforcers are trans-situational. A stimulus that is effective as a reinforcer with one response will be effective with many responses, ideally all responses. There is no reason to believe that food will not be a reinforcer for any response of any hungry organism. Psychologists would pay scant attention to a reinforcer that alters the probability of only one response class for one organism.

3. There are two classes of responses, one that is an accompaniment of reinforcement but not reinforceable, and another that is reinforceable but not an accompaniment of reinforcement. We are always concerned with operations that change the probability of response classes like bar pressing or maze-running, but never eating or drinking.

Premack points out that none of these constitute a theory of reinforcement but rather are the implicit empirical premises that guide all theorists and workers in the field of learning. The first two assumptions unquestionably have empirical foundation but the knowledge is without much formal structure. No one has ever catalogued what is known about what events are reinforcers. Nor has any one bothered to document the trans-situationality of reinforcers, where the range of their effectiveness across response classes and organisms is specified. The third assumption has not been tested at all, perhaps because it is the most low key of the three, and it is this third assumption that Premack turns into a theory of reinforcement.

His theory is one of response relations, which is stated in one generalization: *Of any two responses the more probable response will reinforce the less probable one—the prepotent response is the reinforcer.* There are four implications of this generalization that deserve emphasis:

1. Anatomically different responses can be compared directly. For example, ways can be devised to determine the probabilities of bar pressing and eating, compare them, and determine which one will reinforce the other.

2. The only thing that matters is the probability of the response, not the variables that determine the probability of response. That response probability might be altered by increasing the time of food deprivation is irrelevant in and of itself—only the probability level matters. This is called the "indifference principle."

3. Reinforcement is a relative property. The most probable response of a set will reinforce all of the other responses, the next most probable response will reinforce all responses of lesser probability but not the response of greater probability, and so on down the scale until the least probable response reinforces no response of the set.

4. The reinforcement relation is reversible. By manipulating the probabilities of Responses A and B, we can cause A to reinforce B and vice versa.

Evidence for Premack's theory is all around us. A food-eating response will reinforce bar pressing in an animal because its probability of occurrence is higher than bar pressing. A boy will learn the multiplication tables (a low probability response) for the opportunity to play baseball (a high probability response). It is problematical, however, whether the boy's listening to Handel's *Organ Concerto in F Major* would be an effective reinforcer for learning the multiplication tables because it is a low probability response also.

A marvelous thing about theory worthy of the name is that it will imply the unexpected while, at the same time, accounting for the known and expected. All theories of reinforcement including Premack's would say that eating reinforces an instrumental motor response, but only Premack's theory predicts the unexpected—that an instrumental motor response like running or bar pressing can reinforce the eating response and increase its probability of occurrence.

Every good drive reduction theorist knows that first-grade children will play a pinball machine for candy reward, but would they predict that children will eat candy for the opportunity to play a pinball machine? Premack (1959) used this situation to demonstrate such a reversal of reinforcement relations. Premack's theory requires that the probabilities of the two responses first be determined in a free situation, and in a first session he had both candy and the pinball machine freely available. The number of pinball machine responses and pieces of candy eaten by each child were recorded. Some children played the pinball machine more than they ate candy, and they were called the "manipulators." Others had a preference for candy and they were called "eaters." With respect to the theory, pinball playing should be reinforcing for manipulators because it is their most probable response, and candy eating should be reinforcing for eaters for the same reason. In a second session Premack introduced contingency relationships: The pinball machine could not be played unless the candy was eaten, which has the candy eating reinforced by pinball playing; or the candy could not be eaten unless the pinball machine was played, which has pinball playing reinforced by candy eating. Half of the manipulators were in each of these conditions, as were half of the eaters. The theoretical prediction was that pinball playing should reinforce the eating response and increase its frequency for manipulators but not for eaters. Correspondingly, eating should reinforce pinball playing for eaters but not for manipulators. The data which Premack obtained nicely conformed to this theoretical prediction. In another experiment, Premack (1962) found that the opportunity for a rat to run in an activity wheel was reinforcing for the drinking response and increased the probability of its occurrence, which is also a case of reinforcement reversal. The converse is, of course, easily obtained, and is a routine finding. Similarly, Sawisch and Denny (1973) trained pigeons to peck a key and then made the availability of key pecking dependent upon the eating of free grain. The eating of free grain steadily increased.

A critical test of prepotent response theory lies in verification of the indifference principle. The indifference principle contends that the reinforcing power of a response depends solely on its probability and it makes no difference how response probability was determined. Premack (1963) tested the reinforcing power of drinking sweet-tasting sucrose liquid and running in an activity wheel for the bar-press response. Rats were the subjects. The independent probability of sucrose drinking was assessed in several free response sessions, and the probability was manipulated by using either 16, 32, or 64 percent sucrose in the solution. Free response sessions of wheel running were also held, where the independent probability of running was manipulated by light or heavy force requirements for wheel turning. The various levels of sucrose gave different probabilities for drinking, as did the force requirements for turning the wheel. The results are shown in Figure 3–5, and they meet theoretical expectations. The higher the independent probability of the reinforcer response the greater the power for reinforcing the bar-press response, and it does not matter if reinforcer probability was determined by amount of sucrose or force requirements in wheel turning.

Premack (1959, 1965) recognizes the several problems that exist for his theory, one of which is exemplified by this last experiment, positive though the evidence be. The theory turns on the relations between response probabilities, which means that responses must be counted

FIGURE 3–5
Evidence for Premack's indifference principle. Shown is
the effect of drinking sucrose solution or running in an
activity wheel as reinforcement for bar pressing by the
rat. The probability of drinking the sucrose solution or
running in the activity wheel is given on the horizontal
axis, and it was manipulated by the percent of sucrose
concentration (16, 32, and 64 percent) and the force requirement to turn the wheel (light, LW; heavy, HW).

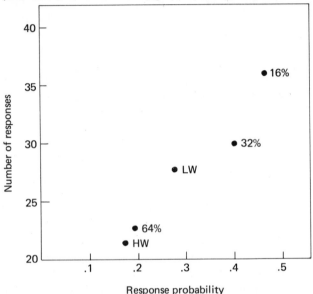

Response probability

Premack, D. Prediction of the comparative reinforcement
values of running and drinking. *Science*, 1963, *139*, 1062–1063.
Reprinted by permission of the American Association for the
Advancement of Science.

in a free response situation to determine their probability of occurrence.
But how is a response defined? Is one occurrence of an eating response
the entire sequence of seizing, biting, chewing, and swallowing the food,
or is each element of the sequence an element to be counted? The
definition of "response" is an old problem for experimental psychology,
and the issue resurfaces again from time to time. What it means for
prepotent reinforcement theory is yet to be determined.

Another difficulty is accounting for learning when no apparent response is associated with the reinforcement. Miller and Kessen (1952)
found that rats could learn a T-maze when milk was injected directly
into the stomach for the correct choice and saline solution injected for
the incorrect choice. Learning was not as fast as when milk reinforcement was taken directly in the mouth in the normal fashion, but learning

nevertheless occurred. Premack cannot apply his theory to this situation because of the absence of an observable response when milk is injected into the stomach as the reinforcing event.

In spite of the problems we must score Premack's theory high in inventiveness. Being able to reverse reinforcement relations is a particularly important finding that cannot be generated by competing theories, and our theories of tomorrow must come to grips with it.

SENSORY REINFORCEMENT

The topic of sensory reinforcement is set off in this separate final section because it does not fit any of the established mechanisms and theories of reinforcement very well. Sensory reinforcement is a young subject matter, being a scant 25 years old, and it will be a while before it fits a larger theoretical scheme.

In one sense "sensory reinforcement" is poorly named because any reinforcement is a sensory event that follows the response being learned. Notwithstanding, the label is appropriate because it refers to learning that occurs for the reinforcement of stimulus change, so it is sensation in a very fundamental sense that induces learning. When we speak of food reinforcers, for example, we are speaking of a particular class of stimuli that are especially effective for learning when the organism is hungry, but sensory reinforcement is different because it does not specify a class of stimuli that will function as reinforcers, only that there be a sufficient change in stimuli, whatever they are.

The origins of sensory reinforcement lie in exploratory and curiosity behavior. Why does a rat walk around, touch objects, look about, engage in play with other rats, and on and on endlessly? Why does a human walk around, touch objects, look about, engage in play with other humans, and on and on endlessly? We say these organisms have curiosity and are exploratory, but this is only a description of behavior, not a scientific explanation. Various explanations are possible within established frames of references, although most certainly speculative. One might say that there is an instinct for exploration, that fearful situations are being avoided, that there is a motivation to explore, or that responses to stimuli like these have been positively reinforced in the past and encountering the stimuli again evokes the responses again. All of these are possibilities, but somehow their use to explain the endless catalog of exploratory and curiosity behavior seems contrived. This topic did not find conceptual direction until the 1950s, when opportunity to explore and encounter (or create) stimulus change was found to be reinforcing for the learning of new responses, just as food might be reinforcing for a hungry animal. The experiments of Harlow, Butler, and Montgomery were pioneering.

Harlow (1950) had a six-unit mechanical puzzle, which is shown in Figure 3–6. At the start of a trial the device was as pictured, and the task was to remove five restraining devices and free the hinge at the bottom. This is child's play for a human, but Harlow's interesting

FIGURE 3–6
Monkeys will learn to solve this mechanical puzzle without primary reinforcement.

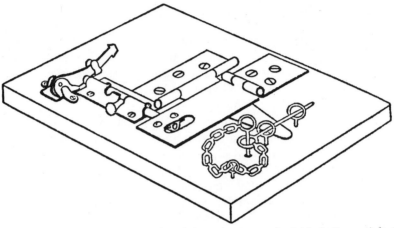

Harlow, H. F. Learning and satiation of response in intrinsically motivated complex puzzle performance by monkeys. *Journal of Comparative and Physiological Psychology*, 1950, *43*, 289–294. Reprinted by permission of the American Psychological Association.

innovation was that he gave it to monkeys to solve without primary reinforcement. Figure 3–7 shows the learning curve, and there is regular learning for no more reinforcement than the stimulation inherent in manipulation of the puzzle. Harlow explained the findings in terms of an externally elicited drive rather than an internal drive like hunger. The stimuli of the puzzle created the motivation to solve it. It was, as Harlow put it, a "manipulation drive."

Butler (1953) also used monkeys and for the experiment he had them in a completely enclosed cage except for two small doors which, when opened, allowed the animal to see the busy laboratory outside. Each door had an identifying colored card, and one of them was designated the correct one and if pressed would come open and give the animal an opportunity to visually explore the laboratory. With no primary reinforcement and only the opportunity for visual exploration as the reward, Butler's monkeys readily learned to press the required door. Butler spoke of a drive for visual exploration; an animal is motivated to seek change in visual stimulation.

FIGURE 3–7

The learning curve of monkeys for solving the puzzle shown in Figure 3–6. The performance measure is a ratio of errors to correct responses which approaches zero as a limit as number of correct solutions increase and number of errors decrease.

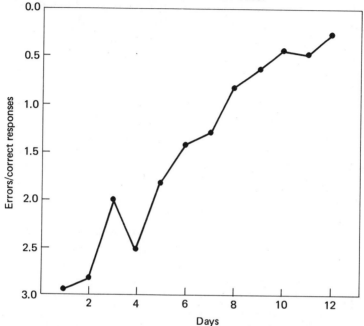

Harlow, H. F. Learning and satiation of response in intrinsically motivated complex puzzle performance by monkeys. *Journal of Comparative and Physiological Psychology*, 1950, *43*, 289–294. Reprinted by permission of the American Psychological Association.

Montgomery (1954) and Montgomery and Segall (1955) found that rats would learn to run a Y-maze and a T-maze simply for the opportunity to explore a more complex maze with a number of turns and passageways. The learning was explained by an increase in an "exploratory drive" aroused by the complex maze that was the reward. About this same time evidence began to appear in psychology literature that rats would learn to press the bar in the Skinner box for only the reinforcement of a light coming on (Kish, 1955; Marx, Henderson, and Roberts, 1955), once again highlighting the significance of stimulus change for learning.

Harlow, Butler, and Montgomery all had notions about stimulus-centered drives determining the behavior. Whether it was manual manipulation, visual exploration, or locomotor exploration, it was a matter of changing patterns of external stimuli, and their effects were assigned the theoretical role of motivation. In one way this was a commendable move because it brought the stimulus effects which these investigators inferred under the heading of motivation, but in another way it was disconcerting to those whose theoretical thinking about motivation was centered on internal homeostatic drives like hunger and thirst. For these theorists drive was an energizer of behavior that heightened activity level as the animal responded to achieve its reward. How, then, could a drive induced by stimulus change *after* the occurrence of the response affect behavior (Brown, 1953)? If the motivation comes after the response, what impelled the animal to action in the first place? Brown (1953, p. 54) correctly saw that the stimulus-centered theorists were offering a drive increase theory of reinforcement in opposition to drive reduction theory of reinforcement.

About this same time there was a relevant thrust from brain physiology. In the late 1940s physiologists began a program of research on the ascending reticular activating system of the brain (Moruzzi and Magoun, 1949), which is sometimes called the brain stem reticular formation or, simply, the reticular formation. Heretofore the emphasis of physiologists had been on the cue function of stimuli being processed by the brain, where the sensory impulse would travel from the receptor to a projection area of the cortex and where we might become aware of it, discriminate it from other stimuli, learn a response to it, etc. Research on the reticular formation, however, revealed that stimuli follow a second, circuitous route through the reticular formation which discharges broadly over the cerebral cortex. This function of the reticular formation came to be known as the arousal function because when it was present in an intact animal the animal was generally alert and responsive, and when the action of the reticular formation was surgically denied the animal was drowsy and indifferent. Psychologists of a physiological persuasion were quick to see that arousal had implications for motivation if not actually being the physiological basis of motivation. Because of the influence of Hull's theory mostly, psychologists conceived of drive as having a general capability for activating any response that might occur, and the general bombardment of the cortex by the reticular formation was nicely parallel to the general energizing effect of drives. Hebb (1955, p. 249) wrote that stimuli had a cue function and an arousal function, and that the arousal function is synonymous with a general drive state.

The theory of stimulus-centered drive by Harlow, Butler, and Montgomery dovetailed with the arousal view of drive—the reticular formation is activated by stimuli, the reticular formation is the basis of drive, and so stimuli are motivating. When an animal is curious and exploring, it is being motivated by the changing stimulus situation. But why does an organism learn for the reinforcement of stimulus change? Needed was the additional assumption that an increase in motivation can be reinforcing—not only does stimulus change produce an increment of motivation but the occurrence of the increment is reinforcing for the response that produced it. This assumption is straightforward enough, but its acceptance was questioned by drive reduction theorists. If hungry and thirsty animals learn by decreasing their hunger and thirst drives, how can drive *increase* produce learning? You cannot have it both ways. Or can you?

The inverted U hypothesis was the arousal theorists answer to the drive reduction theorists' criticism; the hypothesis shows how a theory can explain the reinforcing effects of both drive decrease and drive increase. (Hebb, 1955; Malmo, 1959; Fiske and Maddi, 1961). To accommodate drive-increase and drive-decrease views of reinforcement within the same arousal theory, one must assume that the degree of arousal is important. When the organism is below the optimum point of arousal an increase in drive is rewarding, and when one is above the optimum point the drive level is aversive and a decrease in drive is rewarding. Butler's monkeys were in a dimly lit cage and low in arousal level. When the door opened their arousal level was increased by the stimulation of the visual scene, and the increase was rewarding. A hungry animal, on the other hand, has excessive arousal that is unpleasant for it and the reduction in internal stimulation that eating provides is rewarding. Berlyne (1967, p. 51) reasons in this fashion, but Fowler (1967, p. 159) properly points out that such reasoning is difficult to work out empirically because we cannot specify optimal levels of stimulation for different classes of stimuli and situations, kinds of organisms, and types of responses. Without knowing the optimal point we do not know where we are on the U-function, and we cannot predict whether a change in stimulation will be an increase or a decrease in arousal and be reinforcing or not. Arousal theory has been useful as an attempt to integrate externally-based drives and internally-based drives, and as a link with contemporary findings in brain physiology, but it is not yet a fully functioning theory of reinforcement.

But is it possible that drive reduction theory might explain it all, without the complexities of a U-shaped function and both drive increase and drive decrease as the conditions of reinforcement? Yes, is the answer. Myers and Miller (1954), as drive reduction theorists, proposed such a theory. They assumed that inadequate external stimulation creates a need for stimulation, just as food or water deprivation creates hunger and thirst. When an organism is deprived of sufficient stimulation it develops a *boredom drive,* as it has been called. In accord with drive reduction theory, the boredom drive is reduced by stimulus change and the change is reinforcing for the response that produced it. With this viewpoint, a theoretical economy is achieved because all drives are related to learning in the same way. There is no need for assuming that drive decrease produces learning in some cases and drive increase in others.

The first major clue that too much exposure to a stimulus can produce a need for stimulus change lay in the research on spontaneous alternation in the choices of rats in a T-maze (Dember and Fowler, 1958; Glanzer, 1958). If the animal turns right on a trial in a T-maze and then is immediately returned to the starting point, the likelihood is high that it will turn left on the next trial. Glanzer (1958) wrote in terms of "stimulus satiation," where continuing exposure to a stimulus decreases the responding to it and presumably causes the organism to alleviate the satiation with stimulus change. Spontaneous alternation was not concerned with the learning process but rather with the patterning of responses that occurs over a series of learning trials where the reinforcement is food or water in a goal box of the maze. Nevertheless, at work was the same fundamental phenomenon that caused Myers and Miller (1954) to suggest a boredom drive that can be reduced by stimulus change. The rat's right-turning on the present trial causes boredom (satiation) with the stimuli in that area of the maze, and it is alleviated on the next trial by turning left and finding new stimuli.

The idea of a boredom drive says that the longer you are exposed to stimuli the higher the drive level and the greater the need to reduce it by stimulus change. Earlier in this section we examined an experiment by Butler (1953) where monkeys learned to open a door of an enclosed cage for the reward of visually exploring the laboratory outside. In a later experiment, Butler (1957) used essentially the same procedure but with zero, two, four, or eight hours of visual deprivation in the enclosed cage before the door could be opened momentarily for a brief look. The measure of performance was the number of times after the deprivation period that the door was opened for visual exploration, and Butler found that the frequency of door-opening responses increased as visual deprivation increased from zero to eight hours. As predicted, the greater the boredom drive the greater the need for stimulus change.

In a closely related experiment Fox (1962) kept monkeys in a light-tight box, much the same as Butler, for visual deprivation periods of zero, one, two, three, four, and eight hours after which the pressing of a bar would flash a light for 0.5 seconds and illuminate the inside of the box. The results are shown in Figure 3–8, expressed in terms of number of bar presses. The amount of visual stimulation which the animals generate for themselves is almost directly proportional to the amount of visual deprivation, which corresponds to Butler's findings.

Sensory reinforcement has been provocative for the topic of positive reinforcement. Its beginnings in exploratory and curiosity behavior led us to an appreciation of a new class of reinforcers that seems best described as stimulus change or variety. How to bring these new rein-

FIGURE 3–8

Using light as the reinforcement, number of bar presses made by monkeys as a function of hours in total darkness.

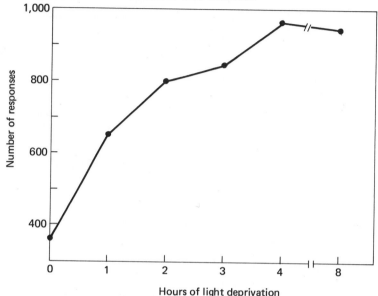

Fox, S. S. Self-maintained sensory input and sensory deprivation in monkeys: A behavioral and neuropharmacological study. *Journal of Comparative and Physiological Psychology,* 1962, *55,* 438–444. Reprinted by permission of the American Psychological Association.

forcers in theoretical line with more conventional reinforcers is a challenge, and the concept of boredom drive and its reduction as reinforcement is an interesting approach.

SUMMARY

The purpose of this chapter was to discuss why positive reinforcers work as they do to produce learning. A distinction was made between primary and secondary reinforcement. Primary reinforcers do not depend on the learning history of the organism. Hungry or thirsty animals learning a response with food or water as reinforcement is an example. Secondary reinforcers, however, are based on learning history. A neutral stimulus gains the power of secondary reinforcement through association with the response being learned with primary reinforcement, the primary reinforcer itself, or both. Secondary reinforcement is often used to explain why a seemingly neutral stimulus like a word of praise can be reinforcing.

Drive reduction theory, contiguity theory, cognitive theory, and prepotent response theory are prominent attempts to explain the action of positive reinforcers. Drive reduction theory says that an event will be a reinforcer if it reduces a biological need. Contiguity theory contends that the response need only occur in the presence of a stimulus for learning to occur and for the stimulus to evoke the response reliably. Reinforcement is important only insofar as it insures the stimulus-response association being learned and discourages the occurrence of unwanted responses. Cognitive theory has learning based on the subject's perception of relationships among events in the situation, with neither the reduction of drive nor stimulus-response contiguity required. Prepotent response theory says that one response will reinforce another; a more probable response like eating will reinforce a less probable response like bar pressing. None of these theories are without their problems, and none have a wholehearted endorsement.

A type of reinforcement that stands apart from primary and secondary reinforcement is sensory reinforcement. Sensory reinforcement occurs when stimulus change is the event which produces learning, as when an animal learns to run a maze for the opportunity to explore. One explanation of how sensory reinforcement produces learning is drive reduction. It is assumed that exposure to stimuli induces boredom, boredom is a drive, and stimulus change reduces boredom.

REFERENCES

Berlyne, D. E.   Arousal and reinforcement. In D. Levine (Ed.), *Nebraska symposium on motivation*. Lincoln: University of Nebraska Press, 1967, pp. 1–110.

Blodgett, H. C.   The effect of the introduction of reward upon the maze performance of rats. *University of California Publications in Psychology*, 1929, *4*, 113–134.

Bolles, R. C.   *Theory of motivation*. New York: Harper & Row, 1967.

Brown, J. S.   Comments on Professor Harlow's paper. *In Current theory and research in motivation: A symposium*. Lincoln: University of Nebraska Press, 1953, pp. 49–55.

Bugelski, B. R.   Extinction with and without sub-goal reinforcement. *Journal of Comparative Psychology*, 1938, *26*, 121–134.

Bugelski, B. R.   *The psychology of learning*. New York: Holt, 1956.

Butler, R. A.   Discrimination learning by Rhesus monkeys to visual-exploration motivation. *Journal of Comparative and Physiological Psychology*, 1953, *46*, 95–98.

Butler, R. A.   The effect of deprivation of visual incentives on visual exploration motivation in monkeys. *Journal of Comparative and Physiological Psychology*, 1957, *50*, 177–179.

Cohen, B. D., Kalish, H. I., Thurston, J. R., & Cohen, E.   Experimental manipulation of verbal behavior. *Journal of Experimental Psychology*, 1954, *47*, 106–110.

Cowles, J. T.   Food-tokens as incentives for learning by chimpanzees. *Comparative Psychology Monographs*, 1937, *14*, No. 5.

Daly, H. B.   Is responding necessary for nonreward following reward to be frustrating? *Journal of Experimental Psychology*, 1969, *80*, 186–187.

Daly, H. B., & McCroskery, J. H.   Acquisition of a bar-press response to escape frustrative nonreward and reduced reward. *Journal of Experimental Psychology*, 1973, *98*, 109–112.

Dember, W. N., & Fowler, H.   Spontaneous alternation behavior. *Psychological Bulletin*, 1958, *55*, 412–428.

DeNike, L. D.   The temporal relationship between awareness and performance in verbal conditioning. *Journal of Experimental Psychology*, 1964, *68*, 521–529.

Egger, M. D., & Miller, N. E.   Secondary reinforcement in rats as a function of information value and reliability of the stimulus. *Journal of Experimental Psychology*, 1962, *64*, 97–104.

Egger, M. D., & Miller, N. E.   When is reward reinforcing? An experimental study of the information hypothesis. *Journal of Comparative and Physiological Psychology*, 1963, *56*, 132–137.

Estes, W. K.   Toward a statistical theory of learning. *Psychological Review*, 1950, *57*, 94–107.

Fiske, D. W., & Maddi, S. R. (Eds.).   *Functions of varied experience.* Homewood: Dorsey, 1961.

Fowler, H.   Satiation and curiosity. In K. W. Spence & J. T. Spence (Eds.), *The psychology of learning and motivation* (Vol. 1). New York: Academic Press, 1967, pp. 157–227.

Fox, R. E., & King, R. A.   The effects of reinforcement scheduling on the strength of a secondary reinforcer. *Journal of Comparative and Physiological Psychology*, 1961, *54*, 266–269.

Fox, S. S.   Self-maintained sensory input and sensory deprivation in monkeys: A behavioral and neuropharmacological study. *Journal of Comparative and Physiological Psychology*, 1962, *55*, 438–444.

Glanzer, M.   Curiosity, exploratory drive, and stimulus satiation. *Psychological Bulletin*, 1958, *55*, 302–315.

Greenspoon, J., & Brownstein, J. A.   Awareness in verbal conditioning. *Journal of Experimental Research in Personality*, 1967, *2*, 295–308.

Guthrie, E. R.   *The psychology of learning* (Rev. Ed.). New York: Harper, 1952.

Harlow, H. F.   Learning and satiation of response in intrinsically motivated complex puzzle performance by monkeys. *Journal of Comparative and Physiological Psychology*, 1950, *43*, 289–294.

Hebb, D. O.   Drives and C.N.S. (Conceptual Nervous System). *Psychological Review*, 1955, *62*, 243–255.

Hull, C. L.   *Principles of behavior.* New York: Appleton-Century, 1943.

Hull, C. L.   *A behavior system.* New Haven: Yale University Press, 1952.

Kanfer, F. H.　Verbal conditioning: A review of its current status. In T. R. Dixon & D. L. Horton (Eds.). *Verbal behavior and general behavior theory.* Englewood Cliffs, N.J.: Prentice-Hall, 1968, pp. 245–290.

Keller, F. S., & Schoenfeld, W. N.　*Principles of psychology.* New York: Appleton-Century-Crofts, 1950.

Kish, G. B.　Learning when the onset of illumination is used as reinforcing stimulus. *Journal · of Comparative and Physiological Psychology,* 1955, *48,* 261–264.

Klein, R. M.　Intermittent primary reinforcement as a parameter of secondary reinforcement. *Journal of Experimental Psychology,* 1959, 58, 423–427.

Kohn, M.　Satiation of hunger from food injected directly into the stomach versus food ingested by mouth. *Journal of Comparative and Physiological Psychology,* 1951, *44,* 412–422.

Levin, S. M.　The effects of awareness on verbal conditioning. *Journal of Experimental Psychology,* 1961, *61,* 67–75.

MacCorquodale, K., & Meehl, P. E.　Edward C. Tolman. In W. K. Estes, S. Koch, K. MacCorquodale, P. E. Meehl, C. G. Mueller, Jr., W., N. Schoenfeld, & W. S. Verplanck (Eds.), *Modern learning theory.* New York: Appleton-Century-Crofts, 1954.

McNamara, H. J., Long, J. B., & Wike, E. L.　Learning without response under two conditions of external cues. *Journal of Comparative and Physiological Psychology,* 1956, *49,* 477–480.

McNamara, H. J., & Paige, A. B.　An elaboration of Zimmerman's procedure for demonstrating durable secondary reinforcement. *Psychological Reports,* 1962, *11,* 801–803.

Malmo, R. B.　Activation: A neuropsychological dimension. *Psychological Review,* 1959, *66,* 367–386.

Marx, M. H., Henderson, R. L., & Roberts, C. L.　Positive reinforcement on the bar-pressing response by a light stimulus following dark operant pre-tests with no aftereffect. *Journal of Comparative and Physiological Psychology,* 1955, *48,* 73–75.

Miles, R. C.　The relative effectiveness of secondary reinforcers throughout deprivation and habit-strength parameters. *Journal of Comparative and Physiological Psychology,* 1956, *49,* 126–130.

Miller, N. E., & Kessen, M. L.　Reward effects of food via stomach fistula compared with those of food via mouth. *Journal of Comparative and Physiological Psychology,* 1952, *45,* 555–564.

Montgomery, K. C.　The role of the exploratory drive in learning. *Journal of Comparative and Physiological Psychology,* 1954, *47,* 60–64.

Montgomery, K. C., & Segall, M.　Discrimination based on the exploratory drive. *Journal of Comparative and Physiological Psychology,* 1955, *48,* 225–228.

Moruzzi, G., & Magoun, H. W.　Brainstem reticular formation and activation of the EEG. *Electroencephalography and Clinical Neurophysiology,* 1949, *1,* 455–473.

Myers, A. K., & Miller, N. E.   Failure to find a learned drive based on hunger: Evidence for learning motivated by "exploration." *Journal of Comparative and Physiological Psychology,* 1954, *47,* 428–436.

Patty, R. A., & Page, M. M.   Manipulations of a verbal conditioning situation based upon demand characteristics theory. *Journal of Experimental Research in Personality,* 1973, *6,* 307–313.

Pavlov, I. P.   *Conditioned reflexes.* Oxford: Oxford University Press, 1927.

Premack, D.   Toward empirical behavioral laws: I. Positive reinforcement. *Psychological Review,* 1959, *66,* 219–233.

Premack, D.   Reversibility of the reinforcement relation. *Science,* 1962, *136,* 255–257.

Premack, D.   Prediction of the comparative reinforcement values of running and drinking. *Science,* 1963, *139,* 1062–1063.

Premack, D.   Reinforcement theory. In M. Jones (Ed.), *Nebraska Symposium on Motivation.* Lincoln: University of Nebraska Press, 1965, pp. 123–180.

Saltzman, I. J.   Maze learning in the absence of primary reinforcement: A study of secondary reinforcement. *Journal of Comparative and Physiological Psychology,* 1949, *42,* 161–173.

Sawisch, L. P., & Denny, M. R.   Reversing the reinforcement contingencies of eating and keypecking behaviors. *Animal Learning & Behavior,* 1973, *1,* 189–192.

Schoenfeld, W. N., Antonitis, J. J., & Bersh, P. J.   A preliminary study of training conditions necessary for secondary reinforcement. *Journal of Experimental Psychology,* 1950, *40,* 40–45.

Sheffield, F. D., & Roby, T. B.   Reward value of a non-nutritive sweet taste. *Journal of Comparative and Physiological Psychology,* 1950, *43,* 471–481.

Skinner, B. F.   *The behavior of organisms.* New York: Appleton-Century, 1938.

Spielberger, C. D., & DeNike, L. D.   Descriptive behaviorism versus cognitive theory in verbal operant conditioning. *Psychological Review,* 1966, *73,* 306–326.

Stein, L.   Secondary reinforcement established with subcortical stimulation. *Science,* 1958, *127,* 466–467.

Taffel, C.   Anxiety and conditioning of verbal behavior. *Journal of Abnormal and Social Psychology,* 1955, *51,* 496–502.

Thorndike, E. L.   Animal intelligence: An experimental study of the associative processes in animals. *Psychological Review Monograph Supplement,* 1898, *2,* No. 4 (Whole No. 8).

Thorndike, E. L.   *The psychology of wants, interests and attitudes.* New York: Appleton-Century, 1935.

Thorndike, E. L., & Rock, R. T., Jr.   Learning without awareness of what is being learned or intent to learn it. *Journal of Experimental Psychology,* 1934, *17,* 1–19.

Tolman, E. C.   *Purposive behavior in animals and men.* New York: Century, 1932.

Tolman, E. C.   Cognitive maps in rats and men. *Psychological Review,* 1948, *55,* 189–208.

Tolman, E. C.   *Behavior and psychological man.* Berkeley: University of California Press, 1958.

Watson, J. B.   Psychology as the behaviorist views it. *Psychological Review,* 1913, *20,* 158–177.

Weiss, R. L.   The influence of 'set for speed' on 'learning without awareness.' *American Journal of Psychology,* 1955, *68,* 425–431.

Wike, E. L.   Secondary reinforcement: Some research and theoretical issues. In W. J. Arnold & D. Levine (Eds.), *Nebraska Symposium on Motivation.* Lincoln: University of Nebraska Press, 1971, pp. 39–82.

Wike, E. L., & Platt, J. R.   Reinforcement schedules and bar pressing: Some extensions of Zimmerman's work. *Psychological Record,* 1962, *12,* 273–278.

Wike, E. L., Platt, J. R., & Knowles, J. M.   The reward value of getting out of a starting box: Further extensions of Zimmerman's work. *Psychological Record,* 1962, *12,* 397–400.

Williams, K. A.   The reward value of a conditioned stimulus. *University of California Publications in Psychology,* 1929, *4,* 31–55.

Wolfe, J. B.   Effectiveness of token-rewards for chimpanzees. *Comparative Psychology Monographs,* 1936, *12,* No. 5.

Zimmerman, D. W.   Durable secondary reinforcement: Method and theory. *Psychological Review,* 1957, *64,* 373–383.

Zimmerman, D. W.   Sustained performance in rats based on secondary reinforcement. *Journal of Comparative and Physiological Psychology,* 1959, *52,* 353–358.

Zimmerman, D. W.   Influence of three stimulus conditions upon the strength of a secondary reinforcement effect. *Psychological Reports,* 1963, *13,* 135–138.

chapter 4

Classical conditioning

Psychologists would be delighted to have all learning of one kind, but they are not so lucky, at least so far. Chapters 2 and 3 were on instrumental learning, which is one main kind of learning, and this chapter is about *classical conditioning*, which is the other main kind. Sometimes it is called *Pavlovian conditioning* or *respondent conditioning* (Skinner, 1938). The first part of this chapter will examine the history of classical conditioning and the main variables that determine it, and the last part will explore the similarities and differences between classical conditioning and instrumental learning.

CLASSICAL CONDITIONING:
BACKGROUND AND DEFINITION

No discussion of classical conditioning dares pass Ivan P. Pavlov (1849–1936) with a polite nod. He sired classical conditioning and gave almost 40 years to its investigation. He was a giant in physiology, having won the Nobel prize for his research on the digestive system (Pavlov, 1902). In fact, Pavlov always regarded himself as a physiologist and had little respect for psychology. He once said (Pavlov, 1927, p. 3), ". . . it is still open to discussion whether psychology is a natural science, or whether it can be regarded as a science at all." Despite his attitudes toward psychology, he had respect for the comparative psychologists of the day who worked with animals and were close to biological traditions (Pavlov, 1927, pp. 5–6).

It may be wrong to say that Pavlov's discovery of conditioning was an act of serendipity, a happy accident like a farmer looking for a cow and discovering a diamond mine, but there seems to have been an element of it. Pavlov was strongly influenced by the mid-nineteenth century writings of the great Russian physiologist I. M. Sechenov (1829–1905), and through Sechenov became attracted to the concept of the reflex, a naturally-given biological response to stimulation that consisted of sensory nerves to a brain connection which in turn fired motor nerves that activated an organ. Under the impact of Darwin's theory of evolution, Pavlov saw the various reflexes as adaptive mechanisms contributing to an organism's survival. With this frame of reference, Pavlov was studying the reaction of the dog's salivary gland to food in the mouth, which was a biological reflex because it facilitated the passage of food in the alimentary canal, when he observed that the salivary glands did not need direct stimulation of food in the mouth but could be activated by the sight or the odor of food, or even the sight of the food dish or the sound of the footsteps of the attendant who ordinarily brought the food. This was not a biological reflex, because nothing had stimulated the salivary glands directly, and the puzzle was one of understanding how stimuli at a distance could activate a reflex. Pavlov was aware that something special was happening, and he placed the phenomenon in the special category of "psychic" activity. Soon he came to call them *conditioned reflexes,* and distinguished them from *unconditioned reflexes* which were biologically endowed and unlearned.

After Pavlov's informal observations on "psychic" activity, he began orderly laboratory studies of the conditioned reflex. (Hereafter the dated term "reflex" will be replaced by "response," in accord with a longstanding practice in psychology.) The experimental arrangement to establish a conditioned response has four standard ingredients:

1. The *unconditioned stimulus* (*UCS*) which has a stable power to elicit a response.
2. The *unconditioned response* (*UCR*) which is elicited by the *UCS.*
3. The *conditioned stimulus* (*CS*) which is a neutral stimulus that has no power to elicit the *UCR.*
4. The *conditioned response* (*CR*) which the *CS* comes to elicit as a learned response. It resembles, but is not the same as, the *UCR.*

Figure 4–1 illustrates a commonly used experimental arrangement of the four ingredients; it is of the kind that has been used to classically condition everything from earthworms to humans. Pavlov used dogs and customarily studied salivation as the response, which is elicited as a *UCR* by such *UCS* as food or weak acid in the mouth. For Pavlov a *UCR* was an inborn, biologically endowed response of the organism that assisted its survival, and an organism has many of them. Typical *CS* stimuli which Pavlov used were such stimuli as a bell, a tone, a

FIGURE 4–1

An example of the four basic events of classical conditioning. The deflection indicates the onset and the offset of the event.

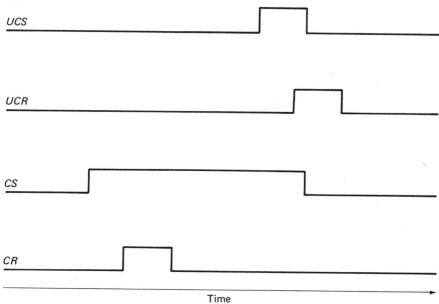

FIGURE 4–2

An experimental arrangement which Pavlov used to study conditioned salivation in the dog.

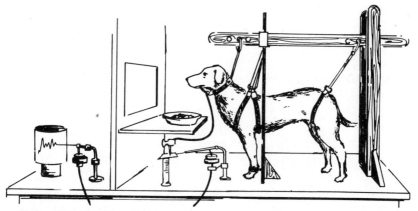

Yerkes, R. M., & Morgulis, S. The method of Pavlov in animal psychology. *Psychological Bulletin*, 1909, *6*, 257–273.

buzzer, or tactual stimuli. With repeated pairings of the CS and UCS, the CS comes to elicit the CR reliably, and the CR now has the status of a learned response. There are two ways of knowing that a CR has been formed. One is CR occurrence after the onset of the CS but before the UCS and the UCR that it induces. The other is the test trial method, where the CS is presented alone to see if a CR occurs. Salivation, the eyeblink, the knee jerk, and the galvanic skin response are among responses that have been classically conditioned.

Figure 4–2 is one of Pavlov's experimental setups for studying conditioned salivation in the dog. The saliva flows through an incision in the mouth and is collected in a beaker and the amount recorded. The dog is in a soundproof room to prevent extraneous stimuli from interfering with the conditioning process.

KINDS OF CLASSICAL CONDITIONING

There are four kinds of classical conditioning, and they are defined by the relationship between the CS and the UCS. If the CS and UCS come on together and go off together, it is *simultaneous conditioning*. For example, a light (CS) and a shock (UCS) to the finger going on and off together is a case of simultaneous conditioning for the finger withdrawal response (CR). When CS onset is before the UCS and persists until UCS onset or later, it is *delayed conditioning*. If the CS is terminated before the onset of the UCS, such that there is a time delay between them, it is *trace conditioning*. Finally, the UCS can precede the CS, which is a case of *backward conditioning*. Little or no conditioning is found with backward conditioning (see below), so it is dubious as one of the main kinds of conditioning.

ACQUISITION VARIABLES

Trials

The heart of classical conditioning is the CS-UCS pairing, and the number of pairings, or practice trials, is the basic condition of learning. Table 4–1 shows learning data obtained by Anrep (1920) in Pavlov's laboratory, and it demonstrates the learning of salivation as the CR. The CS was a tone, and the UCS was food powder. Table 4–1 has the outcome of 50 CS-UCS pairings over 16 days, and there is a regular increase in the flow of saliva (CR) to the CS as a function of the pairings until a maximum is reached in about 10 days.

TABLE 4–1
Example of classical conditioning of a salivation response.

Days	Number of CS-UCS pairings	Drops of saliva for a 30-second CS
1	1	0
3	10	6
7	20	20
10	30	60
13	40	62
16	50	59

Anrep, G. V. Pitch discrimination in the dog. *Journal of Physiology*, 1920, *53*, 367–385. Reprinted by permission of the *Journal of Physiology*.

CS-UCS interval

Once a basic phenomenon has been established by scientists, they begin the long task of systematically varying the independent variables to establish their detailed effects on dependent variables. Key variables for classical conditioning are the time interval between the CS and the UCS, and the order of the CS and UCS in forward and backward conditioning. A good study on the CS-UCS interval is Spooner and Kellogg (1947) who used finger withdrawal as the CR. The CS was a brief buzz for 0.2 seconds and the UCS was a brief shock for 0.2 seconds. The electrodes that delivered the shock were strapped to the finger, making the shock unavoidable, and this was an important procedure because avoidance of the shock by anticipatory finger withdrawal would have eliminated the CS-UCS interval which was under experimental scrutiny. Occasionally during the conditioning trials there was a test trial where the CS alone was presented, and the occurrence of finger withdrawal on these tests was the CR measure. One group of human subjects had simultaneous conditioning where the CS and UCS were presented together, three groups had forward trace conditioning where the CS preceded the UCS by either 0.5, 1.0, or 1.5 seconds, and two groups had backward conditioning where the UCS preceded the CS by either 0.25 or 0.5 seconds. The results are shown in Figure 4–3.

The optimum interval is clearly at .5 seconds, and values in this range often have been found in other studies, although analysts have noted exceptions for certain kinds of responses and animals (Gormezano and Moore, 1969, p. 136). Does backward conditioning occur? Spooner and Kellogg have their doubts even though Figure 4–3 shows a few

FIGURE 4–3

Effect of the time interval between the *CS* and the *UCS,* and the order of the *CS* and the *UCS,* on conditioning. Minus values on the horizontal axis indicate that the *CS* follows the *UCS,* positive values indicate that the *CS* precedes the *UCS.*

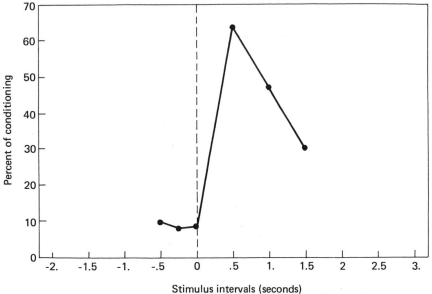

Stimulus intervals (seconds)

Spooner, A., & Kellogg, W. N. The backward conditioning curve. *American Journal of Psychology,* 1947, *60,* 321–334. Reprinted by permission of the University of Illinois Press.

*CR*s when the *UCS* precedes the *CS.* Pavlov was not sure either, citing negative results at one point (Pavlov, 1927, pp. 27–28) and weak evidence at another (Pavlov, 1928, p. 341). Spooner and Kellogg decided that backward and forward conditioning were fundamentally different processes because the forward conditioning groups showed a standard learning curve, where percent of *CR*s increased with trials, and the backward conditioning groups showed an opposite, decreasing curve. One possible explanation for apparent backward conditioning is *pseudoconditioning,* where a noxious stimulus like electric shock places the subject in an aroused state and the occurrence of virtually any stimulus elicits a response resembling the *CR.* That the "learning" curve for backward conditioning decreased with trials could be adaptation to repeated presentations of shock, which is a well-known effect.

Another example of the potency of the *CS-UCS* interval for classical conditioning is an experiment by Reynolds (1945) which used the eyeblink response and human subjects. Trace conditioning was used, with a click as the *CS* and an airpuff to the eye as the *UCS.* Four *CS-UCS* intervals were evaluated: 250, 450, 1,150, and 2,250 milliseconds. The results are shown in Figure 4–4. Notice that the most rapid learning

FIGURE 4–4

Effect of four *CS-UCS* intervals on the acquisition of the conditioned eyeblink response.

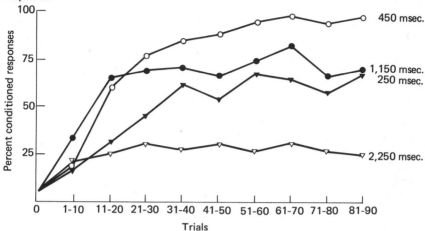

Reynolds, B. The acquisition of a trace conditioned response as a function of the magnitude of the stimulus trace. *Journal of Experimental Psychology,* 1945, *35,* 15–30. Reprinted by permission of the American Psychological Association.

is with the 450-millisecond interval, which is very close to the interval that Spooner and Kellogg found as optimum.

Schedules of reinforcement

We saw in Chapter 2 that one of the most powerful variables for the instrumental learning of a response was the schedule of reinforcement. Performance can be insensitive to the percent of reinforcement or even inversely related to it. Intuition is not assailed so vigorously in classical conditioning because here we find that performance is directly related to the percent of reinforcement which, in the context of classical conditioning, is occurrence of the *UCS.*

Figure 4–5 shows data by Grant and Schipper (1952) on human eyelid conditioning as a function of the percentage of trials that had a *UCS* delivered. Attend only to trial blocks 1–12, which are acquisition data; the last 5 trial blocks are extinction trials and they will be discussed in the next section. Notice that performance is directly related to percent of reinforcement. One could fault this study by saying that with a constant number of acquisition trials the higher the percentage of reinforcements the greater the number of reinforcements, so it is not surprising that performance level was positively related to percent of reinforcement. This criticism was answered by the same laboratory in a study by Hartman and Grant (1960). Again using eyeblink conditioning, they held

FIGURE 4–5

Effect of percent of reinforcement (occurrence of the *UCS*) on occurrence of the conditioned eyeblink response in acquisition and extinction.

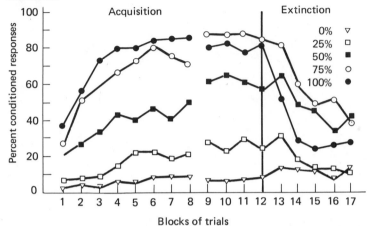

Grant, D. A., & Schipper, L. M. The acquisition and extinction of conditioned eyelid responses as a function of the percentage of fixed-ratio random reinforcement. *Journal of Experimental Psychology,* 1952, *43,* 313–320. Reprinted by permission of the American Psychological Association.

number of reinforcements constant but allowed number of trials to vary, and their findings were very similar to those of Grant and Schipper (1952) in Figure 4–5.

EXTINCTION

Some general features

Extinction is eliminating the occurrence of a learned response by repeatedly eliciting it in the absence of reinforcement, and in classical conditioning it is repeated elicitation of the *CR* by the *CS* without presenting the *UCS.*

Table 4–2 has representative extinction findings from Pavlov's laboratory (Pavlov, 1927, p. 58), and they show how a fully learned response can be diminished in the behavioral repertoire by presentation of the *CS* alone. As usual, a dog was the subject and salivation was the response. The *CS* was sight of meat powder presented a short distance away at ten-minute intervals, and in three trials the *CR* is completely extinguished. A 20-minute rest was given and spontaneous recovery was then observed where the *CR* bounced back to nearly its original level. Pavlov found that salivation in the dog had near 100 percent spontaneous recovery, but it is not always the case. We saw in Chapter 2 that the

TABLE 4–2

Extinction and spontaneous recovery of a conditioned salivation response in the dog.

Time	Drops of saliva
1:42 P.M.	8
1:52 P.M.	3
2:02 P.M.	0
(interval of 20 minutes)	
2:22 P.M.	7

Pavlov, I. P. *Conditioned Reflexes.* (Anrep, trans.). Oxford: Oxford University Press, 1927. Reprinted by permission of the Oxford University Press.

spontaneous recovery of instrumentally learned responses is less than 100 percent, and this can be so for classically conditioned responses also. Grant, Hunter, and Patel (1958) had their subjects learn an eyeblink response to a criterion of eight CRs in ten consecutive trials, and they were then extinguished to a criterion of five successive trials without CRs. A second extinction was one, two, four, or eight hours after the first, and the number of CRs obtained in the second extinction was taken as the amount of spontaneous recovery. The results are shown in Figure 4–6, and the recovery curve levels out at about 60 percent.

FIGURE 4–6

Spontaneous recovery as a function of time for the conditioned eyeblink response.

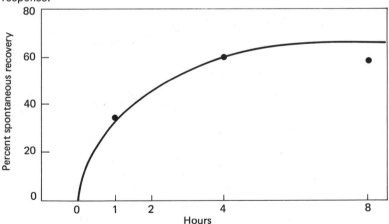

Grant, D. A., Hunter, H. G., & Patel, A. S. Spontaneous recovery of the conditioned eyeblink response. *Journal of General Psychology*, 1958, *59*, 135–141. Reprinted by permission of *The Journal Press*.

The generalization that we have is that extinguished responses, whatever their kind, will show spontaneous recovery, but we have no explanation for why different kinds of responses show different amounts and rates of recovery.

Pavlov also observed that the rate of extinction depended upon the number of times that the response had been extinguished before—the more times the response had been extinguished the faster the extinction until, finally, the animal is extinguished in one application of the CS alone (Pavlov, 1927, pp. 53–54).

Schedules of reinforcement

We saw that the principles governing schedules of reinforcement for the acquisition of classically conditioned responses are different from those of instrumental responses, and this is a temporary complexity on

FIGURE 4–7

Effect of partial reinforcement on extinction of the conditioned eyeblink response. Group II had 50 percent reinforcement, Groups I and III had 100 percent reinforcement. The first point of a curve is the average of the 24 preceding acquisition trials.

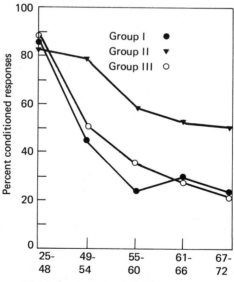

Extinction trials

Humphreys, L. G. The effect of random alternation of reinforcement on the acquisition and extinction of conditioned eyeblink reactions. *Journal of Experimental Psychology,* 1939, *25,* 141–158. Reprinted by permission of the American Psychological Association.

the scientific scene, but happily, schedules of reinforcement relate to extinction in the same way regardless of the kind of learning. Intermittent reinforcement in acquisition gives a slower rate of extinction than continuous reinforcement. The first study (Humphreys, 1939) to show this relationship used a classically conditioned eyeblink reaction, and it has been shown many times since in many kinds of learning situations.

Humphreys conducted an experiment with three groups. Group I had 96 acquisition trials with 100 percent reinforcement, Group II had 96 trials also but with only half of them reinforced on a random basis, and Group III had 48 trials with 100 percent reinforcement and so had the same number of reinforcements as Group II. All groups were then given 24 extinction trials, and the results for extinction are shown in Figure 4–7. Group II with partial reinforcement had an impressively slower rate of extinction than the groups with continuous reinforcement. Figure 4–5 that has the eyeblink conditioning data of Grant and Schipper (1952) also shows the same effect. The last 5 blocks of trials are the extinction trials and 100 percent reinforcement in acquisition had the fastest rate of extinction.

STIMULUS GENERALIZATION

As with so many variables in the psychology of learning, the discovery of them came from Pavlov's laboratory. Using classical conditioning, Pavlov and his colleagues were the first to demonstrate stimulus generalization. In what is the first report of stimulus generalization in the English language, Anrep (1923) gave an account of research conducted in Pavlov's laboratory in 1917–18. Anrep established trace conditioning of salivation in the dog, with a tactile stimulator on the dog's thigh as the CS. Six other stimulators were attached to other parts of the dog's body, and they were activated in generalization tests after the salivation response had been learned to the CS on the thigh. Anrep obtained a gradient of spatial generalization, where there was less salivary secretion for stimuli remote from the CS than for nearby ones. Pavlov (1927, p. 186) believed that stimulus generalization was caused physiologically by a radiation of stimulus events when they project on the cortex; a stimulus not only has a particular projection point on the cortex but also radiates outward from the point with diminishing intensity. The radiating stimuli become conditioned to the response also, and the result is the gradient of responses that we call stimulus generalization. Pavlov called this hypothesized physiological effect spread of excitation or irradiation.

The galvanic skin response (GSR) is an increase in electrical potential between two points on the skin, and it results from bioelectric changes in the sweat glands. The GSR can be elicited by intense stimuli in any modality, and it has been a commonly used response in studies

Learning and memory: An introduction

of classical conditioning. A study by Bass and Hull (1934) further illustrates stimulus generalization, this time with GSR as the response and a
human as the subject. Electric shock was the *UCS* and a tactile stimulator was the *CS*. Figure 4–8 has the experimental arrangement where

FIGURE 4–8
Experimental arrangement used by Bass and Hull to study generalization of the
galvanic skin response on a spatial dimension.

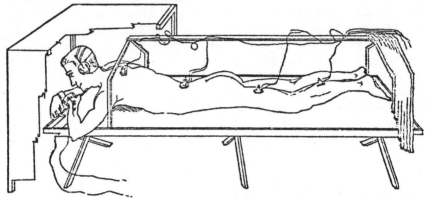

Bass, M. J., & Hull, C. L. The irradiation of a tactile conditioned reflex in man.
Journal of Comparative Psychology, 1934, *17*, 47–65. Reprinted by permission of the
American Psychological Association.

FIGURE 4–9
Generalization of the galvanic skin
response along a spatial dimension.

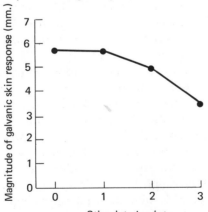

Stimulated points

Bass, M. J., & Hull, C. L. The irradiation of a tactile conditioned reflex in man.
Journal of Comparative Psychology, 1934,
17, 47–65. Reprinted by permission of the
American Psychological Association.

the human was outfitted with four stimulators, somewhat like Anrep's dogs. One of the stimulators was designated the *CS* for a subject, and trace conditioning was used for conditioning of the *GSR*. The generalization tests were trials with the other non-*CS* stimulators without shock, and the results are shown in Figure 4–9 plotted in terms of spatial remoteness from the *CS*. As is customarily found in studies of stimulus generalization, performance level decreases as the similarity between the *CS* and test stimuli decreases (in this case the similarity is along a spatial dimension).

Grant and Dittmer (1940) found the same results for *GSR* when the back of the hand was stimulated, and similar gradients have been reported for *GSR* when tones were stimuli (Hovland, 1937a, 1937b).

CLASSICAL CONDITIONING AND INSTRUMENTAL LEARNING COMPARED

At the outset of this chapter it was said that not all learning can be considered the same, which is another way of saying that one set of laws does not cover all situations. If we were confident in one set of laws, there would be no need to present instrumental learning and classical conditioning as separate chapters. That separate chapters are still maintained represents psychology's uncertainty about one set of laws, and in this section the reasons for that uncertainty are examined. The topic is a long-persisting one in the psychology of learning, bred in many years of pondering the similarities and differences between classical conditioning and instrumental learning.

Similarities between classical conditioning and instrumental learning

There is reason to believe that classical conditioning and instrumental learning are the same if we believe that things equal to the same thing are equal to each other. Many of the standard phenomena of instrumental learning, like changes in performance measures as a function of acquisition trials, extinction, effects of partial reinforcement on extinction, spontaneous recovery, stimulus generalization, etc., are present in both classical conditioning and instrumental learning (Kimble, 1961, pp. 81–98), and they certainly encourage us to believe that the two kinds of learning are probably the same. And, by comparing the procedures for the two kinds of learning, one can see distinct similarities. Consider a salivation response being acquired by classical conditioning, with a tone as the *CS*, food as the *UCS*, and salivation as the *UCR*. Consider a bar press being acquired by instrumental learning, with a tone as the *CS*, food as the positive reinforcement, and salivation and eating the food as the

UCR. Obviously there is a parallel between the two and, when so many behavioral phenomena are common to both kinds, it is easy to see why so many psychologists feel that the two kinds of learning differ only in surface ways and are really the same underneath. The feeling is held in check, however, because there are differences between the two kinds of learning, and for some the differences are more compelling than the similarities.

Differences between classical conditioning and instrumental learning

Skinner (1938, pp. 19–21) pointed out that there is a considerable body of behavior that is emitted rather than elicited by a stimulus; the response simply occurs without an identifiable stimulus. Emitted behavior, whenever it occurs, can be learned instrumentally, and Skinner called this kind of behavior *operant behavior*. Classical conditioning, on the other hand, is a kind of behavior that always has an eliciting stimulus, and Skinner called it *respondent behavior*. Some are tempted to assume that somewhere there is an eliciting stimulus for operant behavior if we were only clever enough to find it but, as Skinner pointed out, the evidence for it is missing and the assumption is rash. Someday we may be able to find eliciting stimuli for all the kinds of operant responses, but until we do we have a class of behavior that is different from classically conditioned responses in a fundamental way.

A second difference is that the *CR* is similar to the *UCR* in classical conditioning, but in instrumental learning the learned response can be totally different from the *UCR* to the reinforcement, and usually is. Pavlov (1927) believed that the *CS* came to substitute for the *UCS*, and the *CR* that was learned in response to it had survival value for the organism. Conditioned salivation, for example, lubricates the mouth in anticipation for the food to follow, and so it is the same as the salivation that accompanies eating. This has been called *stimulus substitution theory*. Instrumental learning, however, ordinarily will have a response learned that is topographically much different than the *UCR* associated with the reinforcement. Bar-pressing is completely different than the eating of the food reward or the drinking of the water reward. As valid as this difference between the two kinds of learning might seem, it is weakened somewhat because the stimulus substitution theory is false in its strong form—a *CR* may be similar to the *UCR*, but it is not the same. In the case of salivation, the amount and rate of conditioned salivation is less than unconditioned salivation, and even the viscosity has been reported as less for conditioned salivation (Terrace, 1973, p. 82). The conditioned eyeblink response, where an airpuff is used to elicit the blink that is the *UCR*, comes to occur in anticipation of the airpuff and is not the same as the *UCR*. Notwithstanding, and without pressing the point too hard, the *CR* and the *UCR* certainly are similar in classical conditioning more often than in instrumental learning.

It was noted earlier that classical conditioning and instrumental learning are similar functions of the same variables, which comforts the view that the same processes underlie both. Partial reinforcement is one notable exception to these similarities, and it is the basis for the third difference between classical conditioning and instrumental learning. In the review of basic variables for classical conditioning earlier in this chapter, the studies by Grant and Schipper (1952) and Hartman and Grant (1960) were on acquisition and partial reinforcement, and they showed that the more frequently the *UCS* was omitted the lower the performance level in acquisition. Performance in instrumental learning, on the other hand, can be insensitive or inversely related to the percent of reinforcement. Opposite effects for the same variable are good reasons for believing that classical conditioning and instrumental learning are not the same.

The fourth difference that has persisted over the years is that classical conditioning and instrumental learning apply to different response classes. The responses that have been classically conditioned usually have been products of the autonomic nervous system which controls glandular and visceral responses, like salivation or the galvanic skin response. Exceptions mainly have been the eyeblink and the knee-jerk response. On the other hand, until very recently, instrumental learning has been found only for nonautonomic responses involving skeletal, or striped, muscle; there has been no evidence of the reward learning of autonomic responses. New evidence has changed all of this, and it deserves featuring in its own right because it is the best hope we have so far of bringing classical conditioning and instrumental learning under one scientific shelter. The topic is closely allied with the emerging area called biofeedback.

Biofeedback. The distinction between responses based on skeletal muscles and responses based on glandular and visceral activity is an old one (Miller, 1969). Ancient Greek philosophers distinguished between the superior rational mind in the head and the inferior body below. Ideas and thoughts were considered to be of a higher form than emotions, for example. Later, neuroanatomists gave this distinction physiological credence when they distinguished between the cerebrospinal nervous system of the brain and the spinal cord that controlled skeletal responses, and the autonomic nervous system that controlled glandular and visceral responses. The autonomic nervous system was considered essentially independent of the cerebrospinal system (its name "autonomic" reflects the belief in autonomy from the cerebrospinal system).

That we can control the movement of a hand but apparently not our heart rate was the kind of evidence taken in support of this distinction. With this distinction in our scientific history, and with many instances of the classical conditioning of glandular and visceral responses, and the many instances of the reward learning of skeletal responses, it is not surprising that learning psychologists have maintained the separation of classical conditioning and instrumental learning for so long.

It has been only recently that learning psychologists have given serious consideration to the instrumental learning of autonomic responses. In retrospect, the tardy concern with this topic is not surprising. A motor act like pressing a bar is observable and available for reward when it occurs, but responses of the autonomic nervous system are remote and hidden, and only when we deliberately seek them out and externalize them with sophisticated instrumentation do they become available for reward. Because reward is an event that is fed back to the subject and informs about the adequacy of the response, and because the responses are physiological events, this research area is known as *biofeedback*. Primarily, it was the work of N. E. Miller and his colleagues at Rockefeller University that caused us to turn toward biofeedback.

Salivation has been a commonly used response for classical conditioning since Pavlov, but Miller and Carmona (1967) viewed it anew and asked if its occurrence could be altered by reward. Dogs were their subjects, and they brought tubing from the parotid duct through a hole in the cheek to a system for measuring the spontaneous flow of saliva. Depending upon the experimental condition, either the spontaneous increase or decrease in the flow of saliva was rewarded with a 20 ml. shot of water in the mouth. Sessions where either increase or decrease in salivation was rewarded lasted for up to 40 days. The results are shown in Figure 4–10. Contrary to long-held beliefs, there can be a clearcut controlling of salivation by reward.

A knotty problem for understanding the instrumental learning of glandular and visceral responses is that it may be mediated by skeletal, or somatic, response learning and not directly learned at all. For example, in the Miller–Carmona study, the water may have rewarded rate of breathing or struggling in the apparatus which in turn affected rate of salivation. Rate of salivation, then, would be a byproduct of reward, not an explicit product. Miller and Carmona recorded additional measures in their study, like frequency of respiration, and they made additional tests to check some of these possibilities. They concluded that somatic mediation was not operating and that true instrumental learning of salivation had occurred. The Miller–Carmona study is a good one, but it would have been more convincing if somehow the mediation of somatic responses was eliminated altogether, and this was the approach taken in other experiments from Miller's laboratory.

FIGURE 4–10

The instrumental learning of salivation. Thirsty dogs were rewarded with water for either an increase or a decrease in salivation.

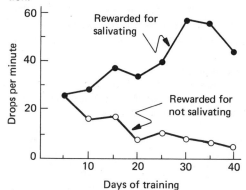

Days of training

Miller, N. E., & Carmona, A. Modification of a visceral response, salivation in thirsty dogs, by instrumental training with water reward. *Journal of Comparative and Physiological Psychology*, 1967, *63*, 1–6. Reprinted by permission of the American Psychological Association.

How related but irrelevant processes can exert an influence on the autonomic response under investigation is best exemplified by the learning of heart rate. Lynch and Paskewitz (1971) capture the flavor of the problem:

> No one would be surprised if an individual claimed he could control his heart rate by jumping up or down, or by running, or holding his breath; in such cases the mediation of heart rate activity via other physiological mechanisms would be clear to us all. In such a case it is also clear that the individual has not "learned" to control his heart rate directly, rather he has altered other mechanisms which in turn reflexively affect heart rate.[1]

Miller and DiCara (1967) used the drug curare as a way of eliminating these influences on heart rate during reward learning. Curare has the interesting property of being able to block neural impulses to the muscles, and so its effect is paralysis, but without blocking the reception and processing of stimuli. The paralysis can be so complete that a respirator must be used for breathing because the muscles of the lungs are inoperative. For some years it has been established that electrical stimulation of the medial forebrain bundle with implanted electrodes

---

[1] *Journal of Nervous and Mental Disease*, 1971, Vol. 153, pp. 207–208. Reprinted by permission of The Williams & Wilkins Co., Baltimore.

is rewarding for responses like bar pressing and maze running, and Miller and DiCara used this as reward for change in the heart rate of the curarized rat when a signal occurred. Heart rate had been instrumentally conditioned before, but none of the earlier work was theoretically decisive because the mediation of skeletal muscles had not been controlled. Animals were rewarded for either low or high heart rates, and the results are shown in Figure 4–11. The heart rate is readily amen-

FIGURE 4–11
The rewarding of dogs for either fast or slow heart rates. The dogs were curarized to eliminate the effect of muscular activity on heart rate.

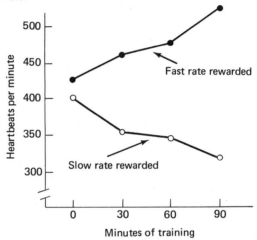

Miller, N. E., & DiCara, L. Instrumental learning of heart rate changes in curarized rats: Shaping, and specificity to discriminative stimulus. *Journal of Comparative and Physiological Psychology*, 1967, *63*, 12–19. Reprinted by permission of the American Psychological Association.

able to instrumental learning when the potential influence of skeletal muscles is ruled out.

The curarizing of skeletal muscles does not rule out all of the possible artifacts that might mislead about the instrumental learning of heart rate. Another possibility is that heart rate learning is associated with changes in general physiological arousal of which heart rate is a function. Like the foregoing argument about the interplay between heart rate and skeletal muscles, learning is not associated with heart rate directly but some other variable on which heart rate depends. Miller and Banuazizi (1968) attacked this possibility by recording two autonomically controlled visceral response simultaneously—heart rate and intestinal contraction (measured with a small balloon inserted through the rectum into the large intestine). If the learning affected a general arousal state then both variables should vary together. On the other hand, if genuine instrumental learning of visceral responses is occurring, then both variables should be independently learnable, with the learning of one leaving the other unaffected. Essentially, Miller and Banuazizi used the same procedures as Miller and DiCara (1967). Electrical stimulation of the brain was the reward for curarized rats, but this time intestinal contractions were recorded along with heart rate. There were four groups of animals: (1) reward when heart rate was faster than normal; (2) reward when heart rate was slower than normal; (3) reward when intestinal contractions were greater than normal; and (4) reward when intestinal contractions were less than normal. Every tenth trial was a test trial where the reward circuitry was turned off, and the test-trial results

FIGURE 4–12

Effect on intestinal contractions when either the contractions or heart rate is rewarded.

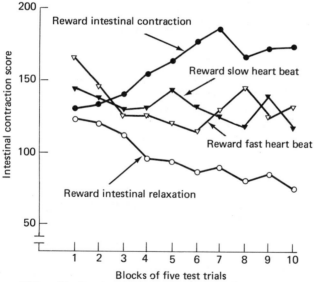

Miller, N. E., & Banuazizi, A. Instrumental learning by curarized rats of a specific visceral response, intestinal or cardiac. *Journal of Comparative and Physiological Psychology,* 1968, *65,* 1–7. Reprinted by permission of the American Psychological Association.

are shown in Figures 4–12 and 4–13. Figure 4–12 has the data of the four groups for intestinal contraction and relaxation. Notice that the intestinal contractions change systematically when they are rewarded but not when heart rate is rewarded. Figure 4–13 presents the data

FIGURE 4–13

Effect of heart rate when either heart rate or intestinal contractions is rewarded.

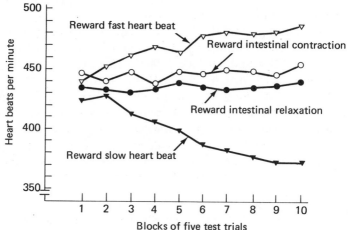

Blocks of five test trials

Miller, N. E., & Banuazizi, A. Instrumental learning by curarized rats of a specific visceral response, intestinal or cardiac. *Journal of Comparative and Physiological Psychology,* 1968, *65,* 1–7. Reprinted by permission of the American Psychological Association.

for heart rate. Heart rate changes where it is rewarded but not when intestinal contractions are rewarded. These results strengthen the position that visceral responses can be learned instrumentally, and are not a correlated consequence of some other learning.[2] Miller and his colleagues also have shown the instrumental learning of urine flow (Miller and DiCara, 1968), changes in peripheral blood flow (DiCara and Miller, 1968b), and blood pressure (DiCara and Miller, 1968a).

The electroencephalogram (EEG) is a record of the minute electrical waves of the brain and it is also a remote physiological response that appears to be subject to instrumental learning effects, although the learning is not without its problems of interpretation. The EEG can have different wave forms, and they are often characterized in terms of levels of wakefulness, ranging from focussed attention and high alertness to deep sleep. For our purposes here we will be concerned only with *alpha waves* and *alpha desynchronization,* both of which are shown in Figure 4–14. Alpha waves have a frequency of 8–13 cycles per second, with

---

[2] For reasons not yet understood, the operant learning of heart rate cannot always be obtained (Miller and Dworkin, 1974). Although the effect can be independently replicated, it is sometimes small or absent, so the findings of Miller and DiCara, and Miller and Banuazizi, must be accepted with caution. But even if the operant learning of heart rate eventually proves spurious, there are enough other lines of evidence to support the assertion that instrumental learning of responses of the autonomic nervous system is a fact.

FIGURE 4–14

EEG alpha waves and their desynchronization.

Desynchronized alpha waves

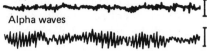

Alpha waves

moderate amplitude, and they often accompany a relaxed, calm state
of wakefulness. Alpha desynchronization has a faster wave, greater than
13 cycles per second, with low amplitude. Alpha waves can be desynchronized by a variety of events, and among them are paying attention,
anxiety and frustration, active thoughts, muscle activity, and, most of
all, visual stimulation.

As with responses of the autonomic nervous system, it was long
thought that EEG was subject only to classical conditioning. The classical conditioning of EEG received preliminary interest in the 1930s, but
by the 1940s there was systematic interest in the topic (e.g., Jasper and
Shagass, 1941; Shagass, 1942; Shagass and Johnson, 1943). A typical
experimental setup would be a light as the *UCS* to desynchronize alpha,
and a tone as the *CS*. At the outset the tone would leave the alpha
waves unchanged but, with repeated pairings of the light and the tone,
the tone alone would come to desynchronize alpha, which is the *CR*.
Not much interest developed in the classical conditioning of EEG because the phenomenon was variable and unstable, although it appears
to be real enough (Albino and Burnand, 1964). The classical conditioning of EEG was a concern with the learning of alpha desynchronization,
which is a lessening of alpha, but the modern work on instrumental
learning is concerned with *increasing* alpha wave production.

Research on the instrumental learning of alpha waves began with
the work of Kamiya and his associates. The approach is illustrated in
a study by Nowlis and Kamiya (1970) who tested their subjects in
a moderately darkened room. A tone was sounded whenever alpha waves
were produced. At the end of training a majority of the subjects were
generating more alpha than in a baseline condition at the start.

Kamiya and his colleagues were working at the frontier where freedom to explore is the charter, so it is overly strict to ask why their
experiment was not better controlled. As a subject matter matures, however, questions of methodology are legitimately raised by investigators
who follow (e.g., Lynch and Paskewitz, 1971). One question concerns
the baseline from which learning is measured. If so many factors affect
alpha waves, just what is a suitable baseline condition? For baseline
alpha performance, Nowlis and Kamiya had subjects hold their eyes

closed for two minutes, with instructions to remain still, and with the
tone accompanying alpha whenever it occurred. There is no assurance
that theirs is a "true" neutral state from which to measure learning.
A second question is that of appropriate controls. How do we know
that a control group without feedback would not show an increase in
alpha over the same period? Subjects ordinarily are apprehensive when
they enter an experiment, which would tend to desynchronize alpha
and, as they become relaxed during the course of the experiment, desynchronization would decrease, alpha would increase, and "learning" would
be observed. Another kind of control group could be given noncontingent
feedback, where feedback and alpha are unrelated. This is a better
control group than one with no feedback because they receive the same
events as an experimental group except that response and reward are
uncorrelated. How do we know that a noncontingent control group
would not show an increase in alpha?

Lynch, Paskewitz, and Orne (1974, Experiment I) compared a contingent feedback group with a noncontingent feedback group in the instrumental learning of alpha waves. Feedback was a green light for alpha
waves and a red light for their absence. The baseline condition at the
start was three minutes in a totally darkened room, and then ten trials
were given, with a trial being two minutes of feedback and one minute
of resting between trials with the feedback lights turned off. The results
are given in Figure 4–15, where the alpha on the feedback and resting
segments of a trial are plotted separately. Feedback, whether contingent
or noncontingent, produced "learning"; both feedback curves steadily
climb over trials. Lynch and Paskewitz (1971) have the hypothesis,
which they apply to this study, that learning-like effects in alpha occur
as a subject ceases to attend to stimuli that desynchronize alpha. As
the power to block incoming stimuli increases, the proportion of alpha
increases and "learning" is observed. Figure 4–15 shows how visual feedback depresses alpha level. If a subject can work out behavioral strategies of ignoring visual stimuli then alpha level should increase, according
to the hypothesis. Lynch, Paskewitz, and Orne (1974), as well as Paskewitz and Orne (1973), contend that feedback training does not produce
alpha levels greater than an optimum baseline level; learning to ignore
stimuli that depress alpha will bring alpha to the baseline but not beyond. Clearly this is different from instrumental learning as we ordinarily
mean it where learning is a response level greater than the initial
baseline.

Alpha waves are often associated with a contemplative, relaxed state
of mind. Because some think that a calm state of mind is desirable,
biofeedback training of EEG is seen as the road to serenity. This line
of thought has not been hurt by the findings that contemplative Indian
Yogis and Zen Buddhists are good at producing alpha waves in an

FIGURE 4–15

The curves on the left show effects of reinforcing the occurrence of EEG alpha waves by making the feedback contingent upon alpha production. The curves on the right show that the same effects are obtained when feedback is noncontingent and unrelated to the occurrence of alpha.

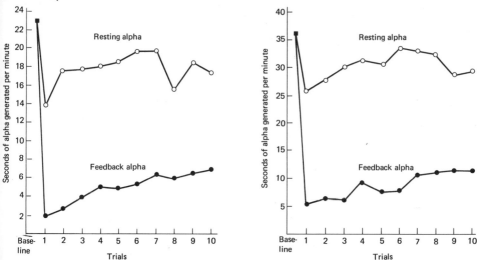

Lynch, J. J., Paskewitz, D. A., & Orne, M. T. Some factors in the feedback control of human alpha rhythm. *Psychosomatic Medicine*, 1974, *36*, 399–409. Reprinted by permission of the American Psychosomatic Society, Inc.

awakened, meditative state. Anand, Chhina, and Singh (1961) obtained EEG recordings on four Indian Yogis before and after meditation. All four showed an increase in alpha activity during meditation. Two of these Yogis were subjected to explicit external stimuli before and during meditation: strong light, loud sound, touching with a hot glass tube, and a vibrating tuning fork. All of these stimuli desychronized alpha before but not during meditation. Kasamatsu and Hirai (1966) conducted a related study of 48 Japanese Zen Buddhist priests and disciples. Experience in meditation ranged from 1 to over 20 years. Comparison was with control subjects with no training in meditation. The control subjects had no change in their EEG records, but the Zen Buddhists increased their alpha production during meditation, and the amount of alpha activity increased with experience in meditation. There is nothing in these studies of Far East meditators to deny the hypothesis of Lynch and Paskewitz (1971) that the learning to produce alpha waves is the learning to ignore stimuli that intrude and desynchronize alpha. Biofeedback may be one route to this skill, but the Yogis and the Zen Buddhists have found another.

Does it follow that acquiring the capability to produce alpha waves will produce a calm state of mind? Obviously not, because sitting quietly with the eyes closed will increase alpha activity, and serenity is not a necessary accompaniment. Walsh (1974) tested the hypothesis that the relaxed mental states are not produced by alpha but by the demands of the experimental situation as the subject perceives them, or by deliberate instructions from the experimenter. Before receiving feedback training, Walsh's subjects received either alpha instructions or neutral instructions. The alpha instructions explained biofeedback training and the "alpha state" as calm, contemplative, and dreamlike. The neutral instructions gave a matter-of-fact account of EEG and biofeedback training. The dependent measure was a description of subjective experiences associated with the feedback signal which judges rated for its correspondence to the "alpha state." The results were that a contemplative "alpha state" accompanied alpha only when the subjects were instructed in it and led to expect it. On the basis of the Walsh experiment it is not surprising that Yogis and Zen Buddhists have serene subjective states that accompany their alpha waves during meditation. Walsh has shown us that these subjective states can be controlled by situational factors, and the situational factors for Yogis and Zen Buddhists are compelling religious ones.

Biofeedback has potential application for psychotherapy (Schwartz, 1973). If it is possible to place certain physiological processes under the control of reinforcement, then would it be possible to eventually place them under a patient's voluntary control in behalf of personal well-being? Excessive heart rate could be dangerous for someone with a bad heart. Could one be trained to slow it? Could someone with high blood pressure be trained to lower it when it soars? The possibility of manipulating "involuntary" functions is exciting a number of therapists, although successes have been limited so far (Blanchard and Young, 1973). There are big problems to overcome with research. Reinforcement delivered by the experimenter in the laboratory for change in physiological functions is one thing, but transferring this operation over to the self-control of the patient in the everyday world is another. Dangerous physiological states, like excessive heart rates, can be induced by environmental stress. Can self-control of these dangerous physiological states ever be strong enough to override environmental stressors?

Conclusion.   The maturity of a science is importantly measured by the ways that it achieves an economy of description for its phenomena, and the reconciliation of classical conditioning and instrumental learning is an example of striving toward this economy. There is still good reason to maintain a separation of the two domains, but there is also good reason to believe that we are closer than ever to erasing the differences between them. It has been about 80 years since Pavlov discovered classical conditioning in Russia, and almost 80 years since Thorndike gave instrumental learning a big boost in the United States (of course, he did not discover it). Let us hope that the centennial celebration of Pavlov's discovery of classical conditioning will see classical conditioning and instrumental learning joined by a common set of principles.

SUMMARY

Classical conditioning is a form of learning that is distinguished from instrumental learning. In classical conditioning there is the presentation of an event called the unconditioned stimulus which reliably elicits an unconditioned response. A neutral stimulus, called the conditioned stimulus, is presented in accompaniment with the unconditioned stimulus and the unconditioned response, and the result of repeated presentation of these events is that the conditioned stimulus comes to evoke a new, learned response called the conditioned response. Everything from primitive organisms to the human have been classically conditioned, and so it is a fundamental kind of learning.

Psychologists have long puzzled about differences between classical conditioning and instrumental learning. They have been unable to reconcile relationships that are different for the two types of learning, and as a result there has been the persisting belief that the two types of learning are fundamentally different. One of the strongest reasons for believing in a difference was that classical conditioning mostly applied to visceral and glandular responses, and instrumental learning applied to muscular responses. The new research area of biofeedback is changing this conception. Reinforcement of visceral and glandular responses has produced the instrumental learning of them, and so they are not linked as strongly with classical conditioning as before. Biofeedback research has raised hopes of bringing the laws of classical conditioning and instrumental learning together.

REFERENCES

Albino, R., & Burnand, G. Conditioning of the alpha rhythm in man. *Journal of Experimental Psychology*, 1964, *67*, 539–544.

Anand, B. K., Chhina, G. S., & Singh, B. Some aspects of electroencephalographic studies in Yogi. *Electroencephalography and Clinical Neurophysiology*, 1961, *13*, 452–456.

Anrep, G. V. Pitch discrimination in the dog. *Journal of Physiology*, 1920, *53*, 367–385.

Anrep, G. V. The irradiation of conditioned reflexes. *Proceedings of the Royal Society of London*, Series B, 1923, *94*, 404–425.

Bass, M. J., & Hull, C. L. The irradiation of a tactile conditioned reflex in man. *Journal of Comparative Psychology*, 1934, *17*, 47–65.

Blanchard, E. B., & Young, L. D. Self-control of cardiac functioning: A promise as yet unfulfilled. *Psychological Bulletin*, 1973, *79*, 145–163.

DiCara, L. V., & Miller, N. E.   Instrumental learning of systolic blood pressure responses by curarized rats: Disassociation of cardiac and vascular changes. *Psychosomatic Medicine*, 1968, *30*, 489–494. (a)

DiCara, L. V., & Miller, N. E.   Instrumental learning of vasomotor responses by rats: Learning to respond differentially in the two ears. *Science*, 1968, *159*, 1485–1486. (b)

Gormezano, I., & Moore, J. W.   Classical conditioning. In M. H. Marx (Ed.), *Learning: Processes*. Toronto: Macmillan, 1969, pp. 119–203.

Grant, D. A., & Dittmer, D. G.   An experimental investigation of Pavlov's cortical irradiation hypothesis. *Journal of Experimental Psychology*, 1940, *26*, 299–310.

Grant, D. A., Hunter, H. G., & Patel, A. S.   Spontaneous recovery of the conditioned eyelid response. *Journal of General Psychology*, 1958, *59*, 135–141.

Grant, D. A., & Schipper, L. M.   The acquisition and extinction of conditioned eyelid responses as a function of the percentage of fixed-ratio random reinforcement. *Journal of Experimental Psychology*, 1952, *43*, 313–320.

Hartman, T. F., & Grant, D. A.   Effect of intermittent reinforcement on acquisition, extinction, and spontaneous recovery of the conditioned eyelid response. *Journal of Experimental Psychology*, 1960, *60*, 89–96.

Hovland, C. I.   The generalization of conditioned responses: I. The sensory generalization of conditioned responses with varying frequencies of tone. *Journal of General Psychology*, 1937, *17*, 125–147. (a)

Hovland, C. I.   The generalization of conditioned responses: II. The sensory generalization of conditioned responses with varying intensity of tone. *Journal of Genetic Psychology*, 1937, *51*, 279–291. (b)

Humphreys, L. G.   The effect of random alternation of reinforcement on the acquisition and extinction of conditioned eyelid reactions. *Journal of Experimental Psychology*, 1939, *25*, 141–158.

Jasper, H., & Shagass, C.   Conditioning the occipital alpha rhythm in man. *Journal of Experimental Psychology*, 1941, *28*, 373–388.

Kasamatsu, A., & Hirai, T.   An electroencephalographic study on the Zen meditation (Zazen). *Folia Psychiatrica Neurologica Japonica*, 1966, *20*, 315–336.

Kimble, G. A.   *Conditioning and learning* (2nd ed.). New York: Appleton-Century-Crofts, 1961.

Lynch, J. J., & Paskewitz, D. A.   On the mechanisms of the feedback control of human brain wave activity. *Journal of Nervous and Mental Disease*, 1971, *153*, 205–217.

Lynch, J. J., Paskewitz, D. A., & Orne, M. T.   Some factors in the feedback control of human alpha rhythm. *Psychosomatic Medicine*, 1974, *36*, 399–409.

Miller, N. E.   Learning of visceral and glandular responses. *Science*, 1969, *163*, 434–445.

Miller, N. E., & Banuazizi, A.   Instrumental learning by curarized rats of a specific visceral reponse, intestinal or cardiac. *Journal of Comparative and Physiological Psychology*, 1968, *65*, 1–7.

Miller, N. E., & Carmona, A.   Modification of a visceral response, salivation in thirsty dogs, by instrumental training with water reward. *Journal of Comparative and Physiological Psychology*, 1967, *63*, 1–6.

Miller, N. E., & DiCara, L.   Instrumental learning of heart rate changes in curarized rats: Shaping, and specificity to discriminative stimulus. *Journal of Comparative and Physiological Psychology*, 1967, *63*, 12–19.

Miller, N. E., & DiCara, L. V.   Instrumental learning of urine formation by rats: Changes in renal blood flow. *American Journal of Physiology*, 1968, *215*, 677–683.

Miller, N. E., & Dworkin, B. R.   Visceral learning: Recent difficulties with curarized rats and significant problems for human research. In P. A. Obrist, A. H. Black, J. Brener, & L. V. DiCara (Eds.), *Cardiovascular psychophysiology*. Chicago: Aldine, 1974, pp. 312–331.

Nowlis, D. P., & Kamiya, J.   The control of electroencephalographic alpha rhythms through auditory feedback and the associated mental activity. *Psychophysiology*, 1970, *6*, 476–484.

Paskewitz, D. A., & Orne, M. T.   Visual effects on alpha feedback training. *Science*, 1973, *181*, 361–363.

Pavlov, I. P.   *The work of the digestive glands*. (W. H. Thompson, trans.). London: Charles Griffin & Co., 1902.

Pavlov, I. P.   *Conditioned reflexes*. (G. V. Anrep trans.). Oxford: Oxford University Press, 1927.

Pavlov, I. P.   *Lectures on conditioned reflexes* (Vol. 1). (W. H. Gantt trans.). New York: International Publishers, 1928.

Reynolds, B.   The acquisition of a trace conditioned response as a function of the magnitude of the stimulus trace. *Journal of Experimental Psychology*, 1945, *35*, 15–30.

Schwartz, G. E.   Biofeedback as therapy: Some theoretical and practical issues. *American Psychologist*, 1973, *28*, 666–673.

Shagass, C.   Conditioning the human occipital alpha rhythm to a voluntary stimulus. *Journal of Experimental Psychology*, 1942, *31*, 367–379.

Shagass, C., & Johnson, E. P.   The course of acquisition of a conditioned response of the occipital alpha rhythm. *Journal of Experimental Psychology*, 1943, *33*, 201–209.

Skinner, B. F.   *The behavior of organisms*. New York: Appleton-Century, 1938.

Spooner, A., & Kellogg, W. N.   The backward conditioning curve. *American Journal of Psychology*, 1947, *60*, 321–334.

Terrace, H. S.   Classical conditioning. In J. A. Nevin (Ed.), *The study of behavior*. Glenview: Scott-Foresman, 1973, pp. 71–112.

Walsh, D. H.   Interactive effects of alpha feedback and instructional set on subjective state. *Psychophysiology*, 1974, *11*, 428–435.

Yerkes, R. M., & Morgulis, S.   The method of Pavlov in animal psychology. *Psychological Bulletin*, 1909, *6*, 257–273.

chapter 5

Punishment and fear

THERE ARE stimuli which innately frighten us. Without learning, a baby is startled by a loud noise, and it will recoil if its hand touches a flame. But a catalog of unlearned reactions to noxious stimuli is of less interest to the learning psychologist than how we become afraid of situations that are ordinarily neutral. Why does a dog cringe and whine when it hears the approaching footsteps of the person who regularly beats it? The rhythmic sound that is approaching footsteps has no innate capability to frighten the animal. Why does the child run away from a home where the tyrannical parent regularly abuses him or her? New-born babies are not genetically endowed with a fear of parents, so the child's fear must have been acquired through experience. It is these learned reactions to punishment that fascinate learning psychologists.

In a pioneering experiment, Watson and Rayner (1920) conditioned a baby (little Albert, as he is affectionately remembered in psychology) to be afraid of stimuli that were previously neutral to him. A classical conditioning procedure was used, with a loud sound as a UCS to arouse fear reliably. The loud sound was a steel bar which was struck behind the child's head. A live white rat was used as the CS. At the outset Albert was unafraid of the rat, but when the loud sound and the rat were paired repeatedly, Albert developed a strong fear of the rat. The investigators then went on to demonstrate stimulus generalization by showing that the fear reactions would occur when Albert was shown a rabbit, a dog, or even a sealskin coat. The importance of this study is that fear can be a learned state and subject to the same laws of learning, such as stimulus generalization, as any response.

Fear has its origins in punishment, so it is appropriate to discuss

118

reactions to punishment before discussing how fear is learned in a punishing situation.

PUNISHMENT

A punishing situation has three levels of analysis. Consider the case of a mother who punishes a child for stealing pennies from her purse. At one level of analysis the punishment stops the stealing. At another level the child develops a fear reaction to the mother, and at still another level the child runs away from home to avoid the feared mother. Only the first level will be discussed in this section, where the concern is with punishment and how it reduces the probability of a response. The other levels of analysis will be discussed in later parts of this chapter where fear and avoidance learning are discussed.

There are two conditions that establish a punishment situation:

1. There is a response that has been rewarded, has strength, and is ongoing. The purpose of punishment is to reduce the occurrence of this response.
2. The ongoing response is delivered a punishing stimulus.

The issue is the reduction in performance produced by the punishing stimulus, and the amount of reduction that is achieved is importantly a function of the strength of the ongoing response and the intensity and duration of the punishment. In experimental work the punishing stimulus almost always is electric shock, and understandably because shock can be painful and because its intensity and duration can be exactly controlled. Psychologists have been slow in studying other kinds of punishing events and their characteristics.

Strength of the ongoing response and punishment

A primary variable for the effectiveness of punishment is the strength of the ongoing response that is punished. The more times the unwanted response has been rewarded the more persistent it will be and the more punishment it will take to eliminate it. The child who has been successfully stealing pennies from mother's purse regularly for a year may not be deterred by one spanking.

The experimental illustration of this principle is a study by Kaufman and Miller (1949). They used five groups of rats and trained them to run down a straight runway for food reinforcement. Different strengths of the running response were defined by the number of reinforcement given to each group, and they were 1, 3, 9, 27, and 81 reinforcements. After this training the animal had four punishment trials where a brief shock was delivered when the rat took the food. Figure

FIGURE 5–1

Data which demonstrate that a punishment situation can be described as approach-avoidance behavior. An approach response in rats is trained with food reinforcement and is deterred when punishing electric shock is delivered.

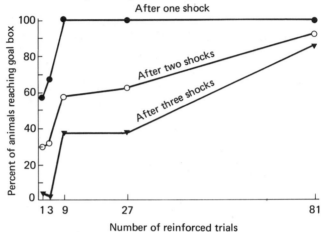

Kaufman, L. E., & Miller, N. E. Effect of number of reinforcements on strength of approach in an approach-avoidance conflict. *Journal of Comparative and Physiological Psychology*, 1949, *42*, 65–74. Reprinted by permission of the American Psychological Asssociation.

5–1 has the findings, plotted in terms of percent of animals who reached the goal box as a function of number of reinforcements in training and number of punishing shocks. The punishment is effective in eliminating the running behavior, and it is least effective for the largest number of reinforcements.

Intensity of punishment

Because of our direct experience with many psychological variables, and in observing their effects on ourselves and others, we sometimes have good intuition on how a variable might effect behavior. The intensity of punishment is one of these variables. We all have been punished and have delivered punishment, and it would be our intuitive feeling that strong punishment eliminates unwanted behavior more quickly than weak punishment. Laboratory research supports this intuition, with the bonus of more detail than common sense provides. Karsh (1962) did a study with rats, where intensity of punishment was the experimental variable. She used a straight runway, where the animals learned to run to the far end for food reward. Speed of running was the measure of performance. After 75 food-rewarded trials she gave 40 punishment trials where the animal was shocked when it touched the food cup. Five groups of animals were used, with each group receiving a different intensity of shock on the 40 punishment trials: 0, 75, 150, 300 and 600 volts. The results are shown in Figure 5–2. The final trials of acquisition show the final preshock performance, and the punishment that followed was effective in lessening performance, with larger consequences for the greater amounts of punishment. With the highest amounts of shock the animals very quickly stopped running altogether, as shown by zero speed in Figure 5–2.

FIGURE 5–2

Effects of intensity of punishment on running speed.

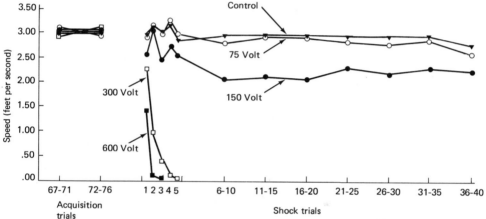

Karsh, E. B. Effects of number of rewarded trials and intensity of punishment on running speed. *Journal of Comparative and Physiological Psychology*, 1962, 55, 44–51. Reprinted by permission of the American Psychological Association.

Duration of punishment

The effects of the duration of punishment are illustrated for us in a study by Church, Raymond, and Beauchamp (1967). Rats and a Skinner box were used, and the rats were first trained to press the lever for food reward, and this went on for five daily sessions. The next ten sessions were punishment sessions, where some of the responses continued to be rewarded with food but some were also punished with shock. There were six groups of animals, with each group receiving a different duration of shock (intensity of shock held constant): 0.00 (control condition), 0.15, 0.30, 0.50, 1.00 and 3.00 seconds. The results are presented in Figure 5–3 in terms of a measure of suppression of the bar-pressing response. There is a clear relationship: The longer the punishment the more effective it is in eliminating a response.

FIGURE 5–3
Effect of duration of punishment on bar-pressing behavior
in the rat. The rat's behavior is represented in terms of
suppression of the bar-pressing that had been trained with
food. Higher values of the index mean less suppression.

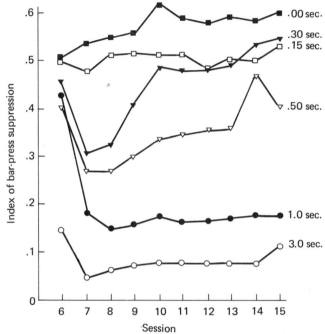

Church, R. M., Raymond, G. A., & Beauchamp, R. D. Response suppression as a function of intensity and duration of
punishment. *Journal of Comparative and Physiological Psychology,*
1967, *63*, 39–44. Reprinted by permission of the American Psychological Association.

AVOIDANCE LEARNING

Reduction in an ongoing response is the most straightforward consequence of punishment but it is only one aspect. Another facet, which
theorists have found more challenging, is behaving to do something about
the punishing situation. Psychologists do not believe that punishing stimuli weaken a response and work in an opposite fashion to the strengthening effects of reward. Instead, subjects actively do something to lessen
the discomfort, and it is this learning of new responses that psychologists
have found so interesting. Basically, this learning occurs in two kinds
of situations, depending whether the subject can avoid the punishment
or not. In *escape learning* it cannot avoid the punishment. The subject
always receives the punishment on a trial but it can escape it by making
a response, and it is the learning of this response which psychologists

study. An example would be a rat placed in a box with an electrified floor. At the start of each trial the shock is delivered and the rat will learn that it can escape it by jumping from the box. But no matter how efficiently it performs its escape response it will always receive the shock at the beginning of each trial. In the second kind of punishment-induced learning, called *avoidance learning*, the subject can learn to avoid punishment all together. Continuing with the rat-in-the-box example, an avoidance learning situation might sound a tone for ten seconds before the shock is delivered on a trial, and the avoidance response which the rat learns is to jump out of the box in the ten seconds before the shock comes on when it hears the tone. Avoidance learning has the anticipatory fear of punishment, and it is a kind of learning which has most fascinated learning psychologists and which will primarily occupy our interests in the remainder of this chapter. The theoretical concern with punishment and fear began in the 1930s, and it has been accelerating ever since.

Consider a puzzle like this, with classical conditioning as the frame of reference. According to the laws of classical conditioning (Chapter 4) the pairing of the CS and the UCS is a fundamental circumstance of learning, with the learning increasing with number of CS-UCS pairings. Brogden, Lipman, and Culler (1938) ran an experiment with guinea pigs which used an activity cage that rotated on a shaft as the animal ran in place with the cage moving beneath its feet. The CS was a tone, the UCS was electric shock, and the UCR was movement; the animal had to learn to move when it heard the tone. One group of animals had the standard classical conditioning arrangement, where the CS and UCS were always paired together and the shock was unavoidable. A second group was treated the same except that its animals could avoid the shock by making a movement in the CS-UCS interval. Figure 5–4 shows the results plotted in terms of anticipatory movements to the CS. The bottom curve is the group which received the standard classical conditioning procedure, and they had a modest amount of learning. But notice the top curve for the second group which could avoid the shock. They had far fewer pairings of the CS and the UCS than the other group because they came to avoid the shock regularly, and yet they learned so much faster. Why this apparent failure of the laws of classical conditioning? How could a few CS-UCS pairings produce better learning than many?

Two-factor theory

In one of the most important papers in the psychology of learning, Mowrer (1947) said that data like Brogden, Lipman and Culler are understandable if we see punishment and avoidance as needing *both*

FIGURE 5–4
With electric shock as the *UCS* in classical conditioning, anticipatory avoidance of the shock speeds the rate of conditioning.

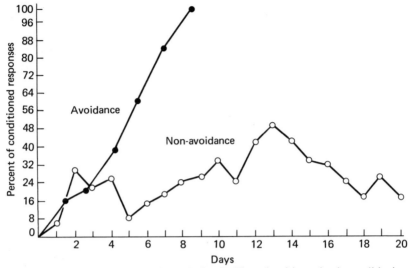

Brogden, W. J., Lipman, E. A., & Culler, E. The role of incentive in conditioning
and extinction. *American Journal of Psychology*, 1938, *51*, 109–117. Reprinted by
permission of the University of Illinois Press.

classical conditioning and instrumental learning to explain them, *and*
if we bring fear into the analysis. He said that fear was an internal
state that was learned, that fear was an uncomfortable motivating state,
and that the fear would motivate the subject to learn forms of behavior
that would remove it. Mowrer said that the fear was an emotion learned
by the principles of classical conditioning and the avoidance behavior
that followed was learned instrumentally. The reward for the instrumental learning was reduction in fear, and any response that eliminated
fear was thereby rewarded and learned. This is the theory of reward
learning called *drive reduction theory* (Chapter 3). Hunger and thirst
are examples of unlearned primary drives because their satisfaction is
necessary for biological survival. Fear, however, is a *secondary drive*
because it is learned.

Mowrer's theory of emotional learning is called *two-factor theory*
because it uses both classical conditioning and instrumental learning
as explanatory tools. In more detail, the theory makes these assumptions:

1. Pain is an innate response of the autonomic nervous system.
2. Pain can be conditioned to any stimulus. The aspect of the pain
    response that is conditioned to a stimulus is called fear (sometimes
    it is called anxiety). The learning of fear is by classical conditioning.
3. Fear is motivating.

4. Fear has cue (stimulus) properties which are called response-produced stimuli.
5. Response-produced stimuli can become the cue for any response through learning.
6. The reduction of the fear motivation is a basis for instrumental learning.

FIGURE 5–5

The stages of Mowrer's two-factor theory. Fear is learned in Stage 1 by classical conditioning, and avoidance behavior is instrumentally learned in Stage 2 when it produces fear reduction.

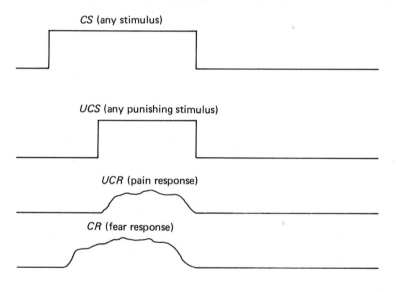

Stage 1: Classical conditioning of the fear response

CS (any stimulus)

UCS (any punishing stimulus)

UCR (pain response)

CR (fear response)

Stage 2: Instrumental learning of an avoidance response

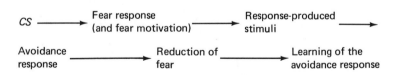

Figure 5–5 shows how these assumptions produce the learning of fear and an avoidance response based on its reduction. A good theory has scope, and two-factor theory has it because it says that fear can become conditioned to any stimulus and that any avoidance response will be learned that reduces fear. Human experience supports this assertion. Can you think of a stimulus to which someone, somewhere, is

not afraid? Can you think of a response that is not made by someone, somewhere, in avoidance of fearful stimuli?

A demonstration of two-factor theory, where fear was classically conditioned and an arbitrary avoidance response was learned to escape a fearful stimulus, was carried out by Brown and Jacobs (1949). They used rats and an apparatus with two compartments separated by a guillotine door which created a wall. With the door lifted, there was a low barrier between the two compartments. The door was down for the classical conditioning of the fear, and an animal was administered 22 training trials where a light–tone combination (*CS*) was paired with shock (*UCS*). Test trials followed, where the door was lifted to reveal the barrier. The *CS* was turned on and when the animal jumped the barrier the *CS* was turned off. Theoretically, fear has been conditioned to the *CS*, and the animal can avoid the fear-arousing *CS* by jumping the barrier. There were two groups of animals: an experimental group that received the treatment just described and a control group that was treated the same except that it was never shocked. The results

FIGURE 5–6

Learning of an avoidance response to escape a stimulus which arouses fear.

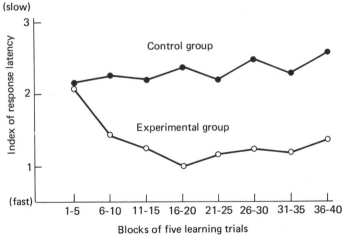

Brown, J. S., & Jacobs, A. The role of fear in the motivation and acquisition of responses. *Journal of Experimental Psychology*, 1949, *39*, 747–759. Reprinted by permission of the American Psychological Association.

given in Figure 5–6 are presented in terms of the time to make the barrier-crossing response. The control animals wandered about in random exploration as animals customarily do, and often crossed the barrier, so a latency measure was obtained for them also. But notice the curve for the experimental group. It is a standard learning curve; the animals respond with increasing speed to escape the fear-producing *CS*. Brown and Jacobs, in their test of two-factor theory, properly interpret the findings in support of it.

Kalish (1954) investigated the learning of an avoidance response as a function of the number of *CS-UCS* pairings which, according to two-factor theory, determines the amount of fear. Different groups of rats were given either 0 (control group), 1, 3, 9 or 27 paired presentations of a light–buzzer *CS* and shock as the *UCS* in a box, and then were transferred to a hurdle-jumping task like Brown and Jacobs used, where the *CS* would sound and then turn off when the animal crossed the barrier. The measure of performance was latency of jumping the hurdle, just as in the Brown and Jacobs experiment. Kalish's results are shown in Figure 5–7. The greater the number of *CS-UCS* pairings and fear, the more readily the avoidance response was learned.

Both the Brown and Jacobs experiment, and the Kalish experiment, had the classical conditioning of fear precede the instrumental learning

FIGURE 5–7

The learning of an avoidance response to escape a stimulus which arouses fear. The curve parameter is the **number of** times the stimulus was paired with electric shock which, according to two-factor theory, determines the degree of fear.

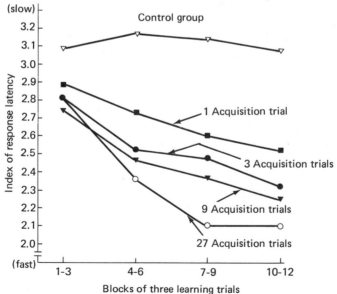

Kalish, H. I. Strength of fear as a function of the number of acquisition and extinction trials. *Journal of Experimental Psychology*, 1954, *47*, 1–9. Reprinted by permission of the American Psychological Association.

of the avoidance response, which has a tidiness about it because it separates the learning of fear and avoidance as two-factor theory does. Commonly, however, research workers in this field will use a task where fear and avoidance are learned together. One such device is the two-way shuttle box, shown in Figure 5–8 (Solomon and Wynne, 1953), and

FIGURE 5–8
A two-way shuttle box for dogs commonly used in research on avoidance behavior.

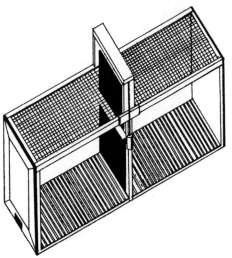

Solomon, R. L., & Wynne, L. C. Traumatic avoidance learning: Acquisition in normal dogs. *Psychological Monographs*, 1953, *67*, Whole No. 354. Reprinted by permission of the American Psychological Association.

it is similar to the hurdle-jumping task. The floor is electrified, and there is a barrier between two compartments. When a guillotine gate is lifted, there remains a hurdle in the center of the box. Any distinctive stimulus can be a *CS*, and its onset is followed by shock. The avoidance response to be learned is jumping over the hurdle and into the other compartment in the *CS-UCS* interval before the shock comes on. The guillotine gate is then closed until the next trial, at which time the animal is required to jump back to the first compartment. The interest in the shuttle box is the study of avoidance learning, but, strictly, it is an escape-avoidance task. In the beginning trials, before it learns to avoid, the animal is shocked each time before the hurdle is jumped, and so at this point it is an escape situation. In the later trials the animal anticipates the shock by jumping over the hurdle when the *CS* comes on, and so it is now an avoidance task.

Representative shuttle box data from one dog are shown in Figure 5–9. (Solomon and Wynne, 1953). The CS was a dimming of lights above the box, and the CS-UCS interval was ten seconds which required that the dog jump over the hurdle within ten seconds or be shocked.

FIGURE 5–9

Representative shuttle box data from one dog. Punishing shock was received when a response took longer than ten seconds. A response in less than ten seconds avoided the shock.

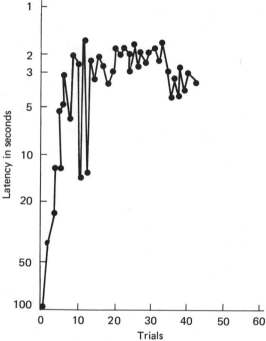

Solomon, R. L., & Wynne, L. C. Traumatic avoidance learning: Acquisition in normal dogs. *Psychological Monographs,* 1953, *67,* Whole No. 354. Reprinted by permission of the American Psychological Association.

It can be seen that the initial responses were longer than ten seconds, which means that the animal was shocked. In these initial trials there was pairing of the CS and UCS for the classical conditioning of fear, but after that the animal learned to avoid shock because responses occurred in less than ten seconds. The learning of the avoidance response was somewhat gradual because there are two responses after the avoidance learning began which had latencies longer than ten seconds and the dog was shocked. Thereafter, the fearful animal always responded

in two to three seconds after onset of the *CS* and was never shocked
again.

EXTINCTION OF AN AVOIDANCE RESPONSE

General characteristics

The extinction of an avoidance response requires withdrawal of the
punishing *UCS*, but there is more to extinction than the withdrawal
of punishment. According to two-factor theory there is the emotional
state of fear that is supporting the avoidance response by the reinforcing
consequences of fear reduction. To extinguish the avoidance response
we must extinguish fear also.

There are many people who never conquer their fear of water and
systematically avoid swimming all of their lives. The punishment that
originally induced the fear of water is long gone, but the avoidance
behavior continues unabated. Such things are common knowledge to
us, and so experimental evidence on the resistance of avoidance responses to extinction will come as no surprise. Figure 5–10 shows data
for the extinction of a hurdle-jumping response. The study is by Solomon,

FIGURE 5–10
Attempt to extinguish the avoidance response
in the two-way shuttle box by withdrawing the
UCS.

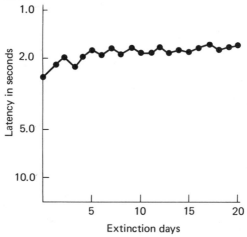

Solomon, R. L., Kamin, L. J., & Wynne, L. C.
Traumatic avoidance learning: The outcomes of
several extinction procedures with dogs. *Journal
of Abnormal and Social Psychology,* 1953, *48,* 291–
302. Reprinted by permission of the American
Psychological Association.

Kamin, and Wynne (1953). They used dogs as subjects and the shuttle box shown in Figure 5–8 as their research apparatus. As in the Solomon and Wynne (1953) study, the CS was a dimming of lights, shock was the UCS, and the CS-UCS interval was ten seconds. After 10 consecutive acquisition trials where shock was administered if the animal did not leap the barrier within 10 seconds, 200 extinction trials were given where shock was always omitted. Notice that over the 200 trials the avoidance response is very efficient, occurring as it does between 1 and 2 seconds after the onset of the CS, and there is no sign of a decrease in response proficiency that ordinarily characterizes behavior in experimental extinction. Two hundred extinction trials without decrement is a long series, certainly longer persistence than one would expect for learning by positive reinforcement. Some investigators have reported many hundreds of extinction trials without a decline in avoidance behavior.

Obviously more must be done to extinguish the avoidance response than withdraw the punishing UCS. The UCS must be withdrawn, of course, but this operation guarantees only that no new fear learning will occur—it does not guarantee the repeated unreinforced elicitation of the fear state and thus its weakening by extinction. That the avoidance response can continue so long in extinction without decline shows that fear is not weakening, and this could be embarrassing for two-factor theory because the occurrence of the avoidance response should bring an unreinforced elicitation of the fear response and its extinction. But maybe two-factor theory is correct in principle but vague on details. Maybe the occurrence of an avoidance response does not bring a full-blown occurrence of the fear response and, thus, a full-fledged extinction trial for it. Maybe the avoidance response is fired by a very slight arousal of fear, so that the full occurrence of the avoidance response does not necessarily mean a full occurrence of the fear response. The result is that the fear response never has full, unreinforced elicitations and so it undergoes little extinction. Solomon and Wynne (1954) conceived this idea and called it the *principle of anxiety conservation*. The person afraid of water does not need a massive fright reaction to avoid swimming, but merely avoids swimming and protests disinterest in it with only the slightest feelings of fear and unpleasantness. The principle of anxiety conservation says that it is the occurrence of the avoidance response to minimal fear cues that minimizes the occurrence of the fear response and thus its extinction.

If the principle of anxiety conservation is true, then the proper extinction procedure is to prevent the avoidance response and repeatedly present the fearful CS in the absence of the UCS so that the fear response is repeatedly elicited in full strength and extinguished. A number of experiments with consistent outcomes have been done using this procedure, which goes under the names of *flooding, blocking,* or *response prevention.* A representative one is by Schiff, Smith and Prochaska (1972). Schiff and his associates used a straight runway with an electrified floor, and the animal (the rat) started a trial in a start box with the door to the runway alley closed. At the start of the trial the CS was sounded (it was "white noise," which sounds like the rush of a waterfall) and the door was opened. If the animal made it to the goal box within ten seconds the CS was turned off and shock was escaped; otherwise the animal was shocked. After an animal reached a criterion of learning, it was administered the flooding treatment, where it was shut in the start box with the CS sounding and the animal blocked from making the avoidance response. The experimental variable was amount of flooding time. The extinction of the avoidance response followed, which was the same as the initial training phase except that shock was never administered, and it was continued to a criterion of not re-

FIGURE 5–11

The extinction of an avoidance response by blocking the avoidance response and forcing the subject to endure the fearful stimulus.

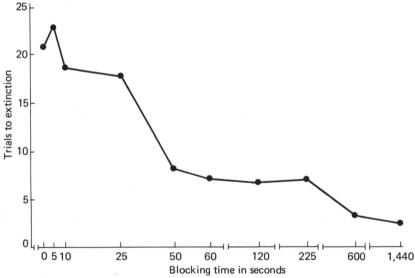

Schiff, R., Smith, N., & Prochaska, J. Extinction of avoidance in rats as a function of duration and number of blocked trials. *Journal of Comparative and Physiological Psychology,* 1972, *81,* 356–359. Reprinted by permission of the American Psychological Association.

sponding. The results are shown in Figure 5–11, where trials to extinction are plotted as a function of blocking time. The more the subject was held in the presence of the fearful CS the less likely it was to make the avoidance response. And, Shipley (1974) has shown that the important thing in flooding is the total exposure time to the CS; it does not matter how the total time is broken up.

Nelson (1967) used these ideas about flooding to evaluate why the tranquilizer chlorpromazine hastened the extinction of fear. One possibility is that the drug works on the fear state itself in a direct physiological way, but another is that it works to increase the amount of exposure to the fear-producing situation. Nelson found that the drug worked through the mechanism of flooding, and that it extinguished the fear level by increasing the amount of time in the fearful situation, just as Schiff and his colleagues found. Nelson's experiment is a nice example of how medicine and psychology can complement one another. If the drug had a special physiological effect, then it would have been a triumph for pharmacology and would have been a unique treatment for fear. But that the drug worked through a behavioral mechanism suggests that the drug is useful for reducing fear but that other methods which prolong the subject in the fearful situation can work equally well.

The elimination of fear is one explanation of extinction of the avoidance response under the two-factor theory. Alternatively it has been suggested that the subject under restraint in the flooding situation learns another response, perhaps one of immobility, as fear is reduced when the CS is terminated, and on the extinction trials this newly learned response to the CS interferes with the execution of the avoidance response and reduces its frequency of occurrence. Fear is unaffected; only a conflicting response has been learned which acts in opposition to the avoidance response and lowers its performance level, making it seem as if the fear supporting the avoidance response has been reduced. This is called the interference, or counterconditioning, hypothesis.

Black (1958) had an inventive test of the counterconditioning hypothesis. He used dogs which were held in a harness, and they were required to learn a head-turning response to a tone CS as an avoidance response to shock. He then placed an experimental group of animals under curare and gave extinction by repeated presentation of the tone. In a final session, with the effects of curare worn off, the experimental animals were given a standard extinction series of the head-turning response, and comparison was with control animals that did not have the extinction treatment under curare but were otherwise treated the same. The idea of the experiment was that the animals under curare could not conceivably learn a competing motor response because their muscles could not function, so any effect of the extinction procedures in the curare session must be on the extinction of fear. The results in the final session supported the view that the extinction of an avoidance response is dependent on the extinction of fear, not the learning of a competing response. The experimental animals required about one sixth as many trials as the control animals to reach a criterion of extinction.

CS termination

All of the studies that have been reviewed on avoidance have one thing in common among themselves and with most other studies in this field: The CS terminates with the occurrence of the avoidance response. An insignificant matter it would seem but, as Kamin (1956) pointed out, the avoidance of shock and termination of the CS occur together, and we cannot tell which is responsible for avoidance learning. His research demonstrated that the time of CS termination was an important variable, and Katzev (1967) followed it with a study showing the importance of CS termination for the speed with which an avoidance response is extinguished. Katzev used rats and a shuttle box (similar to the one shown in Figure 5–8). The CS was a buzzer–light combination, and the UCS was electric shock. All animals were given 200 training trials, where the shock was avoided if the barrier-crossing avoidance response was made within 5 seconds after CS onset and where the CS was terminated promptly when the response occurred. In extinction, where the shock was withdrawn, the animals were divided into two groups. Group 1 had the CS terminate when the avoidance response occurred, or terminate after five seconds if no avoidance response occurred. Group 2 had the same procedure for failure to avoid, but it had the CS continue for 20 seconds after a successful avoidance response. The results are shown in Figure 5–12. The standard extinction procedure gave high persistence of the avoidance response for Group 1, but Group 2 extinguished very rapidly.

A problem with the Katzev experiment is that it confounds the CS termination variable with amount of exposure to the CS. Group 2, which had the CS continue after the avoidance response, had more exposure to the CS than Group 1. Flooding experiments show that exposure to the CS is a fundamental variable for the extinction of fear, and so the more rapid extinction found for Group 2 could be a flooding effect and have nothing to do with the point of CS termination. Katzev and Berman (1974) answered this criticism with an experiment that jointly studied CS termination and CS exposure, and they concluded that the time of CS termination was a genuine variable for the extinction of avoidance behavior. The CS exposure time turned out to be a variable also, however, which is expected from the flooding experiments.

The effect of CS termination on extinction has no established explanation, although there are several to consider. Katzev (1967) entertains a discrimination hypothesis which contends that prompt CS offset in both acquisition and extinction does not allow the subject to tell the two situations apart so he responds in extinction as he did in acquisition. When the CS is terminated promptly in acquisition and delayed in extinction the two situations are discriminated readily and the subject

FIGURE 5–12

Delay of *CS* termination after the avoidance response hastens the extinction process.

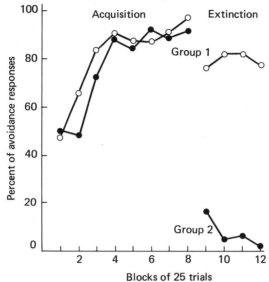

Katzev, R. Extinguishing avoidance responses as a function of delayed warning-signal termination. *Journal of Experimental Psychology*, 1967, *75*, 339–344. Reprinted by permission of the American Psychological Association.

responds differentially. Other possible explanations lie within two-factor theory. If the *CS* arouses fear, and if *CS* offset at the time of the avoidance response reduces fear and reinforces the response, then delay of *CS* offset is delay of reinforcement and it reasonably can be expected to lower the level of the avoidance response. In the same vein, if *CS* offset produces reinforcing effects, its delay until after the avoidance response could reward whatever response happens to be ongoing, like exploring or crouching or relaxing. These could be considered interfering responses that reduce the occurrence of avoidance response.

STATUS OF TWO-FACTOR THEORY

Two-factor theory has explanatory value, but in recent years doubts have arisen about it (Rescorla and Solomon, 1967; Seligman and Johnston, 1973). Psychophysiological measures have been a source of data. The heart beats faster when you are afraid because it receives impulses from the autonomic nervous system which is the main physiological residence of fear, according to two-factor theory, so an experimental test of two-factor theory would be to record heart rate in an avoidance learning situation. Heart rate, as an index of fear, should increase when the CS occurs and subside when the CS is withdrawn, and heart rate should correlate with the extinction of the avoidance response, which is based on fear.

Black (1959) has the most well-known experiment on heart rate and fear. He used the same apparatus and head-turning response as in his earlier study (Black, 1958), which was discussed earlier. Heart rate during acquisition acted about as expected under two-factor theory, although the interpretation is not unequivocal. On an acquisition trial there was a sharp increase in heart rate when the CS came on, and then it subsided in a few seconds after the CS terminated, just as would be expected if the CS was arousing fear and heart rate was an index of it. But body movement increases heart rate also, so was the heart rate increase due to fear or the motor act of head turning? Black had to conclude that muscular activity confounded whatever effects fear had on heart rate. Despite this confounding, the heart rate function had *some* correspondence in acquisition to theoretical expectations, but even that was not found for extinction. If heart rate is an index of fear that is sustaining the avoidance response, it should be high at the start of extinction and return to normal when the avoidance response is extinguished. Black found that heart rate returned to normal in one sixth the trials it took the avoidance response to extinguish. This is small comfort for two-factor theory.

Thus, there are problems with some of the details of two-factor theory as it was originally formulated. What remains of the theory today is the central thesis that the laws of fear conditioning are the same as the laws of classical conditioning, that this conditioning has important effects on avoidance learning, and that fear is probably motivational (Rescorla and Solomon, 1967; Maier, Seligman, Solomon, 1969). This is a weaker statement than the original two-factor theory because it does not state how fear and an avoidance response are related. It is far from an inconsequential statement, however. To know that the laws of fear learning are the same as the laws of classical conditioning, and to know that avoidance behavior is importantly determined by them, is an important scientific generalization.

THE COGNITIVE VIEWPOINT

The two-factor theory of fear and avoidance learning is in the stimulus/response, drive/reduction tradition of learning (Chapter 3). Fear is a learned response, and the avoidance response which is instrumental in reducing the aversive motivation accompanying the fear response is learned also. Because of problems that are developing for two-factor theory, however, there is interest in cognitive interpretations of fear and avoidance behavior (e.g., Seligman and Johnston, 1973).

Chapter 3 discussed cognitive theorizing which assumes that through learning the subject comes to know the patterning and timing of events and can specify a course of behavior on the basis of them. Responses are not learned to stimuli, as in two-factor theory. Rather, information about stimuli, responses, and behavioral outcomes, is learned. This *information hypothesis* is derived from the cognitive theorizing of Tolman, and one use that we saw for it was as an explanation of secondary reinforcement (Egger and Miller, 1962; 1963). Cognitive theorizing about fear and avoidance still preserves a distinction between the classical conditioning of fear and instrumental learning of the avoidance response, but the learning is now described in informational terms.

Information and the classical conditioning of fear

A theory of classical conditioning since the time of Pavlov has been one of contiguity, where the essential condition of learning is the pairing of the CS and the UCS (the pairing usually has to be repeated, and the order has to be CS-UCS, in addition). Contiguity says that learning depends upon the number of times that the CS and the UCS are experienced together, but as one begins to think in terms of information it becomes meaningful to think in terms of correlations and their learning. Given the CS, what are the chances of the UCS occurring? What is the probability of a UCS in the absence of a CS?

Rescorla (1967; 1972) has been an advocate of the informational point of view. He contends that learning occurs when a correlation exists between the CS and the UCS but not when the correlation is absent and the UCS cannot be predicted from the CS. Rescorla (1968) used the *conditioned emotional response* technique, which is a method of measuring fear, to test his idea. Rescorla's use of this technique took the standard form of teaching a rat to press a bar for food. Once this act had been acquired the animal underwent classical conditioning of fear, where a tone CS was paired with shock UCS. Later the animal was returned to bar pressing for food, and occasionally the tone was sounded. The tone had acquired the power to elicit fear, and the amount of fear was measured by suppression of the bar-pressing behavior (sometimes this approach is properly called *conditioned suppression*). The experimental variable was the probability that the UCS would occur in the presence or absence of the CS. Conditioned suppression occurred only when the CS had some correlation with the UCS. When the correlation was absent, and the UCS was just as likely to occur in the absence as in the presence of the CS, suppression was absent. Contiguity does not seem to be the basis of learning because the CS and the UCS occurred together on occasion when the correlation was absent. Primarily when there was information in the events and some prediction was possible did the conditioning of fear occur.

Information and the instrumental learning of avoidance

If the fear state is learned by classical conditioning and the processing of information in the CS and UCS events, why cannot the avoidance response be learned in the same way by processing the information in response and outcome events? Seligman, Maier, and Solomon (1971) have spoken for this point of view and it runs in parallel with Rescorla's view of classical conditioning. The subject can learn the regularities between his responding and outcome, it is hypothesized. If the response regularly leads to avoidance of a punishing stimulus the subject can learn it, and if the punishment and the behavior are uncorrelated the subject can learn this state of affairs also. In this latter case he will be punished regardless of his behavior, and he will learn that there is nothing he can do about punishment. Later on, when the circumstances have been changed and the subject is given the opportunity to make an avoidance response, he may be indifferent to the opportunity because the uncorrelated behavior and punishment in his past ill-suits him for adaptive responding. This line of thinking supports the rapidly expanding research on *helplessness*. The gist of helplessness is that the experience of unavoidable and unpredictable punishment creates a reluctance to avoid punishment when it becomes predictable and possible.

Helplessness

Mowrer and Viek (1948, p. 193) wrote that "A painful stimulus never seems so objectionable if one knows how to terminate it as it does if one has no control over it." They reported an experiment where hungry rats were more likely to eat food when the electric shock that followed the eating could be turned off with a jump in the air than when it could not. The rats in the two kinds of situation were equated for amount of shock received, and so according to two-factor theory the same amount of fear should have developed. Yet, unpredictable shock produced a greater suppression of eating behavior than predictable shock. This provocative finding lay dormant until Overmier and Seligman (1967) reopened the topic.

Overmier and Seligman used two apparatus units in their experiment. One unit was a cloth hammock in which their dog subjects were slung for receiving unsignaled, inescapable shocks. The other unit was a two-way shuttle box for the learning of avoidance behavior. The procedure was to give experimental animals strong, unsignaled, unpredictable shocks in the hammock, followed 24 hours later by avoidance training in the shuttle box, where the CS was the dimming of illumination and the CS-UCS interval was 10 seconds. The control animals received no treatment prior to avoidance training. The avoidance behavior of the control and the experimental animals differed in striking ways. The experimental animals were much slower than the controls in their avoidance response and about half of them never escaped shock at all. And, the experimental dogs were qualitatively different than the control dogs in the shuttle box. In the initial trials they acted like the naive control dogs—whimpering, howling, and urinating as they were shocked, and there was a strong tendency to give up and accept the shock. Sometimes an experimental dog would cross the barrier and escape the shock, but learning was not affected very much because on the next trial the dog was likely to sit passively and accept the shock. In appearance it was helpless and depressed, and it was experimentally made that way.

There are other lines of evidence which indicate that predictability is an important consideration for understanding the consequences of punishment. Lockard (1963) administered unavoidable shocks to rats in a two-compartment chamber. Her experimental animals always had a CS (blinking light) signal shock onset in one side of the apparatus and not the other. The control animals had shock and the CS paired randomly. She found a reliable preference of the experimental animals for the side of the chamber with signaled shock; the control animals showed no preference. To try for a subjective grasp of the rat's perceptions and emotions, the signaled shock in the Lockard experiment is more tolerable because the rat need only be afraid when the CS is on, but when the shock is unpredictable the animal never knows when punishment will strike, and it has a general fear all of the time. Another possibility is that the CS gives the animal time to prepare itself by crouching and freezing, which may reduce impact of the shock somewhat. There is more to signaled versus unsignaled punishment than preference, however. Weiss (1968), Seligman (1968), and Seligman and Meyer (1970) found that punishment with unsignaled shock produced a higher incidence of gastrointestinal ulcers than signaled shock.

Tests of a cognitive view of helplessness. Before one launches on a test of theory it is desirable to eliminate nontheoretical explanations of the phenomenon. One such explanation of helplessness is motor interference. The subject acquires motor responses in the inescapable punishment situation that are incompatible with the avoidance response, and so it appears helpless because its dominant response is a nonavoidance one. Motor interference in this case might be seen as superstitious responding, where the response that is fortuitously occurring at the time of inescapable shock offset is reinforced. As reasonable as interference might seem as a hypothesis, it slipped from stature when Overmier and Seligman (1967) showed that helpless behavior occurred even when the unsignaled, inescapable shocks were administered to curarized dogs. Curare prevents any motor response whatsoever, and so it becomes difficult to hold a hypothesis which says that helplessness is based on competing motor activity.

Seligman and Maier (1967) made a test of the cognitive view by assuming that prior experience in controlling shock should allow the subject to perceive the effectiveness of its own behavior and should offset the effects of unsignaled, inescapable shock on avoidance behavior. Dogs were their subjects. An escape group was first trained to turn off a shock by turning the head and pressing a panel. The escape group was then given the same unsignaled, inescapable shocks and avoidance training in the same harness and shuttle box apparatus that was used by Overmier and Seligman (1967). A yoked control group received the same treatment as the escape group except that panel pressing was ineffective in controlling the shock. A normal control group received only avoidance training in the shuttle box. The results supported the cognitive theory of helplessness. The escape group which had prior training in shock control performed about the same as the normal control group—both had good success in learning the shuttle box avoidance task. The yoked control group, by contrast, showed typical helplessness behavior by failing to avoid shock on a majority of their trials. As long as experience taught a relationship between behavior and punishment there was adaptive behavior in the avoidance situation. But, when experience left the perception that punishing events are uncontrollable, maladaptive helplessness occurred.

The alleviation of helplessness. The control of behavior is a scientific goal of psychology, and so we are as interested in undoing helplessness as in creating it. The passage of time is one tentative variable for the alleviation of helplessness, and compelling the subject to make a response that eliminates punishment is another.

The first indication that time was a variable for helplessness came in the paper by Overmier and Seligman (1967), discussed earlier. Overmier and Seligman ordinarily used 24-hour intervals between inescapable shocks and avoidance training, but in one of their experiments they had time as the experimental variable, with 24, 48, 72, and 144 hours between the inescapable shock and avoidance. They found that the helplessness effect dissipated rapidly, leaving a normal subject (the dog, in this case) after 48 hours. A finding like this can jeopardize a learning interpretation of helplessness. Unpredictable shocks may do no more than induce a transient emotional stress effect. The problem with the transient stress interpretation is that the time effect has not held up well in other experiments. Seligman and Maier (1967, Experiment I) found a retention of helplessness over seven days, as did Seligman, Maier, and Geer (1968), and Seligman and Groves (1970). Either the

Overmier and Seligman finding is fortuitous, or variables are operating that we do not understand.

Seligman and Maier (1967) showed that prior acquaintance with shock-behavior contingencies prevented helplessness from occurring, and this idea can be used to alleviate helplessness after it is formed. Seligman, Maier, and Geer (1968) used the same apparatus and about the same procedures as Overmier and Seligman (1967), discussed above. Their treatment for modifying helplessness had two phases, and their approach, which has its roots in cognitive view, was to expose the dog to the punishment/response contingency after it had acquired helplessness so it could perceive a relationship between behavior and punishment. The first phase was to lower the barrier of the shuttle box and call to the dog while it was being shocked, trying to induce its escape. One dog responded to this treatment, but the remainder of the dogs were subjected to a second phase where they were placed on a leash and dragged from shock to the safe area of the shuttle box. The forcible procedure worked. The helplessness syndrome was broken up in all cases. Avoidance tests in a shuttle box followed, and all animals learned to avoid.

Helplessness and human depression.   The similarities between human depression and learned helplessness may be more than accidental, and Miller and Seligman (1973) and Seligman (1975) believe that the principles of helplessness explain depression. The natural world contains events like wars, accidents, and economic catastrophes that occur independently of our behavior, and these can be forms of unpredictable punishment that contribute to human depression. Depression and helplessness have much in common—passivity, inability to cope, and paralysis of the will. We saw in laboratory work that this kind of behavior in dogs can be alleviated by showing them relationships between their behavior and events in the world. Like the laboratory dog, the human can become helpless when a behavior repeatedly fails to cope with situational demands. And, like the dog, the human can be adaptive again when taught effective coping behavior. Caution must be used in drawing correspondence between helplessness in the dog and depression in the human, because the same behavior can have different causes. But with this caution in mind, one should not pass up the possibility that the same variables and laws operate in helplessness and depression, and that our knowledge gained in the laboratory can be tailored to the human circumstance and be used to ease human despair.

PRACTICAL APPLICATIONS

So far this chapter has covered basic research and theory on punishment and avoidance, and the work has been with animals because they can be punished in the interest of science and humans cannot be. In recent years an interesting development in psychotherapy is the application of learning principles to deviant and distressful human behavior that the psychotherapist must try to change for the better. Since the time of the Viennese physician Sigmund Freud (1856–1939), psychotherapy has been dominated by psychoanalytic theory and practices. Psychoanalysis emphasizes subconscious mental processes that are influential in normal and abnormal behavior, and it uses a historical method of psychotherapy that works over many sessions to reveal the events of the past which have shaped the unconscious forces that are determining the troublesome behavior. The behavior therapist, as the clinical psychologist is called who works from learning principles, has an approach that is much less historical, much more of the here and now, than psychoanalysis. It is not that behavior therapists deny the importance of past events for present behavior, but rather that they start from the assumption that the troublesome behavior is learned and therefore manipulable by the laws of learning. A psychoanalyst might interpret a child's bed-wetting during sleep as an example of urinary eroticism which gives the child sexual pleasure, and when it occurs during sleep it is accompanied by sexual fantasies that a puritanical society forces him to repress during waking hours. A behavior therapist would dismiss this psychoanalytic account as fanciful, and might cite in counterargument the research of Mowrer and Mowrer (1938) which used a specially constructed bed pad that rang a bell at the onset of urination and woke the child for a trip to the toilet. Mowrer and Mowrer saw getting out of bed and going to the toilet as a response to be learned to the cue of a full bladder, and with their learning approach they had 100 percent success in curing 30 chronic bedwetters ages 3 to 13 years.

We saw in Chapter 2 that the principles of positive reinforcement had various applications in changing behavior, and the same is true for the principles in this chapter. Punishment can change behavior just as reward, and the extinction of unrealistic human fear is a therapeutic process in great demand.

Some therapeutic uses of punishment

Any parent who has ever slapped the bottom of a child for doing the wrong thing once too often knows that punishment can work, and the experimental work reviewed earlier in this chapter demonstrated in detail how punishment can reduce the frequency of a response. Sylvester and Liversedge (1960) report an interesting study where punishment was used to cure writer's cramp. Writer's cramp is an ailment where spasms and tremors develop in the hand and prevent writing, although it is not limited to writing behavior because it has been found among such occupations as typists and musicians. Notwithstanding, it is most prevalent among those who write regularly in their work, such as book-keepers, and so the name. Psychotherapists are agreed that the ailment is behavioral and lacks a direct physiological cause. Sylvester and Livers-edge devised three tasks that punished the behavioral characteristics of writer's cramp with electric shock. One task required the holding of a stylus in a small hole so that a tremor brought contact with the side of the hole and produced shock. A second task required the tracing of an irregular path with a stylus and any deviation from it gave a shock. The third task was an ordinary pen rigged so that too much thumb pressure gave a shock. The intent is obvious—avoidance of writer's cramp behavior will avoid punishment. After several sessions on these three tasks were given each patient, a number of cures was obtained. Of 39 cases treated, 24 had definite improvement and returned to normal employment. In the world of psychotherapy, this is a high cure rate.

Lovaas, Schaeffer, and Simmons (1965) used electric shock to instill social behavior in two five-year old autistic children who had not responded to conventional psychiatric treatment. The children did not speak or show any social responsiveness to people whatsoever. They spent most of the day in dreamy self-stimulatory behavior like rocking back and forth. Lovaas and his associates devised an experimental room so that shock could be delivered through the floor, and they punished the autistic behavior and withheld shock when the child made a social response by moving toward an experimenter when called. The sequence of events in the experiment and the results are shown in Figure 5–13. The proportion of responses to the experimenter's command is the measure of performance. At the start, before shock, neither child paid any attention to the experimenter. With shock they readily came to respond in the desired fashion, and in a subsequent extinction period of ten months, when the shock was withheld, the children maintained their social behavior at a high level for nine months before it finally declined. At this point, shock was reintroduced, and it took only one shock to re-turn the social behavior to a high level.

Practical uses of punishment, as in these studies, may seem harsh, even brutal, to some, but let us remember a couple of things. We are dealing with people in misery, and the discomfort of the shock may be a small price to pay for a chance to return to normalcy. Writer's cramp is an occupational ailment, and the patient having it can be threatened with the loss of employment. Autistic children might not be miserable because their rich inner life may be calm and peaceful, but their maladaptive behavior dooms them to the drabness of institu-tional life. They are moved a step closer to normal, productive lives as therapy helps them build a storehouse of socially useful responses.

FIGURE 5–13

Use of punishment to shape social behavior in two autistic children.

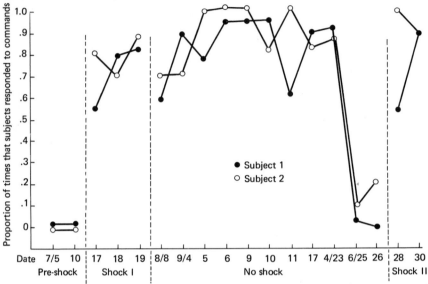

Lovaas, O. I., Schaeffer, B., & Simmons, J. Q. Building social behavior in autistic children by use of electric shock. *Journal of Experimental Research on Personality,* 1965, *1,* 99–109. Reprinted by permission of Academic Press, Inc.

Psychotherapy and the extinction of fears

Many fears are beneficial, such as the fear of fire which keeps you from putting your hand in a flame. Other fears can be beneficial under some circumstances and absurd under others. Consider a fear of height. It is a healthy attitude to be respectfully fearful when on the edge of a 1,000-foot cliff, but it is abnormal for your heart to pound wildly when standing on a chair in your kitchen. It is a wise person who does not put a hand in a nest of cobras, but it is abnormal to break into a sweat when handed a plastic snake. The psychotherapist does a lively business in the extinction of abnormal fears such as these.

Psychoanalytic theory would hold that fear of snakes is because of sexual impulses repressed in the unconscious, and that snakes are phallic symbols. Only by prolonged psychoanalysis would one come to free the impulses from the unconscious and gain freedom from the fear. Bandura, Blanchard, and Ritter (1969), however, experimentally showed that a fear of snakes can be largely overcome with approaches that have been rationalized by learning theory. They began by publicizing the purpose of their experiment and recruiting subjects who wanted to eliminate their fear of snakes. Not willing to take the volunteers' word about their fear, they gave each volunteer a test of fear that used a live, four-foot-long king snake (nonpoisonous). The test had a graded series of 29 performance tasks involving increasing interactions with the snake. A score of zero was complete unwillingness to enter the room with the snake, and a top score was holding the snake with a gloved hand. Those volunteers who earned the top score were not used as experimental subjects because they showed no fear of snakes and so had no fear to extinguish.

Four groups of subjects were used, each receiving a different treatment.

Systematic desensitization. This is a technique where muscular relaxation is paired with a graded series of imagined snakes, going from mildly fearful situations to frightening ones. Psychologists know that densitization can sometimes work, although it is not clear theoretically why it does. The imagining could be a sort of mental flooding, and provide a poorly understood kind of experimental extinction, or the relaxation along with the imagined snake stimuli could be a counterconditioning activity that works against the snake-avoiding response.

Symbolic modeling. These subjects were shown a graduated film of people handling snakes, with scenes ranging from the handling of plastic snakes to those where the live snake crawled all over a person's body.

Live modeling with participation. The subject watched the experimenter fearlessly handle the snake in various situations, and was gradually led to handling the snake.

Control. No treatment.

All subjects had received the avoidance test of fear in the beginning, and after the experiment they were given the same test again. The change from pretest to posttest was the measure of treatment effectiveness.

The results are shown in Figure 5–14. The control group had no change from pretest to posttest, as might be expected, but all of the other groups showed a substantial increase in the willingness to approach and handle snakes, with the greatest increase for live modeling with actual participation. Ninety-two percent of the subjects in this latter treatment came to actually handling the snake, while only 33 percent of the symbolic modeling group, 25 percent of the systematic desensitization group, and 0 percent of the control group did so. None of the subjects were able to handle the snake in the pretest, it will be recalled.

Applied research, like this study by Bandura and his colleagues, looks for the best overall way to achieve a practical goal, and in so doing it does not hesitate to use a mix of basic principles. Desensitization is a mixture of flooding where faint (imagined) fearful stimuli occur, and counterconditioning where relaxation presumably works in opposition to the avoidance response. The symbolic modeling treatment appears to be a case of flooding where the fearful stimuli are similar

FIGURE 5–14

Effects of three experimental treatments on the extinction of fear of snakes. All treatments produced an increase in the tendency to approach snakes.

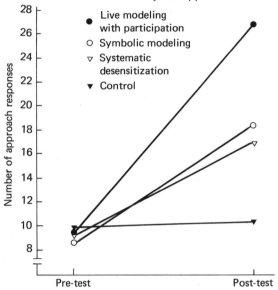

Bandura, A., Blanchard, E. B., & Ritter, B. J. Relative efficacy of modeling therapeutic changes for inducing behavioral, attitudinal, and affective changes. *Journal of Personality and Social Psychology,* 1969, *13,* 173–199. Reprinted by permission of the American Psychological Association.

to the real ones. Live modeling with participation is flooding with the actually feared stimuli and with the counterconditioning of approach responses that are in direct opposition to the avoidance responses. Moreover, the feared snake stimulus persisted after the avoidance response had stopped for many of the subjects in all of the experimental treatments, and we saw that extinction was speeded when *CS* termination was delayed past the time of occurrence of the avoidance response. Later, when these basic principles are better understood, one of the principles in a pure form might prove to be the most effective of all.

SUMMARY

A punishing, aversive stimulus, and the fear that results from it, have strong effects on behavior. A punishing stimulus has the effect of reducing the probability of response occurrence, and its effectiveness is positively related to stimulus intensity and duration.

A consequence of punishment is fear and avoidance of the fearful situation, and Mowrer's two-factor theory has been a prominent attempt to explain them. Two-factor theory assumes that fear is a learned emotional state acquired by classical conditioning (one factor), and that avoidance behavior is instrumentally learned by fear reduction as the avoidance response takes the subject from the fearful situation (the second factor). Extinction of an avoidance response is accomplished by prevention of the avoidance response and the repeated presentation of the stimulus which controls the fear. The unreinforced elicitation of fear brings its extinction and a decrease in the avoidance response based on it.

Another explanation of fear and avoidance learning is the information hypothesis, which is a cognitively oriented theory. The information hypothesis assumes that the subject learns the correlation between stimulus events presented to it and its response and the resulting outcome. Avoidance will be learned when there is a regular relationship between the avoidance response and elimination of the punishing, fearful stimuli but, when correlation is absent, the subject will perceive that there is nothing it can do to eliminate the punishment and fear and so it will not avoid. The failure to avoid an aversive situation and the willingness to endure it is called helpless behavior.

Our scientific knowledge of punishment, fear, and avoidance is being used in clinical situations to eliminate undesirable or uncomfortable behavior. This is called behavior therapy. Punishment is used on occasion by some therapists to reduce the occurrence of unwanted behavior. Patients with uncomfortable, maladaptive fears are commonplace in psychological clinics, and the therapist uses psychology's knowledge of fear extinction to eliminate the fears.

REFERENCES

Bandura, A., Blanchard, E. B., & Ritter, B. J.   Relative efficacy of modeling therapeutic changes for inducing behavioral, attitudinal, and affective changes. *Journal of Personality and Social Psychology*, 1969, *13*, 173–199.

Black, A. H.   The extinction of avoidance responses under curare. *Journal of Comparative and Physiological Psychology*, 1958, *51*, 519–524.

Black, A. H.   Heart rate changes during avoidance learning in dogs. *Canadian Journal of Psychology*, 1959, *13*, 229–242.

Brogden, W. J., Lipman, E. A., & Culler, E.   The role of incentive in conditioning and extinction. *American Journal of Psychology*, 1938, *51*, 109–117.

Brown, J. S., & Jacobs, A.   The role of fear in the motivation and acquisition of responses. *Journal of Experimental Psychology*, 1949, *39*, 747–759.

Church, R. M., Raymond, G. A., & Beauchamp, R. D.   Response suppression as a function of intensity and duration of punishment. *Journal of Comparative and Physiological Psychology*, 1967, *63*, 39–44.

Egger, M. D., & Miller, N. E.   Secondary reinforcement in rats as a function of information value and reliability of the stimulus. *Journal of Experimental Psychology*, 1962, *64*, 97–104.

Egger, M. D., & Miller, N. E.   When is reward reinforcing? An experimental study of the information hypothesis. *Journal of Comparative and Physiological Psychology*, 1963, *56*, 132–137.

Kalish, H. I.   Strength of fear as a function of the number of acquisition and extinction trials. *Journal of Experimental Psychology*, 1954, *47*, 1–9.

Kamin, L.   The effects of termination of the CS and avoidance of the US on avoidance learning. *Journal of Comparative and Physiological Psychology*, 1956, *49*, 420–424.

Karsh, E. B.   Effects of number of rewarded trials and intensity of punishment on running speed. *Journal of Comparative and Physiological Psychology*, 1962, *55*, 44–51.

Katzev, R.   Extinguishing avoidance responses as a function of delayed warning-signal termination. *Journal of Experimental Psychology*, 1967, *75*, 339–344.

Katzev, R. D., & Berman, J. S.   Effect of exposure to conditioned stimulus and control of its termination in the extinction of avoidance behavior. *Journal of Comparative and Physiological Psychology*, 1974, *87*, 347–353.

Kaufman, E. L., & Miller, N. E.   Effect of number of reinforcements on strength of approach in an approach-avoidance conflict. *Journal of Comparative and Physiological Psychology*, 1949, *42*, 65–74.

Lockard, J. S.   Choice of a warning signal or no warning signal in an unavoidable shock situation. *Journal of Comparative and Physiological Psychology*, 1963, *56*, 526–530.

Lovaas, O. I., Schaeffer, B., & Simmons, J. Q.   Building social behavior in autistic children by use of electric shock. *Journal of Experimental Research on Personality*, 1965, *1*, 99–109.

Maier, S. F., Seligman, M. E. P., & Solomon, R. L.   Pavlovian fear conditioning and learned helplessness: Effects on escape and avoidance behavior of (a) the CS-US contingency and (b) the independence of the US and voluntary responding. In B. A. Campbell and R. M. Church (Eds.), *Punishment and aversive behavior*. New York: Appleton-Century-Crofts, 1969, pp. 299–342.

Miller, W. R., & Seligman, M. E. P.   Depression and the perception of reinforcement. *Journal of Abnormal Psychology*, 1973, *82*, 62–73.

Mowrer, O. H.   On the dual nature of learning: A re-interpretation of "conditioning" and "problem-solving." *Harvard Educational Review*, 1947, *17*, 102–148.

Mowrer, O. H., & Mowrer, W. M.   Enuresis: A method for its study and treatment. *American Journal of Orthopsychiatry*, 1938, *8*, 436–459.

Mowrer, O. H., & Viek, P.   An experimental analogue of fear from a sense of helplessness. *Journal of Abnormal and Social Psychology*, 1948, *83*, 193–200.

Nelson, F. Effects of chlorpromazine on fear extinction. *Journal of Comparative and Physiological Psychology*, 1967, *64*, 496–498.

Overmier, J. B., & Seligman, M. E. P. Effects of inescapable shock upon subsequent escape and avoidance responding. *Journal of Comparative and Physiological Psychology*, 1967, *63*, 28–33.

Rescorla, R. A. Pavlovian conditioning and its proper control procedures. *Psychological Review*, 1967, *74*, 71–80.

Rescorla, R. A. Probability of shock in the presence and absence of CS in fear conditioning. *Journal of Comparative and Physiological Psychology*, 1968, *66*, 1–5.

Rescorla, R. A. Informational variables in Pavlovian conditioning. In G. H. Bower (Ed.), *The psychology of learning and motivation* (Vol. 6). New York: Academic Press, 1972, pp. 1–46.

Rescorla, R. A., & Solomon, R. L. Two-process learning theory: Relationships between Pavlovian conditioning and instrumental learning. *Psychological Review*, 1967, *74*, 151–182.

Schiff, R., Smith, N., & Prochaska, J. Extinction of avoidance in rats as a function of duration and number of blocked trials. *Journal of Comparative and Physiological Psychology*, 1972, *81*, 356–359.

Seligman, M. E. P. Chronic fear produced by unpredictable electric shock. *Journal of Comparative and Physiological Psychology*, 1968, *66*, 402–411.

Seligman, M. E. P. *Helplessness*. San Francisco: Freeman, 1975.

Seligman, M. E. P., & Groves, D. P. Nontransient learned helplessness. *Psychonomic Science*, 1970, *19*, 191–192.

Seligman, M. E. P., & Johnston, J. C. A cognitive theory of avoidance learning. In F. J. McGuigan and D. B. Lumsden (Eds.), *Contemporary approaches to conditioning and learning*. New York: Wiley, 1973, pp. 69–110.

Seligman, M. E. P., & Maier, S. F. Failure to escape traumatic shock. *Journal of Experimental Psychology*, 1967, *74*, 1–9.

Seligman, M. E. P., Maier, S. F., & Geer, J. H. Alleviation of learned helplessness in the dog. *Journal of Abnormal Psychology*, 1968, *73*, 256–262.

Seligman, M. E. P., Maier, S. F., & Solomon, R. L. Unpredictable and uncontrollable aversive events. In F. R. Brush (Ed.), *Aversive conditioning and learning*. New York: Academic Press, 1971, pp. 347–400.

Seligman, M. E. P., & Meyer, B. Chronic fear and ulcers in rats as a function of the unpredictability of safety. *Journal of Comparative and Physiological Psychology*, 1970, *73*, 202–207.

Shipley, R. H. Extinction of conditioned fear in rats as a function of several parameters of CS exposure. *Journal of Comparative and Physiological Psychology*, 1974, *87*, 699–707.

Solomon, R. L., Kamin, L. J., & Wynne, L. C. Traumatic avoidance learning: The outcomes of several extinction procedures with dogs. *Journal of Abnormal and Social Psychology*, 1953, *48*, 291–302.

Solomon, R. L., & Wynne, L. C.   Traumatic avoidance learning: acquisition in normal dogs. *Psychological Monographs,* 1953, *67,* No. 354.

Solomon, R. L., & Wynne, L. C.   Traumatic avoidance learning: the principles of anxiety conservation and partial irreversibility. *Psychological Review,* 1954, *61,* 353–385.

Sylvester, J. D., & Liversedge. L. A.   Conditioning and the occupational cramps. In H. J. Eysenck (Ed.), *Behaviour therapy and the neuroses.* New York: Pergamon, 1960, pp. 334–348.

Watson, J. B., & Rayner, R.   Conditioned emotional reactions. *Journal of Experimental Psychology,* 1920, *3,* 1–14.

Weiss, J. M.   Effects of coping responses on stress. *Journal of Comparative and Physiological Psychology,* 1968, *65,* 251–260.

chapter 6

Biological constraints on learning

THE TRADITIONAL VIEW OF LEARNING

THE PREVIOUS chapters implicitly represent a scientific model of learning that can be called the *traditional view*. The traditional view is fashioned after the Newtonian model in physics in the sense that it seeks general laws that cover a full range of the phenomena, from smallest to largest. Laws of motion and gravitational forces apply to a falling pea and a falling star, and similarly learning psychologists have sought principles that embrace learning phenomena from amoeba to humans. Guthrie, Hull, Skinner, Thorndike, and Tolman were systematizers for the psychology of learning, and none of them for a moment doubted the eventual realization of general laws of learning.

Seligman (1970, p. 407) said that the traditional view was guided by the *assumption of equivalence of associability*, which holds that any response of any animal can be associated with any stimulus, and the laws of acquisition, extinction, delay of reinforcement, etc., can be worked out with any arbitrary animal, response, or stimulus. Studying a simple animal was perfectly acceptable because it had learning processes in common with all animals and, being simple, was amenable to good scientific control. The rat and the pigeon have been studied extensively by psychologists because it was believed that general laws of behavior can be found for all animals, and that something can be learned about them by studying the rat and the pigeon. Of course complex animals like humans would have more complex functions than simple animals but this obvious fact altered nothing. It is possible for complex relations to be derived from combinations of simple laws, and so the complexities of behavior deterred no one. Animal psychologists and human psychologists stood shoulder to shoulder in a grand search for the general laws of learning. It was "a period of heroic optimism" (Hinde, 1973, p. 1).

Underlying the traditional view and its faith in general laws was the assumption of an orderly biological universe, progressing from simple animals to complex ones. Aristotle proposed a classification of animals that was of graded complexity, and a scale of animals on a dimension of complexity has been called the *scala naturae* or the *phylogenetic scale*. At the bottom of the scale were simple animals like sponges, in the middle of the scale were animals of intermediate complexity like fish, reptiles, and birds, and at the top were humans. The scala naturae had its origins in a concern with the organization of the biological world but, as Hodos and Campbell (1969) point out, it also had theological ramifications where God was perfect, angels somewhat less perfect, humans more imperfect, and so on down the scale to formless blobs like the sponge. Too, the scala naturae was seemingly compatible with Charles Darwin's biological theory of evolution, where animals were seen on a continuum, evolving from simple to complex. This conception of evolution was consistent with the traditional view of learning because the belief in general laws was complemented by a belief in general biological processes.

Another thrust of the traditional view of learning, usually unverbalized, was that instinct, or the genetic determinants of behavior, mattered little. Instinct as a topic has had an uneven history in psychology, with its lowest point being a facile process where every aspect of behavioral activity was explained by an instinct which determined it. There was an instinct for eating, playing, smiling, fighting, and so on, and instinct psychology fell into low repute because behavior was being explained by naming it. Behaviorism, or stimulus-response psychology as it is so often called, was given its first strong statement by John B. Watson (Watson, 1913), and as it became a powerful influence on the American psychological scene there was an elevation of learning to the top of psychology's scientific hierarchy and a downgrading of instinct. Behaviorism was a scientific philosophy of environmentalism, where behavior was controlled by environmental circumstances and learning was the mechanism of adjustment to the environment. In the long-running nature-nurture controversy, nurture won for behaviorism. If pressed, a staunch behaviorist might have admitted that genetics was a determinant of certain features of behavior, such as primary drives like hunger and thirst, and the senses, but learning was master and pursuit of the general laws of learning was a prime goal of experimental psychology. The result was thousands of experiments on rats and pigeons in standardized laboratory apparatuses like Skinner boxes, with the confidence that general laws of learning would someday emerge. The observing of rats and pigeons, or any other animal for that matter, outside the laboratory where they normally live, was virtually unheard of. This was not a wholly misspent emphasis because many important behavioral regularities were uncovered, as we saw in preceding chapters.

Learning and instinct

Somewhat parallel with American behaviorism was a scientific effort called ethology, which was centered in Europe (e.g., Tinbergen, 1951; Eibl-Eibesfeld, 1970). Ethologists are one kind of zoologist, and they prefer to observe animals in their natural setting and constrain them as little as possible. Each scientist must seek the phenomena which will best yield important regularities for him or her, and ethologists chose behavior in the natural, free setting, just as American experimental psychologists chose the restricted laboratory setting. Instinct rather than learning became the focus of ethology. Ranging far beyond the rat and the pigeon, they unobtrusively observed a generous portion of the animal kingdom and saw a rich array of behaviors that existed at the time of the animal's birth, or came to exist with some maturation, and all without learning. Without denying learning, they found a central place for the genetic determinants of behavior that are shaped by forces defined by Darwin's theory of evolution.

Evolution theory says that organisms are modified by change in the genetic composition of the species and natural selection. Genetic combinations emerge by mating, and rarely, by mutation which is a fundamental alteration of gene structure. Gene variability gives variability in the characteristics of a species, and natural selection operates on this variability to produce characteristics that help in the struggle for existence. Life is hard, and members of a species compete in a brutish struggle for food, water, survival against enemies, etc. Members of the species who have the most favorable characteristics emerge victorious in the competition and are naturally selected to breed new generations who also will tend to have good survival characteristics, and so on. It is "survival of the fittest," as the classic phrase has it, and the important thing to remember is that behavior is every bit as important for survival as anatomical characteristics. It is important for evolution to have produced a long neck for the giraffe so that it can reach the high leaves of trees on the East African plains where it lives, but it is also important the evolutionary processes give it the behavior to flee the leopards that lurk in wait for it. A newborn giraffe must have an instant, unlearned capability to flee if it is to survive. Certainly giraffes would be doomed if the fleeing behavior was dependent upon a gradual learning process.

Concern with instinct in modern American psychology came late. In 1950 the American comparative psychologist, Frank A. Beach, published a prophetic article (Beach, 1950) that suggested a usefulness of the ethological approach, but it aroused only minor attention at the time because the learning-centered view was so strong in experimental psychology. It was not until some years later when Breland and Breland (1961) published an article entitled "The Misbehavior of Organisms" that American psychologists began to have cautious second thoughts about the traditional view that had dominated for so long. The Brelands were putting their psychological skills to work in training animals for zoos, television commercials, and various other commercial exhibits. The nature of their work required them to train a variety of animals, and they found that the "general laws" of learning from laboratory work with the rat and pigeon were not as general as they had surmised.

One of their projects was the teaching of raccoons to pick up coins and deposit them in a small box. The raccoon has "hands" like a primate, and it seemed a simple matter to reinforce it with food for putting coins in the container. Teaching it to pick up one coin and deposit it in the box was easy enough, but trouble came when the problem was changed to picking up and depositing two coins. The raccoon would not let go of the coins. Instead, its time was spent in rubbing the coins together and dipping them into the container. This seemingly eccentric behavior produced no reinforcement, and it would seem that nonreinforcement would extinguish the behavior, but not so. The rubbing behavior became worse and worse until the project had to be abandoned. In a similar project the Brelands set to train a pig to drop large wooden coins in a "piggy bank." The coins were placed several feet from the bank and the pig was required to carry them to the bank and deposit them. A partial reinforcement schedule of one reinforcement for four of five coins deposited was used, and the pig readily learned the act. But as the training regime progressed the pig's behavior degenerated. The coin would be picked up well enough but on the way to the bank the pig would drop the coin, root it, toss it up in the air, root it along, and so on. This problem behavior might have been dismissed as the unknown peculiarities of a particular pig, but it was found in other pigs as well.

The Brelands came to the conclusion that the behavior of these animals represented a failure of learning theory—the animals simply did not do what they were trained to do. The particular behaviors to which these animals drifted were examples of instinctive food-getting behavior which no training could overcome. The raccoon exhibited its well-known "washing behavior," and the rooting behavior of pigs is known to the most casual visitor of a farm. The Brelands did not throw out the learning principles that they were trying to use, for that would have been hasty, but they did conclude that the rejection of instinct has weakened the psychologists power to predict and control behavior. Specie differences are not insignificant.

Evidence for biological constraints on learning

There is a wealth of data to consider once one begins to face the issue of unlearned, instinctive behavior (e.g., Bolles, 1970, 1971, 1973; Eibl-Eibesfeldt, 1970; Hinde, 1969; Hinde & Stevenson-Hinde, 1973; Hodos & Campbell, 1969; Seligman, 1970; Scott, 1967), and the theoretical thrust of these data is to urge a reappraisal of the traditional view about general laws of learning. The traditional view has established opinions about stimuli, responses and the reinforcers that associate them, and all of this becomes attenuated when instinct enters the picture.

Stimulus specificity. It is the traditional view that all stimuli bombarding the senses have equal potentiality for response until learning operations give some stimuli control over behavior and denying it to others. This view has truth in it, but it is also true that evolution has tuned some receptors for a highly selective reaction to stimuli. Some aspects of the impinging stimulus energy fire an adaptive response and others do not. Hinde (1969, p. 43) cites von Uexküll's observation about the mated female tick who climbs to the top of a bush so that mammals can rush beneath her. She can hang there for a month ignoring all stimuli until she smells butyric acid, a product of mammalian skin glands and the sign of a blood meal. Out of the rich variety of stimuli that impinge on her senses she has her neural circuitry tuned by evolution to respond only when food is signaled. "Like a gourmet who picks the raisins out of the cake," von Uexküll said.

Evolutionary forces also shape selective reactions through learning by making it easier to learn some responses than others to stimuli. It is critical for movement in the visual field to connote danger and for the animal to be able to learn various avoidance responses. On the other hand, there is little adaptive value in stomach upset becoming associated with visual movement, because movement can hardly ever be the cause of the upset, but it is important for flavors to become associated with illness so that avoidance can be learned, and this is especially important for animals like the rat which has poor vision and would have trouble discerning whatever distinctive visual features that poisons sometimes have. If evolution is a factor in behavior, then natural selection should cause some responses to be associated more readily with certain classes of stimuli than others as a way of optimizing survival. Garcia and Koelling (1966) did an experiment that demonstrated just this phenomenon, and discounted the traditional view that any response can be learned to any stimulus.

Garcia and Koelling trained one group of rats to drink "bright, noisy water," which was accomplished by a drinkometer that detected the contact of a rat's tongue with the water outlet. Whenever the rat licked the spout, the circuitry of the drinkometer produced a flash of light and click of an electrical relay. Another group was given flavored water containing saccharin. Each group was then divided in half, with one half having electric shock (externally-produced pain) following drinking and the other half made ill by the administration of X rays (internally-produced pain). They were subsequently tested with either bright, noisy water or the saccharin water, and the results are shown in Figure 6–1.

FIGURE 6–1
Evidence that the consequences of responding determine the stimuli that come to control the response.

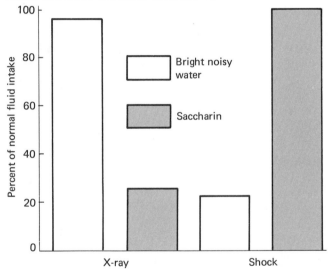

Revusky, S., & Garcia, J. Learned associations over long delays. In G. H. Bower (Ed.), *The psychology of learning and motivation* (Vol. 4). New York: Academic Press, 1970, pp. 1–84. Reprinted by permission of Academic Press, Inc.

Notice that the X-ray punishment inhibited drinking only when the stimulus was saccharin water, not bright, noisy water. The converse was true for shock punishment; only the bright, noisy water inhibited drinking. As Garcia and Koelling (1966, p. 124) said: "The cues, which the animal selects from the welter of stimuli in the learning situation, appear to be related to the consequences of the subsequent reinforcer." Electric shock is an external punishment which can be associated with external stimuli, and taste cues can be associated with internal discomfort, but not vice versa.

The Garcia and Koelling experiment might suggest that illness cannot be associated with visual stimuli, but it seems more likely that this is a special feature which evolution has given the rat in deference to its poor vision, highly developed senses of taste and smell, and nocturnal feeding habits. Animals with superior visual equipment that rely on vision in seeking food and drink can learn to avoid ingesting substances that are distinctive in appearance only. Wilcoxon, Dragoin, and Kral (1971) compared rats and bobwhite quail, a bird with a high-quality visual system. Both learned to avoid flavored water when it had been followed by illness induced by a drug, but only the quail learned to avoid distinctively colored water that had been associated with illness.

Avoidance learning. Additional evidence that any response cannot be learned in any situation is avoidance behavior in rats. As we saw in Chapter 5, the rat has been a principal vehicle for the study of punishment and fear, and we have learned a great deal from it. But Chapter 5, like the chapters that preceded it, carried the implication that any response can be learned in any situation, and this implication must now be qualified: There are avoidance situations which rats learn poorly if at all. The occasional failure of avoidance behavior in rats has appeared in the research literature from time to time as a puzzling item. In 1956, Solomon and Brush observed:

> We somehow assume that it is *natural* for organisms to "anticipate" noxious events in an "adaptive" fashion. But it is only after we set up certain special types of environmental event sequences that the avoidance phenomenon emerges. Failure of subjects to learn to avoid are *not* rare, but they are less apt to be reported in scientific papers than are the successes. And the conditions surrounding failures to learn to avoid are as instructive to the investigator, in many cases, as are the optimum conditions for producing avoidance phenomenon.[1]

Only with the recent interest in biological constraints on learning has this phenomenon come into focus.

Meyer, Cho, and Wesemann (1960) publicly puzzled about the failure of rats to avoid shock by pressing a bar. Their experimental situation was a standard one. A light was the CS and shock was the UCS, and if the animal pressed the bar between light onset and shock onset the light was turned out and the punishing shock was avoided. They had instances of rats being unable to learn this simple avoidance task in several thousands of trials, and it was difficult to understand because they knew that rats could learn avoidance in a running wheel in less than 100 trials (Mote, 1940). And in Chapter 5 we saw the avoidance learning

---

[1] Jones, M. R. (Ed.). *Nebraska symposium on motivation.* Lincoln: University of Nebraska Press, 1956, pp. 215–216. Reprinted by permission of the University of Nebraska Press.

of other locomotor acts. Their puzzlement took the form of two questions. If light produces fear and pressing the bar eliminates the light and the fear, how can avoidance learning fail? Why is the particular form of the response important, with avoidance failing for bar pressing and succeeding with a running response?

Using about the same bar-pressing task as Meyer and his associates, D'Amato and Schiff (1964) also were frustrated in teaching rats to avoid. They ran three experiments. In Experiment I they administered 1,080 avoidance training trials and only 2 out of 8 rats conditioned to any appreciable extent. In Experiment II, after 7,330 trials, only 4 out of 8 attained a reasonable level of performance. In Experiment III, after 1,082 trials, 1 out of 8 animals learned to avoid.

Bolles (1969) attacked the question of response form and its relevance for avoidance learning. He found that rats would readily learn a running response to avoid but not one of rearing up and standing on the hind legs. Bolles (1970, 1971, 1973) has been an active analyst of biological constraints on learning, and he interpreted his findings as evidence of *species-specific behavior,* which is another name for biological evolutionary influence on behavior and is a more acceptable term than "instinct." An animal will learn an avoidance response if it is consistent with its natural defensive reactions that are part of its innate endowment. Running is such a response for a rat. It runs when it is afraid and does not lurch forward and press bars or rear up and stand on its hind legs.

Boice (1970) found avoidance learning of frogs and toads in a shuttle box task (electric shock as the *UCS,* opening of the guillotine door as the *CS*) to be directly proportional to their natively endowed activity level in the natural setting. The leopard frog and the spade-foot toad are decidedly passive, the green frog is moderately active, and the Woodhouse toad is very active. The leopard frog and the spade-foot toad showed no avoidance responding, the green frog showed only a little, and the Woodhouse toad showed substantial avoidance learning. The toad can be extremely efficient in avoidance learning if a response is chosen that is particularly relevant to survival in its natural environment. Using the Southern toad's eating response for study and bumblebees as food, Brower and Brower (1962) found that it took only one or two experiences for the toad to learn that bumblebees are noxious. Contrast this swift avoidance learning to Boice's spadefoot toads who could not learn to avoid in the shuttle box task. Findings such as these would be considered mysterious if the animal's behavior in the natural environment was not included in the explanation.

In an open environment rats are known to show *positive thigmotaxis,* or the tendency to remain in contact with objects, like remaining close to a wall while running from one point to another. Grossen and Kelley

(1972) hypothesized that this thigmotactic tendency was a species-specific defensive reaction because predators like birds would have a harder time attacking a rat that was hugging a wall. To test the hypothesis, they asked if rats would become more thigmotactic under defensive motivation. Their apparatus was a large box with an electrifiable grid floor, and the thigmotactic behavior was defined as amount of time spent in contact with the box wall. A 30-minute no-shock session was followed by a 30-minute session of periodic shocks, with the wall-hugging behavior measured throughout. The rats exhibited thigmotactic behavior 67 percent of the time in the no-shock session and 91 percent of the time in the shock session. In a second experiment they asked if rats would learn an avoidance response faster if it capitalized on the thigmotactic tendency. The same apparatus was used as before, and the avoidance response was jumping on a small platform. The platform was placed either in the center of the box or along the wall, and they reasoned that the avoidance response would be learned more readily when the platform was along the wall because it would be consistent with a rat's defensive behavior. One group of rats had the platform along the wall, another had it in the center, and a third had platforms in both positions and had a choice between them. The rat was placed in the box and given ten seconds to make the avoidance response before being shocked. The group with the platform at the wall avoided on 77 percent of the trials, while the group with the platform in the center avoided only 57 percent of the time. The group given choice chose the platform along the wall 92 percent of the time. A third experiment essentially repeated the second one except that the animals were reinforced with food for jumping onto the platform. In this case there were no differences between the three groups, indicating that the behavior shown in the first two experiments was particularly associated with defensive reactions. Here again we have data that are much clearer when we take into account the species-specific behavior of the animal.

Imprinting.   The phenomenon of *imprinting* in newly born animals is a fascinating case of learning that is neither instrumental learning nor classical conditioning, is biologically adaptive for the animal in its natural environment, and is species dependent. Imprinting is the acquisition of an identification response by exposure to a stimulus, and it is learning that can occur at only one period in an animal's lifetime. Imprinting was first reported in 1873 by D. A. Spalding (Spalding, reprinted 1954). Spalding wrote (p. 6):

> Chickens as soon as they are able to walk will follow any moving object. And, when guided by sight alone, they seem to have no more disposition to follow a hen than to follow a duck, or a human being. Unreflecting on-lookers, when they saw chickens a day old running after me, and older ones following me miles and answering to my whistle,

imagined that I must have some occult power over the creatures, whereas I simply allowed them to follow me from the first.

The more contemporary research of Hess (1959) puts imprinting on a firm experimental footing and illustrates it nicely.

Hess used wild mallard ducks as his experimental subjects. The eggs were hatched in an incubator and the newly born ducks were kept in a small box until the imprinting experience, which was conducted with the apparatus shown in Figure 6–2. Following time intervals ranging

FIGURE 6–2
Apparatus used for the imprinting of ducklings. A duckling was given systematic exposure to the decoy as it moved around the runway.

Hess, E. H. Imprinting. *Science,* 1959, *130,* 133–141. Reprinted by permission of the American Association for the Advancement of Science.

from 1 to 32 hours after birth, the young mallard was put in the imprinting apparatus with a decoy model of a male duck which moved along a circular runway and gave out with duck-like sounds. This procedure went on for about an hour, after which the duckling was returned to the incubator and subsequently tested. The test was four discrimination tests, where the duckling had to chose between the male mallard model and a female model which differed from the male in its coloration. The male model gave the same duck-like sound as before and the female model emitted a recording of the actual call of a mallard female calling her young. The duckling was released between the two models who were four feet apart and the interest was in the one it chose. The four tests were: both models stationary and silent; both models stationary and calling; the male stationary and the female calling; and the male stationary and silent and the female moving and calling. The percentage of times which the duckling chose the male model on all four tests is shown in Figure 6–3 as a function of the time between birth and

FIGURE 6–3

In a choice discrimination test, percent of time that duck-lings chose the imprinted decoy as a function of time between birth and the imprinting experience.

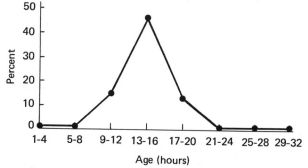

Age (hours)

Hess, E. H. Imprinting. *Science,* 1959, *130,* 133–141. Re-printed by permission of the American Association for the Advancement of Science.

the imprinting experience. Notice how critical that time is as a variable for learning. Imprinting in the duckling is only possible in a narrow span of hours after birth.

It is not necessary that the imprinted object resemble the species of the young subject. Hinde, Thorpe, and Vince (1956) imprinted coots and moorhens to follow a box or a man, just as if it were the mother, al-though not all stimuli imprint with equal effectiveness (Bateson, 1973, p. 102). Hess (1959, p. 140) was the imprinting stimulus for a jungle fowl cock and succeeded in alienating its affections. Even after five years it was attracted to humans and had nothing to do with the female of its spe-cies. A lay person looks affectionately at an animal mother and its baby fol-lowing along and speaks of infant love of the mother, but maybe there is nothing more involved than the mother being present during the critical imprinting period. Infant devotion or not, the baby that is imprinted by its mother and stays close to it greatly enhances its chances of survival.

As with any behavioral phenomenon, there are a number of variables involved in imprinting, and the underlying processes are not understood very well (Sluckin, 1965; Bateson, 1973). Nor do all species imprint with equal efficiency. Hess (1959, p. 140) reports that some species visually imprint poorly if at all. For example, Hess was unable to visually imprint the wood duck with the same success as the mallard. Klopfer (1959), however, cautions that the behavior of the species in its natural environment must be considered if we are to determine the conditions of imprinting. The mallard lives in open nests and natural selection would tune it to be responsive to visual stimuli. The wood duck, on the other hand, lives in holes in trees and imprinting to auditory stimuli would be most adaptive for it. Presumably Hess would have had more luck with the wood duck if an auditory pattern like a duck call was used as the imprinting stimulus.

Imprinting is a kind of learning that we have not encountered before. It results from direct exposure to a stimulus and does not need the usual operations of reinforcement as in instrumental learning, or the pairing of the CS and the UCS as in classical conditioning. Hess (1959, pp. 140–141) argues against imprinting being associative learning of a conventional kind like instrumental learning and classical conditioning, as does Sluckin (1965, Chapter 9). Sluckin calls imprinting "exposure learning," and his definition of it gives it the same properties as perceptual learning (Gibson, 1969). Bateson (1973) considers imprinting to be perceptual learning also, where the imprinting experiences give an animal the flexible powers of responding to wide variation in the stimulus. In form constancy, for example, the subject can recognize a table no matter what its size and orientation on the retina. Similarly, through imprinting experiences, the baby mallard comes to recognize its mother at varying distances and at any angle. The survival advantages of being oriented to the mother under a variety of circumstances are obvious.

Broad implications for laws of learning

The implications of this chapter are that the traditional view of learning which seeks general laws of learning that sweep across animals, responses, and stimuli must be revised. The adaptive pressures of the environment cause genetic differences between behaviors within a specie and between species, as Darwin's theory of evolution said, and these innate differences undermine transcendent laws of learning. Darwin's theory has been with us for over 100 years, and the scientific study of learning for a bit more than half of that. How could the psychology of learning have missed the implications of Darwin's exquisite scientific achievement? Where did the psychology of learning go wrong? There are three main influences that obscured learning's scientific vision, and although they have been mentioned earlier in this chapter they bear mentioning again for the sake of summary and elaboration.

First was the powerful influence of behaviorism on the American scene. Its environmentalism gave experimental psychology in the United States a powerful interest in learning. The concern with environmentalism and learning was so strong that it led to cursory dismissal of innate influences on learning. The pursuit of environmentalism has not been an empty scientific effort because environmental variables are obviously of enormous significance and we have learned a great deal about them under behaviorism's flag.

Second, the psychology of learning was enamored with models from the physical sciences which have wide, general laws; we saw a science of behavior that eventually would have the same form as physics and chemistry. That we should envy success and seek it for ourselves is understandable, but perhaps our efforts were too imitative. There is no necessity for lawfulness to have the same form in different sciences, and perhaps we should have been more sensitive to the special direction that behavioral laws might take. Physics and chemistry have nothing like evolution that would restrict the generality of their laws.

Third has been the false belief in the scala naturae, or the phylogenetic scale. Whatever touch that the psychology of learning has had with evolution theory has been here, and unfortunately it has been in touch with the wrong theory. Hodos and Campbell (1969, p. 338) see the problem as mistaking the phylogenetic scale and the *phylogenetic tree*. Figure 6–4 is a phylogenetic tree showing the approximate times of origin and the probable lineages of various living vertebrates and related groups of animals. The animals along the top approximate the phylogenetic scale (the sequence of lineages from left to right have been arbitrarily arranged to achieve this). The phylogenetic scale from simple animals to complex has led us to believe that there is a common underlying unity to biological nature, and yet the various lineages of the phylogenetic tree represent a number of independent lines of evolutionary development. Figure 6–5 is a closeup of the primate lines. Apes and monkeys have their linkages to humans, but they also have independent lines of development. Biological adaptation to the demands of their environment has given them their own physical and behavioral characteristics that is neither inferior nor superior to other species but is simply adaptation to environmental circumstances. As Scott (1967, p. 72) said:

> Subhuman primates are not small human beings with fur coats and (sometimes) long tails. Rather they are a group which has diversified in many ways, so that they are different from each other as are bears, dogs, and raccoons in the order Carnivora. The fact that an animal is a primate therefore does not automatically mean that its behavior has special relevance to human behavior.[2]

[2] *Annual Review of Psychology*, 1967, Vol. 18, p. 72. Reprinted by permission of Annual Reviews, Inc.

FIGURE 6-4

Phylogenetic tree showing the probable time of origin and relationships of vertebrates and some related groups of animals.

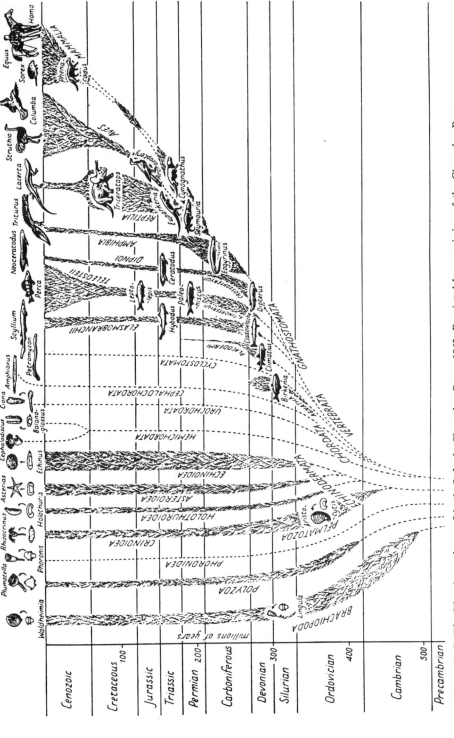

Young, J. Z. *The life of vertebrates*, 2d ed. Oxford: Clarendon Press, 1962. Reprinted by permission of the Clarendon Press.

FIGURE 6–5

Phylogenetic tree showing the probable time of origin and relationships of primates.

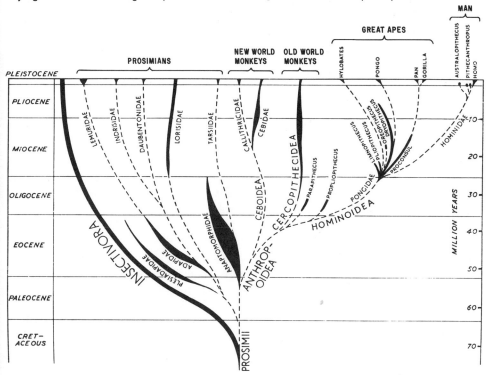

Young, J. Z. *The life of vertebrates.* 2nd ed. Oxford: Clarendon Press, 1962. Reprinted by permission of the Clarendon Press.

Henry Beston (1928), in his book *The Outermost House,* said it in the special way that gifted writers have:

> Remote from universal nature, and living by complicated artifice, man in civilization surveys the creature through the glass of his knowledge and sees thereby a feather magnified and the whole image in distortion. We patronize them for their incompleteness, for their tragic fate of having taken form so far below ourselves. And therein we err, and greatly err. For the animal shall not be measured by man. In a world older and more complete than ours they move finished and complete, gifted with extensions of the senses we have lost or never attained, living by voices we shall never hear. They are not brethren, they are not underlings; they are other nations, caught with ourselves in the net of life and time, fellow prisoners of the splendour and travail of the earth.[3]

---

[3] Beston, H. *The outermost house.* New York: Holt, Rinehart & Winston, 1928, p. 25. Reprinted by permission of Holt, Rinehart and Winston, Inc.

What is the future of law and theory in the psychology of learning? The neglect of evolution and the innate determinants of behavior is a significant omission, and it must be remedied. Lockard (1971, p. 172) believes that the answer lies in adoption of evolution theory as the "one great theoretical principle that unites all of behavior." Lockard is correct in implying that we must embrace evolution more warmly than before, but he oversteps when he dismisses learning almost entirely (p. 174) and says that it is not the key to animal behavior because most behavior is not acquired. There is truth in this statement, particularly if one has a biologist's view of the animal kingdom, which is mostly insects. Lockard says that most behavior is instinctive, which to most of us means rigid behavioral forms that are innately determined and run off spontaneously in the absence of experience. But what this viewpoint ignores is that evolution gave many, many animals, including some insects (Eibl-Eibesfeldt, 1970, Chapter 13; Hinde, 1973, p. 9), the power of plasticity, or *learning*. If evolution is master as Lockard says, then evolutionary processes must have recognized the environment as an inconstant, uncertain place, and the animals that can readily cope with its new events and relationships through learning have a marvelous adaptive mechanism. Indeed, learning is the supreme adaptive mechanism, and we should see it as evolution's finest achievement. Learning is not something to be replaced by biology and evolution but to be reconciled with it.

Accommodation must be made to evolutionary influences on behavior, and one possible direction is to accept evolutionary determinants of the myriad units of behavior for over a million species on earth and proceed to study and record them. These behavioral elements could have independent genetic determinants, and so there would be a near-infinite number of behavior elements to investigate, without hope for or attempts at integration. Libraries of disconnected fact and descriptions would be produced. Psychology would have some lawfulness and predictive power under these circumstances but it would be of low order.

A more reasonable approach is to believe that any science worthy of the name must have laws and theory of some generality and, while the great dreamed-of generalizations of yesteryear may not be achieveable, laws of some limited generality probably are. Many animals have common environmental problems, and have comparable drives to satisfy, and it is likely that laws can be found for these communalities. Principles of positive reinforcement that mainly have been worked out on rats and pigeons are now regularly applied to human behavior under the heading "behavior modification." Principles of fear learning and extinction, from rats, pigeons, and dogs, have some success at the human level and are used for the treatment of fear under the name of "behavior therapy." Such generalizations across species give us hope for laws of some scope.

Biological constraints on learning are just that—constraints. They are not the destroyers of laws of learning but the framework within which learning operates, the intra- and inter-species differences that evolution has produced for us. Within these constraints laws of learning of some generality might be found. The early faith that any animal can learn any response to any stimulus is in doubt. A more viable faith may be that many animals can learn many responses to many stimuli, and we can find the laws that relate them. Biology can be a source for explanation when we apply a law and, say, find that one species learns slowly and another rapidly even though the same law is at work. And, biology will help us understand why a law breaks down and has the limits that it does.

SUMMARY

The traditional view of the laws of learning has physics as the model, where laws of very wide scope are possible. Psychology has assumed that a law of learning will specify the conditions under which virtually any organism can learn any response to any stimulus. The present evidence is that biological factors restrict the scope of behavioral laws. Instinctive response patterns can interfere with an arbitrary response that has been selected for learning. For example, evolution has endowed the rat with positive thigmotaxis, which is the tendency to remain close to objects and avoid open spaces, and it is a factor when the behavior being learned involves movement in open spaces and with respect to objects. Another example of biological constraints is imprinting, where certain responses can be learned only at a specific time in an organism's life.

Today we have doubts about general laws of learning. Some generality is undoubtedly possible, but biological constraints will define limitations on the stimuli that can come to control responses through learning, on the responses that can be learned, and on the organisms that can learn them.

REFERENCES

Bateson, P. P. G. Internal influences on early learning in birds. In R. A. Hinde and J. Stevenson-Hinde (Eds.), *Constraints on learning*. New York: Academic Press, 1973, pp. 101–116.

Beach, F. A. The snark was a boojum. *American Psychologist*, 1950, 5, 115–124.

Beston, H. *The outermost house*. New York: Holt, Rinehart & Winston, 1928.

Boice, R. Avoidance learning in active and passive frogs and toads. *Journal of Comparative and Physiological Psychology,* 1970, *70,* 154–156.

Bolles, R. C. Avoidance and escape learning: Simultaneous acquisition of different responses. *Journal of Comparative and Physiological Psychology,* 1969, *68,* 355–358.

Bolles, R. C. Species-specific defense reactions and avoidance learning. *Psychological Review,* 1970, *77,* 32–48.

Bolles, R. C. Species-specific defense reaction. In F. R. Brush (Ed.), *Aversive conditioning and learning.* New York: Academic Press, 1971, pp. 183–233.

Bolles, R. C. The comparative psychology of learning: The selective association principle and some problems with "general" laws of learning. In G. Bermant (Ed.), *Perspectives on animal behavior.* Glenview: Scott, Foresman, 1973, pp. 280–306.

Breland, K., & Breland, M. The misbehavior of organisms. *American Psychologist,* 1961, *16,* 681–684.

Brower, L. P., & Brower, J. V. Z. Investigations into mimicry. *Natural History,* April 1962, 8–19.

D'Amato, M. R., & Schiff, D. Long-term discriminated avoidance performance in the rat. *Journal of Comparative and Physiological Psychology,* 1964, *57,* 123–126.

Eibl-Eibesfeldt, I. *Ethology: The study of behavior.* New York: Holt, Rinehart & Winston, 1970.

Garcia, J., & Koelling, R. A. Relation of cue to consequence in avoidance learning. *Psychonomic Science,* 1966, *4,* 123–124.

Gibson, E. J. *Principles of perceptual learning and development.* New York: Appleton-Century-Crofts, 1969.

Grossen, N. E., & Kelley, M. J. Species-specific behavior and acquisition of avoidance behavior in rats. *Journal of Comparative and Physiological Psychology,* 1972, *81,* 307–310.

Hess, E. H. Imprinting. *Science,* 1959, *130,* 133–141.

Hinde, R. A. *Animal behaviour.* New York: McGraw-Hill, 1969.

Hinde, R. A. Constraints on learning—An introduction to the problems. In R. A. Hinde & J. Stevenson-Hinde (Eds.), *Constraints on learning.* New York: Academic Press, 1973, pp. 1–19.

Hinde, R. A., & Stevenson-Hinde, J. (Eds.). *Constraints on learning.* New York: Academic Press, 1973.

Hinde, R. A., Thorpe, W. H., & Vince, M. A. The following response of young coots and moorhens. *Behaviour,* 1956, *9,* 214–242.

Hodos, W., & Campbell C. B. G. Scala naturae: why there is no theory in comparative psychology. *Psychological Review,* 1969, *76,* 337–350.

Klopfer, P. H. Imprinting. *Science,* 1959, *130,* 730.

Lockard, R. B. Reflections on the fall of comparative psychology: Is there a message for us all? *American Psychologist,* 1971, *26,* 168–179.

Meyer, D. R., Cho, C., & Wesemann, A. F. On problems of conditioning discriminated lever-press avoidance responses. *Psychological Rev*, 1960, *67*, 224–228.

Mote, F. A.   Correlations between conditioning and maze learning in the white rat. *Journal of Comparative Psychology*, 1940, *30*, 197–219.

Revusky, S., & Garcia, J.   Learned associations over long delays. In G. H. Bower (Ed.), *The psychology of learning and motivation* (Vol. 4). New York: Academic Press, 1970, pp. 1–84.

Scott, J. P.   Comparative psychology and ethology. *Annual review of psychology*, 1967, *18*, 65–86.

Seligman, M. E. P.   On the generality of the laws of learning. *Psychological Review*, 1970, *77*, 406–418.

Sluckin, W.   *Imprinting and early experience.* Chicago: Aldine, 1965.

Solomon, R. L., & Brush, E. S.   Experimentally derived conceptions of anxiety and aversion. In M. R. Jones (Ed.), *Nebraska symposium on motivation.* Lincoln: University of Nebraska Press, 1956, pp. 213–305.

Spalding, D. A.   Instinct. *MacMillan's Magazine*, 1873. Reprinted in *British Journal of Animal Behaviour*, 1954, *2*, 2–11.

Tinbergen, N.   *The study of instinct.* Oxford: Clarendon Press, 1951.

Watson, J. B.   Psychology as the behaviorist views it. *Psychological Review*, 1913, *20*, 158–177.

Wilcoxon, H. C., Dragoin, W. B., & Kral, P. A.   Illness-induced aversions in the rat and quail: Relative salience of visual and gustatory cues. *Science*, 1971, *171*, 826–828.

Young, J. Z.   *The life of vertebrates* (2nd ed.). Oxford: Clarendon Press, 1962.

r 7

Verbal learning

THE CHAPTERS on positive reinforcement, classical conditioning, and punishment and fear, were intended to express widely applicable laws of learning for all kinds of responses, including verbal responses. Why, then, a special chapter on verbal learning? The answer is that there are verbal learning methods, findings, and explanations which do not fit the standard paradigms of learning very well and deserve examination in their own right. There is nothing in previous chapters to suggest that people might use mental images in the formation of associations, and yet it is a viable point of view in verbal learning. Moreover, there are procedures, materials, and ideas that were born in the study of verbal learning which came to have impact on the field of human memory, and so an engagement of these matters at this point will ease passage through the latter half of the book where human memory is treated.

The chapter is entirely about recall, where the subject must reproduce a response that was learned before. Recall is distinguished from recognition, where the subject must indicate whether a stimulus has occurred before (Chapter 13).

ASSOCIATIONISM

Some history and background

The concern with verbal associations is a much older concern than reward learning. The far-ranging minds of Plato and Aristotle, those ancient Greek philosophers with whom we are all familiar, discussed the association of thoughts and images as part of people's mental apparatus and as a theory of thought. They wrote how events are related in memory and arouse one another in recollection. Aristotle said that mental associations are governed by *similarity* (bronze reminds us of gold), *contrast* or opposites (black reminds us of white), and *contiguity* in space or time (a book reminds us of school). These principles of Aristotle were gradually formed into laws of the association of ideas, which became the foundation of British Associationism, an important philosophical and psychological movement of the 17th–19th century. It was Thomas Hobbes (1588–1679) who was the founder of British Associationism, and with it we associate such prominent names in philosophy as George Berkeley, Thomas Brown, David Hartley, David Hume, John Locke (he gave us the expression "association of ideas"), and James Mill. For them there were four basic laws of the association of ideas: similarity, contrast, temporal contiguity, and spatial contiguity (the debt to Aristotle is obvious). From these four laws they sought to describe the properties of mind as a kind of derivative, building block process. Thus, not all thought processes are simple A-to-B kinds of associations; obviously longer associative chains occur. Using the basic laws of association, they derived *mediate association* from *immediate association.* If, in immediate association, A leads to B and B leads to C, then mediate association of A to C will occur via the route of B.

The British empirical school of psychology probably would not have come to much if they did nothing but proclaim and elaborate their four laws of association. What they did, however, was couple the laws with John Locke's empirical theory of knowledge, and this had vast ramifications that are still debated. All knowledge comes from experience, according to this theory. The mind is a blank tablet at the outset, and all knowledge is acquired through the senses. As events and their associations are experienced, the mind acquires them and gradually comes to build up the structure that is the mature mind. The mind only receives and records; it contributes no relations of its own. It is evident now why this empirical theory of knowledge that relies on the laws of association to populate the mind with ideas and percepts, and relations among ideas and percepts, is so important for the experimental psychology of learning and memory. The organization of events in the mind is determined by the organization of events in experience, so by controlling the organization of events in the world we can control the organization of events in the mind and come to understand them.

Hermann Ebbinghaus (1850–1909) is notable in the history of associationism, learning, and memory because he introduced the experimental study of associations. Before Ebbinghaus, in the tradition handed from Aristotle and the British Associationists, the interest was a descriptive, nonexperimental one for the existing associative processes in the mind.

Ebbinghaus changed all of this, and secured his position in the history of psychology. He published a thin book in 1885 (Ebbinghaus, translated edition, 1964) about his research, and each generation of students rediscovers this volume and comes to know on whose shoulders it stands.

Ebbinghaus saw the study of words as too complex for determining the essentials of association because words come with many built-in associations (later investigators saw this as a challenge to be met, rather than a barrier). To meet this difficult challenge as he saw it, he invented the nonsense syllable, or, to be exact, a pool of 2,300 of them consisting of all consonant-vowel-consonant combinations. Ebbinghaus presumed that this minimal verbal unit was free of complicating associations and the investigation of its learning would reveal the conditions under which the mind forms associations. His procedure was to make up a list of syllables and read through it at a uniform, rapid rate (Ebbinghaus was his own patient subject). Occasionally Ebbinghaus would stop and test himself without looking at the items, and he would continue in this fashion until he could recite the items in their correct order without error. This was *serial learning*. Theoretically, it is important to see that Ebbinghaus was proceeding according to the tenets of association theory, where the *contiguity* of items in experience placed the items in memory, and the *frequency* of that experience, or practice trials, determined the strength of the relations between items. And, for the thousands of verbal learning studies that followed, it is worth noting that Ebbinghaus began the list tradition, where the number of items correct or number of errors made on a list was the measure of performance.

Ebbinghaus' method of serial learning was gradually changed. Ebbinghaus had the items spread out in front of him, and with the items arrayed in front of him there was the possibility that the time devoted to each was uncontrolled, even though Ebbinghaus was a disciplined subject. Stimulated by the work of Ebbinghaus, G. E. Müller and F. Schumann in 1887 undertook work on serial verbal learning, and to control presentation time exactly they arranged the items on a drum and presented them one at a time at a fixed rate through a slit in a screen (Angell, 1894). This was the invention of the memory drum, and a picture of a modern memory drum is shown in Figure 7–1. More than a device for serial learning, a modern memory drum is a device for presenting verbal items at a constant rate, whatever the method.

Two traditional methods of verbal learning

Serial anticipation learning. The *method of serial anticipation* came into use with the memory drum. The task in serial anticipation learning is to look at the item that is showing and use it as a cue to respond with the next item of the list before it appears. When the next item

FIGURE 7–1

The memory drum is a device for controlled presentation of a verbal list. The knob at the top controls the rate at which the items are presented at the opening in the front. The tape behind the cover can have up to four different orders of the list typed on it, and the flaps on the front control which order the subject sees on a trial.

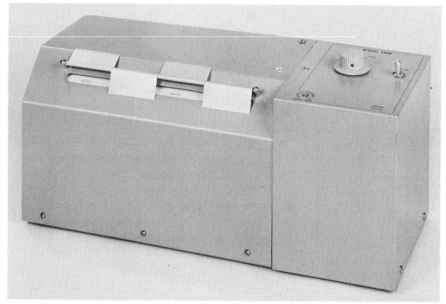

Reprinted by permission of the Lafayette Instrument Co., Inc.

appears, the subject uses it to verify the response just given, tries to anticipate the next item before it comes into view, and so on through the list. Once through the list is a trial, and practice repetitions continue until a criterion of performance has been met. Thus, practice might continue until the subject meets the criterion of two consecutive errorless trials, and each subject's score would be the number of trials to achieve the criterion. Or, a fixed number of practice trials could be administered, and the score on each trial would be the number of responses correctly anticipated or number of errors. This latter method is the best for plotting a learning curve and showing how performance changes with trials.

After Ebbinghaus the study of verbal associations accelerated, and by the 1920s and the 1930s the psychological literature was generously dotted with studies of serial verbal learning. Starting in the 1940s, however, the method of paired associate learning began to replace serial learning and, although serial learning continued well into the 1960s, it went into decline. By the late 1960s, the method that had given birth to verbal learning was defunct. One reason was a strong interest in memory that brought new methods and techniques, but another reason was a weakness in the method of serial anticipation learning itself. The stimuli and response roles of items were confounded, which made analysis difficult for those of behaviorist persuasion who sought to determine the separate effects of eliciting stimuli and the responses made to them (Young, 1968).

Paired-associate learning. *Paired-associate learning,* which was mentioned in passing above, came into favor because it lacked the confounding of stimulus and response that plagued serial anticipation learning. Being able to study the association of verbal responses to verbal stimuli was commendable in the pre-1960s because animal learning and conditioning studies also were seen in terms of responses being associated with stimuli. Presumably, all of these approaches were reflecting the same laws of learning in different ways, and this was seen as a sound scientific strategy because it was establishing the wide generality of the laws.

Each item of the list to be learned in paired-associate learning is a pair of verbal units (words, nonsense syllables, etc.), with the left-hand unit the stimulus term and the right-hand unit the response term. The subject must learn to respond with the response term in the time that the stimulus term is exposed. The three basic methods of paired-associate learning are the study-test method, the anticipation method, and the correction method (Battig, 1965). Paired-associate learning was first used by Mary Calkins, and she used the study-test method (Calkins, 1894).

The learning of the verbal pair, and the testing of the learning, are separated in study trials and test trials in the *study-test method.* On a study trial both terms of each pair are presented together for a fixed period of time, and the subject studies each pair and tries to learn it. Each study trial is followed by a test trial, where the stimulus term of each pair is presented for a fixed interval and the subject attempts to give the response term paired with it. Thus:

Stimulus term	*Response term*
Study trial	
DOG	STORE
CAR	HOUSE
BICYCLE	GIRL
LADY	TREE
Test trial	
DOG	–
LADY	–
BICYCLE	–
CAR	–

The sequence is study-test, study-test, etc., with a different order of the pairs on each trial, until a criterion of learning is met. Trials to achieve the criterion can be the measure of performance when learning is carried to a criterion. Or, a fixed number of trials can be given, where number correct on each test trial is the performance measure.

The *anticipation method* alternates study and test within the trial:

Stimulus term	Response term
DOG	–
DOG	STORE
CAR	–
CAR	HOUSE
BICYCLE	–
BICYCLE	GIRL
LADY	
LADY	TREE

The stimulus term is displayed for a fixed interval and in that time the subject is tested and must give (that is, anticipate) the response term that is paired with the stimulus term. When the time is up the complete pair is presented for a fixed interval and the subject uses it to check the correctness of each response given, as well as for further learning of the pair. As with the study-test method, practice can be continued until a criterion is met or until a specified number of trials has passed.

A problem with the study-test method and the anticipation method for some purposes is that the number of correct responses for each pair is unequal. If the subject learns to a criterion, the easy items are given correctly first, and the subject continues to give them correctly as the more difficult items are being learned. The result is overlearning of the easy items. The *correction method* remedies this problem by removing a pair from the list when it has met a criterion of learning. Here is an example of two trials of our short example list being learned by the correction method:

Stimulus term	Response term
Trial 1–Study	
DOG	STORE
CAR	HOUSE
BICYCLE	GIRL
LADY	TREE
Trial 1–Test	
LADY	TREE
CAR	HOUSE
BICYCLE	WIFE
DOG	–

Only the responses to CAR and LADY are correct, so they are omitted on the next trial:

Stimulus term	Response term
Trial 2–Study	
DOG	STORE
BICYCLE	GIRL
Trial 2–Test	
BICYCLE	FEMALE
DOG	–

And so on, until one correct response is given each item.

Any device that presents material at a standard rate can be used for any of the three methods. A memory drum or a slide projector is common for the study-test and the anticipation methods. The memory drum and the slide projector cannot be used very efficiently for the correction method because the pairs must be manually restructured on each trial. Placing the items on cards allows the items to be easily reorganized on each trial, although the presentation time lacks the precision of the memory drum and the slide projector. A signal light for timing the presentation interval, or a tone through a headset, can easily be rigged for the experimenter, however.

The study of serial learning and paired-associate learning was sometimes seen as the investigation of rote learning, or unmediated learning. The associative bond was commonly seen as "habit," and was conceived in the same conceptual terms as the habit of the rat for bar pressing. A somewhat more elaborate, and realistic, conception of the verbal learning process depended on processes akin to mediate association which the British Associationists described. Verbal units can have verbal associations, and these associations can be a variable for the verbal learning process. Investigators have scaled verbal items for the number of associations which they elicit, and these scaled values have been used as an experimental variable. C. E. Noble (1952) has been prominent among those who have scaled verbal items in this fashion, and this scaling has come to be called the *meaningfulness* of an item (as distinct from the meaning of an item).

Noble's scaling method was to present a subject with an item and allow 60 seconds to write down as many other words as the stimulus word brought to mind. Noble used two-syllable items, ranging from meaningless artificial words such as NEGLAN, which had few or no associations for most subjects, to meaningful, common words that had many associations for all subjects. Cieutat, Stockwell, and Noble (1958) used these scaled items to investigate the effects of number of associations on paired-associate learning. They had lists of paired associates where the stimulus terms were either high (*H*) or low (*L*) in meaningfulness, as were response terms. There were four groups for these four conditions: *H-H, L-H, H-L,* and *L-L,* where the first letter designates the meaningfulness of the stimulus term and the second letter the meaningfulness of the response term for the pairs that a group used. Learning was by the anticipation method, and twelve practice trials were given. The results are shown in Figure 7–2, and it can be seen that meaningfulness is a strong variable for verbal learning. High meaningfulness of the stimulus term produced more rapid learning than low meaningfulness, whether the meaningfulness of the response term was low or high; the greater the number of associations for the stimulus term the easier a response term can be hooked to it. Meaningfulness of the response

FIGURE 7-2

Effects of high (*H*) and low (*L*) meaningfulness of the stimulus and response terms on paired-associate learning.

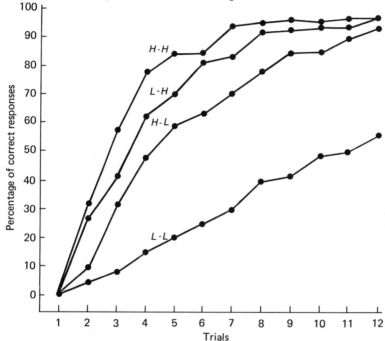

Cieutat. V. J., Stockwell, F. E., & Noble, C. E. The interaction of ability and amount of practice with stimulus and response meaningfulness (*m, m'*) in paired-associate learning. *Journal of Experimental Psychology,* 1958, *56,* 193–202. Reprinted by permission of the American Psychological Association.

terms also made a difference, with high meaningfulness producing a faster rate of learning than low meaningfulness. Pronunciation case could be a factor for response term effects. The low meaningfulness response terms were artificial words which the subject had never encountered before. The subject first must learn the new elements of the strange word and how to pronounce it before learning to give it as an associate of the stimulus term. A slower learning rate is the result.

THE COGNITIVE VIEW OF ASSOCIATIVE LEARNING

Some history and background

In the scientific drama that is the psychology of learning, association-ists, or behaviorists as the latter-day ones are often labeled, and cognitive psychologists, are antagonists. In Chapter 3 we saw that E. C. Tolman was the chief advocate of cognitive psychology in the realm of positive reinforcement and animal learning, and an influence on him was Gestalt psychology. Gestalt psychology, which had its origins in Germany in 1912, was an intellectual reaction to elementarism in psychology; it emphasized the properties of the whole and the relations among the elements rather than the elements themselves. Gestalt psychology was most interested in perception, but their theoretical ideas about perception had a spinoff for learning. In perception they reacted to structuralist psychology of the late 19th and early 20th centuries that analyzed complex visual forms and sounds into the elementary parts that comprised the whole pattern. For example, the Gestaltists said that it was meaningless to analyze a tune into its notes, ignoring the relations among the notes. The relations are fundamental, and as evidence they cite the ability to sing a tune in the wrong key—the elements are wrong but the pattern is correct. A key point of disagreement between Gestaltists and associationists is this matter of relations. Gestalt psychology says that the mind directly apprehends relations (Köhler, 1947; Asch, 1968), along with the parts, whereas associationists hold that both the relations and the parts are learned. This associationist position is consistent with John Locke's philosophy that the mind is a blank tablet at the start, and that all mental content is acquired in experience.

The issue of relations clearly divides the associationists and the Gestaltists in their interpretation of the verbal learning process. The associationists, who work out of the Ebbinghaus tradition, turn heavily on the principles of contiguity and frequency in the acquiring of a stable relation between verbal units. Experience the pair LAKE-SUGAR enough times and they will come to be associated, and when LAKE is presented as a stimulus SUGAR will occur as a response. Wolfgang Köhler, as a leading theorist for Gestalt psychology, saw it differently (Köhler, 1947, p. 265). He said that LAKE-SUGAR can evoke pictures, or images, in the mind, and it is these images that give the words of the pair an organization into a whole. Moreover, organization of the elements *is* the learning. Contiguity in experience, and frequency of experience, are fundamental for verbal learning but only insofar as they affect the organizational process. Not all verbal learning uses imagery; patterns might be wholly verbal. But, no matter what they are, learning is the meaningful organization of elements of experience.

Another tenet of cognitive psychology is the belief in the active mind. Associationism has a passive subject as an unwritten premise. If specified events with a specified temporal relationship occur in experience, learning will occur, otherwise not, according to associationism. There is nothing the subject need do about the events, or, indeed, can do about them. If the events are properly experienced the learning automatically will happen. Cognitive psychology, on the other hand, has a mentally active subject. No matter whether human or lower animal, there is the active relating of information in the environment, thinking about it, hypothesizing about it, judging it, and deciding about it. Associationism is much more of a psychology of the "out there," where events in the environment are the prime determiners of behavior. Cognitive psychology would hardly deny the importance of events "out there," but it imputes significance to them only insofar as they are used by the subject's active mind. Events in the environment are objective, and their touchable, seeable, hearable quality has given the advocates of associationism strong feelings of being objective. Everyone accepts the objectivism of associationism, but the inner events of cognitive psychology can be studied with objectivity too. Inner events are untouchable, unseeable, and unhearable, but they can be objectified by empirical operations and studied, just as physicists study the unobservable electron and atom.

The balance of this chapter will review natural language mediation, imagery, and free recall. All are in the tradition of cognitive psychology.

Natural language mediation

The associationist model is weak in any good way to handle what W. E. Montague (1972) calls "elaborative strategies in verbal learning." He writes (p. 225): "During the last ten years or so research and theorizing on verbal learning and memory has gone in a new direction. Gradually, it has been apparent that the learner controls much, and in some cases all of what he learns in experiments relatively independently of the experimenter." Montague goes on to say, "In memorizing, subjects elaborate tasks and materials; they transform, recode, encode, reorganize, give meaning to, or make sense out of seeming nonsense." The associationist model has a passive subject implicit among its premises, where the stimulus term is presented by the experimenter, associations perhaps are aroused, and the response is learned regardless of what the subject thinks about it. Montague, however, sees the subject as an active agent in the learning process, which is a cognitive model.

The active subject can choose a mode of learning. The *rote learning* of an item in a paired-associates task is one strategy that subjects can elect to use, where they repeat the item over and over to themselves until they can successfully give the response term when they are tested for it. Or they can form a *natural language mediator,* where they organize the two items of the pair with any verbal association that meaningfully relates them. Suppose the pair to be learned is DOG-HOG. When confronted with this pair a subject might organize these two words by thinking to herself that DOG and HOG are both animals, that a DOG is a smaller animal than a HOG, that DOG is the name of another animal that rhymes with HOG, or that both are three-letter words for the names of domesticated animals. There are no restraints in the formation of a natural language mediator; it is up to the subject and will vary from subject to subject and item to item. And natural language mediators are not dependent on meaningful words being in the item. Many nonsense syllables induce easy natural language mediators. The pair BUS-BUT might be translated into "The bush is beautiful." Ebbinghaus was wrong when he thought that nonsense syllables were free of associations.

Having acquired a natural language mediator in learning, the subject is faced with the problem of making use of it at recall. When the stimulus word appears the subject must remember the natural language mediator and must remember how to decode it and obtain the response word which is required. If the natural language mediator is that the response term is the name of an animal that rhymes with the stimulus term DOG, the subject must not only recall the aid but also remember how to use it and obtain the response term HOG. The natural language mediator could be a poor one and yield the response POLLYWOG. With all these problems of getting a good natural language mediator in the first place, remembering it, and properly decoding it, one would think that natural language mediators might be a hindrance. Not so, as will be documented shortly.

Natural language mediators are complex events that are hidden determiners of the behavior we observe, and we must have an index that represents them if we are to relate them to the responses being learned. Montague and Kiess (1968) scaled verbal pairs for their power to elicit a natural language mediator of any sort, similar to the way that Noble (1952) scaled items for simple associations. They called their scale *associability*. With these materials one can make up lists of word pairs with a high and low probability of evoking natural language mediators in subjects, and one could, for example, do an experiment on associability as Cieutat, Stockwell, and Noble (1958) did on meaningfulness. Another approach is to use verbal reports as a way of documenting natural mediators, where the subject is asked to describe the natural language mediator for an item if she/he had one. Items can then be divided into those that were mediated and those that were not (rote learning), and the effect of mediation on learning calculated. Some have skepticism about verbal reports, however, and this matter will be discussed in a later section on natural language mediators and their methodological problems.

The effect of natural language mediators on the learning process is to make it faster than when learning is by rote. Adams, McIntyre, and Thorsheim (1969) gave their subjects a list of ten paired associates to learn over eight trials by the anticipation method. The procedure was to have the subject report the response term, if possible, when the stimulus term alone was showing, as is standard for the anticipation

method. The next presentation for the item was the stimulus and response terms together, which is also standard for the anticipation method
as an informing and study event, except here the subject also was asked
to report his natural language mediator to the experimenter if he had
one. If he did not have a mediator, then he was to report "Rote," and
it was presumed that the item was being learned by rote practice
repetitions. A four-second rate was used so there was ample time for
these reports. The reason for obtaining the verbal report at each presentation of each item was to place the recording of the natural language
mediator very near the point of its use. When a subject is asked about
his mediators only at the end of the experiment there is the possibility
that faulty memory of some mediators may cause errors to creep in.

The results of the study were that subjects were mediating 46 percent
of their items at the end of practice. The percent of responses correctly
anticipated on each trial is shown in Figure 7–3, and they are shown

FIGURE 7–3

A comparison of mediated and rote verbal learning. Paired
associates were learned by the anticipation method.

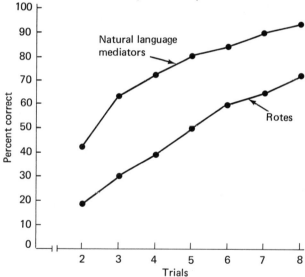

Adams, J. A., McIntyre, J. S., & Thorsheim, H. I. Natural
language mediation and interitem interference in paired-associate
learning. *Psychonomic Science,* 1969, *16,* 63–64. Reprinted by
permission of The Psychonomic Society, Inc.

for both rote and mediated items. A substantial advantage was found
for mediated items. Over all 8 trials, the average superiority of mediated
over rote items was 28 percent.

Köhler (1947, Chapter 8) said that organizing the item is equivalent to learning the association. A natural language mediator is an organizing device for the units of an item, and Masters (1970) found evidence that Köhler was more right than wrong. She studied paired-associate learning by the anticipation method and, like Adams, McIntyre, and Thorsheim (1969), recorded mediated or rote learning for each item on each trial. Using this approach, she related the first occurrence of a natural language mediator for an item and the first occurrence of the correct response for the item. If Köhler is right and learning depends on organization, then the first occurrence of a natural language mediator and the first correct anticipation of a response for an item should go hand in hand. Masters found this to be the case. The joint occurrence of the response and the natural language mediator occurred 64–80 percent of the time among the groups of her experiment for the items that were mediated. This finding should not imply that a verbal association cannot be formed without a mediator. Depending on the group, Masters found that only 25–40 percent of the items were learned by mediation.

Another way of looking at natural language mediation is that the mediator is a mechanism by which a subject meaningfully processes the item, whether it is intrinsically meaningful in its own right or not. Some investigators have thought that providing the subject with a mediator rather than letting her find her own was a superior approach because it takes the natural language mediator under explicit experimental control and it avoids the problems of verbal reports. If the pair to be learned was CAT-BIRD, the experimenter would give the subjects instructions about the requirements of paired-associate learning and then would present the pair in a mediational context like "The CAT chased the BIRD." Bobrow and Bower (1969) found that this was ineffective and that learning was much better when the subject was asked to make up her own sentence mediator. They had a number of items where the self-generated sentences in one condition were the same as those that were provided by the experimenter in another, so all factors were equated, and the recall of responses from self-generated sentences was superior by a factor of almost three.

There are a couple of good reasons for the finding that mediators provided by the experimenter can be ineffective. One is that the subject can ignore the sentence mediator that the experimenter provides. The other is that the subject might dutifully read the sentence but treat it superficially and not process its meaning. Bobrow and Bower (1969), in another experiment, experimentally manipulated the level of processing that the subjects used in learning. The pair to be learned was imbedded in a sentence, where the stimulus term of the pair was the subject of the sentence and the response term was the object, e.g., "The COW chased the rubber BALL." All sentences had an ambiguous word like "ball," which can refer either to a round object or an elegant dance.

One experimental condition had superficial processing of the sentence where, after reading it, the subject was given a word of the sentence and asked if it had been misspelled. A second condition was asked the meaning of the ambiguous word within the context of the sentence ("Did BALL refer to a round object or an elegant dance?"), which required that the subject think about the sentence. This second condition that required the processing of meaning was superior in recall of response terms by a factor of almost three.

A way to have rapid verbal learning, then, is to set up procedures guaranteeing that the subject will think about the material, elaborate it, and process it. It is not necessary that the learner create a natural language mediator of his own, although this is certainly one way to insure processing because the subject must think and process while creating his own mediator. Any technique that requires the subject to process the meaning of the material, whether it is self-generated or provided to the subject, will work to speed the rate of verbal learning.

Methodological problems for natural language mediators. Natural language mediators nicely fit the cognitive, organizational view of verbal learning. The subject is given a verbal item to learn and does so by integrating it into verbal thought processes. Modern investigators in the cognitive tradition accept this point of view, although they qualify it somewhat by finding a place for rote learning, which is in the associationist tradition. They identify *rote learning* by the absence of a verbal report of a natural language mediator. One could, of course, adopt a severe cognitive position and say that all verbal learning is really mediated but that our verbal reporting methods are insufficient to tap the mediator, or that the mediator exists but it is "unconscious" and cannot be reported at all. Less severe cognitive psychologists are less prone to force their thinking and data into the one classical cognitive slot. They think in terms of elaborative strategies (Montague, 1972) where the circumstances of the verbal materials, the subject, and the learning situation can produce a natural language mediator, rote learning, or an image mediator (as we shall see in the next section). Several verbal learning options are available to the adult learner, and it is the charge of the psychologist to determine them and relate them to the learning process. An interesting research question is how these strategies are related to age (Flavell, 1970).

Scientific life in the psychology of learning would be placid if everyone would accept the cognitive viewpoint that was just described, but it is not destined to be and should not be. The associationists, who are historically older, have some interesting, hard-to-beat arguments against the cognitive account of natural language mediation, and they are not about to step aside. The refinement of scientific law and theory comes from scientists hurling data and arguments at one another. If there were only two learning psychologists in the world, be assured there would be two opposing theoretical camps.

A primary associationist objection to natural language mediators is that they are epiphenomenal and have nothing to do with the basic learning process; they are the frosting on the doughnut, so to speak. If verbal learning is conceived as habit formation, then the natural language mediator is considered an accompaniment of habit formation with nothing to do with habit formation. The natural language mediator might be a correlate of the learning process, even a close correlate, but it is not the learning process itself, as cognitive psychologists contend. Implicit in this contention is that the experimental response defined by the experimenter and the natural language mediator are independent responses, and in the course of the learning experience both are acquired. That which causes learning of the experimental response also causes learning of the response that is the natural language mediator. If this is so, it should be possible to structure the verbal learning situation so that the separate learning of the natural language mediator and the experimental response could be independently controlled. So far, this possibility has not been tested empirically.

Another associationist objection is that the verbal reporting procedures cause natural language mediators. When asked if a mediator was used for the learning of an item, the obliging subject under the demands of the experimental situation will often give a natural language mediator, thinking it is part of the experiment. There is no evidence that this is so, although its possibility cannot be denied.

A third major problem is that the verbal reports of natural language mediators are an introspective account of conscious processes, which are suspect. The rise of behaviorism early in this century in the United States, and the corresponding decline of structuralist psychology which relied on a verbal description of one's own conscious processes for its data, turned importantly on problems of consciousness and knowing it through introspection and verbal reports. A long-standing skepticism about verbal reports of conscious processes is part of psychology's history in the United States, and these sentiments are still with us. The verbal reporting of consciousness is still a controversial source of data, and the issues are complex (e.g., Radford, 1974).

What is the resolution of controversies like these between cognitive psychology and associationist psychology? Probably there is none. Historically, controversies in science are not solved by a brilliant theoretical insight or a crucial experiment that tilts the balance forevermore. Rather, the balance shifts gradually, as more and more data are more congenial to one theory than another, until eventually all of a science has a dominant mode of theoretical thinking and regards the other theoretical position only as an interesting part of the past. Associationist psychology has been the dominant theoretical camp in psychology until the recent swing toward cognitive psychology.

IMAGERY

Natural language mediation is a verbal strategy for the learning process, and *imagery* is nonverbal strategy. Anyone who has ever had a dream knows what an image is, and in recent years there has been an active concern with developing objective indices of imagery and relating them to verbal learning and retention.

There is a general sentiment in psychology today that the source of the image is concrete sensory experience, and that its arousal is a kind of re-creation of that experience. David Hartley, the 18th century British associationist, wrote of the image as a conditioned sensation. There are several things to notice about this conception of an image. First, it is objective in principle because it derives from experience, and experience can be manipulated. Second, it does not necessarily imply that consciousness and images are the same; there is no reason why one cannot have unconscious images. Third, images can be in any sense modality even though the term "image" has an implication of visual experience. Considering images as coming from sensory experience, there is no reason why we should not have images in any sense modality. And fourth, images should not necessarily be considered high fidelity representation of sensory experience; a visual image is not necessarily a clear color photograph in the head.

Much of the modern revival of interest in imagery is due to A. Paivio (1971). Paivio's thinking basically turns on the *dual-coding hypothesis,* which has both images and verbal processes as codes in verbal learning, and the degree that these two processes operate depends upon the type of verbal material. Images alone cannot carry the mediational burden for verbal learning because there are abstract words like TRUTH and INFINITY that have no basis in sensory experience, and it is difficult to see how images can be associated with them. Concrete words, like HOUSE and CAR, have been associated with sensory experience of the objects that they connote, and they develop the power to arouse the images that have come from sensory experience. Pictures of the objects would have even a greater power of eliciting images than the words that represent them.

In a standard paired-associate learning task, the choice of words would determine whether images would be available as a potential mediator, according to Paivio's thinking. Consider the pair of concrete words BOAT-LAKE presented for learning by the study-test method. When the pair is presented for study they each arouse their respective images, and the compound image of a boat on a lake could be an image mediator. At the test, when BOAT is presented alone as the stimulus term, its image-arousing value is particularly crucial because it must stimulate the compound image from which the response term LAKE must be decoded. Paivio, using this reasoning, gives the stimulus term special status because the image of relevance must be attached to it, and this is his *conceptual-peg hypothesis.* The paired-associate learning of abstract words should be more difficult than concrete words because their potential for imagery is weak or absent.

Paivio, Smythe, and Yuille (1968) tested the conceptual-peg hypothesis in an experiment that varied the imagery value of nouns on both the stimulus and the response side in paired-associate learning. In a different study, Paivio, Yuille, and Madigan (1968) scaled words for their imagery-evoking powers as well as meaningfulness, and it was from this study that the nouns were chosen. Paivio and his colleagues had high and low imagery for the stimulus terms and the same for the response terms. Examples of high imagery words were ACCORDION and ACROBAT, and examples of low imagery words were DIFFUSION and DUTY. All words were equated for meaningfulness and frequency of occurrence in the English language, so whatever effects that were found could be assigned to the imagery variable and not to nonimagery verbal factors. Four trials were given by the study-test method. The results are shown in Figure 7–4, and they are in support of the conceptual-peg hypothesis. The highest recall was when high imagery words were in the stimulus position, facilitating arousal of the image mediator.

Methodological problems for imagery. Imagery nicely fits the cognitive mold. Like natural language mediators, images are a way of organizing the verbal item and, like natural language mediators, there are benefits for the learning process, or so it seems for cognitive psychology. But, unfortunately, imagery mediators are beset with the same methodological problems that were listed for natural language mediators, as well as one or two more. A primary argument, which is an old one in associationist psychology, is that the image is epiphenomenal to the learning process; no one denies the existence of images but one can deny the relevance of images for the learning process. They are an acknowledged correlate of the learning process, but that does not mean that they are causal for learning. Also, verbal reports of images are sometimes recorded, and they have the same problems as verbal reports of natural language mediators.

Furthermore, how do we know that imagery is *really* operating rather than some other mediational state? Paivio, Smythe, and Yuille (1968) scaled words for both imagery and meaningfulness, and varied imagery while holding meaningfulness constant in their experiment. By this method they had some assurance that the verbal influences of single-word associations defined by meaningfulness were ruled out. But what

FIGURE 7–4

Effects of high (*H*) and low (*L*) imagery values of the stimulus and response terms on paired-associate learning. The total recall over four trials is shown.

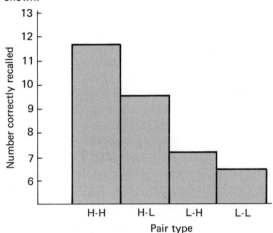

Paivio, A., Smythe, P. C. & Yuille, J. C. Imagery versus meaningfulness of nouns in paired-associate learning. *Canadian Journal of Psychology,* 1968, *22,* 427–441. Reprinted by permission of Editor, *Canadian Journal of Psychology.*

about natural language mediators? The same concrete nouns that are high in imagery would also be high in their potential for verbal elaboration. Unfortunately, no one has yet scaled words for both imagery and natural language mediation, so it is not possible to vary one and hold the other constant. One method to sort out the influences of different encoding strategies is the instructional approach, which assumes that a subject will follow directions. Bower and Winzenz (1970) used the paired-associate learning of concrete nouns—four groups each had a different way of learning specified for them: (1) repetition, where the pair was to be repeated over and over and learned by rote, (2) sentence reading, where the pair was the subject and object of a sentence which was an experimenter-provided natural language mediator, (3) sentence generation, where the subject made up a sentence as a natural language mediator, and (4) imagery, where the subject was to visualize the objects denoted by the words in vivid interaction. If imagery is nothing more than natural language mediation, then we would expect Conditions 3 and 4 to be the same, but they were not. The order of proficiency in recall for the four groups, from worst to best, was repetition, sentence reading, sentence generation, and imagery. That sentence generation is the road to a better natural language mediator than sentence reading is the same finding as Bobrow and Bower (1969), and that imagery was the best of all shows effects over and beyond those that can be ascribed to natural language mediation. Of course, one could say that the imagery condition was actually using natural language mediators of a superior quality to those used by the sentence reading and sentence generation conditions, and so the effects were entirely from verbal causes, not imagery. This may be so but there is no evidence for it, and in the absence of evidence, the argument in favor of imagery mediation must stand.

Even more convincing evidence for imagery is reported by Bower (1970), where the experimental procedure was to interfere with the formation of visual images. The underlying idea was that visual perceptual centers are of limited capacity, and one cannot form visual images in verbal learning and carry out a parallel visual activity at the same time. Subjects were instructed to use either a rote or imagery learning strategy for learning word pairs. While learning, the subjects during one experimental condition had to visually track a wavy, erratic line with the finger, and under another condition the subjects had to tactually track, with eyes closed, a raised string that moved erratically. The expectation was that imagery instructions would produce better performance than rote instructions, as Bower and Winzenz found, and that performance would be better with tactile than visual tracking under imagery instructions because it would not interfere with the visual imagery being used to learn the pairs. Rote learning should be unaffected by both types of tracking.

TABLE 7–1

Proportion of paired associations recalled correctly when they were learned by visual imagery or rote repetition and when the auxillary task was tactile or visually guided tracking.

	Tracking	
	Tactile	Visual
Imagery	66	55
Rote repetition	28	28

Bower, G. H. Analysis of a mnemonic device. *American Scientist,* 1970, *58,* 496–510. Reprinted by permission, *American Scientist,* journal of Sigma Xi, The Scientific Research Society of North America.

The results are given in Table 7–1, and they nicely fit the expectation. Atwood (1971) performed a similar experiment that confirmed and extended Bower's. He found that a visual signal presented between concrete verbal phrases interfered with their recall when compared with an auditory signal, and that the opposite was found when abstract

phrases were used. In addition to supporting a role for imagery mediation, Atwood's results are compatible with Paivio's dual-coding
hypothesis.

FREE RECALL

Each response in serial anticipation learning and in paired-associate
learning has its own identifiable stimulus, but there is no necessity in
the study of verbal learning for an identifiable stimulus. A list of words
or nonsense syllables can be presented and the subject then can be
asked to recall as many as possible in any order of recall. This is the
method of *free recall,* and it is in common use today.

An effect in free recall which has attracted the theoretical interests
of cognitive psychologists is *clustering* because it says something about
how the mind organizes and structures the elements of the world that
impinge on it. The gist of clustering is that words which are presented
in an unsystematic way will show some degree of organization in recall.
The basic clustering effect was demonstrated in a study by Bousfield
(1953), where it was discovered. Bousfield presented his subjects a list
of 60 nouns, with 15 in each of 4 different categories: animals, proper
names, vegetables, and professions. The 60 words were presented in
a random order, and in free recall Bousefield found a significant tendency
for words of a category to be recalled together, or cluster. This should
not imply that a subject would necessarily recall, say, all the animals
from the list that he could remember, followed by all the vegetables
that he could remember, and so on. Rather, he might recall three animal
words, one vegetable word, four professions words, two vegetable words,
etc. As the name of the phenomenon says, there is clustering. Bousfield
set the direction of research on clustering by using lists with words
of several conceptual categories, but clustering is not limited to words
of conceptual categories. Apparently any dimension of a list which the
subject can perceive can be used as a basis for clustering. Hintzman,
Block, and Inskeep (1972) and Nilsson (1973, 1974) found that clustering occurred on the basis of sensory modality when some of the words
of the list were visually presented and some were auditorily presented.
In other experiments of Hintzman et al., they found that the type of
lettering for visually-presented words was a basis of clustering, as was
the voice of the speaker in auditory presentation.

What are some of the other variables that determine clustering? An obvious one is amount of practice. Using Bousfield's list of 60 nouns with 4
conceptual categories, Bousfield and Cohen (1953) gave 5 groups of
subjects 1 to 5 presentations of the list. The number of words correctly
recalled increased with practice, and the number of clusters essentially
doubled from one presentation to five. Another fundamental variable

is whether the words of a category are blocked together or not when they are presented. As might be expected, it is easier to relate items and promote their clustering at recall when the category words are presented together. Cofer, Bruce, and Reicher (1966) found that blocking increased the clustering of conceptually related words by about 50 percent. To the extent that the presentation becomes less and less blocked and more and more disorganized and random, the clustering will decline. Kintsch (1970, pp. 368–369) observed that items presented together tend to cluster, and as the number of items between any two words of a category increases, their tendency to be recalled together decreases.

Psychologists have had a theoretical interest in clustering because it pits the old rivals, cognitive and associationist psychology, against one another again. Cognitive psychology sees clustering as an example of the organizing powers of the mind that perceives the regularities among the randomly presented words and uses these regularities in guiding the recall (Tulving, 1968). A strong cognitive position would contend that learning in free recall is a matter of giving organization to the list's items, and that increasing amount recalled over practice trials is a function of increasing organization of the items. This cognitive stance is very similar to Köhler's position, mentioned earlier in this chapter when natural language mediation was discussed, that organizing is the fundamental nature of associative learning (Köhler, 1947).

Does the amount of clustering for a subject influence the number of items recalled, as the cognitive view says? Does learning in free recall depend on clustering? "Not necessarily" seems to be the answer. Shapiro and Bell (1970) separated their subjects in a free recall experiment into low, moderate, and high "organizers" based on a clustering score. A series of practice trials was given on a list, and Shapiro and Bell related the number of words recalled on each trial to the level of clustering shown by each type of organizer. They found that only high organizers had increases in clustering over trials that paralleled increases in recall. Low and moderate organizers also had increases in recall over trials, but no appreciable change in clustering; they learned without clustering, as if there was some rote learning where subjects repeated an individual item over and over without relating it to other items. The data of Shapiro and Bell show that there is something to the cognitive view, but that it is not a general principle because some subjects are not structuring and organizing the material one bit. Perhaps this should not be surprising. In paired-associate learning some subjects learn some items by rote and do not use natural language mediators or images and, similarly, a certain amount of rote learning should be expected in free recall.

Associationist psychologists can contend that there is no need to invoke the organizing powers of the mind to explain clustering in free recall. Words that tend to cluster at recall can be words that have been associated in past experience, and the strength of the clustering is a function of the strength of association. These associative relationships between words can be known in free association tests. Suppose, in a free association test, you were given the stimulus word HORSE and you gave RIDER as the first response that came to mind. Then, if HORSE and RIDER were items in a list presented to you it would not be surprising if they occurred together in free recall, and all in the absence of conceptual relatedness.

Jenkins and Russell (1952) and Jenkins, Mink, and Russell (1958) were the first to show that free association norms can predict clustering in free recall. Pairs of words from a free association test were randomly presented in a list for free recall, and there was a significant tendency for them to occur together in recall.

Marshall (reported by Cofer, 1965) presented data which showed how clustering in free recall is a function of association, and that associative relatedness is not the whole story. He calculated an index based on all the associations that any two words had in common, and with the index he was able to define lists for free recall whose words were associatively related in varying degrees. Figure 7–5 shows a clustering score plotted as a function of four practice trials and six values of the index. The greater the number of associations between words the greater the clustering. But is this all there is to clustering? It could be, because

FIGURE 7–5

The tendency to cluster items in free recall as a function of an index of the associative related-ness among items. The value for the index is specified beside each curve.

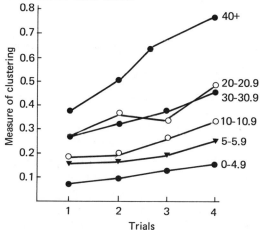

Cofer, C. N. On some factors in the organizational characteristics of free recall. *American Psychologist,* 1965, *20,* 261–272. Reprinted by permission of the American Psychological Association.

words which are conceptually related also tend to be associatively related, so maybe the explanation in terms of association is the more fundamental one. DOG and CAT are conceptually related as animals but they are also associates of one another in a free association test. Marshall went on to evaluate the contributions of cognitive and associative relations by using lists of words that had the index of association held constant but which were conceptually related or unrelated. The results in Figure 7–6, presented in terms of a clustering score, show

FIGURE 7–6

The tendency to cluster items in free recall when associative relatedness is held constant and items differ in being categorically (conceptually) related or not.

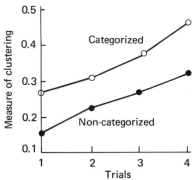

Cofer, C. N. On some factors in the organizational characteristics of free recall. *American Psychologist,* 1965, *20,* 261–272. Reprinted by permission of the American Psychological Association.

that conceptual categories contribute something in their own right, over and beyond the associative relations among words. The associative position and the cognitive position both seem correct. That associations contribute to clustering is true, but that they cannot account for all of the clustering is also true.

How can clustering occur for items that have neither conceptual nor associative relatedness from past language experience? Tulving (1962) demonstrated increasing clustering with practice for unrelated nouns, and Allen (1968) found increasing clustering over practice trials with unrelated nonsense syllables. How can a subject come to give XIB, JEK, and LAV together? The answer is rote practice. Rundus (1971) had his subjects vocalize their rehearsal patterns of unrelated nouns that were presented for free recall, and he found there was much more going on than studying the item that was being displayed. Rundus found that at any particular moment a subject was rehearsing a set of items. He was rehearsing the item that was showing, he was usually rehearsing the immediately preceding item also, and he had some chance of rehearsing items more distant in the list. The probability of any two items being recalled together in a cluster depended upon the number of times that the two were rehearsed together. Rehearsal was the sole explanation of clustering of unrelated words in Rundus' experiment but, when the words were conceptually related and categorized, apparently the categories were perceived because the rehearsal rate and the performance level were higher. The cognitive organization of the material determined the amount of rehearsal and the level of performance that is a function of it.

SUMMARY

Verbal learning has associationism as its ancestor. As far back as ancient Greek philosophers, but most notably the British empirical philosophers of the 17th–19th centuries, there has been concern with the association of ideas and how these associations are related to a theory of thought. Hermann Ebbinghaus, in the 19th century, began the experimental study of verbal learning and how verbal items are associated.

There are three main verbal learning procedures: serial learning, paired-associate learning, and free recall. Serial learning requires that a list of verbal items be recalled in the order presented. Paired-associate learning presents the verbal items in pairs, where one item is the stimulus term and the other the response term. The subject must learn to associate the two items and give the response term when the stimulus term is presented. Free recall allows a subject to recall a list of verbal items in any order.

There are three primary ways that verbal associations are formed. One is rote rehearsal where the items to be associated are repeated over and over until they are learned. A second way of verbal learning is natural-language mediation, where the subject conceives any kind of verbal elaboration for an item or an item pair. At recall the natural language mediator must be recovered and decoded to obtain the item. The third way is imagery, where the to-be-remembered material is embodied in an image. The processing of the image at recall proceeds the same as for a natural language mediator. Both natural language mediation and imagery are methods of learning in the tradition of cognitive psychology, and both are more effective modes of learning than rote rehearsal.

REFERENCES

Adams, J. A., McIntyre, J. S., & Thorsheim, H. I.   Natural language mediation and interitem interference in paired-associate learning. *Psychonomic Science*, 1969, *16*, 63–64.

Allen, M. Rehearsal strategies and response cueing as determinants of organization in free recall. *Journal of Verbal Learning and Verbal Behavior,* 1968, *7,* 58–63.

Angell, J. R. Memory. *Psychological Review,* 1894, *1,* 435–438.

Asch, S. E. The doctrinal tyranny of associationism: Or what is wrong with rote learning? In T. R. Dixon & D. L. Horton (Eds.), *Verbal behavior and general behavior theory.* Englewood Cliffs: Prentice-Hall, 1968, pp. 214–228.

Atwood, G. An experimental study of visual imagination and memory. *Cognitive Psychology,* 1971, *2,* 290–299.

Battig, W. F. Procedural problems in paired-associate learning research. *Psychonomic Monograph Supplements,* 1965, *1,* No. 1, pp. 1–12.

Bobrow, S. A., & Bower, G. H. Comprehension and recall of sentences. *Journal of Experimental Psychology,* 1969, *80,* 455–461.

Bousfield, W. A. The occurrence of clustering in the recall of randomly arranged associates. *Journal of General Psychology,* 1953, *49,* 229–240.

Bousfield, W. A., & Cohen, B. H. The effects of reinforcement on the occurrence of clustering in the recall of randomly arranged associates. *Journal of Psychology,* 1953, *36,* 67–81.

Bower, G. H. Analysis of a mnemonic device. *American Scientist,* 1970, *58,* 496–510.

Bower, G. H., & Winzenz, D. Comparison of associative learning strategies. *Psychonomic Science,* 1970, *20,* 119–120.

Calkins, M. W. Association. In Münsterberg, H. (Ed.), Studies from the Harvard Psychological Laboratory (II.). *Psychological Review,* 1894, *1,* 441–495.

Cieutat, V. J., Stockwell, F. E., & Noble, C. E. The interaction of ability and amount of practice with stimulus and response meaningfulness (m, m') in paired-associate learning. *Journal of Experimental Psychology,* 1958, *56,* 193–202.

Cofer, C. N. On some factors in the organizational characteristics of free recall. *American Psychologist,* 1965, *20,* 261–267.

Cofer, C. N., Bruce, D. R., & Reicher, G. M. Clustering in free recall as a function of certain methodological variations. *Journal of Experimental Psychology,* 1966, *71,* 858–866.

Ebbinghaus, H. *Memory: A contribution to experimental psychology.* (H. A. Ruger & C. E. Bussenius, trans.). New York: Dover, 1964.

Flavell, J. H. Developmental studies of mediated memory. In H. W. Reese & L. P. Lipsitt (Eds.), *Advances in child development and behavior* (Vol. 5). New York Academic Press, 1970, pp. 181–211.

Hintzman, D. L., Block, R. A., & Inskeep, N. R. Memory for mode of input. *Journal of Verbal Learning and Verbal Behavior,* 1972, *11,* 741–749.

Jenkins, J. J., Mink, W. D., & Russell, W. A. Associative clustering as a function of verbal association strength. *Psychological Reports,* 1958, *4,* 127–136.

Jenkins, J. J., & Russell, W. A.   Associative clustering during recall. *Journal of Abnormal and Social Psychology*, 1952, 47, 818–821.

Kintsch, W.   Models for free recall and recognition. In D. A. Norman (Ed.), *Models of human memory*. New York: Academic Press, 1970, pp. 331–373.

Köhler, W.   *Gestalt psychology*. New York: Liveright, 1947.

Masters, L.   Knowledge of results and item associability in paired-associates learning. *American Journal of Psychology*, 1970, 83, 76–85.

Montague, W. E.   Elaborative strategies in verbal learning and memory. In G. H. Bower (Ed.), *The psychology of learning and motivation* (Vol. 6). New York: Academic Press, 1972, pp. 225–302.

Montague, W. E., & Kiess, H. O.   The associability of CVC pairs. *Journal of Experimental Psychology Monograph*, 1968, 78, No. 2, Part 2.

Nilsson, L.   Organization by modality in short-term memory. *Journal of Experimental Psychology*, 1973, 100, 246–253.

Nilsson, L.   Further evidence for organization by modality in immediate free recall. *Journal of Experimental Psychology*, 1974, 103, 948–957.

Noble, C. E.   An analysis of meaning. *Psychological Review*, 1952, 59, 421–430.

Paivio, A.   *Imagery and verbal processes*. New York: Holt, Rinehart and Winston, 1971.

Paivio, A., Smythe, P. C., & Yuille, J. C.   Imagery *versus* meaningfulness of nouns in paired-associate learning. *Canadian Journal of Psychology*, 1968, 22, 427–441.

Paivio, A., Yuille, J. C., & Madigan, S. A.   Concreteness, imagery, and meaningfulness values for 925 nouns. *Journal of Experimental Psychology Monograph Supplement*, 1968, 76, No. 1, Part 2.

Radford, J.   Reflections on introspection. *American Psychologist*, 1974, 29, 245–250.

Rundus, D.   Analysis of rehearsal processes in free recall. *Journal of Experimental Psychology*, 1971, 89, 63–77.

Shapiro, S. I., & Bell, J. A.   Subjective organization and free recall: Performance of high, moderate, and low organizers. *Psychonomic Science*, 1970, 21, 71–73.

Tulving, E.   Subjective organization in free recall of "unrelated" words. *Psychological Review*, 1962, 69, 344–354.

Tulving, E.   Theoretical issues in free recall. In T. R. Dixon & D. L. Horton (Eds.), *Verbal behavior and general behavior theory*. Englewood Cliffs: Prentice-Hall, 1968, pp. 2–36.

Young, R. K.   Serial learning. In T. R. Dixon & D. L. Horton (Eds.), *Verbal behavior and general behavior theory*. Englewood Cliffs: Prentice-Hall, 1968, pp. 122–148.

chapter 8

Motor learning

THE HUMAN learning of movement has had a spottier scientific history than the other areas of learning that we have reviewed, and the reasons for it are not clear. A complete science of behavior turns on an understanding of motor learning, just as it does on verbal learning, animal learning, and conditioning. Why then, did motor learning get off to a slower start? A possible reason is that a topic gathers momentum in a science, once research on it has begun, and the momentum causes it to roll on for a long time. The study of verbal learning got underway in 1885 with the research of Ebbinghaus, and it has held the interests of experimental psychologists ever since. The same can be said of reinforced learning (Thorndike) and classical conditioning (Pavlov). Once a topic gets rolling it creates puzzles and problems which, invariably, create new puzzles and problems, and so on. Motor learning did not pick up an early momentum like other learning topics, but research on motor learning and theory has accelerated in recent years, and this chapter will examine these recent trends.

KNOWLEDGE OF RESULTS

What are the defining conditions for the learning of a motor response? We saw in Chapter 2 that a positive reinforcer is any event which increases the probability of a response when it is delivered along with, or shortly after, the occurrence of the response. The increase in response probability is identified with learning and, to the extent that the principle of positive reinforcement has good generality, it can be applied to human motor behavior, just as it can be applied to other human response classes and to animal behavior. While there is no reason to believe that a hungry human would not learn with food as a primary reinforcer, just as a rat, there is a wide range of secondary reinforcers that work very well. Symbolic language rewards work nicely with humans, and for motor learning they are customarily called *knowledge of results*.

E. L. Thorndike was a strong figure on the American scene in behalf of reinforced learning, as we saw in Chapter 3. On occasion he studied motor learning, and a task that he used was line-drawing. A subject would be given the task of learning to draw a three-inch line, for example. The subject would be blindfolded, and not told the length of line to be drawn. Knowledge of results as "Right" and "Wrong" were delivered by the experimenter, with "Right" being delivered whenever the subject drew a line $3 \pm \frac{1}{8}$ inches and "Wrong" otherwise. As you might guess, a subject learns under these circumstances. The percentage of lines drawn that fell within the $3 \pm \frac{1}{8}$-inch bounds steadily increased with practice trials.

Turning a motor learning task into the pass-fail, qualitative act of drawing a proper line is parallel to many animal learning situations where an act is defined and reward depends upon the occurrence of the act or not. Bar pressing with rats and key pecking with pigeons are examples. More often than not, the psychology of learning has been concerned with the learning of *acts* rather than the learning of the continuous, graded sequences that we commonly call *skills*. An act is performed or it is not, and so is rewarded or not; the act and the reward are qualitative. A continuous sequence can be quantitatively conceived, however, and the information on the adequacy of the act can be quantitative. Motor learning most often is the concern with continuous behavioral sequences, and quantitative knowledge of results is the most effective for their learning. This principle is demonstrated in a study by Trowbridge and Cason (1932). They had type of knowledge of results as the variable in their experiment.

Trowbridge and Cason had their blindfolded subjects draw 100 3-inch lines. There were four experimental conditions. One condition had qualitative knowledge of results, as in the Thorndike experiment just described, where the experimenter said "Right" whenever the line was drawn within the bounds $3 \pm \frac{1}{8}$ inches and "Wrong" otherwise. A second condition had quantitative knowledge of results where error was graduated in $\frac{1}{8}$-in units. If the subject's movement was $\frac{7}{8}$ inches too long the experimenter would say "Plus seven," or if the movement was $\frac{3}{8}$ inches too short the experimenter would say "Minus three." A third condition had no knowledge of results, and a fourth condition had irrelevant knowledge of results, where a nonsense syllable was reported after each response. This latter condition controlled for the possibility that saying anything to a subject could affect performance, and that the effects of knowledge of results may not be due wholly to the information about performance that it provides.

The results are shown in Figure 8–1. The strong superiority of quantitative knowledge of results (abbreviated as *KR* in the figure) is the

FIGURE 8–1

Effects of type of knowledge of results on motor learning.

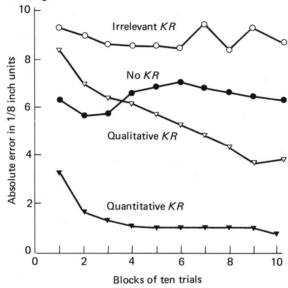

Trowbridge, M. H., & Cason, H. An experimental study of Thorndike's theory of learning. *Journal of General Psychology*, 1932, 7, 245–258. Adapted from tabled values by permission of *The Journal Press*.

most striking feature of the graph. Most of the learning was completed in about 20 trials or so when information was quantitative. Satisfactory learning, but at a slower rate, occurs with qualitative knowledge of results. No learning occurred without knowledge of results, and irrelevant knowledge of results degraded motor performance. Maybe the nonsense syllables were distracting, or maybe the subjects imputed meaning to the meaningless syllables and led themselves into maladaptive modes of responding.

Problems with the reinforcement interpretation of knowledge of results

A reinforcement interpretation of knowledge of results is sound, at least at one level of analysis. Any event whose occurrence increases the probability of a response qualifies as a positive reinforcer, and some positive reinforcers are better than others. Quantitative knowledge of results has been established as better than qualitative knowledge of results in the Trowbridge and Cason experiment, for example. But at another level of analysis the reinforcement position is wanting because it describes only surface empirical relations and is insensitive to underlying processes in motor learning. Adams (1971, p. 115) discusses three of these, and he feels that motor learning will not go very far until they find their way into law and theory:

1. A reinforcement interpretation of knowledge of results would hold that information about the correctness of a response increases the chances of repeating the response. Elwell and Grindley (1938), who did several experiments on knowledge of results with several kinds of motor tasks, made the perceptive observation that a subject does not repeat rewarded responses, as a rat repeats the bar pressing. Instead, on the next trial after knowledge of results, he attempts to correct his error. Rather than repeating a response, the subject seeks to vary it.

2. A moment's introspection during the learning of a motor response will tell you that motor activity is not the only kind of behavior going on. Subjects talk to themselves in the early stages of motor learning, formulating ideas and hypotheses about achieving the movement that is expected of them. Trowbridge and Cason (p. 252) made this observation back in 1932 when they said that their subjects verbalized and that the motor act of drawing a line was not the only psychological activity taking place. In short, motor behavior, which has sometimes been identified with the "lower senses," is far more cognitive than most analysts have been willing to admit. This does not mean that motor behavior is always accompanied by covert verbal activity. A long time ago William James (1890a, p. 114; 1890b, pp. 496–497) held that motor activity was under verbal control ("conscious" control, in the terminology of his day) early in learning, and that the control diminishes as practice progresses. Eventually verbal control drops out altogether and the motor sequence becomes "automatic." Something like James' hypothesis probably applies. As Adams (1971) wrote:

> James was on the right track in saying that verbal control is a variable early in motor learning and eventually drops out. Something like this must be so if verbal behavior controls motor behavior at all. It would be silly to postulate a theory where *all* motor behavior is under verbal control because words are crude when compared with the fineness of motor movements. The fingers of a concert violinist are not under verbal control, but they probably were in the beginning when he first started with his teacher.[1]

---

[1] *Journal of Motor Behavior*, 1971, 3, p. 115. Reprinted by permission of the *Journal of Motor Behavior*.

3. A performer "knows" the correctness and incorrectness of a move-ment as it is made, and continues to adjust the movement until he "knows" that it is correct. Self-knowledge of our competence, and responding on the basis of that knowledge, is not part of any reinforce-ment theory.

Motor learning will not collapse if these three processes are not taken into account. A reinforcement view that simply relates measures of motor performance to knowledge of results is an order of scientific description that will produce prediction and control, but it is also true that the degree of prediction and control will be modest when significant pro-cesses are left out.

CLOSED-LOOP AND OPEN-LOOP SYSTEMS

The point that subjects respond to error information and try to correct for it on the next trial is an important point for theory, and it can be the basis for an entirely different theoretical approach. It suggests that motor behavior is closed-loop instead of open-loop, which is the way it has been ordinarily conceived. Adams (1971, p. 116) defines open-loop and closed-loop systems as follows:

> An *open-loop system* has no feedback or mechanisms for error regula-tion. The input events for a system exert their influence, the system effects its transformation on the input, and the system has an output. A poorly operating open-loop system (error) is because of characteristics of the input and/or the transformations imposed by the system. A traffic light with fixed timing snarls traffic when the load is heavy and impedes the flow when traffic is light. The system has no compensatory capability.
>
> A *closed-loop system* has feedback, error detection, and error correc-tion as key elements. There is a reference that specifies the desired value for the system, and the output of the system is fed back and compared to the reference for error detection and, if necessary, corrected. The automatic home furnace is a common example. The thermostat setting is the desired value, and the heat output of the furnace is fed back and compared against this reference. If there is a discrepancy the furnace cuts in or out until the error is zero. A closed-loop system is self-regulat-ing by compensating for deviations from the reference.[2]

Until recently, all of our theories of learning have been open-loop. If the stimuli are adequate, and if the internal states of the organism such as habit and motivation and the like are sufficient, the response will occur. If there is error, where the response does not occur or occurs in an improper form, then the stimuli or the transformations imposed by the internal states of the organism are inadequate. For example, response error might be due to inadequate habit strength for the criterion response relative to other responses. The solution would be to change

---

[2] *Journal of Motor Behavior*, 1971, 3, p. 116. Reprinted by permission of the *Journal of Motor Behavior*.

the state of the system by more reinforcement for the criterion response. A closed-loop theory would have information about the wrong response fed back to the subject, error determined, and a corrective response made.

Closed-loop theory may be new for learning but it is not new in the world of engineering systems where it wears such labels as servo-theory and cybernetics. In engineering, closed-loop theory became practical in World War II as the basis of sophisticated weaponry, and it has had a variety of uses since then, ranging from automatic control of the common household furnace, which was mentioned, to the autopilot of the airplane where values of basic flight parameters are set and the airplane is automatically flown to adjust error with respect to each of them. Such systems seem intelligent to the lay person because they continually adjust themselves and find a goal. Actually, all that they are doing is correcting errors with respect to a reference. The transition of closed-loop thinking from equipment engineering to the realms of behavior was begun in a paper by Rosenblueth, Wiener, and Bigelow (1943). They discussed purposeful, goal-seeking behavior which always has such an intelligent character for the observer, and they saw it as an attempt to reduce the error discrepancy, as known by feedback, between the organism's present state and the reference, or goal. But the most influential work on the closed-loop conception was a thin volume by Wiener (1948) entitled "Cybernetics"; it ranged freely over such domains as anti-aircraft guns, vehicular control, physiology, psychology, and the social implications of automation. In writing about closed-loop control of human behavior and the processing of errors, Wiener described the simple act of picking up a pencil:

> To perform an action in such a manner, there must be report to the nervous system, conscious or unconscious, of the amount by which we have failed to pick the pencil up at each instant. If we have our eyes on the pencil, this report may be visual, at least in part, but it is more generally kinaesthetic or to use the term now in vogue, proprioceptive.[3]

A closed-loop model has three essentials: feedback, a reference mechanism, and error detection and correction. Before turning to the closed-loop model and learning, it is useful to summarize the evidence which shows the relevance of these ingredients for various kinds of ordinary behavior.

Essentials of a closed-loop system of behavior

Feedback. Feedback means about what it says: It is information that is fed back and informs a system about its own actions. An open-

---

[3] Wiener, N. *Cybernetics*. New York: Wiley, 1948, p. 14. Reprinted by permission of John Wiley & Sons.

loop system responds and has no information about the suitability of its behavior, but a closed-loop system behaves and through feedback has information about the adequacy of its own responding. Much of animal and human behavior has multiple feedback channels which inform about the response in progress. When you walk across the room you have visual feedback from the changing room cues, auditory feedback from the rhythmic sound of your footsteps, proprioceptive feedback from the sensors in the muscles and joints that inform about limb position, and tactual feedback that comes from your feet on the floor. Or consider speaking. The air-conducted sound provides auditory feedback, as does the bone-conducted sound that is transmitted through the head. Proprioceptive and tactual feedback come from the vocal cords, the tongue, the lips, and the moving jaw.

One need not go far to find compelling evidence for feedback as a determiner of behavior. Walk with your eyes closed and be convinced of the value of visual feedback. Deafferentation is the severing of the neural paths that carry the proprioceptive feedback stimuli from the body sensors in the muscles and the joints to the brain, and a large number of animal experiments show that motor behavior becomes disorganized after deafferentation (Adams, 1968). Humans have motor disorganization also when disease or injury impairs proprioceptive feedback (Lashley, 1917; Gibbs, 1954). A technique called *delayed auditory feedback* dramatically demonstrates the importance of air-conducted sound for the smooth regulations of speech (Yates, 1963). The sound is electronically delayed for a fraction of a second before it is transmitted to the ear, and the quality of speech is badly disturbed under these circumstances. The speaking takes longer, is louder, and has higher pitch.

The reference mechanism.   The reference mechanism is the standard against which feedback is compared for a determination of error. No independent evidence exists for the reference mechanism. Rather, there is evidence for the detection and correction of errors, which depends on a standard of correctness, and so implies a standard for error determination. Evidence for the detection and correction of error is given in the next section.

The detection and correction of errors.   None of us think much about it but we all have a capability for detecting and correcting errors. Consider a slip of the tongue. You say, "I'm going to the hog, I mean dog show." How could you do this without a reference mechanism that specified "dog" as the correct response, and without a comparison of "hog" with the reference mechanism for a determination of error?

Laboratory studies have turned up evidence of error detection and correction in motor tasks. West (1967) was interested in the ability of typists to detect and correct their errors, both with the visual feedback of their typed copy and without. Visual feedback was eliminated by a shield that blocked the subject's view of the typewriter. Different skill levels of typists were used. West found a definite capability of typists to know when they have made an error and to correct it, both with and without vision, but not as good a capability as typists like to believe. Without vision, and being required to detect errors by "feel" alone, the best typists (100 words per minute) detected and corrected only 50 percent of their errors. Beginning typists (11 words per minute) had a detection and correction rate of only 20 percent without vision. These percentages increased when visual feedback was available, as might be expected. Here the detection and correction of errors went as high as 76 percent.

Rabbit (1967, 1968) used a choice reaction time task in his research, where a subject had his fingers on four keys, and where different fingers must respond as rapidly as possible to different signals when they appear. With several fingers involved, it is possible to respond with the wrong finger on occasion, and if the subject has the capability to detect and correct errors he will know an error when he makes it and he will correct it by responding belatedly with the correct finger. There was no information on the display to inform the subject that he had made an error, so his power to detect and correct errors must have come from within him. In one of his studies Rabbitt (1967) found that 9 of his 12 subjects detected and corrected all of their errors. In other experiments Rabbitt (1968) found detection of 70–80 percent of the errors and correction of most of them.

A CLOSED-LOOP THEORY OF MOTOR LEARNING

The foregoing has been a case for the usefulness of a closed-loop description of behavior, but none of it applies to learning directly. A closed-loop theory of learning must show how the elements of closed-loop theory are acquired, and the variables that define them. The processing of errors is fundamental to the closed-loop conception, and it requires a reference mechanism that defines correct behavior and is the basis for knowing that an error has occurred. But theories of learning have never been concerned with a learning of standards of desired behavior. What is the role of feedback for defining the reference? Knowledge of results? Adams (1971) has specified a closed-loop theory of human motor learning that tries for an answer to some of these issues.

How knowledge of results works

We saw earlier that a reinforcement interpretation of knowledge of results has problems, and a main one is that it fails to consider the thinking human who has ideas and hypotheses about what is required of him. In short, a cognitive conception of knowledge of results is needed. Instead of knowledge of results producing an increment of habit as a reinforcement operation, Adams' theory sees motor learning as a problem-solving situation, where knowledge of results is information which the subject uses in a problem-solving activity. This does not mean that knowledge of results is used in a simple, straightforward way in the problem solving. Depending upon the task and the type of knowledge of results, the subject may form a variety of hypotheses about the movements that are required, and the hypotheses may be an elaborate transform of knowledge of results.

Reference mechanism

The main dimensions of a movement are that it starts, it has a direction, and it has an extent. The extent of movement will be dealt with first, and the starting and the direction of the movement will be treated in the next section.

The learning of a movement requires: a reference about past movements that have been made in the situation which is the reference for correctness insofar as the subject has learned it; knowledge of results about the effectiveness of the last movement that was made; and feedback stimuli that inform about the progress of the ongoing movement. The reference mechanism is called the *perceptual trace* in Adams' closed-loop theory. At the start of a trial the perceptual trace is aroused, and as the subject moves, the response-produced feedback stimuli that accompany the movement are compared with the perceptual trace. The matching of the feedback and the perceptual trace is a signal that the correct movement is being made, and a discrepancy signifies an error to be corrected. The strength of the perceptual trace is a positive function of experience with feedback stimuli. The perceptual trace is not a unitary entity. Rather, it is a distribution of traces formed by the various movements that have been made on the previous practice trials, and it is the mode of the distribution that governs the responding.

One might think that the execution of a motor movement is no more than comparing the feedback with the perceptual trace and adjusting the error difference between them. This is part of it, but it is not the whole story. Early in learning, when the subject is making substantial errors, the values of knowledge of results are sizable. At this time the subject must do more than respond solely to the perceptual trace because this would cause him to repeat past responses which have been wrong. Repeating wrong responses is maladaptive and would appear as a failure to learn. For adaptive learning to occur, the subject must use hypotheses based on knowledge of results to improve upon past behavior; the subject must vary the response and make it *different* from previous ones. The theory contends that for adjusting the response on the next trial, the perceptual trace is used *in relation* to hypotheses based on knowledge of results. This early stage of learning, where corrections are substantially derived from knowledge of results and hypotheses based on it, is called the *Verbal-Motor Stage.*

The Verbal-Motor Stage has a somewhat indefinite end point, and it will vary from subject to subject, but it comes to an end when knowledge of results has been signifying trivial error for some time and that the response is being successfully made. At this point the subject can switch wholly to the perceptual trace as the reference for responding because it now defines the·correct response. The subject can now behave without knowledge of results and the hypothesis behavior based on it. He is in the "automatic" phase of responding which William James described, and which here is called the *Motor Stage.*

More than being able to respond without knowledge of results, the subject can actually learn without knowledge of results in the Motor Stage, according to the theory. The perceptual trace in the Motor Stage is a reliable reference about correctness of the response, and adjustment of response error with respect to it should produce learning, just as adjustment of response based on externally observed error, or knowledge of results. For learning, it should make no difference whether error information is externally or internally derived. This learning from an internal error source is called *subjective reinforcement* (Adams & Bray, 1970; Eimas & Zeaman, 1963).

The perceptual trace is a theoretical abstraction, remote and unobservable. Remote and unobservable it is, as theoretical constructs usually are in psychology, but it can lose its mystery when we see it as another version of the image. In Chapter 7 we discussed images as the product of sensory experience, and their uses in verbal learning were examined. The common sense meaning of "image" is a photographic representation, which is unfortunate for psychology. All that psychologists today mean by "image" is an internal representation of sensory experience, and it can be in any sense modality. There can be a tactual image for a pattern of touching, an olfactory image for an odor, or a motor image from the various feedback stimuli generated by movement. The perceptual trace, then, is a motor image. Adams's closed-loop theory has motor learning as a special case of recognition behavior. Consider the Motor Stage of learning. When feedback stimuli from the current movement match the motor image, the subject confidently recognizes the movement as the correct one and continues it to completion because it is known to be correct. We can recognize a movement that we made before, just as we can recognize a face that we have seen before. Recognition behavior will be discussed fully in Chapter 13.

Starting of a movement

It is tempting for a theorist to use the perceptual trace as the agent which initiates the movement as well as guides it, and some closed-loop theorists have succumbed to this seductive lure (e.g., Bernstein, 1967). Adams rejects this approach in favor of a two-state theory where, in addition to the perceptual trace, there is a second construct called the *memory trace* whose job is to select and initiate the movement. Use of the perceptual trace alone would make the error detection process difficult to explain. Consider an example from verbal behavior. Suppose you corrected a slip of the tongue by saying, "Please pass the nickels—I mean pickles." If there was only the perceptual trace to select and initiate the responses as well as to verify it, then "nickels" would have been selected and initiated by the perceptual trace, and the feedback from the utterance would have been tested against the same perceptual trace and would have been verified as correct. The response generator and the reference mechanism are the same, and the response that is made is necessarily verified and accepted as correct by the speaker. The subject would have said, "Please pass the nickels." and would have been satisfied with its correctness. But this is not what happened. The speaker rejected "nickels" as correct, and changed it to "pickles." One state must have insisted on "nickels" and another must have appraised it as error and forced a substitute response which was accepted as correct.

The same reasoning can be applied to motor behavior. If the single state that defines and initiates the movement is also used to verify its correctness the movement is reflected upon itself and must necessarily be judged as correct. Two states, the perceptual trace and the memory trace, are judged as necessary in Adams' theory to avoid this problem.

Evidence for the theory

The evidence for the theory has been gathered with simple motor tasks of the complexity of Thorndike's line-drawing task. While some might protest that such tasks are too simple to tell us much about motor skills as we know them in our ordinary lives, it is nevertheless true that a simple movement like drawing a line is a continuous, graded movement that must be carefully controlled for accuracy and so has embodied in it the essence of all skills. Those who need realism in research will not find much of it in the scientist's laboratory, regardless of the science. Scientists, in their search for laws, seek to isolate independent variables and to understand their effects on dependent variables, and the enterprise pushes them toward unrealistic laboratory situations.

Figure 8–2 shows the events in a typical motor learning situation

FIGURE 8–2

Events and variables in a typical motor learning situation.

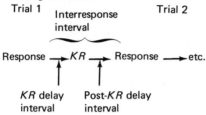

Adams, J. A. A closed-loop theory of motor learning. *Journal of Motor Behavior,* 1971, 3. 111–149. Reprinted by permission of *Journal of Motor Behavior.*

and some of the variables that are involved. Evidence for knowledge of results will be discussed first.

The application of knowledge of results in acquisition. Earlier, in our introduction to knowledge of results, the experimental findings of Trowbridge and Cason (1932) were reviewed. Motor error was shown to be related to the type of knowledge of results which was delivered. How is this explained in terms of Adams' closed-loop theory?

Motor learning is seen as a cognitive activity in the theory, where the subject devises hypotheses about the next movement and uses knowledge of results as information in the planning. Trowbridge and Cason demonstrated, as Thorndike (1927) had done before them, that there is no learning without knowledge of results—the amount of error was essentially unchanged over 100 practice trials. This finding is a straightforward expectation from the theory because there can be no meaningful plans for improvement in the next movement if there is no information on the adequacy of the last movement. Qualitative knowledge of results, where the experimenter says "Right" or "Wrong," definitely produces learning but its rate is slow (Figure 8–1). Subjects have no difficulty with hypothesis formation when knowledge of results is "Right" because they have made a movement of the correct length and the simple hypothesis to repeat the movement is all that is needed. But, when the experimenter says "Wrong" a number of hypotheses are possible. Was the movement too long? Too short? Just a bit long? A bit short? The efficiency of hypothesis-making is low with qualitative knowledge of results, and the rate of learning is slow as a result. Quantitative knowledge of results, where the amount and the direction of error is specified, is different. Subjects have an accurate statement of their error, and their hypotheses about what to do next can be accurate and beneficial to the movement on the next trial; the result is rapid learning

(Figure 8–1). Thus, if the experimenter said "Three long," the subject could easily infer that the last movement was just a trifle long on the last trial and that it should be shortened a bit on the next trial. The hypothesis could even be more accurate if the knowledge of results had common units of measurement and the experimenter reported "Three-eighths of an inch long." When the knowledge of results is "Three long" the subject may have to expend trials and hypotheses to learn about the units of measurement and discover what three of them are.

Given how knowledge of results works in the theory, the *KR* delay interval (Figure 8–2) would not be expected to have much of an effect on learning rate. The subject uses knowledge of results in the covert hypothesis behavior and so the *KR* delay interval would be an empty waiting period, where only minor forgetting might occur. That delay of knowledge of results has no effect on the rate of motor learning has been repeatedly confirmed (Adams, 1971; Bilodeau, 1966).

The post-*KR* delay interval (Figure 8–2), however, is another matter because the arrival of knowledge of results is the information the subject has been waiting for to plan the next response. If the interval is too short there will not be enough time for planning and the learning will suffer as a result. Weinberg, Guy, and Tupper (1964) had their blind-folded subjects learn a simple positioning task of displacing the arm ten inches. The knowledge of results was delivered immediately after the response, but the post-*KR* interval was either 1, 5, 10, or 20 seconds for a group. The one-second group had reliably poorer performance than the other three groups, who had about the same level of performance. Theoretically this finding is expected. When the interval is as short as one second there is no time to process the knowledge of results and formulate a sound hypothesis for the next trial. The result is degraded performance. From these data it appears that something like five seconds is necessary for the planning of the simple motor response that was used.

The dependence of learning rate on the post-*KR* interval has been amply confirmed in nonmotor areas. Learning to identify a concept is an activity replete with hypothesis behavior, and the length of the post-*KR* interval should be a particularly potent variable. Bourne and Bunderson (1963), Bourne et al. (1965), and White and Schmidt (1972) have all demonstrated a positive relationship between learning rate and the length of the post-*KR* interval. Croll (1970) has demonstrated the same relationship for discrimination learning in children.

The post-*KR* interval and the activities in it should be most influential in the Verbal-Motor Stage of the early trials where hypothesis behavior is most active, and the least in the Motor Stage of the late trials. Boucher (1974) tested this implication of the theory, using a simple task of learning to displace the arm ten centimeters. The design of the experiment had the interpolation of interfering verbal activity in the post-*KR* interval, either early or late in practice. On the assumption that covert hypothesis behavior was occurring in the post-*KR* interval, and that it was greater early in learning than late, there should be more interference of the interpolated task with the hypothesis behavior early than late, and it should show in the accuracy of the motor response. The interpolated task was the reading of words aloud (a subject, however, had his hand screened from view). Fifty trials were given, and the early trials were the first 25 and the late trials were the last 25. Boucher found, as the theory predicts, that the interpolated task degraded motor performance early but not late in learning.

The withdrawal of knowledge of results. For a long time, under the aegis of the reinforcement view, the withdrawal of knowledge of results was considered the same as the withdrawal of reinforcement in animal learning and conditioning, which is extinction. Performance level deteriorates in extinction. This expectation was not disappointed in a number of studies, and an example of one of them is shown in Figure 8–3. It is an experiment by Bilodeau, Bilodeau, and Schumsky (1959), where

FIGURE 8–3
Effects of withdrawal of knowledge of results on motor performance.

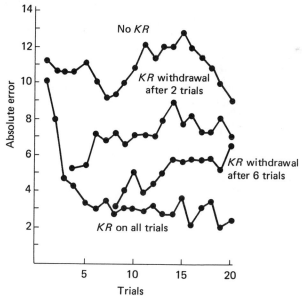

Bilodeau, E. A., Bilodeau, I. McD., & Schumsky, D. A. Some effects of introducing and withdrawing knowledge of results early and late in practice. *Journal of Experimental Psychology* 1959, *58,* 142–144. Reprinted by permission of the American Psychological Association.

the task was learning the displacement of a lever 33 degrees. Four groups of subjects had no knowledge of results over the 20 trials, knowledge of results on every trial, or knowledge of results withdrawn after 2 or 6 trials. Figure 8–3 shows that both of the latter two groups have extinction-like performance after knowledge of results is withdrawn. Performance level steadily degrades which, in this case, is an increase in lever positioning error.

The cause to challenge the reinforcement view of knowledge of results comes in findings which show that results like those of Bilodeau, Bilodeau, and Schumsky are of limited generality, and hold only when the trials with knowledge of results are small in number. When number of trials with knowledge of results is not small, performance deterioration is absent. A recent experiment by Newell (1974) shows these effects nicely, and demonstrates the local nature of extinction-like effects when knowledge of results is withdrawn. Newell's motor task was a rate learning task, where the subject had to learn to move a slide 9.5 inches in 150 milliseconds. Seventy-seven trials were given, and knowledge of results was withdrawn not at all, or after 2, 7, 17, 32, or 52 trials. His results are shown in Figure 8–4. Consistent with Bilodeau, Bilodeau, and Schumsky (1959), performance deteriorated when knowledge of results was withdrawn after a small or intermediate number of trials. But observe the condition that had knowledge of results withdrawn late in learning, after 52 trials. Their performance on the final trials, where knowledge of results was withheld, is the same as the group which received knowledge of results throughout; the extinction-like effect is missing.

If a reinforcement interpretation of these data is wanting, can closed-loop theory do any better? Yes, it seems. Early in learning, when the subject is in the Verbal-Motor Stage, the perceptual trace is ill-defined and the subject is relying importantly on covert hypothesis behavior in the responding. When knowledge of results is withdrawn in this stage the subject lacks information to direct the hypothesis behavior and also lacks a well-defined perceptual trace for inner guidance of the response. The result is response attempts without much guidance, and performance degrades as a result. Withdrawal of knowledge of results in the Motor Stage, late in learning, is another matter, however. Here the perceptual trace is well-defined and is fully capable of providing accurate guidance of the motor movement. When knowledge of results is withdrawn performance level should hold steady because accurate guidance for it is coming from a strong perceptual trace, and performance level should hold indefinitely without knowledge of results. Such thinking squares with our everyday experience. An athlete's skill does not fall away when the coach stops correcting him. Nor does a child lose his arithmetic skill when the teacher stops saying "Right" or "Wrong." Without denying

FIGURE 8–4

Effects of withdrawal of knowledge of results on motor performance. These findings supplement those in Figure 8–3 where only a small number of trials with knowledge of results was given before knowledge of results was withdrawn.

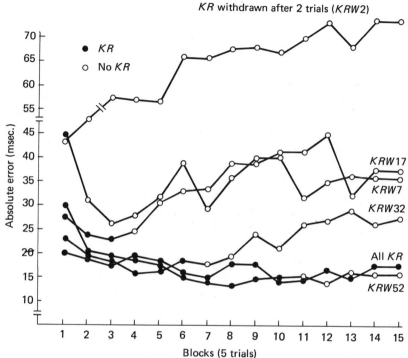

Newell. K. M. Knowledge of results and motor learning. *Journal of Motor Behavior* 1974, 6, 235–244. Reprinted by permission of Journal Motor Behavior.

the importance of external reinforcers (for it would be folly to do so), we seem to have placed an overreliance on them.

But Adams' closed-loop theory says that *learning gains* can occur in the Motor Stage. More than hold its own, performance actually can improve because the subject has a well-developed perceptual trace which defines the correct response and can be an accurate source of error information, just as external knowledge of results from the experimenter. Decisive data on the subjective reinforcement effect is not yet forthcoming, although Schmidt and White (1972) found limited evidence for it. One of the procedures which they used to get at internal error sensing was to ask the subject for an estimate of response speed after a trial and before knowledge of results. The subject who was able to do it well would be receiving accurate internal information about the accuracy of personal responding. After extended training, Schmidt and White found that their subjects could judge the speed of movement with an accuracy of about six percent. Newell (1974) found evidence along the same lines. There is no doubt that the skilled performer has mechanisms which allow self-judgment of error in behavior. The issue for subjective reinforcement is whether this error information can be used to promote learning, just as error information from the experimenter does.

Feedback stimuli. The closed-loop theory that we are examining turns critically on the response-produced stimuli that are the after-effects of a response. These stimuli lay down the perceptual trace, and they provide the data that are compared with the perceptual trace and used to calculate the subject's perception of error. If all of this is so, then the manipulation of type and amount of feedback should have an effect on performance. Several lines of evidence were reviewed earlier in this chapter which showed sizeable effects of feedback on behavior. That these findings are all consistent with the theory is not surprising because they were known at the time of the theorizing. But more than organize old findings, a good theory must imply new findings and guide discovery.

Implied and untested in Adams' closed-loop theory is that error detection and correction are a function of feedback stimuli. They need not be a function of feedback, of course. One could conceive of a theoretical system where the movement-to-be is centrally communicated to the reference mechanism and the error calculated, without any involvement of feedback. Adams' closed-loop theory is an alternate view that places feedback squarely at the heart of error processing. A recent experiment by Adams and Goetz (1973) tested this key implication. The strength of the perceptual trace, as the reference mechanism for the perception of error, is basically a function of amount of practice (experience with feedback) and amount of feedback, and Adams and Goetz had both of these variables in their experiment. They ran two experiments, one on error detection and one on error correction. Low and high amounts of practice were administered in the error detection experiment, as was low and high amounts of feedback, which they designated as minimal and augmented feedback. They used guided motor practice where the subject moved a slide along a linear track until it hit a stop, which defined the length of the movement. The number of times moved to the stop defined amount of practice, and this was either two (low amount of practice) or 10 times (high amount of practice). A movement was practiced under either minimal or augmented feedback from the visual, auditory, and proprioceptive channels. Augmented feedback for vision was lights on and minimal feedback was lights off. Auditory feedback came from the slide moving along the track. Minimal auditory feedback was the masking of the moving slide with loud white noise, and augmented feedback was removal of the noise. Proprioceptive feedback was controlled by the amount of tension required to move the slide. Augmented proprioceptive feedback was a coiled clock spring attached to the slide which the subject moved, and minimal feedback was absence of the spring which left the slide with a very light action (the slide had ball bearings and moved along a stainless steel rod).

Each trial had a learning phase and a test phase. In the learning phase the subject moved the slide to the stop either two or ten times, and with minimal or augmented feedback, depending upon the experimental condition. In the test phase the subject had to make two movements. One was the practiced movement and the other was a new movement whose length differed from the other by anywhere from 3 to 25 percent. The subject had to report which was the movement practiced in the learning phase. The question was how well the error difference between the new movement and the old one could be discriminated, and whether the discrimination was a function of amounts of practice and feedback.

The results of the error detection experiment are shown in Table 8–1. As the theory says, augmented feedback gives better error detection

TABLE 8–1

Experimental findings relating amount of practice and type of feedback to error detection and correction.

Experimental condition		Error detection experiment (percent correct error detection)	Error correction experiment (average absolute error in inches after error correction)
Amount of practice	Type of feedback		
Low	Minimal	70	.83
High	Minimal	70	.87
Low	Augmented	83	.47
High	Augmented	93	.18

Adams, J. A., and Goetz, E. T. Feedback and practice as variables in error detection and correction. *Journal of Motor Behavior,* 1973, *5,* 217–24. Reprinted by permission Editor, *Journal of Motor Behavior.*

than minimal feedback, and the high amount of practice averages out better than the low amount of practice. Interestingly, practice is a functioning variable only when there is plenty of feedback. Movement repetition alone is insufficient for error detection.

The error correction experiment had the same experimental design and procedures as the error detection experiment except that the two-choice discrimination on the test phase of a trial was replaced by a single move to a stop which defined an error movement. The stop was then removed and the subject attempted to correct the error by adjusting the slide so that it corresponded to the length of the movement practiced in the learning phase. The measure of performance was amount of error remaining after the correction, which averaged 1.0 inches before correction. The results are shown in Table 8–1. The findings for error correction parallel those for error detection. Augmented feedback gives better error correction than minimal feedback, and the high amount of practice averages better correction than the low amount. Here, again, practice is only a variable with augmented feedback. Taken together, these two experiments of Adams and Goetz are in support of Adams' closed-loop theory of motor learning.

THE MOTOR PROGRAM

The *motor program* is a theoretical idea that rivals Adams' closed-loop theory because it downplays feedback as a primary agent for movement (e.g., Keele, 1973, Chapter 6; MacNeilage, 1970). The gist of the motor program is that there is a central sequencing mechanism that runs off the motor movement without the necessity of moment-to-moment feedback control. Presumably, motor learning is the development of a program.

Evidence for the motor program

Deafferentation studies.   *Deafferentation* is the cutting of neural fibers from the muscles and the joints that go to the brain; it is a surgical denial of proprioceptive feedback (for review, see Adams, 1968). Historically, the idea of the motor program came from the deafferentation research of K. S. Lashley, who was a prominent physiological psychologist from the 1920s until his death in 1958. Lashley and his associates (Lashley and McCarthy, 1926; Lashley and Ball, 1929) found that deafferented rats retained some competence in maze running. The animals had motor disorganization, but nevertheless they had some success in maze running, and so Lashley assumed there must be a central plan, or program, that dictates the behavioral sequence. More recent studies (e.g., Taub and Berman, 1968) have verified and extended Lashley's original work, and so the motor program idea remains with us.

The weakness of deafferentation studies as support of the motor program is that they eliminate only one of the feedback channels that guide behavior, and usually there are others. Years ago, in criticism of Lashley's research, Hunter (1930) discussed the behavioral complexity of maze running, and he said that denial of only one feedback channel should not destroy the behavioral sequence. Vision and proprioception are obvious sources of sensory feedback for a rat in a maze, but there is also touch (different parts of the maze may feel differently to the feet or whiskers), olfaction (an animal may follow its own odor trail or the trail of other animals), and audition (the sound of movement down the maze, as well as sound in the surrounding room, could be informing). Any of these other feedback channels, singly or in combination, could provide information for an animal's movements in the absence of proprioception, and it is not necessary to assume the control of a central motor program. The removal of all feedback channels for a strong test of the motor program idea seems a near insurmountable task, although it appears to have been achieved by Wilson in his work on the locust, as we shall see in the next section. Wilson's work does not involve learning, however.

Insect behavior. The most convincing evidence for the motor program comes from biology. Humans are not the only coordinated animal, and it is not surprising that biologists have concerned themselves with the coordinated movements of animals' legs, tails, and wings. Wilson's research on the rhythmic wing movements of the locust (Wilson, 1961, 1964, 1966, 1968; Wilson and Gettrup, 1963; Wilson and Wyman, 1965) is the best evidence for the motor program. He found that the rhythmic wing movements of flight persisted with all sources of feedback removed, and Wilson concluded for a motor program as the primary determiner of wing movement. Feedback was not dismissed as a variable, however. Feedback stimuli were seen as a general source of information about local flight conditions, but it is a genetically-endowed motor program that controls the moment-to-moment positions of the wings.

The control of fast movements. A convincing line of evidence for advocates of the motor program is that motor movements are too fast for closed-loop proprioceptive control so, therefore, they must be centrally controlled. Lashley (1951) was the originator of this argument with an example of a pianist's fingers that moved at the rate of 16 per second. This is faster than proprioceptive feedback can possibly control, it was contended. Recent physiological evidence has weakened this argument, however.

The best evidence against this point of view comes from research on the tongue. The tongue ordinarily is not regarded as a skillful organ, and yet its elaborate positioning and timing in the mouth is a primary determiner of that complex behavior we call speech. Bowman (1968), and Bowman and Combs (1968, 1969a, 1969b), report a comprehensive series of experiments on the tongue, and they conclude that the tongue has the neural basis for full feedback control of movement in the three-dimensional oral cavity. They have shown that a neural impulse from the tongue to the brain can occur in as little as four to five milliseconds. Fuchs and Kornhuber (1969) have shown that the neural travel time from an eye muscle to the brain is 4 milliseconds, and Cohen et al. (1965) have shown that the return trip from the brain to the eye takes only 5.5 milliseconds. With the round trip from the eye to the brain and back being only about ten milliseconds, it is obvious that closed-loop control of fast movements is possible. For other motor responses, physiological research has found the round trip to take 30–40 milliseconds (Evarts, 1973) or 50–60 milliseconds (Sears and Davis, 1968), but even this is very fast. Feedback neural circuitry seems far faster than we have believed. Perhaps Lashley's pianist is a closed-loop, feedback-determined system after all.

The motor program, feedback, and learning. It is a bit difficult to say how feedback, learning, and the motor program are related because the interrelationships have not been fully specified by motor program theorists. Does feedback play a role early in learning, with the program being an independence of feedback that develops with practice? Adams, Goetz, and Marshall (1972) changed the conditions of feedback during motor learning to infer about this possibility, and they found evidence against it. If a program was developing during learning then feedback change should be more damaging early in learning than late. After a large amount of practice, late in learning, the motor program should be well-developed and a change in feedback should not be so impairing. This expectation for the motor program idea was not confirmed. They found big impairing effects for a feedback change, whether the change was early or late, and the biggest effect was late in learning, which is contrary to the possibility that feedback has a lessening of influence with practice. A way of looking at their findings is this: The motor program notion says that the concert pianist, who has been practicing eight hours a day since childhood, can show her great competence in the absence of all feedback. The Adams, Goetz, and Marshall data say that this is not so. The concert pianist needs feedback as much today as when she was a child, and perhaps more.

SUMMARY

The human learning of motor movement is based on knowledge of results, or information about error in responding. Knowledge of results can be coarse, like "Right" or "Wrong," or it can be fine grain, like "You moved 2.5 inches too long." The traditional conception of knowledge of results is reinforcement, or an event that increases the probability of occurrence of a designated response. Motor learning tasks usually require the learning of continuous graded sequences, which are commonly called skills.

That motor learning is based on error information has been the basis of a theoretical approach called closed-loop theory, whose conceptual antecedents are cybernetics and servotheory in engineering. Closed-loop theory is based on error processing. Feedback stimuli, like proprioceptive stimuli from the muscles and joints, or visual stimuli, inform about the response and are compared to a learned reference of correctness. The difference between feedback and the reference is error, and the detection of error leads to its correction, much in the same fashion as an automatic furnace senses and adjusts error in room temperature.

A theoretical rival to closed-loop theory is the motor program. The motor program is hypothesized to be a central mechanism which runs off substantial segments of a motor response without feedback playing a role. The evidence for the motor program lies mostly in studies of deafferentation, where sources of feedback stimuli are experimentally denied, and studies of motor movements that appear too fast for feedback. to operate.

REFERENCES

Adams, J. A.   Response feedback and learning. *Psychological Bulletin*, 1968, *70*, 486–504.

Adams, J. A.   A closed-loop theory of motor learning. *Journal of Motor Behavior*, 1971, *3*, 111–149.

Adams, J. A., & Bray, N. W.   A closed-loop theory of paired-associate verbal learning. *Psychological Review*, 1970, *77*, 385–405.

Adams, J. A., Goetz, E. T., & Marshall, P. H.   Response feedback and motor learning. *Journal of Experimental Psychology*, 1972, *92*, 391–397.

Adams, J. A., & Goetz, E. T.   Feedback and practice as variables in error detection and correction. *Journal of Motor Behavior*, 1973, *5*, 217–224.

Bernstein, N.   *Co-ordination and regulation of movements.* New York: Pergamon, 1967.

Bilodeau, E. A., Bilodeau, I. M. & Schumsky, D. A.   Some effects of introducing and withdrawing knowledge of results early and late in practice. *Journal of Experimental Psychology*, 1959, *58*, 142–144.

Bilodeau, I. M.   Information feedback. In E. A. Bilodeau (Ed.), *Acquisition of skill.* New York: Academic Press, 1966, pp. 255–296.

Boucher, J.-L.   Higher processes in motor learning. *Journal of Motor Behavior*, 1974, *6*, 131–138.

Bourne, L. E., Jr., & Bunderson, C. V.   Effects of delay of informative feedback and length of postfeedback interval on concept identification. *Journal of Experimental Psychology*, 1963, *65*, 1–5.

Bourne, L. E., Jr., Guy, D. E., Dodd, D. H., & Justesen, D. R.   Concept identification: The effects of varying length and informational components of the intertrial interval. *Journal of Experimental Psychology*, 1965, *69*, 624–629.

Bowman, J. P.   Muscle spindles in the intrinsic and extrinsic muscles of the rhesus monkey's (macaca mulatta) tongue. *Anatomical Record*, 1968, *161*, 483–488.

Bowman, J. P., & Combs, C. M.   Discharge patterns of lingual spindle afferent fibers in the hypoglossal nerve of the Rhesus monkey. *Experimental Neurology*, 1968, *21*, 105–119.

Bowman, J. P., & Combs, C. M.   The cerebrocortical projection of hypoglossal afferents. *Experimental Neurology,* 1969, *23,* 291–301. (a)

Bowman, J. P., & Combs, C. M.   Cerebellar responsiveness to stimulation of the lingual spindle afferent fibers in the hypoglossal nerve of the Rhesus monkey. *Experimental Neurology,* 1969, *23,* 537–543. (b)

Cohen, B., Goto, K., Shanzer, S., & Weiss, A. H.   Eye movements induced by electrical stimulation of the cerebellum in the alert cat. *Experimental Neurology,* 1965, *13,* 145–162.

Croll, W. L.   Children's discrimination learning as a function of intertrial interval duration. *Psychonomic Science,* 1970, *18,* 321–322.

Eimas, P. D., & Zeaman D.   Response speed changes in an Estes' paired-associate "miniature" experiment. *Journal of Verbal Learning and Verbal Behavior,* 1963, *1,* 384–388.

Elwell, J. L., & Grindley, G. C.   The effect of knowledge of results on learning and performance. *British Journal of Psychology,* 1938, *29,* 39–54.

Evarts, E. V.   Motor cortex reflexes associated with learned movements. *Science,* 1973, *179,* 501–503.

Fuchs, A. F., & Kornhuber, H. H.   Extraocular muscle afferents to the cerebellum of the cat. *Journal of Physiology,* 1969, *200,* 713–722.

Gibbs, C. B.   The continuous regulation of skilled response by kinaesthetic feed back. *British Journal of Psychology,* 1954, *45,* 24–39.

Hunter, W. S.   A consideration of Lashley's theory of the equi-potentiality of cerebral action. *Journal of General Psychology,* 1930, *3,* 455–468.

James, W.   *Principles of psychology* (Vol. 1). New York: Holt, 1890. (a)

James, W.   *Principles of psychology* (Vol. 2). New York: Holt, 1890. (b)

Keele, S. W.   *Attention and human performance.* Pacific Palisades: Goodyear, 1973.

Lashley, K. S.   The accuracy of movement in the absence of excitation from the moving organ. *American Journal of Physiology,* 1917, *43,* 169–194.

Lashley, K. S.   The problem of serial order in behavior. In L. A. Jeffress (Ed.), *Cerebral mechanisms in behavior.* New York: Wiley, 1951, pp. 112–136.

Lashley, K. S., & Ball, J.   Spinal conduction and kinaesthetic sensitivity in the maze habit. *Journal of Comparative Psychology,* 1929, *9,* 71–106.

Lashley, K. S., & McCarthy, D. A.   The survival of the maze habit after cerebellar injuries. *Journal of Comparative Psychology,* 1926, *6,* 423–434.

MacNeilage, P. F.   Motor control of serial ordering of speech. *Psychological Review,* 1970, *77,* 182–196.

Newell, K. M.   Knowledge of results and motor learning. *Journal of Motor Behavior,* 1974, *6,* 235–244.

Rabbitt, P.   Time to detect errors as a function of factors affecting choice-response time. *Acta Psychologica,* 1967, *27,* 131–142.

Rabbitt, P. M. A.   Three kinds of error-signalling responses in a serial choice task. *Quarterly Journal of Experimental Psychology,* 1968, *20,* 179–188.

Rosenblueth, A., Wiener, N., & Bigelow, J.   Behavior, purpose and teleology. *Philosophy of Science*, 1943, *10*, 18–24.

Schmidt, R. A., & White, J. L.   Evidence for an error detection mechanism in motor skills: A test of Adams' closed-loop theory. *Journal of Motor Behavior*, 1972, *4*, 143–153.

Sears, T. A., & Davis, J. N.   The control of respiratory muscles during voluntary breathing. *Annals of the New York Academy of Science*, 1968, *155*, 183–190.

Taub, E., & Berman, A. J.   Movement and learning in the absence of sensory feedback. In S. J. Freedman (Ed.), *The neuropsychology of spatially oriented behavior*. Homewood: Dorsey Press, 1968, pp. 173–192.

Thorndike, E. L.   The law of effect. *American Journal of Psychology*, 1927, *39*, 212–222.

Trowbridge, M. H., & Cason, H.   An experimental study of Thorndike's theory of learning. *Journal of General Psychology*, 1932, *7*, 245–258.

Weinberg, D. R., Guy, D. E., & Tupper, R. W.   Variation of postfeedback interval in simple motor learning. *Journal of Experimental Psychology*, 1964, *67*, 98–99.

West, L. J.   Vision and kinesthesis in the acquisition of typewriting skill. *Journal of Applied Psychology*, 1967, *51*, 161–166.

White, R. M., Jr., & Schmidt, S. W.   Preresponse intervals versus postinformative feedback intervals in concept identification. *Journal of Experimental Psychology*, 1972, *94*, 350–352.

Wiener, N.   *Cybernetics*. New York: Wiley, 1948.

Wilson, D. M.   The central nervous control of flight in a locust. *Journal of Experimental Biology*, 1961, *38*, 471–490.

Wilson, D. M.   The origin of the flight-motor command in grasshoppers. In R. F. Reiss (Ed.), *Neural theory and modeling*. Stanford: Stanford University Press, 1964, pp. 331–345.

Wilson, D. M.   Insect walking, *Annual review of entemology*, 1966, *11*, 103–122.

Wilson, D. M.   Inherent asymmetry and reflex modulation of the locust flight pattern. *Journal of Experimental Biology*, 1968, *48*, 631–641.

Wilson, D. M., & Gettrup, E.   A stretch reflex controlling wingbeat frequency in grasshoppers. *Journal of Experimental Biology*, 1963, *40*, 171–185.

Wilson, D. M., & Wyman, R. J.   Motor output patterns during random and rhythmic stimulation of locust thoracic ganglia. *Biophysics Journal*, 1965, *5*, 121–143.

Yates, A. J.   Delayed auditory feedback. *Psychological Bulletin*, 1963, *60*, 213–232.

part TWO

Memory

chapter 9

An overview of memory

THE AVERAGE person has a good deal of practical wisdom about learning, undoubtedly because learning is the source of so many skills that are necessary for livelihood, and, indeed, survival. The parent will have plenty of advice about learning for a child whose school grades are deficient, and the advice can be sound and lead to improvement in grades. But what advice does the lay person have when poor performance is caused by a deficiency in memory methods? The remembering of knowledge and skills is just as important for livelihood and survival as learning, and yet the experiences of lay people with remembering do not produce much practical wisdom.

Actually people know more about memory than they think they do because learning and memory are not independent processes, and so the person's knowledge about learning also represents some knowledge about memory. Chapter 1 said that learning and memory are different sides of the same behavioral coin, and so to know something about one is to know something about the other. Learning is concerned with the operations that place a relatively stable behavior potential in memory in the first place, and memory is the storage of that potential over time and its activation when recollection takes place. The time between learning and the attempt to activate the memory is called the *retention interval*, and any loss that occurs between learning and test is called a *retention loss* or *forgetting*.

The first half of this book was devoted to learning, and the last half will be devoted to storage and retrieval, which is the topic of memory. In the study of *storage* we ask such questions as: How does rehearsal affect the retention of material? What are the effects of encoding with natural language mediation and imagery? How is material lost from storage? *Retrieval* is getting the response out of storage, and it has status as a topic of memory because an item can be in storage in full strength and would occur if only it could be found and stimulated. Subjectively, we all have faced retrieval problems when we have a response on the tip of our tongue, have a feeling of knowing the response, and have searched our memory for it.

SOME HISTORY AND BACKGROUND OF MEMORY

The interest in memory goes back to the very beginnings of recorded civilization (Gomulicki, 1953). The ancient Greeks, who are among the earliest of our intellectual forebears, had memory in their mythology as the goddess Mnemosyne. Zeus was the supreme god of the ancient Greeks, and through Mnemosyne he fathered nine daughters who were called the Muses and who were the patron saints of the various arts. Plato (427–347 B.C.) was a philosopher among those ancient Greeks, and he asked what form memory might take in people and what some of its properties are. Plato (translated edition, 1892) wrote:

> I would have you imagine, then, that there exists in the mind of man a block of wax, which is of different sizes in different men; harder, moister, and having more or less purity in one than another, and in some of an intermediate quality. . . . Let us say that this tablet is a gift of Memory, the mother of the Muses, and that when we wish to remember anything which we have seen, or heard, or thought in our own minds, we hold the wax to the perceptions and thoughts, and in that material receive the impression of them as from the seal of a ring; and that we remember and know what is imprinted as long as the image lasts; but when the image is effaced, or cannot be taken, then we forget and do not know. (Pp. 254–255.)

Plato was saying that memory must be soft (change with experience) and erode with time (show forgetting).

Aristotle (384–322 B.C.) was another famous philosopher among the ancient Greeks, and was a student of Plato's. He began a long line of physiological speculation about the location of memory in the body. The significance of the brain was unappreciated by Aristotle because he assigned most of the brain's functions to the heart, and memory was among them. From Aristotle we still have the expression "learned by heart," and even today young children know that learning something by heart is to have it completely in memory and available on call. Aristotle's ideas about the heart as the locus of memory were short-lived, however. Erasistratus (310–250 B.C.), who was Aristotle's own grandson, doubted Aristotle's ideas about the heart. He did the first dissections of the brain and concluded that the nervous system was the seat of mental functions, and from that time on the brain was properly cited as the location of mental functions. Not all concerns with memory were physiological. In addition to his physiological interests, Aristotle undertook a description of mental activity at the level of ideas or behavior, and he outlined principles about how one thought would lead to another. The concern with the association of ideas reached its peak in 17th–19th century England among the British Associationists (Chapter 7).

Perhaps a more direct, visible ancestor for the behavioral study of memory is Hermann Ebbinghaus (1850–1909). He was interested in the association of ideas also, and he took his interests and moved them from armchair speculation, which was the style of the British Associationists, to objective research in the laboratory (Ebbinghaus, translated edition, 1964). Chapter 7 discussed Ebbinghaus as the founder of the objective study of verbal learning, which indeed he was, but left unsaid was that he developed an objective method of verbal learning as the route to an objective study of human memory. Ebbinghaus varied the amount of practice of the lists that he learned, and he was the first to show that the more rehearsal the less forgetting. Ebbinghaus also varied the length of the retention interval and became famous for the "curve of forgetting," showing recall as a function of the time between learning and recall. His procedure was to learn 8 lists of 13 nonsense syllables each to a criterion of 2 errorless repetitions, put them aside for the duration of the retention interval, and then relearn them to the same criterion as before. His measure of forgetting was the savings score, or the amount of time to relearn relative to the time to learn originally. If it took 1,000 seconds to learn a list originally and only 300 seconds to relearn it after the retention interval, the savings would be 700 seconds or 70 percent. Savings should be less as the retention interval increased because less would be remembered as time went on and more time would be required for relearning. The curve of forgetting, plotted in terms of the saving score as a function of time, is shown in Figure 9–1. The curve of forgetting was entrenched in psychology for a long time, but modern textbooks shy from it because psychologists no longer think in terms of *the* curve of forgetting. Forgetting is a function of many factors and there are many curves of forgetting.

Ebbinghaus set the objective tone for research on memory, and later investigators often used verbal lists in their investigation of it, although occasionally they branched out and studied the retention of other forms of behavior, like prose passages and motor skills. It is fair to say that memory was a low key interest of psychologists for about 75 years after Ebbinghaus. Learning, as discussed in the first half of this book, became one of the dominant research interests of experimental psychologists, and memory remained in the background. The period of the 1930s to the 1950s was one of intensive theorizing about learning, much of it

FIGURE 9–1

Classic curve of forgetting by Ebbinghaus.

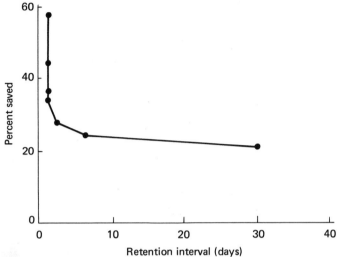

Retention interval (days)

Ebbinghaus, H. *Memory: A contribution to experimental psychology.*
(Ruger and Bussenius, trans.) New York: Dover, 1964. Adapted from
tabled values by permission of Dover Publications, Inc.

animal learning, and the theories contained little or no mention of memory (e.g., Hull, 1943). If a theory of memory existed at all it was a
theory of habit. The conditions of learning strengthened the habit for a
response, and forgetting processes operated on the habit to induce loss
over the retention interval. Psychology might have continued on this
course if it had not been for two papers on short-term verbal retention
in the late 1950s, one by Brown (1958) in England and the other by
Peterson and Peterson (1959) in the United States.

Short-term verbal retention

The Ebbinghaus tradition was a verbal list as the unit of study and
retention intervals that were long—hours and days. There is nothing
wrong with the Ebbinghaus method, but Brown (1958), and Peterson
and Peterson (1959), set it aside and studied the retention of a single
nonsense syllable over intervals of seconds. To the astonishment of psychologists they found that human subjects had dramatic forgetting in
but a few seconds, and this caused psychologists to think that memory
might have unsuspected complexities.

The Peterson and Peterson data, which have been replicated many
times, are shown in Figure 9–2, and the method for getting them was
simple. The experimenter spelled a three-unit consonant syllable (e.g.,

FIGURE 9–2

Short-term retention function for a single verbal item.

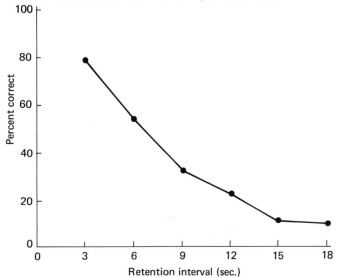

Retention interval (sec.)

Peterson, L. R., and Peterson, M. J. Short-term retention of individual verbal items. *Journal of Experimental Psychology,* 1959, *58,* 193–198. Adapted by permission of the American Psychological Association.

BDX) as the item for the subject to learn and remember, and then spoke a three-digit number as a cue for the subject to immediately begin counting backwards by threes (or fours). Retention intervals were 3 to 18 seconds before recall was attempted. The purpose of counting backwards was to prevent the subject from covertly rehearsing the item in the retention interval and offsetting any forgetting that might occur. The data in Figure 9–2 are no surprise when one stops and thinks about everyday experiences in forgetting. Who among us has not forgotten a telephone number in the few seconds between finding it in the telephone book and dialing it?

Visual memory

There was another line of research, occurring at about the same time as the work on short-term verbal retention, which was influential in directing research and theory about memory. This research was on *visual memory* or *iconic memory,* and it opened the general topic of sensory memories. Neisser (1967) was the first to use the term "iconic," which is based on the Greek word meaning "likeness" or "image." This implied use of "image" is different than that in Chapter 7 where image was defined as a learned product of sensory experience. There should be no problem in keeping a learned image separate from the momentary visual trace that is under scrutiny here.

Sperling (1960) and Averbach and Coriell (1961) were the first to document the temporal characteristics of the visual trace for verbal materials. They found that verbal information typically persisted as a trace in the visual system for about 200 milliseconds, and if it was not extracted or "read out" in that time it would be completely faded away and unavailable for later processing. The implication was a very short-term storage system based on the visual system, and different from the short-term memory system implied by the work of Brown (1958) and Peterson and Peterson (1959). The senses are the first way station of environmental stimuli that impinge on the subject, and the short-term memory system was ordinarily considered to be the second stop. Beyond short-term memory was long-term memory, the residence of relatively stable, well-learned material. An implication of research on visual memory is that all senses have memories, and time has amply borne out this implication. The next chapter will give a more detailed account of research on sensory memories.

MODELS OF MEMORY

The common distinction that came to be made in modern models of memory was between sensory memory, short-term memory, and long-term memory, and William James, the American psychologist and philosopher, had these distinctions in hand when he described after-image, primary memory, and secondary memory (James, 1890). *After-image* is a temporary sensory persistence when stimulation has ceased, such as the momentary persistence of objects in the room when the lights are turned off. James saw *primary memory* as the basis of short-term retention and different from after-image; it makes us aware of the "just past" (James, 1890, p. 646). *Secondary memory* was a long-term memory system that holds the stable behavioral repertoire from a lifetime of experience. James's insightful distinctions were not the goad for modern model-building on memory, however. Research like that of Brown (1958) and Peterson and Peterson (1959) was far more influential. Only after the modern work began to have structure did we look back and appreciate James's perceptiveness. An idea is exploited when its historical timing is right, and James' ideas were before their time.

The most influential model of human verbal memory was by Atkinson and Shiffrin (1968), and it used the three compartments of memory that were implied by James. An important characteristic of the Atkinson-Shiffrin model is that it expresses an information-processing point of view, where the flow and transformation of information is emphasized, and it is often expressed as a digital computer analogy. The human memory and a digital computer have a number of similarities. A computer has the input and the output of information, a working memory of limited capacity and a central memory of large capacity. Information is transferred from one memory to the other, and information is processed, transformed, compared, decided upon, searched, scanned and retrieved. By introspection of our own memory we can come up with operations that are similar to these, and it is easy to assume that the digital computer and human memory have the same, or closely analogous, processes.

The Atkinson and Shiffrin model is shown in Figure 9–3. The model has three stores: sensory memory (actually it is visual memory because

FIGURE 9–3

Information-processing model of verbal memory by Atkinson and Shiffrin.

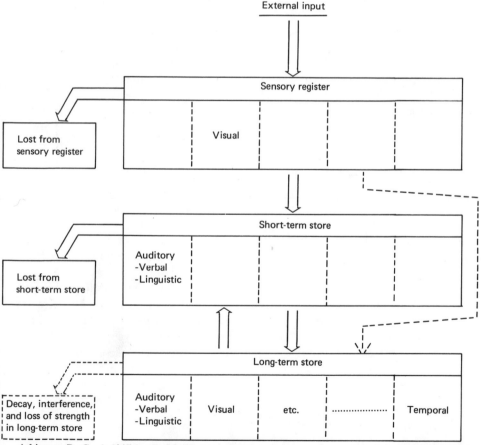

Atkinson, R. C., & Shiffrin, R. M. Human memory: A proposed system and its control processes. In K. W. Spence & J. T. Spence (Eds.), *The psychology of learning and motivation* (Vol. 2). New York: Academic Press, 1968, pp. 89–195. Reprinted by permission of Academic Press, Inc.

insufficient evidence existed at the time to justify memories for the other sense modalities), short-term memory, and long-term memory. The sensory store provides brief persistence of the material when it is presented. Loss from the sensory store is through rapid decay and interference from newly arriving information in the same modality.

The short-term memory is a temporary store of limited capacity, but not as temporary as sensory memory. The limited capacity of short-term memory is commonly called memory span, which is the number of items that can be immediately recalled without error, and Atkinson and Shiffrin derived it from the decay of items in short-term memory and from rehearsal that restores the decaying item. Considering the decay rate and the rehearsal rate, there is a limited number of items which can be processed, and this limited number is the capacity, or memory span. Memory span is five to eight items, and the transfer of these items from short-term memory to long-term memory is determined by amount of time in short-term store. Decay and rehearsal are determiners of time in short-term memory, but so is interference from incoming items which knocks out old items and replaces them with new ones.

Long-term verbal memory is the repository of established knowledge and language (and might better be called semantic memory—see Chapter 14). Information is retrieved from long-term memory by searching for it, although it might not always be there to be found because it could be lost through decay or interference. Sometimes the searching is easy, as when we immediately recall an item, but other times it can be difficult, as when an item is on the tip of the tongue and it takes a long search to find it. The subject's memory and its utilization are under conscious control—the subject can decide what information to take in, what and when to rehearse, whether to form a natural language mediator or an image, and when to search memory and retrieve information or not. Atkinson and Shiffrin call these voluntary actions in behalf of memorization and recall "control processes," and in giving a central place to them makes the model undeniably cognitive.

What can we say in criticism of the Atkinson and Shiffrin model and variants of it that populate the psychological literature? The sensory memory concept seems to be on sound research turf. Similarly, the defense of long-term memory is easy. Who can deny the storage of stable information from a lifetime of experience? Criticism, if it can be made at all, turns primarily on short-term memory. What case can be made for and against short-term memory?

Arguments for a short-term memory system

Rapid forgetting. One of the standing arguments for a short-term memory system is rapid forgetting, where the complete loss of information is believed to occur in about 30 seconds. Thirty seconds is a convention, based on data like those in Figure 9–2. Fast forgetting is taken to define a short-term memory system because long-term memory, the major compartment of memory, retains information for so much longer than 30 seconds that a short-term memory system with special properties is implied.

Memory span.   An old finding in experimental psychology is *memory span* (Jacobs, 1887). Memory span is defined as the ability to reproduce immediately, after one presentation, a series of discrete stimuli in their original order (Blankenship, 1938). Any normal person can recall one item immediately after it is presented, but what about five items? Ten? The number that can be reliably recalled without error is the memory span and it is commonly believed to be about seven (Miller, 1956). The literature of memory span is large, and representative findings are found in a study by Jahnke (1963). Either five, six, seven, eight or nine randomly ordered consonants were read to college student subjects at a rate of one per second for immediate recall. The recall for 5, 6, 7, 8 or 9 items was, respectively, 100, 96, 83, 62, and 57 percent. The ability for immediate recall of briskly presented verbal material is very definitely limited.

Prior to our modern concern with memory, the interpretation of memory span was in terms of individual differences, not memory theory. Jacobs (1887), in the first report of memory span, described how it was related to age, sex, and academic achievement. The memory span correlated with intelligence, and it has received considerable attention in the field of mental testing. In more recent times the memory span has been seen as the capacity of short-term memory. The reasoning went like this: We have a vast capability to recollect the material in long-term memory, like yesterday's argument, last year's funeral, and the arithmetic that was learned in primary school. The store of material in long-term memory is enormous. Why, then, is immediate recall so poor? Part of the answer came to be that short-term memory, which is used for immediate recall, has a limited capacity.

Acoustic coding.   Suffice to say at this point that there are circumstances where the learning of one response will interfere with the recall of another. There is a large literature on verbal interference, and one of the variables established for it is semantic similarity—words that are similar in meaning tend to interfere (Adams, 1967, Chapter 4). It was Conrad (1964) who did the basic study which showed that verbal items that sound alike can also interfere with one another, and it was this finding that had implications for short-term memory.

Conrad's approach to acoustic interference required two experiments. His first experiment was an auditory discrimination experiment. Letters were recorded on tape against a background of white noise at a rate of one per five seconds, and the task of the subject was to write down the letter that she or he thought was spoken. The results were not unexpected. Letters that sounded alike, like B, T, and V, or S, F, and X, were often confused. Conrad's second experiment was short-term retention, where 6-letter sequences were presented *visually* at a 0.75-second rate for immediate recall. The finding which became of interest for memory theory is that subjects confused letters that sounded alike, just as they had in the auditory discrimination experiment.

The puzzle in Conrad's data had two dimensions. One was the finding of acoustic interference when the history of interference research had targeted only semantic interference, where only words of similar meaning would interfere. The other was that visually presented material produced errors along an acoustic dimension. Memory theorists decided that short-term memory is fundamentally an acoustic store, and it differs from long-term memory which is semantic in character. The theoretical assumption came to be that verbal material presented in any sense modality is transformed into acoustical form and stored in short-term memory. It was never quite clear how the transformation was accomplished. Presumably auditory inputs could enter the acoustically-based short-term memory directly, and visual inputs would undergo transformation to acoustic form, perhaps by the act of covert verbalization (Sperling, 1967).

Recency in free recall. A line of evidence for short-term memory came from the free recall of word lists (Chapter 7). The evidence came from the serial position curve (Figure 9–4).

A serial position curve is a plot of words correctly recalled as a function of an item's position in the list when it was presented. The characteristic serial position curve shows better recall of items at the beginning and the end of the list, with the middle faring least well. The prominent initial segment of the curve is called the *primacy effect,* and the prominent end segment is called the *recency effect.* It was Glanzer and Cunitz (1966) who opened up exploitation of the serial position curve for short-term memory by suggesting that recency represents items in short-term memory. After presenting a list of 15 nouns for free recall, they interpolated a delay between the end of presentation and the start of recall, with the delay filled with counting to prevent the rehearsal of the items that had just been presented. The delays were 0, 10, and 30 seconds. Their results are shown in Figure 9–5. Intriguing was that short-term retention losses occurred only in the recency part of the serial position curve; the brief retention intervals had no effect on primacy. The implication of these data was that the items represented in the recency part of the curve were in short-term memory, and by investigating the variables that influence recency we study the determinants of short-term memory. It follows, and Glanzer (1972) makes this generalization, that

FIGURE 9–4
Serial position curve.

anything which contributes to the thorough learning of verbal material and secures it in long-term memory will influence the primacy part of the curve.

Convincing evidence for the Glanzer-Cunitz hypothesis is research on free recall by Rundus (1971). Rundus had his subjects rehearse items out loud during presentation rather than rehearse them covertly as they ordinarily would do. At any time during presentation subjects could rehearse any item, or any combination of items, as often as they wished. We saw in Chapter 7 that rote rehearsal is one of the strategies that subjects used in verbal learning, and Rundus related the rehearsal strategy to free recall and the serial position curve. There were 20 nouns in a list, and the results are shown in Figure 9–6. One curve is number of rehearsals given the item in each serial position, and the other is percent of items correctly recalled. Number of rehearsals is closely related to primacy, but there is a dramatic dissociation of rehearsal and recall in the recency part of the curve. Analysts mostly agree that a primary variable for securing items in long-term memory is rehearsal, and in Figure 9–6 it is rehearsal that determines primacy. The items in the recency part of the curve are recalled very well hardly without any rehearsal at all, however, and so one is urged to consider a short-term memory system that has powers of retention in the absence of rehearsal.

FIGURE 9–5
Brief delays between presentation and free recall
affect only the recency part of the serial position
curve, suggesting that recency particularly reflects short-term memory.

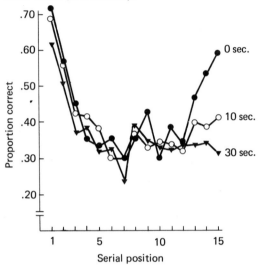

Glanzer, M., & Cunitz, A. R. Two storage mechanisms in free recall. *Journal of Verbal Learning and
Verbal Behavior,* 1966, *5,* 351–360. Reprinted by permission of Academic Press, Inc.

Another line of evidence from free recall for short-term memory is
the *negative recency effect.* Craik (1970) presented ten lists of nouns,
and had immediate free recall of each. After recall of the tenth list
he had his subjects free recall as many words as they could from all
ten lists. The results for the ten lists for immediate recall and final
recall are shown in Figure 9–7. Immediate recall shows the standard
serial position curve, with positive primacy and positive recency. Final
recall, however, has positive primacy but *negative* recency. The items
which have the best immediate recall have the poorest final recall, suggesting that they are particularly unstable and are in a temporary short-
term memory system rather than a long-term memory system like the
primacy items.

Brain trauma. In these enlightened times epileptic seizures are usually
held in check with drugs, but success is not 100 percent. There are
an unfortunate few among epileptics who cannot benefit from drugs.
They can have several grand mal seizures a day where they are smitten
unconscious and fall down, twitching and contorting. These severe cases
can be helped with brain surgery (e.g., Penfield and Jasper, 1954; Penfield and Perot, 1963). For our purposes here, surgical relief from epi-

FIGURE 9–6

Rehearsal affects the primacy but not the recency part of the serial position curve. That primacy and recency are not affected in the same way suggests that recency reflects something different, presumably short-term memory.

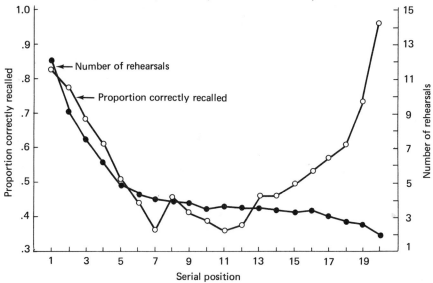

Rundus, D. Analysis of rehearsal processes in free recall. *Journal of Experimental Psychology,* 1971, *89,* 63–77. Reprinted by permission of the American Psychological Association.

leptic seizures can be at the price of new learning, and this has implications for memory theory. Milner (1959, 1966), who has been the most systematic analyst of these cases, cites a post-operative patient who could not learn the address of his new house, or know that he had read a magazine the day before (he would read the same magazine over and over with no sense of familiarity with the contents). He could not find the lawnmower that he had put away after using it yesterday, and he would do a jigsaw puzzle over and over with no knowledge of having seen it before. Yet the patient was not stupid because his IQ from before the operation was intact. Nor did he lack memory. His long-term memory was sound because all of his preoperative skills and knowledge were intact, and he had short-term retention if he rehearsed the item over and over to himself. When he stopped refreshing the item with rehearsal it quickly became unavailable for recall, however. Thus, he had all the mechanisms of a normal mind but he lacked the capability of change through experience. Barbizet (1963) calls this misfortune *amnesie de memoration* (defect of memorizing). What was interesting for memory theory is that a short-term and a long-term memory system were separately identifiable by an absence of the mechanism which transferred material from one to the other.

FIGURE 9–7
The negative recency effect. The recency items
with the best immediate recall have the poorest
delayed recall. This is another line of evidence
taken in support of a short-term memory system.

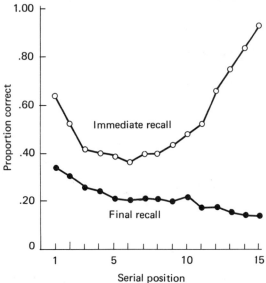

Craik, F. I. M. The fate of primary memory items
in free recall. *Journal of Verbal Learning and Verbal
Behavior*, 1970, *9*, 143–148. Reprinted by permission of
Academic Press, Inc.

Arguments against a short-term memory system

The arguments in the foregoing section flowered in the 1960s and
led to models of verbal memory like that of Atkinson and Shiffrin, but
doubts for some of the arguments began to arise along the way.

Rapid forgetting. Speedy forgetting in 30 seconds or so is no cause
to assume a special short-term memory system. In an older conceptualization of memory, where a habit would reside in memory, there could
be fast or slow forgetting depending upon strength of the habit. A
weak habit could have very fast forgetting, perhaps not unlike that
found with the Brown-Peterson paradigm (Figure 9–2). Short-term
retention does not mean short-term memory.

Memory span. There is too much of a tendency to think of memory
span as a constant, as if there was a box with seven slots in it. One
does indeed find seven or thereabouts appearing many times in the
literature of memory span, but there is also a disconcerting number
of times when it does not appear. Rather than a near constant, the
memory span is a response and like any response has multiple determi-

nants. In the first paper on memory span, Jacobs (1887) emphasized age, sex, and academic variables as correlates of memory span. Blankenship (1938), in a well-known review, cited many variables that influence memory span. Among them were characteristics of the material, rhythm and grouping of the material when it was presented, rate of presentation, time of day, practice, age, and sex. We saw in Chapter 7 that the subject is an active agent in the verbal learning process, and we saw that Atkinson and Shiffrin found a big place for conscious control processes in their theory. The subject can be expected to rehearse the material, form natural language mediators, or form images. These learning strategies are variables for retention also, and if they occur when memory span is being measured then they distort the estimate of span. Crowder (1969, p. 527) makes the perceptive observation that memory span "is not so much a restriction on what humans can *store* but instead a limit on what they can (or are willing to) *learn* in the first place."

A further difficulty for memory span is that it is affected by input-output interference—the occurrence of an item when it is presented for memorization interferes with those that are already in store (input interference), and the recall of an item also interferes (output interference). The tradition of the memory span has it that items entering and exiting short-term memory do not interfere with one another, and that all items within the memory span will be recalled. Input-output interference can go unnoticed by theorists, although the psychological literature has generous examples of it (e.g., Tulving and Arbuckle, 1963).

Units of measurement are a problem. Digits have dominated the study of memory span, but letters, nonsense syllables, words, sentences, and pictures have been used. Can seven of *anything* be held in short-term memory? Miller (1956) suggested as much by saying that any identifiable "chunk" can be the unit. Elementary units like digits can be accommodated in immediate memory, but then so can an encoding of the digits as new units. The digits 111213 fill six slots in the memory span, but they can be encoded as the words "eleven," "twelve," and "thirteen" and they are units also, now occupying only three slots. Or do the 20 letters in the 3 words signify that a memory span of seven is false and that 20 units can be accommodated? But each letter is composed of phonemes, the elementary speech sounds in the language, and if the unit is seen as a phoneme then even more than 20 units are being handled. Units, then, are in the eye of the beholder, and a memory span of seven becomes meaningless.

An alternative to the computer analogy of memory

With decline in status for a short-term memory "box," the analogy to a digital computer is strained. Craik and Lockhart (1972) and Craik

(1973) have proposed an alternative model based on *levels of processing* that does not rely on the computer analogy.

The basic idea of the Craik and Lockhart model is that there are levels of processing, and the greater the depth of processing the less the forgetting. The first level is a preliminary stage, where the processing is concerned with the sensory and physical features of the stimulus input. At a somewhat deeper level of processing the stimulus might be recognized, and at the deepest level the stimulus can engage the mature, sophisticated knowledge of the perceiver. An example of levels of processing is reading. We can handle the material at a simple sensory level, where we are aware of the printed page but do not recognize or understand the words. We can process at a somewhat deeper stage and recognize that we have experienced the material before. Or, we can process it at the deepest level where associations are aroused and where meaning is explored.

There is more to the theory, however. There is a mechanism called the central processor. The central processor is free-floating and can be diverted to any processing level. Items that are in the central processor are receiving attention, are in consciousness, and are in a kind of short-term memory of limited capacity (they do not question limited capacity as much as has been done in this chapter). There is no forgetting so long as items are in the central processor, but once the central processor is diverted from them the rate of forgetting is determined by the level of processing for the material.

It is difficult to say what will come of this level of processing idea. Maybe nothing will come of it because level of processing which determines rate of forgetting cannot always be independently determined, and so rate of forgetting cannot be predicted. This model could turn out to be mostly circular—rate of forgetting is determined by level of processing but level of processing cannot be determined until rate of forgetting is determined; the predicted and the predictor are hopelessly confounded. But the difficulty may not be all that great. We will see in the next chapter that sensory processing, which is Craik and Lockhart's first processing level, can be meaningfully studied. In Chapter 7 we discussed the research of Bobrow and Bower (1969) on natural language mediation, and they used a levels of processing approach.

Levels of processing means the degree to which we attend and think about verbal material, and operations of this sort have been used in psychology for a long time under the heading of intentional and incidental learning. Intentional learning is honestly telling the subjects what is expected of them in the task, and cooperative subjects will intentionally do as they are asked. Incidental learning diverts subjects by having them work on one task and then testing them on another to which they have been giving only off-hand attention. It is reasonable to say that intentional learning is a deeper level of processing than incidental learning, and so intentional and incidental learning should be considered a good approach for testing the levels of processing idea.

SUMMARY

This chapter has traced the concern with memory from ancient times to the present. Plato, the great philosopher of ancient Greece, viewed memory metaphorically as a wax tablet that was soft and could change with experience, and which would erode with time as a means of accounting for forgetting. In the 19th century, Hermann Ebbinghaus introduced the experimental study of verbal learning and forgetting, and the decay curve of forgetting over hours and days which he obtained was commonly cited into the 1950s as the nature of the forgetting function. In the late 1950s, however, rapid short-term forgetting in a matter of seconds was established, causing psychologists to think that memory was more complex than had been suspected. At about the same time, research established that human sensory systems had short-term forgetting characteristics also. Starting in the early 1960s, the output of research on memory vastly increased, and new theorizing about memory accompanied it.

One of the prominent theoretical viewpoints was information-processing, which emphasized the flow and transformation of data as a computer might do. The information-processing model of verbal memory ordinarily had the three compartments of sensory memory, short-term memory, and long-term memory for the storage of material to be remembered, and the subject using voluntary processes like rehearsal and imagery for the transformation and the control of the material. The short-term memory compartment, where material supposedly resides for 30 seconds or so after it has been read out of sensory memory and before being transferred to long-term memory or recalled, eventually came under criticism and its scientific usefulness has been questioned.

A new theoretical conception, intended to replace the information-processing point of view, is called levels of processing. The levels of processing viewpoint says that the more the subject operates upon the data and processes it, the greater the resistance to forgetting. Whether this new theory is rich enough to account for the many facets of memory data, and hardy enough to survive the challenge of the experimental attacks that are certain to come, remains to be seen.

REFERENCES

Adams, J. A. *Human memory.* New York: McGraw-Hill, 1967.

Atkinson, R. C., & Shiffrin, R. M. Human memory: A proposed system and its control processes. In K. W. Spence & J. T. Spence (Eds.), *The psychology of learning and motivation* (Vol. 2). New York: Academic Press, 1968, pp 89–195.

Averbach, E., & Coriell, A. S. Short-term memory in vision. *Bell System Technical Journal,* 1961, *40,* 309–328.

Barbizet, J. Defect of memorizing of Hippocampal-mammillary origin: A review. *Journal of Neurology, Neurosurgery and Psychiatry,* 1963, *26,* 127–135.

Blankenship, A. B. Memory span: A review of the literature. *Psychological Bulletin,* 1938, *35,* 1–25.

Bobrow, S. A., & Bower, G. H. Comprehension and recall of sentences. *Journal of Experimental Psychology,* 1969, *80,* 455–461.

Brown, J. Some tests of the decay theory of immediate memory. *Quarterly Journal of Experimental Psychology,* 1958, *10,* 12–21.

Conrad, R. Acoustic confusions in immediate memory. *British Journal of Psychology,* 1964, *55,* 75–84.

Craik, F. I. M. The fate of primary memory items in free recall. *Journal of Verbal Learning and Verbal Behavior,* 1970, *9,* 143–148.

Craik, F. I. M. A "levels of analysis" view of memory. In P. Pliner, L. Krames, and T. Alloway (Eds.), *Communication and affect.* New York: Academic Press, 1973, pp. 45–65.

Craik, F. I. M., & Lockhart, R. S. Levels of processing: A framework for memory research. *Journal of Verbal Learning and Verbal Behavior,* 1972, *11,* 671–684.

Crowder, R. G. Behavioral strategies in immediate memory. *Journal of Verbal Learning and Verbal Behavior,* 1969, *8,* 524–528.

Ebbinghaus, H. *Memory: A contribution to experimental psychology.* (H. A. Ruger and C. E. Bussenius, trans.). New York: Dover, 1964.

Glanzer, M. Storage mechanisms in recall. In G. H. Bower (Ed.), *The psychology of learning and motivation* (Vol. 5). New York, Academic Press, 1972, pp. 129–193.

Glanzer, M., & Cunitz, A. R. Two storage mechanisms in free recall. *Journal of Verbal Learning and Verbal Behavior,* 1966, *5,* 351–360.

Gomulicki, B. R. The development and present status of the trace theory of memory. *British Journal of Psychology Monograph Supplements,* 1953, No. 29.

Hull, C. L. *Principles of behavior.* New York: Appleton-Century, 1943.

Jacobs, J. Experiments on "prehension." *Mind,* 1887, *12,* 75–79.

Jahnke, J. C. Serial position effects in immediate serial recall. *Journal of Verbal Learning and Verbal Behavior,* 1963, *2,* 284–287.

James, W. *Principles of psychology* (Vol. 1). New York: Holt, 1890.

Miller, G. A. The magical number seven, plus or minus two: Some limits on our capacity for processing information. *Psychological Review,* 1956, *63,* 81–97.

Milner, B.   The memory defect in bilateral hippocampal lesions. *Psychiatric Research Reports,* 1959, *11,* 43–52.

Milner, B.   Amnesia following operation on the temporal lobes. In C. W. M. Whitty & O. L. Zangwill (Eds.), *Amnesia.* London: Butterworths, 1966. Pp. 109–133.

Neisser, U.   *Cognitive Psychology.* New York: Appleton-Century-Crofts, 1967.

Penfield, W., & Jasper, H.   *Epilepsy and the functional anatomy of the human brain.* Boston: Little, Brown, 1954.

Penfield, W., & Perot, P.   The brain's record of auditory and visual experience: A final summary and discussion. *Brain,* 1963, *86,* 595–696.

Peterson, L. R., & Peterson, M. J.   Short-term retention of individual verbal items. *Journal of Experimental Psychology,* 1959, *58,* 193–198.

Plato.   *The dialogues of Plato* (Vol. 4) (3rd ed.). (B. Jowett, trans.). Oxford: Clarendon Press, 1892.

Rundus, D.   Analysis of rehearsal processes in free recall. *Journal of Experimental Psychology,* 1971, *89,* 63–77.

Sperling, G.   The information available in brief visual presentations. *Psychological Monographs,* 1960, *74,* (Whole No. 498).

Sperling, G.   Successive approximations to a model for short term memory. *Acta Psychologica,* 1967, *27,* 285–292.

Tulving, E., & Arbuckle, T. Y.   Sources of intratrial interference in immediate recall of paired associates. *Journal of Verbal Learning and Verbal Behavior,* 1963, *1,* 321–334.

chapter 10

Sensory memories

THE ATKINSON AND Shiffrin model, which we examined in the last chapter was a good example of the information processing point of view that schematizes human memory as a flow of information in and out of "boxes," as a computer might be schematized. The first stop which incoming information made was sensory memory. Atkinson and Shiffrin had sensory memory as visual memory because evidence for it was available for theorizing, but they acknowledged that a sensory memory could exist for each sense modality, in principle. Since that time there has been a lively acceleration of research on sensory storage, and it has been broadened to include nonvisual sensory memories. This chapter documents the modern work on sensory memories. The remarks that were made about visual memory in the last chapter are expanded, and research on other sensory memories is presented.

VISUAL MEMORY

Basic data on visual memory

The last chapter said that the visual trace lasts but a fraction of a second, and such ephemeral phenomena require special apparatus for their study. Typically, a laboratory device called a tachistoscope is used. A tachistoscope is a device for controlling the time of visual presentation, often measured in milliseconds. A tachistoscope might be used to present a word for 50 milliseconds, or it might be used for more elaborate sequences like a word for 50 milliseconds, a blank time interval of 100 milliseconds, and a second word for 75 milliseconds.

Very brief presentation of visual events can preclude the occurrence of eye movements, which take about 200 milliseconds to get underway. There are times when it is desirable to eliminate the effects of eye movements, and the study of visual memory is one of them. A movement of the eye to a new position creates a second visual input which complicates the study of a single input.

Sperling (1960) and Averbach and Coriell (1961) were the first to define the properties of visual memory, and their research methods are in common use today. Averbach and Coriell used a tachistoscope to present a 2×8 array of randomly chosen letters for 50 milliseconds (Figure 10–1). The display went blank after the letters appeared, which

FIGURE 10–1

The visual array which Averbach and Coriell used in their research on the visual trace. Either the circle indicator or the bar marker occurred at the end of the retention interval to indicate the letter for recall.

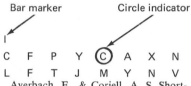

Bar marker   Circle indicator

Averbach, E., & Coriell, A. S. Short-term memory in vision. *Bell System Technical Journal*, 1961, *40*, 309–328. Reprinted with permission from *The Bell System Technical Journal*, Copyright, 1961. The American Telephone and Telegraph Company.

signified a delay interval whose length varied from trial to trial and which was the retention interval for the visual input. At the end of the delay a signal appeared at one of the positions and the subject attempted recall of the letter that had appeared at that position. Before a trial the subject never knew which 16 letters would be shown. Depending on the experiment, a bar marker above the top row or beneath the bottom row, or a circle around the letter, was used to designate the letter for recall. Figure 10–2 shows the order of events that was used. Figure 10–3 has the results of the three subjects of the experiment, and the measure of performance is percent of letters correctly named adjusted for guessing. Notice that the longer the items are in visual memory the greater the forgetting, with the trace dissipated and leveled off at about 200 milliseconds (that the curves level off at a non-zero

FIGURE 10–2
Sequence of events on a trial which Averbach and Coriell used in their research on the visual trace.

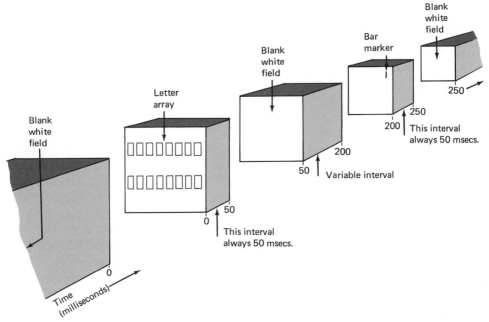

Averbach, E., & Coriell, A. S. Short-term memory in vision. *Bell System Technical Journal,* 1961, *40,* 309–328. Reprinted with permission from the *Bell System Technical Journal,* The American Telephone and Telegraph Company.

value suggests the operation of unknown long-term memory factors as a minor contaminant of the sensory memory data). Two hundred milliseconds is not a fixed constant for the visual trace. The brightness of the display makes a difference, with better performance associated with the brighter display (Keele and Chase, 1967). Averbach and Sperling (1961) also found that brightness of the screen before and after item presentation is a variable for duration of the visual trace. When the preexposure and postexposure fields are bright the trace fades rapidly, as in the Averbach-Coriell study, but when they are dark the duration of the trace is increased several times.

Another approach to the visual trace has been by Posner and his associates (Posner, Boies, Eichelman, & Taylor, 1969; Posner, 1969, 1973). Rather than the tachistoscope, which is the device commonly used by investigators of the visual trace, they used a reaction time situation. A pair of letters was presented on a display, and the speed of a judgement about them recorded. The first letter would be presented and it remained there while a second letter was introduced anywhere from zero to two seconds later. The letters could be different, could be

FIGURE 10–3

Primary findings of the experiment by Averbach and Coriell on the visual trace. The three curves represent three different subjects. The decay of the trace is complete in about 200 milliseconds.

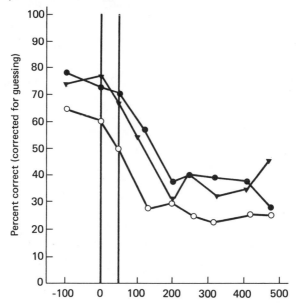

Time in milliseconds between array and bar marker

Averbach, E., & Coriell, A. S. Short-term memory in vision. *Bell System Technical Journal*, 1961, *40*, 309–328. Reprinted by permission from *The Bell System Technical Journal*, The American Telephone and Telegraph Company.

physically identical (e.g., two uppercase As), or identical in name but physically different (e.g., an uppercase *A* and a lowercase *a*). The subject had two keys, one under each index finger, which stopped a clock when released and gave the reaction time. One key was the "same" key which the subject released if the two letters had the same name. The other key was the "different" key for when the two letters were different. The main finding was that reaction time for physical identity was faster than for name identity, and the time difference between the two was a decay function that dropped to zero in about two seconds. The interpretation of these data is that the subject verbally encodes the letters whether they have physical or name identity, but the presence of the visual trace when a stimulus is first presented makes the judgement of physical identity easier. The advantage persists for about two seconds, by which time the visual trace has completely dissipated and only the verbal description remains. Two seconds is a longer persistence time than inferred from the tachistoscopic method (Averbach & Coriell, 1961). It would have been gratifying if the two different methods of measuring the visual trace had converged on the same time function. Convergence of this sort is desirable in science. Evidence for convergence on the Averbach and Coriell results is a study by Eriksen and Collins (1968) which used a different approach (see below).

Forgetting in visual memory

Why are items lost (forgotten) from the visual trace? *Trace decay* and *interference* are two theories of forgetting that have concerned psychologists for a long time (see Chapter 12), and both of them can apply to the visual trace. Trace decay is spontaneous degeneration of the trace. Time alone, in the absence of any other variables, is sufficient to produce forgetting. Forgetting is inevitable. Interference, on the other hand, ascribes forgetting to events that occur in time, not time itself. Forgetting may or may not occur, depending on the intruding events.

Trace decay. The experimental proof of trace decay requires empty time, assurance that intervening events have not occurred as a potential source of interference, and guarantees that rehearsal to offset the forgetting has not occurred. We are confident that trace decay is operating for the visual trace because the retention intervals that were studied were brief, and it is difficult to believe that interfering or rehearsal events could occur.

The experimental data by Eriksen and Collins (1968) speak explicitly for a decaying visual trace. Their approach was based on Figure 10–4. When the two nonsense patterns in Figure 10–4 are presented simultaneously with a tachistoscope the letters HOV are seen. But, if the two nonsense patterns are presented with a delay between them, then integration of the two should depend on the amount of decay that has taken place for the one presented first (if trace decay is true). When the delay is short the first nonsense pattern should still be strong, fuse readily with the second nonsense pattern, and be read easily as HOV. As the delay increases, however, the trace of the first nonsense pattern should become weaker and weaker, decreasing the chances that enough of the first nonsense pattern will be available when the second one occurs to be readable as HOV. Another variable should be the intensity of the nonsense pattern. The brighter the first nonsense pattern the stronger its visual trace and the greater the chances that it will be available when the second one occurs. Eriksen and Collins found support for both of these implications. Decay of the visual trace was definitely established, with persistence being in the same 100–200 millisecond range that has been inferred by other techniques (Averbach and Coriell, 1961).

FIGURE 10-4

The successive presentation of the two nonsense patterns at the top will result in the pattern HOV at the bottom. Experimental study of the time between presentations permitted the decay function for the visual trace to be inferred.

Eriksen, C. W., & Collins, J. F. Sensory traces versus the psychological moment in the temporal organization of form. *Journal of Experimental Psychology,* 1968, *77,* 376–382. Reprinted by permission of the American Psychological Association.

The brightness level of the first nonsense pattern also met expectations. Higher brightness levels gave the best accuracy in reading the meaningful letters.

Interference. It would be theoretically tidy if trace decay were the entire explanation of forgetting in visual memory, but the world is not so simple. Interference applies also. Averbach and Coriell found that if they designated the letter to be recalled with the circle instead of the bar marker (Figure 10–1), there was a marked decrement in recall beyond that normally found for the bar marker. Figure 10–5 shows a comparison of the circle and the bar marker. The individual recall functions for the three subjects show substantially poorer performance with the circle indicator. Somehow, the circle interferes and makes the letter less available. The two principal theories of interference in visual memory are *interruption* and *integration* (Kahneman, 1968). Interruption theory says that the second, or masking stimulus, stops the visual action of the criterion stimulus (it has been called "erasure"). Averbach and Coriell believe that erasure is adaptive in a normal, constantly changing environment because it always insures that old information is out of the visual system when new information occurs. Without erasure, they

FIGURE 10–5

Figure 10–1 had the circle indicator and the bar marker as two different ways to cue the letter to be recalled. Here we see that the effects of the two indicators are not the same for the three subjects. The circle indicator exerts an interference effect.

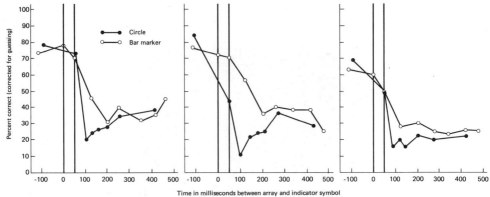

Time in milliseconds between array and indicator symbol

Averbach, E., & Coriell, A. S. Short-term memory in vision. *Bell System Technical Journal,* 1961 *40,* 309–328. Reprinted with permission from the *Bell System Technical Journal,* The American Telephone and Telegraph Company.

argue, old and new visual information would be merged and the world would be blurred. Eriksen and his associates (e.g., Eriksen and Hoffman, 1963), favor a version of integration theory where, instead of interruption, the second stimulus combines with the first and makes it less discriminable. Two stimuli, each with sufficient brightness and contrast for clear discriminability, combine and can have insufficient discriminability for clear perception.

Readout

How do we get verbal information out of the visual code so that we might operate upon it? The process is called *readout,* or scanning. The visual trace need not necessarily be translated into a verbal code. The translation could be from the visual trace to a nonverbal visual image.

Readout is a process that is poorly understood, but nevertheless there are three points to be made about it:

1. It is similar to attention; without it we have no perception of the input.

2. Readout is a matter of making contact with stable, well-learned elements in long-term memory. A digit 9 is unavailable for recall while in visual memory, and only after it has made contact with well-learned representations of the digit does a potential for recall exist. And the better the internal representation has been learned the faster and more accurate the readout. Mewhort, Merikle, and Bryden (1969), using a

tachistoscope and procedures like those of Averbach and Coriell, presented arrays of letters that were either random or an approximation to English words. The best performance was with the letters that approximated words and where well-established language habits were being used.

3. Readout is very rapid. Sperling (1963) collected data on readout and demonstrated its speed. A tachistoscope was used and the experimental variable was amount of exposure time for an array of letters before an undifferentiated visual pattern was switched on to "erase" the letters just entered into visual memory. Sperling related number of letters correctly read to exposure time, and he found that the letters could be read out at the rate of 10–15 milliseconds per letter, which is 65–100 letters per second. Eriksen and Eriksen (1971) criticize Sperling's finding because it asserts the interruption theory of interference and assumes that the undifferentiated visual pattern erases the letters from visual memory and stops their processing. If the integration theory of interference is true, however, then the letters might have had some continued availability after the undifferentiated visual pattern came on, but with reduced clarity.

AUDITORY MEMORY

There is an auditory memory system, just as there is a visual memory system, and it has been called by several names. Neisser (1967) called it *echoic memory*. Crowder and Morton (1969), and Crowder (1970, 1972), call it *precategorical acoustic storage*, where by "precategorical" they mean that the items are being held in unprocessed sensory form before being read out. Here, this auditory system will be called *auditory memory* to imply in a direct way that it is one of the sensory memories.

A main difference between visual memory and auditory memory is that items in auditory memory have a longer persistence. The decay time in visual memory is probably a fraction of a second, but the time in auditory memory seems to be much longer.

Incidents in conversation suggest the operation of auditory memory. Consider the example of a father at dinner who asks his son, "Pass the salt, please." The son continues to eat as if nothing had been said to him. After a polite waiting period the father says impatiently, "The salt!" The son passes the salt, and thinks to himself that the father is becoming cantankerous in his old age. In turn, the father thinks that the boy might be a bit deaf. The father may be ill-humored but the boy is not deaf. Psychologically, the auditory input was unprocessed in the boy's auditory memory when the salt was first requested. At the second request the boy read out his auditory trace and acted upon the information in it. It is likely that auditory memory is a significant factor in the processing of all speech. The processing of words when we listen to someone speak could be one word at a time, with each word being processed as it is heard. Alternatively, we may store segments of incoming speech in auditory memory and then process the segment as a whole. Sentences, and clauses of sentences, are integrated, meaningful units of speech, and it is reasonable that they are temporarily stored so that they may be processed as a unit.

Basic data on auditory memory

Effects of vocalization.   There is a body of experimental literature which shows that saying material aloud during learning will improve its retention, presumably because it is the condition of a strong auditory trace. Consider an experiment by Pollack (1963) on the short-term retention of digits. A subject was presented a 6-digit sequence visually, followed by reading other digits in a 12-second retention interval to prevent rehearsal before recall of the 6 was signalled. Pollack had his subjects say the six digits silently without moving the lips, silently with lips moving, or speaking aloud. The percent correct for these three conditions, respectively, was 72, 80, and 87. A clear advantage occurs when an item is vocalized during learning. Tell (1971) reported similar findings from an experiment which used the Brown–Peterson method (Chapter 9) for studying short-term verbal retention. Subjects were presented a nonsense syllable visually and were required to say it to themselves, whisper it, or say it aloud. The best recall was for the vocalized item, whispering next best, and silent study the worst of all.

Conrad and Hull (1968) are among those who have shown that vocalization produces its advantage by reducing errors in the recency part of the serial position curve (Chapter 9). Sequences of seven digits were presented visually for immediate recall in order, with either silent reading or vocalization during presentation. The results are shown in Figure 10–6. Saying the item aloud benefits recency, not primacy. The Conrad and Hull finding is replicable (e.g., Kappel et al, 1973) and is a reliable one, as a good scientific finding must be. That vocalization affects the recency part of the serial position curve has theoretical significance, as we shall see later on in this chapter when the relationship between auditory memory and short-term memory is discussed.

There is the possibility that amount of rehearsal is not equated for silent reading and vocalization, but this possibility does not upset the interpretation of data in Figure 10–6. It is generally acknowledged that subvocal rehearsal is faster than overt rehearsal, and so the expectation would be that the silent reading would be the circumstance of more rehearsal and better performance. But just the opposite is true (Figure 10–6). The vocalization condition has the best performance, so something

FIGURE 10–6

Vocalization of verbal items aids their recall. The benefit for a series is in the recency part of the serial position curve.

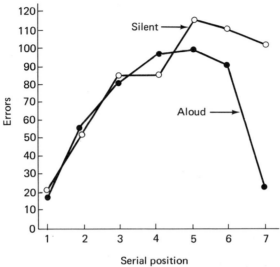

Serial position

Conrad, R., & Hull, A. J. Input modality and the serial position curve in short-term memory. *Psychonomic Science*, 1968, *10*, 135–136. Reprinted by permission of The Psychonomic Society, Inc.

else must be operating to offset the effects of uncontrolled rehearsal, presumably auditory memory.

Effects of sense modality. The second line of evidence that urges an auditory memory upon us is research on sense modality and retention, where the visual and auditory modes of presenting verbal items are compared. The evidence is that the auditory mode of presentation produces retention that is superior to the visual mode. And, the retention advantage appears in the recency part of the serial position curve, just as with vocalization. A representative experiment is by Craik (1969) (also see Madigan, 1971). His subjects had either visual or auditory presentation of 12 common words, with immediate recall. Recall was either forward from the beginning of the list or backward from the end of the list. The results are shown in Figure 10–7. The auditory mode was superior to visual in the recency part of the curve only when recall was forward. Let us consider a subject's behavior in the situation. By the time of recall, under the visual mode of presentation, there is no trace in visual memory to rely on because it lasts for only a fraction of a second, but we can expect that a subject will say the words as they are presented and make a low-level input into auditory memory (Sperling, 1967). For the auditory mode, of course, there is

FIGURE 10–7
Auditory presentation of a verbal list produces better recall than visual presentation, and the magnitude of the effect depends on whether the recall is forward or backward.

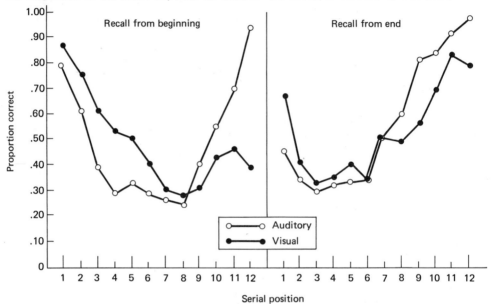

Craik, F. I. M. Modality effects in short-term storage. *Journal of Verbal Learning and Verbal Behavior,* 1968, *8,* 658–664. Reprinted by permission of Academic Press, Inc.

a full input into auditory memory. When recall is backwards, the items in auditory memory are recalled first and the low-level auditory input during visual presentation produces a sufficient auditory trace for a sizable recency effect, almost equal to that of auditory presentation. In forward recall the weak auditory trace for the visual condition has faded by the time the final items are recalled and the recency part of the serial position curve is absent. Auditory presentation, however, produces a strong trace that is available even when recall of the final items are delayed in forward recall, and the result is a recency effect. This interpretation may seem a bit involved, but it is an example of how a theoretical notion like auditory memory can unify various findings. Craik's data would be an unexplained curiosity without the assumption of auditory memory with a few seconds' persistence.

Forgetting in auditory memory

We saw that both trace decay and interference were plausible mechanisms of forgetting for visual memory, and the same applies to auditory memory.

Trace decay. Relative to visual memory, decay of the auditory trace is considered to be long, and this makes for possibilities for rehearsal and interfering events in the retention interval. How to control for rehearsal and interference is not yet defined, so what is said here about the time course of auditory trace decay must be accepted with caution.

Estimates of decay time for the visual trace are accurate when compared to estimates of the auditory trace. Crowder (1970, p. 159) has the estimate at two seconds, and Glucksberg and Cowen (1970) have it at about five seconds. About ten seconds is another estimate and, while it is long by some theorists' thinking, there are three experiments that agree on it. Consider an experiment by Estes (1973). The item for short-term retention was four consonants. The subject either vocalized each of the letters aloud or categorized it as "high" if a letter fell in the first half of the alphabet or "low" if the letter fell in the second half of the alphabet. The purpose of vocalization was to create a strong acoustic trace, and the purpose of categorization was to create suppression of the acoustic trace. The retention interval ranged from .4 to 14.4 seconds and during the interval the subjects read digits aloud as a rehearsal-preventing measure. The retention curves for the two conditions are shown in Figure 10–8, and they again show that vocalization produces superior recall. Of importance for our purposes here is the time course of the decay—the advantage for vocalization ceases

FIGURE 10–8

Vocalization improves short-term verbal recall, and the time course of the advantage lasts about ten seconds.

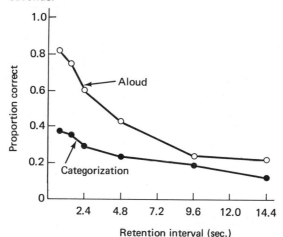

Estes, W. K. Phonemic coding and rehearsal in short-term memory for letter strings. *Journal of Verbal Learning and Verbal Behavior,* 1973, *12,* 360–372. Reprinted by permission of Academic Press, Inc.

at 9.6 seconds. Estes also examined confusion errors, or the substitution of a letter that sounds like the correct one. These acoustic confusions lasted for about 9.6 seconds also. It will be remembered that our first hint of acoustic factors in memory came from the work of Conrad (1964), and he based his analysis on confusion errors of this type. In an experiment which has its similarities to Estes' study, Tell and Ferguson (1974) found the positive effects of vocalization on retention to persist for 8 seconds, which is comfortably close to Estes' finding.

Using an entirely different approach, Eriksen and Johnson (1964) also found decay time in the ten-second range. Their subjects were comfortably seated in an experimental room with the main task of reading an interesting novel. Occasionally a brief low-intensity tone would sound, and after a delay the reading lamp would go off and the subject would indicate whether he heard the tone or not by pressing a key. The time interval between the tone and the reading lamp going off varied from zero to ten seconds. They found that detection of the tone decreased steadily from zero to ten seconds. Even at ten seconds the detection of the tone was slightly higher than chance guessing, suggesting that the duration of the acoustic trace may be even slightly longer than ten seconds.

Interference. Interference in auditory memory is best documented by the *suffix effect*. Crowder and Morton (1969) have been visible in their efforts for defining the properties of auditory memory, and they have relied heavily on the suffix effect. The experimental procedure for demonstrating the suffix effect is simple. A typical experiment has a short string of digits presented aurally for immediate recall. In a control condition the subject hears 296714385 (for example) and she tries to recall 296714385. In the experimental, or suffix condition, she hears 2967143850 and, like the control condition, must try and respond with 296714385. The only difference is that the experimental condition has a single digit added by the experimenter, and the result of it is a large recall decrement in the recency part of the curve. Typical serial position data by Crowder (1972) are shown in Figure 10–9, where the word "zero" was the suffix and a simple tone was a control event administered in the same place in the sequence as "zero." In later work, Morton, Crowder and Prussin (1971) manipulated the characteristics of the suffix in a number of ways and obtained the suffix effect consistently. The experimenter could say "Naught," "Recall," or any of a number of random words, as the suffix, and they all produced a decrement in the recall of digits. Instead of digits, lists of common words were the items for recall in another study of theirs, and the suffix was a word either similar or dissimilar in meaning to the words of the list. In both cases decrement was obtained, and it was uninfluenced by meaning. Whether the voice that spoke the suffix was the same or different from that which

FIGURE 10–9

The suffix effect, where the occurrence of a single stimulus after the item series to be remembered will interfere and produce an increase in errors. The increase occurs primarily in the recency part of the serial position curve.

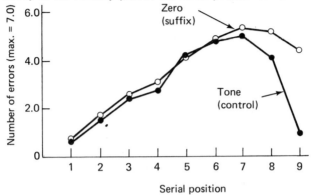

Serial position

Crowder, R. G. Visual and auditory memory. In J. F. Kavanagh and I. G. Mattingly (Eds.), *Language by ear and eye: The relationships between speech and reading.* Cambridge, Massachusetts: M. I. T. Press, 1972, pp. 251–275. Reprinted by permission of the M. I. T. Press.

spoke the items to be remembered made a difference in decrement, however. Decrement occurred for any voice, but it was greatest for the same voice. There is no doubt that the acoustic trace is subject to broad-band acoustic interference and the absence of effects from word meaning implies operation of a precategorical sensory trace before it has been read out.

Is auditory memory really short-term memory?

The information-processing point of view discussed in Chapter 9 found reasons to define a temporary store called short-term memory where incoming verbal items persist for a few seconds before forgetting processes materially weaken them. One cannot help but wonder whether short-term memory could be replaced by auditory memory as it has been defined in this chapter. Auditory memory has the power to hold verbal material for several seconds, perhaps ten seconds. Much of the data on short-term verbal retention could be accommodated by a system which holds information for about ten seconds.

Another reason for suggesting the correspondence of short-term memory and auditory memory is that the effects of vocalization, sense modality, and the suffix effect, all reveal their influence on the recency part of the serial position curve. We saw in Chapter 9 that analysts have had cause to identify recency with short-term memory. If recency is particularly sensitive to variables that define auditory memory, then perhaps it is theoretically advantageous to identify recency with auditory memory rather than a special short-term memory system. There is a theoretical economy in being able to throw out the short-term memory system as the box that lies between sensory memory and long-term memory. Science gains whenever a concept is dropped and the functions assigned to it are replaced by others. Maybe auditory memory can carry the explanatory burden for much of short-term verbal retention.

MOTOR MEMORY

Just as with vision and audition, the sensory trace of motor movement has both trace decay and interference as forgetting processes.

Trace decay. The first research statement in behalf of decay of the motor trace was a study by Adams and Dijkstra (1966). The movement was a displacement of the arm, whose distance was defined by having the blindfolded subject move a slide along a linear track until it hit a stop. Amount of practice was a variable in their experiment, and the number of times that the subject made the movement to the stop before the retention interval began defined amount of practice. One, 6, and 15 practice repetitions were made, and retention intervals of 5, 10, 15, 20, 50, 80, and 120 seconds were used. Recall after the retention interval was with the stop removed and was an attempt to reproduce the length of the movement that was made originally. The results are shown in Figure 10–10 in terms of absolute error in movement (regardless of whether it was too short or too long) at recall. There are two distinctive features to the curves. One is that error decreases as a function of amount of practice, which is a routine rehearsal effect and nothing new. The other is the rate at which error increases as a function of the retention interval. Error increases steadily over 80 seconds, at which time it levels off. Adams and Dijkstra interpret the forgetting as decay of the motor trace. Adams, Marshall, and Goetz (1972) and Burwitz (1974) have since added support to the decay interpretation with their motor retention studies.

The estimate of an 80-second motor trace has explanatory power that goes beyond motor movements. Both overt vocalization and subvocalization have motor elements accompanying them in the act of speaking (Hardyck and Petrinovich, 1970; McGuigan and Winstead, 1974), and so their motor traces would combine with the auditory trace to influence the course of short-term verbal retention and undoubtedly prolong it. Behavior can often have multiple sensory consequences, and so we must be alert to the effects of the compound. Hintzman (1967) pointed out that the auditory consequences of speech are confounded with motor

FIGURE 10–10

Motor recall error as a function of length of the retention interval and amount of rehearsal. The decay appears to continue for about 80 seconds.

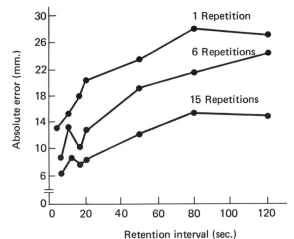

Retention interval (sec.)

Adams, J. A., & Dijkstra, S. Short-term memory for motor responses. *Journal of Experimental Psychology*, 1966, *71*, 314–318. Reprinted by permission of the American Psychological Association.

elements, and so it is hard to untangle their influences on short-term verbal retention. Untangling the auditory and motor influences is a scientific assignment that we must accept, but understanding the effects of them together in a sensory compound is an equally important assignment.

Interference. The motor trace does not appear to be different from the visual and auditory traces; it is susceptible to interference from motor events that occur in the retention interval. Kantowitz (1972) gives us an example of interference with the motor trace. Using a task like that which Adams and Dijkstra used, where position of the displaced arm had to be remembered, the subjects were required to freely move the control slide during a 20-second retention interval. The outcome was decrement in the movement that was being remembered and unmistakable evidence for motor interference. Stelmach (1974) provides a thorough review of research on motor interference.

TACTILE MEMORY

The sensory memory for touch is subject to forgetting from both interference and trace decay.

Forgetting in tactile memory

Interference. In our discussions of visual, auditory, and motor memories, we saw that events in the same modality as the criterion
material to be remembered will cause a decrement in recall, and the
same phenomenon holds for tactile memory. Abramsky, Carmon and
Benton (1971) used an electromechanical stimulator for the study of
interference (or masking, as it is often called in sensory psychology)
among tactile stimuli. The instrument stimulates the skin by dropping
and holding weights on it, which permits accurate control of the force
duration, rate of application, and area of stimulation. The stimulator
in this experiment controlled two tactile stimuli and the time interval
between them. The masking stimulus and the criterion stimulus could
occur together, the masking stimulus could follow the criterion stimulus
by 30, 60, or 100 milliseconds, or the masking stimulus could precede
the criterion stimulus by these same intervals. Thus, both forward and
backward masking were studied. The locations of the two stimuli on
the forearm were different, and the subject's task was to respond with
a footswitch upon feeling the touch of the criterion stimulus. The results
are shown in Figure 10–11, plotted in terms of an index of masking.

FIGURE 10–11

The masking (interference) function generated by the successive
presentation of two tactile stimuli. The vertical axis is an index
of masking, with a value of 1.0 being no masking. The horizontal
axis has the order and the time separation of the two stimuli.
+ means that the masking stimulus precedes the criterion
stimulus, — means that the masking stimulus follows the criterion
stimulus.

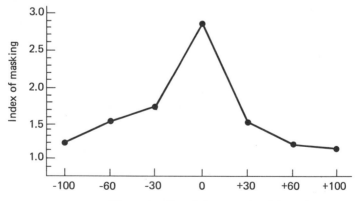

Time separation of the two stimuli (msec.)

Abramsky, O., Carmon, A., & Benton, A. L. Masking of and by
tactile pressure stimuli. *Perception & Psychophysics*, 1971, *10*, 353–355.
Reprinted by permission of The Psychonomic Society, Inc.

A value of 1.0 is no masking, and values greater than 1.0 signify masking. The greatest interference is when the two stimuli occur together, and the greater their temporal separation the less the masking. Coquery and Amblard (1973) have findings in close agreement with these. In another experiment reported in this same paper, Abramsky et al. found that masking is directly related to the force of the masking stimulus and inversely related to the force of the criterion stimulus.

Trace decay. A study by Schurman, Bernstein, and Proctor (1973) is the main one which demonstrates trace decay for tactile stimuli and reports the time function for retention. They stimulated the skin with a "von Frey hair," which is a pressure control device. The experimenter strikes the skin vertically with the hair (it is often made of nylon today), and the touch to the skin has a controlled intensity because the hair bends at a known pressure. Schurman and his colleagues touched a subject on the skin with the hair, and then one to ten seconds later touched the skin again and the subject judged whether or not the same point on the skin had been touched. One group of subjects was a counting group, where the subjects counted backward by threes from a number spoken by the experimenter at the start of each retention interval (except the one-second interval, which was too brief). And, of course, there was a no-counting group. If the subjects were remembering the location of the touch with the aid of verbal factors then counting should reduce their rehearsal and lower the accuracy of tactile judgments relative to the no-counting group.

The results are shown in Figure 10–12. The curve represents the counting and no-counting group combined because there was no difference

FIGURE 10–12
The decay function for touch lasts about four seconds.

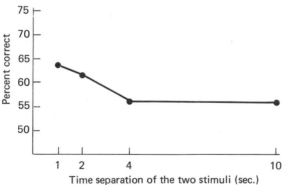

Time separation of the two stimuli (sec.)

Schurman, D. L., Bernstein, I. H., & Proctor, R. W. Modality-specific short-term storage for pressure *Bulletin of the Psychonomic Society,* 1973, *1,* 71–74. Reprinted by permission of The Psychonomic Society, Inc.

between them, demonstrating an absence of verbal factors in the judgments. The decay was largely completed in 4 seconds, although the curve does not plunge to the 50 percent chance level. Rather, it levels off slightly above 50 percent, and the investigators suggest that long-term memory factors may be present. As we shall see in the next section on olfactory memory, the intrusion of long-term memory is a problem for it also.

OLFACTORY MEMORY

Investigation of the short-term retention of odors, as another domain of sensory memory, is new. Engen, Kuisma, and Eimas (1973) tested the retention of odors over intervals of 3 to 30 seconds. They used a recognition procedure where the subject sniffed an odor on cotton held under the nose, and at the end of the retention interval an odor was again placed under the nose and the subject had to judge whether it was the same as or different from the first one. Sometimes the same odor was presented for test, and sometimes not. Using the same procedures as Schurman et al (1973) to control verbal factors, the investigators had one group that counted backwards by threes during the several retention intervals that were used in the various tests (the three-second interval was too short to allow this), and another group which did not. If the memory for odor was related to rehearsal of a verbal description of the odor, then the counting activity should offset rehearsal and decrease recollection of the odor. They used 100 different odors in the testing, ranging from the odors of household products (e.g., garlic) and chemical compounds (e.g., alcohol) to perfumes, and no evidence of forgetting was found. The subjects averaged about 80–85 percent correct for all retention intervals. Counting backwards had no effect on retention.

Why is forgetting mostly absent for the olfactory trace? An effective verbal labeling system could possibly offset the sensory forgetting, but absence of an effect for counting backwards denies this possibility. Another possibility is that the olfactory trace has long persistence. In fact, in a study on the long-term retention of odors, Engen and Ross (1973) found no forgetting over intervals ranging from an immediate test to 30 days. They concluded that trace decay is a minor factor in the retention of odors, and they find no value for interference as an explanation either (there have been no explicit studies of interference and the retention of odors, however). Odor processes in memory have a considerable degree of uniqueness, they decide, with little likelihood of interference. Uniqueness or not, it is too early to decide about odors and memory. Findings like these which do not fit the mainstream of data and theory challenge scientists, and clarifying studies will not be long in coming.

SUMMARY

The first stage of processing information for retention is one or more sensory memories. For example, visual memory alone would be involved if a verbal item is presented visually for immediate recall but, if the subject vocalizes the visually presented item before recall, then the act of speaking will add the effects of auditory, motor and tactual memories to visual memory.,

Both trace decay and interference are the processes of sensory forgetting. Trace decay is the spontaneous degeneration of the material in store, and interference is the action of new inputs in the same modality that degrade those in storage. Trace decay in visual memory may be complete in 200 milliseconds. Other sensory memories appear to have longer storage times, although their duration is the subject of investigation and sometimes controversy. Auditory memory may range from 2–10 seconds, tactual memory about 4 seconds, and motor memory as long as 80 seconds. Olfactory memory is the most recent of sensory memories to receive experimental examination, and its time characteristics are yet to be estimated.

REFERENCES

Abramsky, O., Carmon, A., & Benton, A. L. Masking of and by tactile pressure stimuli. *Perception & Psychophysics*, 1971, *10*, 353–355.

Adams, J. A., & Dijkstra, S. Short-term memory for motor responses. *Journal of Experimental Psychology*, 1966, *71*, 314–318.

Adams, J. A., Marshall, P. H., & Goetz, E. T. Response feedback and short-term motor retention. *Journal of Experimental Psychology*, 1972, *92*, 92–95.

Averbach, E., & Coriell, A. S. Short-term memory in vision. *Bell System Technical Journal*, 1961, *40*, 309–328.

Averbach, E., & Sperling, G. Short-term storage of information in vision. In C. Cherry (Ed.), *Information theory*. London: Butterworth, 1961, pp. 196–211.

Burwitz, L. Short-term motor memory as a function of feedback and interpolated activity. *Journal of Experimental Psychology*, 1974, *102*, 338–340.

Conrad, R. Acoustic confusions in immediate memory. *British Journal of Psychology*, 1964, *55*, 75–84.

Conrad, R., & Hull, A. J. Input modality and the serial position curve in short-term memory. *Psychonomic Science*, 1968, *10*, 135–136.

Coquery J.-M., & Amblard B. Backward and forward masking in the perception of cutaneous stimuli. *Perception & Psychophysics*, 1973, *13*, 161–163.

Craik, F. I. M. Modality effects in short-term storage. *Journal of Verbal Learning and Verbal Behavior*, 1969, *8*, 658–664.

Crowder, R. G. The role of one's own voice in immediate memory. *Cognitive Psychology,* 1970, *1,* 157–178.

Crowder, R. G. Visual and auditory memory. In J. F. Kavanagh and I. G. Mattingly (Eds.), *Language by ear and eye: The relationships between speech and reading.* Cambridge: M.I.T. Press, 1972, pp. 251–275.

Crowder, R. G., & Morton, J. Precategorical acoustic storage (PAS). *Perception & Psychophysics,* 1969, *5,* 365–373.

Engen, T. Kuisma, J. E., & Eimas, P. D. Short-term memory of odors. *Journal of Experimental Psychology,* 1973, *99,* 222–225.

Engen, T., & Ross, B. M. Long-term memory of odors with and without verbal descriptions. *Journal of Experimental Psychology,* 1973, *100,* 221–227.

Eriksen, C. W., & Collins, J. F. Sensory traces versus the psychological moment in the temporal organization of form. *Journal of Experimental Psychology,* 1968, *77,* 376–382.

Eriksen, C. W., & Eriksen, B. A. Visual perceptual processing rates and backward and forward masking. *Journal of Experimental Psychology,* 1971, *89,* 306–313.

Eriksen, C. W., & Hoffman, M. Form recognition at brief durations as a function of adapting field and interval between stimulations. *Journal of Experimental Psychology,* 1963, *66,* 485–499.

Eriksen, C. W., & Johnson, H. J. Storage and decay characteristics of non-attended auditory material. *Journal of Experimental Psychology,* 1964, *68,* 28–36.

Estes, W. K. Phonemic coding and rehearsal in short-term memory for letter strings. *Journal of Verbal Learning and Verbal Behavior,* 1973, *12,* 360–372.

Glucksberg, S., & Cowen, G. N., Jr. Memory for nonattended auditory material. *Cognitive Psychology,* 1970, *1,* 149–156.

Hardyck, C. E., & Petrinovich, L. F. Subvocal speech and comprehension level as a function of the difficulty level of reading material. *Journal of Verbal Learning and Verbal Behavior,* 1970, *9,* 647–652.

Hintzman, D. L. Articulatory coding in short-term memory. *Journal of Verbal Learning and Verbal Behavior,* 1967, *6,* 312–316.

Kahneman, D. Method, findings, and theory in studies of visual masking. *Psychological Bulletin,* 1968, *70,* 404–425.

Kantowitz, B. H. Interference in short-term motor memory: Interpolated task difficulty, similarity, or activity? *Journal of Experimental Psychology,* 1972, *95,* 264–274.

Kappel, S., Harford, M., Burns, V. D., & Anderson, S. Effect of vocalization on short-term memory for words. *Journal of Experimental Psychology,* 1973, *101,* 314–317.

Keele, S. W., & Chase W. G. Short-term visual storage. *Perception & Psychophysics,* 1967, *2,* 383–386.

McGuigan, F. J., & Winstead, C. L., Jr. Discriminative relationship between covert oral behavior and the phonemic system in internal information processing. *Journal of Experimental Psychology,* 1974, *103,* 885–890.

Madigan, S. A. Modality and recall order interactions in short-term memory for serial order. *Journal of Experimental Psychology,* 1971, *87,* 294–296.

Mewhort, D. J. K., Merikle, P. M., & Bryden, M. P. On the transfer from iconic to short-term memory. *Journal of Experimental Psychology,* 1969, *81,* 89–94.

Morton, J., Crowder, R. G., & Prussin, H. A. Experiments with the stimulus suffix effect. *Journal of Experimental Psychology Monograph,* 1971, *91,* 169–190.

Neisser, U. *Cognitive psychology.* New York: Appleton-Century-Crofts, 1967.

Pollack, I. Interference, rehearsal, and short-term retention of digits. *Canadian Journal of Psychology,* 1963, *17,* 380–392.

Posner, M. I., Boies, S. J., Eichelman, W. H., & Taylor, R. L. Retention of visual and name codes of single letters. *Journal of Experimental Psychology Monograph,* 1969, *79,* No. 1, Part 2.

Posner, M. I. Abstraction and the process of recognition. In G. H. Bower & J. T. Spence (Eds.), *The psychology of learning and motivation* (Vol. 3). New York: Academic Press, 1969, pp. 43–100.

Posner, M. I. Coordination of internal codes. In W. G. Chase (Ed.), *Visual information processing.* New York: Academic Press, 1973, pp. 35–73.

Schurman, D. L., Bernstein, I. H., & Proctor, R. W. Modality-specific short-term storage for pressure. *Bulletin of the Psychonomic Society,* 1973, *1,* 71–74.

Sperling, G. The information available in brief visual presentations. *Psychological Monographs,* 1960, *74,* Whole No. 498.

Sperling, G. A model for visual memory tasks. *Human Factors,* 1963, *5,* 19–31.

Sperling G. Successive approximations to a model for short term memory. *Acta Psychologica,* 1967, *27,* 285–292.

Stelmach, G. E. Retention of motor skills. *Exercise and Sport Sciences Reviews,* 1974, *2,* 1–31.

Tell, P. M. The influence of vocalization on short-term memory. *Journal of Verbal Learning and Verbal Behavior,* 1971, *10,* 149–156.

Tell, P. M., & Ferguson, A. M. Influence of active and passive vocalization on short-term recall. *Journal of Experimental Psychology,* 1974, *102,* 347–349.

chapter 11

Coding strategies and verbal memory

CHAPTER 7 described the strategies of rote rehearsal, natural language mediation, and imagery in verbal learning, and this chapter shows how research has related them to verbal memory.

ROTE REHEARSAL

Always, in studies of verbal learning and retention, it has been common to give unstructured periods of silent study for the practicing of an item. In the history of this topic there have been those who have assumed that subjects were diligently repeating the items to themselves, all earnestly applying the rote rehearsal strategy. Most assuredly some of the subjects were learning some of the items by rote, but also some were forming natural language mediators and images. Experiments which have used silent study actually do not tell us much about rote rehearsal because there is no way of knowing which of the learning strategies were being used.

The best guarantee of rote rehearsal is to have the subject repeat the item aloud. By setting a brisk pace the subject is denied time to form a natural language mediator or an image, and so can do nothing but rehearse by rote. An example of rote rehearsal by repeating the item aloud is an experiment on short-term retention by Hellyer (1962). The item to be remembered was a consonant syllable (e.g., XBJ), visually presented, which a subject had to repeat aloud either one, two, four, or eight times before reading digits as the activity that filled the retention interval and prevented informal and unwanted rehearsal. Retention intervals were either 3, 9, 18, or 27 seconds. The results are

FIGURE 11–1

Short-term retention of single verbal items as a function of number of rehearsal repetitions.

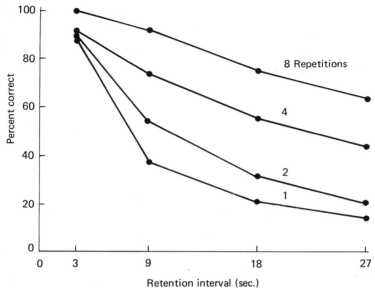

Hellyer, S. Supplementary report: Frequency of stimulus presentation and short-term decrement in recall. *Journal of Experimental Psychology*, 1962, *64*, 650. Reprinted by permission of the American Psychological Association.

shown in Figure 11–1. Forgetting steadily increased over the retention interval, but the greater the amount of rote rehearsal the less the forgetting.

In Chapter 9 we reviewed an experiment by Rundus (1971) that used the method of free recall and recorded the spontaneous rehearsal of subjects who were instructed to rehearse aloud. The Rundus study allowed inferences about short-term memory, but his procedure also allows inferences about recall and amount of overt rehearsal. A closely related study was by Rundus and Atkinson (1970), and here again there was free recall of verbal lists where the subjects rehearsed aloud and where any item in the list could be rehearsed any time and as often as desired. From the recordings of rehearsal, the amount of rehearsal given each item was tabulated and related to level of recall for each item. The results are shown in Figure 11–2 and they confirm the Hellyer experiment: Recall is positively related to amount of rehearsal. From Ebbinghaus on, the positive relationship between retention and rote rehearsal has been a secure generalization.

There is no doubt that people use the rote rehearsal strategy in everyday life because it is easy and everybody knows that it benefits retention. Rote rehearsal is undoubtedly the best, and maybe the only, strategy

FIGURE 11–2
Another example of how rehearsal repetitions benefit verbal recall.

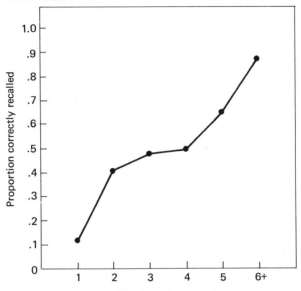

Number of rehearsals

Rundus, D., & Atkinson, R. C. Rehearsal processes in free recall: A procedure for direct observation. *Journal of Verbal Leaning and Vebal Behavior,* 1970, *9,* 99–105. Reprinted by permission of Academic Press, Inc.

in a small child's mental arsenal. Rote rehearsal is handy for adults too. Who wants to bother with finding an image or a natural language mediator for a telephone number that must be remembered for a few seconds? How much easier it is to repeat the number two or three times to yourself.

Theories of rehearsal

The number of times that a response is repeated is the empirical operation that defines rote rehearsal. Why does this operation benefit retention as it does? Some adopt a strict empirical stance and are satisfied with knowing only the positive relationship between number of rehearsal repetitions and retention, but others who are theoretically inclined ask why.

Theorists have offered four hypotheses for the effects of rehearsal:

1. Rehearsal affects the strength of the item in memory. This explanation is the oldest one, coming as it does from a habit-oriented psychology of learning. Rehearsal is positively related to habit strength, and the greater the habit strength the better the recall.

2. Rehearsal affects the number of associations or traces for an item, and these richer connections within the existing network of associations and semantic relations in memory give positive benefits for retention. In some respects, this consequence of rehearsal is very much like finding a natural language mediator. A problem with this hypothesis is that it fails to say how learning occurs in a completely naive subject who totally lacks a network of associations, like a newborn infant. The merit of the first hypothesis above is that it works for the most innocent of subjects.

3. Rehearsal affects the transfer from short-term memory to long-term memory. One presentation of an item will have it in transitory short-term memory, but repeated repetitions move it to long-term memory and increase the chances of its survival over the retention interval.

4. Assuming the trace decay theory of forgetting, Brown (1958) theorized that rehearsal refreshed the memory trace that was being weakened by decay. This hypothesis has turned out to have plausibility when we see it as implying that auditory and motor sensory memories (Chapter 10) are replenished during the act of verbal rehearsal, but the hypothesis fails to account for the relatively long-term retention that we can have when rehearsal stops. Why do we remember so long after rehearsal has ceased to replenish the sensory traces? To accommodate long-term retention, Atkinson and Shiffrin (1968), whose information-processing model of verbal memory was reviewed in Chapter 9, used Brown's idea in combination with the assumption that time in short-term memory determined the transition to long-term memory. The more the rehearsal the longer the time in short-term memory and the greater the transfer to long-term memory. The result: Rehearsal and retention are positively related, as the long-standing generalization in psychology says.

There is little direct evidence for any of these four accounts of rehearsal, although recently the Atkinson and Shiffrin version of rehearsal received a test by Craik and Watkins (1973) and it was found wanting. They used the free recall method, and after a list of words was presented they had the subjects give extra rehearsal aloud to the final four items of the list. The last four items of the list fall in the recency part of the serial position curve, which some theorists see as the reflection of short-term memory (Chapter 9). The extra rehearsal given the last four items should prolong their stay in short-term memory, increase their transfer to long-term memory, and increase their retention, according to the Atkinson and Shiffrin model. The results were negative for the model. The extra rehearsal did not benefit immediate or delayed recall. Craik and Watkins conclude for two kinds of rehearsal: Maintaining rehearsal and elaborative rehearsal. Maintaining rehearsal is in keeping with Brown's hypothesis and refreshes the fading sensory traces, it would seem. Presumably there is repeated input to auditory and motor memories, without reading them out. Elaborative rehearsal differs in that it places the item in touch with associative and semantic networks, and it is the kind of rehearsal that gives long-term stability. In effect, Craik and Watkins elected as theory a combination of sensory memory and the second of the four rehearsal hypotheses that were reviewed above. What will come of any of these hypotheses is hard to say—perhaps it is a time for watchful waiting. Psychologists are just beginning to have ideas and conduct research about rehearsal mechanisms, and it will be a while before our knowledge is sufficient for a confident stand on theory.

NATURAL LANGUAGE MEDIATION

A powerful mechanism for remembering is natural language mediation. Good advice that can be given about increasing retention is this: Form an association, any association, for the material at the time of learning. Then, try and remember the association at recall, and from it recover the material that is to be remembered. There are a number of experiments that support this generalization, and prominent ones will be reviewed. The most up-to-date review of natural language mediation for the student who wishes to pursue the topic further is by Montague (1972).

Short-term retention

Kiess (1968) compared mediated and rote learning for the short-term retention of single nonsense syllables. The experimental procedure was to present a syllable visually for three seconds, at which time the subject would report a natural language mediator if one came to her. She then read from arrays of random digits as the rehearsal-preventing activity during the retention interval, which could range from 0 (immediate recall) to 30 seconds. The recall attempt for the item and the natural language mediator, if one had been reported, followed. Association value of the syllables was a main variable of the study because Kiess hypothesized that the number and the quality of natural language mediators would depend on it. A low association value item might be ZOJ, which is unlike a word and for which an association is difficult. A high association value syllable is a word (SUN), or nearly a word (TEL), and associations should be easy for them. Kiess found association value to be related positively to the formation of natural language mediators, as expected, with natural language mediators occurring for 32 percent of low association value items and 87 percent of high association value items. The recall of natural language mediators was virtually perfect, so the forgetting of syllables could not be assigned to the forgetting of mediators. The syllable retention data appear in Figure 11–3. For items of both low and high association value, the mediated ones were recalled best, with the largest benefits going to unfamiliar items of low

FIGURE 11–3

Effect of low and high association value of nonsense syllables on short-term verbal retention. Learning was either by rote or natural language mediation.

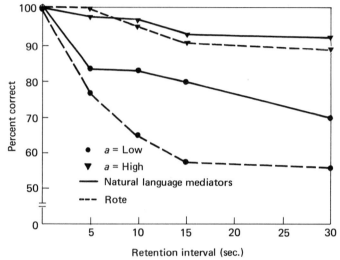

Kiess, H. O. Effects of natural language mediators on short-term memory. *Journal of Experimental Psychology,* 1968, *77,* 7–13. Reprinted by permission of the American Psychological Association.

association value. The low association value items are rare in everyday experience and the natural language mediation is a way of making them memorable by converting them to the familiar and commonplace. The high association value items are common in everyday experience, and benefit far less from natural language mediation.

Long-term retention

Montague, Adams, and Kiess (1966) conducted an experiment similar to the Kiess study but with a retention interval of 24 hours. The outcome of the two studies is similar but Montague et al. had substantial forgetting of natural language mediators whereas Kiess (1968) did not, and the consequences of it are interesting and important. A long list of 96 nonsense syllable pairs was used, and each pair was presented once. The study time for a pair in acquisition was an experimental variable, and was either 15 or 30 seconds. Mediation takes time, and the number of natural language mediators should be determined by the amount of study time for an item. The other variable was low (e.g., TAC-ZIG) and high (e.g., VET-BAT) association value of the nonsense syllables that made up the pairs, much the same as in the Kiess study. During the study of a pair, the subject wrote down a natural language mediator if one occurred to him, and at recall with the stimulus term displayed he wrote the response term of a pair if he could remember it as well as the natural language mediator if the item had been mediated originally. Recording the mediator at both learning and recall was to assess effects of forgetting the mediator at recall.

The results of the study by Montague et al. are shown in Tables 11–1 and 11–2. Table 11–1 has percent of items that had a natural lan-

TABLE 11–1

Percent of items mediated for each of four experimental conditions.

Study time (seconds)	*Association value*	
	Low	*High*
15	33	62
30	53	78

Montague, W. E., Adams, J. A., & Kiess, H. O. Forgetting and natural language mediation. *Journal of Experimental Psychology,* 1966, *72,* 829–833. Reprinted by permission of the American Psychological Association.

TABLE 11–2

Percent of items correctly recalled after 24 hours.

Experimental condition		*Item category*		
Association value	*Study time (seconds)*	*Mediator remembered*	*Mediator forgotten*	*Rote learning*
Low	15	46	1	3
Low	30	46	0	5
High	15	80	2	8
High	30	86	3	11

Montague, W. E., Adams, J. A., and Kiess, H. O. Forgetting and natural language mediation. *Journal of Experimental Psychology,* 1966, *72,* 829–833. Reprinted by permission of the American Psychological Association.

guage mediator in acquisition. As anticipated, the longer the study time the more frequently a mediator is formed. Number of mediators was also related positively to association value, which is the same finding as the Kiess experiment. Table 11–2 has the recall data. There are three categories of items in Table 11–2: (1) rote learning, where there was no natural language mediator reported, (2) mediated learning, where a natural language mediator was formed in acquisition and remembered at recall, and (3) mediated learning, where the natural language mediator was formed in acquisition and forgotten at recall. Recall after rote learning was poor, which is not unexpected because not much study time was allowed for an item. The forgetting of a natural language mediator had a devastating effect on recall, with recall level near zero. By contrast, the remembering of the natural language mediator gave an excellent level of recall, particularly for items of high association value. Natural language mediation is a very successful memorization strategy providing that the mediator is correctly recalled.

Smith (1969) extended the study by Montague, Adams, and Kiess (1966). He demonstrated that the trends in Table 11–2 for a 24-hour retention interval also hold for longer intervals. Each of Smith's three groups learned a list of nonsense syllable pairs of intermediate association value by the correction method (Chapter 7). After the criterion of learning had been met the subject wrote the natural language mediator for each item if one was used; otherwise the subject indicated rote learning. A group then had a retention interval of either one, three, or nine days, and was tested at recall for both the response term of the pair and the natural language mediator. His results are shown in Table 11–3. Notice that the very high retention which Montague et al. found when the natural language mediator was remembered holds up for at least nine days, and is not limited to the modest one-day interval which Montague et al. used. Notice, too, that the most forgetting occurred when learning was mediated and the natural language mediator went unremembered. Rote learning occupies an intermediate level of retention, also confirming Montague et al. The absolute level of the percentages in Tables 11–3 and 11–2 cannot be compared, only the relative trends, because different acquisition methods and materials were used in the two studies.

Encoding and decoding of the natural language mediator

What is the nature of learning and recall processes for mediated items? During acquisition there is mental exploration for a suitable association to encode the item, and the success of the exploration increases with longer study time and higher association value (Table 11–1). Over the retention interval the subject must not only remember the natural

TABLE 11–3
Percent of items correctly recalled after 1, 3, and 9 days.

Retention interval (days)	Item category		
	Mediator remembered	*Mediator forgotten*	*Rote learning*
1	98	70	72
3	97	62	75
9	96	17	35

Smith, W. R. Retention as a function of natural language mediation and of time. *Psychonomic Science,* 1969, *14,* 288–289. Reprinted by permission of The Psychonomic Society, Inc.

language mediator, which now embodies the item to be remembered, but also how to decode the mediator at recall and obtain the item from it. WESTERN as the natural language mediator for the pair WES-TER would be easy to decode, but THE PIZZA HAS MOZZARELLA CHEESE for the item PIZ-MOL should be difficult because the element PIZ and MOL are both imbedded in words of a sentence and somehow must be extracted and verified at recall. The column *mediator remembered* in Table 11–2 shows that this process is relatively easy for pairs of high association value, which often yield simple natural language mediators that preserve the item in a rather direct form (e.g., WESTERN for the item WES-TER) and are easily decoded into the correct response at recall. Low association value items are another matter. The level of correct recall for them is only 46 percent, indicating unsuccessful decoding of mediators even though they were successfully recalled. Undoubtedly their mediators were complex with more decoding steps (e.g., THE PIZZA HAS MOZZARELLA CHEESE for the item PIZ-MOL), and the decoding procedure could not always be remembered at the time of recall. Natural language mediation is very helpful for remembering a verbal item *if* the mediator can be remembered *and* decoded.

The best research on the decoding of natural language mediators is by Prytulak (1971). Consonant-vowel-consonant nonsense syllables were used. They were presented one at a time, and the subject wrote a natural language mediator for each one. At the completion of the series, the subject was given the natural language mediators and asked to reconstruct the nonsense syllable from each one. Table 11–4 lists various nonsense syllables, examples of natural language mediators that were formed for them, and the probability of correctly decoding the natural language mediators. The decoding probability was high when

TABLE 11-4

Examples of nonsense syllables, natural language mediators, and the probability of correctly decoding the natural language mediators.

Nonsense syllables and their natural language mediators	Probability of correct decoding
PIN-PIN	.88
LOV-LOVE	.89
WOD-WOOD	.88
FEX-FLEXIBLE	.78
PYM-PAYMENT	.71
JEK-JERK	.68
ZEL-ZEAL	.59
FOH-FOREHEAD	.57
KUT-CUT	.52
VAQ-VANQUISH	.44
KOZ-COZY	.40
YIT-YET	.36
BYF-BYE	.36
WIQ-WICK	.29
BUH-BUNCH	.24
ZYT-ZEST	.20
JYZ-JAZZ	.20

Prytulak, L. S. Natural language mediation. *Cognitive Psychology,* 1971, *2,* 1–56. Reprinted by permission of Academic Press, Inc.

the natural language mediator had the same letters as the nonsense syllable preserved in the same order. But, when the natural language mediator did not preserve all of the letters of the syllable, then the probability of correct decoding was low. Decoding the nonsense syllable LOV from the natural language mediator LOVE is easy, but decoding JYZ from JAZZ is not.

Prytulak took the natural language mediators which his subjects gave him and developed a classification system for the kind and number of transformations relating the nonsense syllable and the natural language mediator. Consider the nonsense syllable WOD. One type of transformation was the internal addition of a constant, giving the natural language mediator WORD. This is a one-step transformation. The internal addition of a constant, and the addition of a suffix, gives the natural language mediator WONDER, which is a two-step transformation. And so on. Prytulak correctly surmised that the probability of correctly decoding a natural language mediator is inversely related to the number of transformation steps, and the plot of his data for this relationship are given in Figure 11–4. Prytulak theorized that the transformations are "stacked" in the subject's mind according to complexity, and in encoding an item the subject works down the stack until finding one that applies.

FIGURE 11–4
Verbal recall as a function of the number of steps in decoding the various natural language mediators that were used.

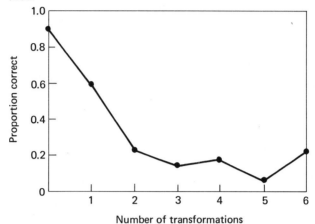

Prytulak, L. S. Natural language mediation. *Cognitive Psycology*, 1971, *2*, 1–56. Reprinted by permission of Academic Press, Inc.

The decoding of the natural language mediator to retrieve the item requires an application of the transformation in reverse.

IMAGERY

It has been said that if you doubt a role for mental imagery in memory, then ask yourself how you know the answer to this question: How many windows do you have in your house? Almost certainly you have never made a deliberate count of your windows, so a verbal response from previous experience is not available to you in memory. What is available to you are the products of sensory experience with your house, which are memory images with spatial representation. In a manner that is hardly understood at all, you stroll through the mental image of your house, as a Victorian lady through her garden, and count the windows.

The method of loci

Remembering a speech without notes has always been an art, and it was a valued art among the ancients. Before printing, all was oral communication, and effective oral communication placed a premium on the memory for events and their organization. The art of rhetoric undoubtedly was a more refined skill then than now, and the Roman Cicero (106–43 B.C.) in his treatise *De Oratore* (Cicero, translated edition, 1959), discussed the importance of memory for rhetoric. He tells a story about the discovery of the first mnemonic device:

> There is a story that Simonides was dining at the house of a wealthy nobleman named Scopas at Crannon in Thessaly, and chanted a lyric poem which he had composed in honour of his host, in which he followed the custom of the poets by including for decorative purposes a long passage referring to Castor and Pollux; whereupon Scopas with excessive meanness told him he would pay him half the fee agreed on for the poem, and if he liked he might apply for the balance to his sons of Tyndareus, as they had gone halves in the panegyric. The story runs that a little later a message was brought to Simonides to go outside, as two young men were standing at the door who earnestly requested him to come out; so he rose from his seat and went out, and could not see anybody; but in the interval of his absence the roof of the hall where Scopas was giving the banquet fell in, crushing Scopas himself and his relations underneath the ruins and killing them; and when their friends wanted to bury them but were altogether unable to know them apart as they had been completely crushed, the story goes that Simonides was enabled by his recollection of the place in which each of them had been reclining at table to identify them for separate inter-ment; and that this circumstance suggested to him the discovery of the truth that the best aid to clearness of memory consists in orderly arrangement. He inferred that persons desiring to train this faculty must select localities and form mental images of the facts they wish to remember and store those images in the localities, with the result that the arrangement of the localities will preserve the order of the facts, and the images of the facts will designate the facts themselves, and we shall employ the localities and images respectively as a wax writing tablet and the letters written on it.[1]

Cicero goes on to relate the principles of this memory technique that came to us from Simonides:

> . . . The most complete pictures are formed in our minds of the things that have been conveyed to them and imprinted on them by the senses, but that the keenest of all our senses is the sense of sight, and that consequently perceptions received by the ears or by reflexion can be most easily retained in the mind if they are also conveyed to our minds by the mediation of the eyes, with the result that things not seen and not lying in the field of visual discernment are earmarked by a sort of outline and image and shape so that we keep hold of as it were by an act of sight things that we can scarcely embrace by an act of thought. But these forms and bodies, like all the things that come under our view require an abode, inasmuch as a material object without a locality is inconceivable. Consequently (in order that I may not be

---

[1] Cicero. *De Oratore* (Books I and II.) (Rev. ed.) (E. W. Sutton and H. Rackham, trans.). Cambridge: Harvard University Press, 1959, pp. 352–355. Reprinted by permission of Harvard University Press.

prolix and tedious on a subject that is well known and familiar) one must employ a large number of localities which must be clear and defined and at moderate intervals apart, and images that are effective and sharply outlined and distinctive, with the capacity of encountering and speedily penetrating the mind; the ability to use these will be supplied by practice, which engenders habit. . .[2]

The technique has come to be known as the *Method of Loci*, based as it is on the placing of distinctive visual images of the items to be remembered in the locations of a spatial image. Retrieval at the time of recall is a matter of mentally moving through the locations of the spatial image, finding the images of the item that are stored, and recalling them. The same locations can be used repeatedly for an indefinite number of memory tasks, it is contended.

Suppose you have ten items to remember. Recollect the image of a familiar place, like your kitchen, and then imagine each of the ten items and place it in a distinctive location in the kitchen image—one in the oven, one under the sink, and so on. At recall you imagine your kitchen again, image the item in the oven, the item under the sink, etc. Cicero recommended that the imagery be vivid and distinctive, and about the only change (from unknown sources) in the Method of Loci in 2,000 years is the suggestion that images be not only vivid but bizarre. Do not simply put the item in the oven. Put it in the mouth of a one-eyed suckling pig wearing sunglasses that you imagine is cooking there.

Does the Method of Loci work? It seems far-fetched to some, and yet the Method of Loci has persisted throughout the ages and has been regularly endorsed as a memory aid (Yates, 1966). Memory experts who perform on the stage claim it as one of their techniques. Only in very recent times, however, has the Method of Loci come under experimental scrutiny. Since the mid-1960s, research on imagery has accelerated (Bower, 1970; 1972), and one thrust of research has been the Method of Loci. Some of the research has been demonstration exercises, which is a beginning, but Groninger (1971) has a suitably designed experiment on the topic.

After instructing them in the Method of Loci, Groninger sent each subject of an imagery group into a booth to work out a spatial image with 25 locations that could be easily ordered and was very familiar. A typical subject took about 10 minutes to do this, then was given a pack of 25 cards and told to learn them in order, using the Method of Loci. A control group of subjects was simply given the cards and told to learn them in order, using any method they wished. That all subjects knew the words when they came out of the booth was verified,

---

[2] Ibid, pp. 357–358.

and they were then instructed to return after one week and five weeks. On their return they were administered retention tests. The imagery group recalled 92 percent of the words in correct order after one week and 80 percent after five weeks. Corresponding values for the control group were 64 percent and 36 percent. Interviews of the control group subjects found that most of them learned the list by rote rehearsal, so the data are a comparison of imagery mediation and rote learning as mechanisms of remembering. Imagery clearly wins.

Is it necessary that images be bizarre? Nappe and Wollen (1973) gave their subjects one study-test trial on a list of 48 noun pairs. The nouns were of high imagery value as scaled by Paivio, Yuille, and Madigan (1968), so mostly they were concrete objects, like TREE or DOG, and would easily arouse an image. The study time for each pair was self-paced because a subject was required to form an image for each pair and the time for it varied from item to item and subject to subject. A memory drum was used for presentation. Written beside each pair was "common" or 'bizarre," indicating the kind of image that should be conceived for the item. Half of the items were designated "common" and half "bizarre." The act of image creation was timed, with the subject pressing a switch after forming an image. The subject then gave a verbal description of the image, which was tape-recorded, before going on to the next pair. No evidence was found that bizarre images benefitted retention. Sixty-eight percent of the pairs with common images were recalled correctly, and 65 percent of the pairs with bizarre images were correct—an inconsequential difference. Common images had the advantage of faster formation time. On the average, common images were formed in four seconds and bizarre images in six seconds. As a check on the commonness and bizarreness of the images, judges rated the decriptions of the images that had been recorded. The judges concluded that "common" images were indeed commonplace, and "bizarre" images were typically unusual.

In another experiment on bizarreness, Wollen and his associates (Wollen, Weber, and Lowry, 1972) tested the hypothesis that image bizarreness might be concealing a more fundamental variable for imagery and retention. Their example of the problem is the pair SOFA-ELEPHANT to be learned with imagery. For a bizarre image, undoubtedly you would come up with something like an elephant sitting on a sofa, but in creating this bizarre image you also have an image where the two elements are interacting. Is it bizarreness or interaction that is important? Most cases of bizarre imagery would involve interacting elements, so the two variables are confounded. Wollen et al. performed an experiment that untangled these two variables. They had their subjects learn noun pairs like PIANO-CIGAR by the study–test method, and with each pair there was one of four possible line drawings depicting the objects as bizarre or not and interacting or not. This approach deliberately gave the subject the image, rather than letting a subject freely create an image of his own. An example of the four kinds of drawings is given in Figure 11–5. The four line drawings constitute

FIGURE 11–5

Example of the four kinds of drawings that accompanied word pairs when they were presented for study in the Wollen et al. experiment. The intent was to encourage bizarre imagery or not, and interaction among image elements or not.

Noninteracting, nonbizarre

Noninteracting, bizarre

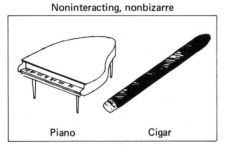
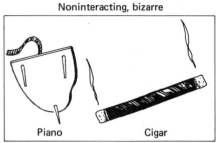

Interacting, nonbizarre

Interacting, bizarre

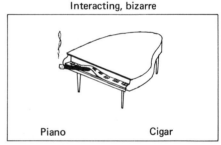

Wollen, K. A., Weber, A., & Lowry, D. H. Bizarreness versus interaction of mental images as determinants of learning. *Cognitive Psychology*, 1972, *3*, 518–523. Reprinted by permission of Academic Press, Inc.

four experimental conditions of the study where each of four experimental groups learned a list with one type of drawing. A control condition learned the pairs without a drawing. Recall was immediate, and the results indicated benefits for retention when elements of the image interacted, not when they were bizarre. In fact, bizarreness affected retention adversely, giving a level of recall below that of the control group.

At this stage of our knowledge the rule seems to be that elements of the image should be integrated in a way that is meaningful and consistent with everyday experience. For the Method of Loci it is better to place the item to be remembered in the oven amidst the baking potatoes rather than in the mouth of a one-eyed suckling pig wearing sunglasses.

The pegword method

The Method of Loci can be used to recall items in order or otherwise. You can choose to wander through your mental locations sequentially if you wish for the retrieval of items in order, or you can wander through the locations aimlessly and retrieve items in any order. When the interest is solely order information, however, there is an imagery mnemonic system called the *Pegword Method* designed solely for that purpose. You can use the Pegword Method to recall ten items in their correct order, or you could give the ninth item on request, or any other item for that matter. A nightclub memory expert, using the Pegword Method, can stand by the door, meet the guests as they enter, and then flawlessly recall all their names in a flashy display of recollection. Or, if asked, he can recall the name of the 63d person that entered the club.

The Pegword Method requires the memorization of a jingle which has the pegs on which the items to be remembered are hung with imagery. The most common jingle in use today goes on in this vein: One is a bun, two is a shoe, three is a tree," etc. After learning this mnemonic device you can take on the learning of any series of items, with imagery as the mechanism. Suppose the first word of a list is LADY. Conjure an image of a LADY sitting on a bun, as if she were a hot dog. If the second word is SCISSORS, image a scissors cutting a shoe in half. And so on. At recall you go through the jingle, and the rhyme arouses the image that you constructed for it and allows you to retrieve the item.

Does the Pegword Method work? In a laboratory evaluation, Bugelski (1968) instructed the subjects of an experimental group in the uses of imagery, thoroughly schooled them in the One-Bun mnemonic device, and then had them learn six lists of ten nouns each. There was a control group, and they were given the lists and instructed to learn them in serial order, with nothing said about imagery or mnemonic devices. The outcome was that the experimental group recalled 63 percent of the words in their correct positions, and the control group only 22 percent.

Bower and Reitman (1972) compared two ways of using the Pegword Method with the Method of Loci. The jingle they used for lists of 20 noun pairs to be learned by the Pegword Method is given in Table 11–5. A Separate Images Group learned five lists by the Pegword Method, with a separate set of images for each list. A Progressive Elaboration Group learned the five lists by the Pegword Method also, but by progressively enlarging the imagery scene around each pegword. Suppose the first words of Lists 1, 2, and 3 were HUNTER, HOUND, and FOX. The peg is "One is a gun." For List 1 the subject might get the image of a hunter with a gun, and for List 2 he might elaborate this to be

TABLE 11–5

Rhymes for numbers 1–20 used by Bower and Reitman (1972) in their experiment on mnemonic devices and imagery.

One is a gun	Eleven is penny-one, hotdog bun
Two is a shoe	Twelve is penny-two, airplane glue
Three is a tree	Thirteen is penny-three, bumble bee
Four is a door	Fourteen is penny-four, grocery store
Five is knives	Fifteen is penny-five, big bee hive
Six is sticks	Sixteen is penny-six, magic tricks
Seven is oven	Seventeen is penny-seven, go to heaven
Eight is plate	Eighteen is penny-eight, golden gate
Nine is wine	Nineteen is penny-nine, ball of twine
Ten is hen	Twenty is penny-ten, ball point pen

Bower, G. H., & Reitman, J. S. Mnemonic elaboration in multilist learning. *Journal of Verbal Learning and Verbal Behavior*, 1972, *11*, 478–485. Reprinted by permission of Academic Press, Inc.

a hunter with a gun who has his hound beside him, and for List 3 the image might be a hunter with a gun and his hound who are pursuing a fox. The idea was that separate images might cause some confusion among items of the lists and cause errors at recall, whereas progressive elaboration has all of the items of a given serial position in a single integrated image, which should lessen the chances of confusion. The third group was the Loci Group, which used the Method of Loci, with locations of the subject's own choosing. The Loci Group also used progressive elaboration. Needless to say, all groups were thoroughly pretrained in imagery and the mnemonic device assigned to them. At the end of the learning session of 1 trial per list all subjects attempted immediate recall of the 100 items of the 5 lists, and then attempted recall once again a week later. The results for items in their correct list positions are shown in Figure 11–6. The strongest variable for recall is the progressive elaboration technique, regardless of the mnemonic device used, and it remains effective over the one-week retention interval. Separate images serve the most recently learned lists reasonably well for an immediate recall test, but after a week their effectiveness is negligible. That the progressive elaboration technique yields special benefits for recall is a new and important finding.

Commentary on imagery and retention

Imagery is one of the most elusive and complex topics in the experimental psychology of learning and retention, but the topic will lose its mystery as research progresses. How one can encode and decode

FIGURE 11–6

A comparison of the Pegword Method and the Method of Loci as mnemonic devices that use imagery. Whether the image was separately conceived for each item of each list or progressively elaborated across items of the several lists that were learned, was also studied.

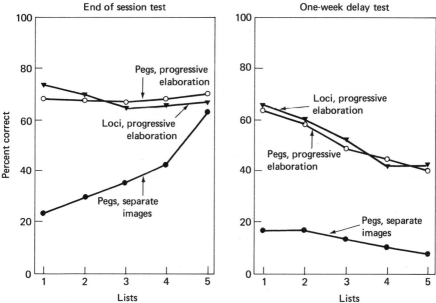

Bower, G. H., & Reitman, J. S. Mnemonic elaboration in multilist learning. *Journal of Verbal Learning and Verbal Behavior*, 1972, *11*, 478–485. Reprinted by permission of Academic Press, Inc.

the nonverbal products of past sensory experience in relation to the present learning situation is a dark jungle of unknowns. The most perplexing problem in the field of imagery is the separation and control of verbal and image influences on behavior. Many of the findings on verbal learning and retention that are ascribed to imagery can be equally ascribed to verbal mediators. Of course a staunch advocate of imagery could contend that verbal mediators are internal sequences that have images associated with them as part of their meaning, and it is these images that are the most fundamental influence for learning and retention. But to contend that images are *really* the underlying influence for learning and retention or, conversely, that verbal mediators are *really* the most influential, is sophistry, not science. A good research direction will be the study of the acquisition of new images and their influences on learning and retention, with the aim of controlling verbal factors, rather than the study of established images which can be so easily mixed in a compound with verbal mediators.

SUMMARY

Chapter 7 discussed rote rehearsal, natural language mediation, and imagery as strategies of verbal learning, and this chapter has related them to verbal memory.

Rote rehearsal is the best known strategy to insure the retention of verbal information in memory, and for good reason because it works well. Retention is related positively to the number of rote practice repetitions. The theory of rote rehearsal is underdeveloped, and only recently has a concern with it awakened. We are only beginning our understanding of why rote rehearsal benefits retention as it does.

Natural language mediation is the verbal elaboration of a verbal item to be remembered, and it is positively related to retention also. A natural language mediator is an effective mnemonic aid only if the subject remembers it and can remember how to decode it and retrieve the to-be-remembered item. When these requirements are met a natural language mediator is several times more effective than rote rehearsal.

Imagery and retention are positively related. Embodying a to-be-remembered verbal item in an image has the same requirements as the natural language mediator if it is to be effective: The image must be remembered, as must the method of decoding it.

Imagery is the oldest strategy of memorization. A technique called the Method of Loci goes back to the ancient Greeks, and it uses a spatial image in which the items to be remembered are stored. At recall the spatial image is remembered and the items are retrieved from it. The Pegword Method is another imagery device to aid retention, and it is tailored for the remembering of items in a sequence. Modern research has supported the effectiveness of these well-known mnemonic devices.

REFERENCES

Atkinson, R. C., & Shiffrin, R. M. Human memory: A proposed system and its control processes. In K. W. Spence & J. T. Spence (Eds.), *The psychology of learning and motivation* (Vol. 2). New York: Academic Press, 1968, pp 89–195.

Bower, G. H. Analysis of a mnemonic device. *American Scientist,* 1970, *58,* 496–510.

Bower, G. H. Mental imagery and associative learning. In L. Gregg (Ed.), *Cognition in learning and memory.* New York: Wiley, 1972, pp. 51–88.

Bower, G. H., & Reitman, J. S. Mnemonic elaboration in multilist learning. *Journal of Verbal Learning and Verbal Behavior,* 1972, *11,* 478–485.

Brown, J. Some tests of the decay theory of immediate memory. *Quarterly Journal of Experimental Psychology,* 1958, *10,* 12–21.

Bugelski, B. R. Images as mediators in one-trial paired-associate learning.

II: Self-timing in successive lists. *Journal of Experimental Psychology,* 1968, 77, 328–334.

Cicero. *De Oratore* (Books I and II). (Rev. ed.) (E. W. Sutton and H. Rackham, trans.). Cambridge: Harvard University Press, 1959.

Craik, F. I. M., & Watkins, M. J. The role of rehearsal in short-term memory. *Journal of Verbal Learning and Verbal Behavior,* 1973, *12,* 599–607.

Groninger, L. D. Mnemonic imagery and forgetting. *Psychonomic Science,* 1971, *23,* 161–163.

Hellyer, S. Supplementary report: Frequency of stimulus presentation and short-term decrement in recall. *Journal of Experimental Psychology,* 1962, *64,* 650.

Kiess, H. O. Effects of natural language mediators on short-term memory. *Journal of Experimental Psychology,* 1968, 77, 7–13.

Montague, W. E. Elaborative strategies in verbal learning and memory. In G. H. Bower (Ed.), *The psychology of learning and motivation* (Vol. 6). New York: Academic Press, 1972, pp. 225–302.

Montague, W. E., Adams, J. A., & Kiess, H. O. Forgetting and natural language mediation. *Journal of Experimental Psychology,* 1966, *72,* 829–833.

Nappe, G. W., & Wollen, K. A. Effects of instructions to form common and bizarre mental images on retention. *Journal of Experimental Psychology,* 1973, *100,* 6–8.

Paivio, A., Yuille, J. C., & Madigan, S. A. Concreteness, imagery, and meaningfulness values for 925 nouns. *Journal of Experimental Psychology Monograph Supplement,* 1968, *76,* No. 1, Part 2.

Prytulak, L. S. Natural language mediation. *Cognitive Psychology,* 1971, *2,* 1–56.

Rundus, D. Analysis of rehearsal processes in free recall. *Journal of Experimental Psychology,* 1971, 89, 63–77.

Rundus, D., & Atkinson, R. C. Rehearsal processes in free recall: A procedure for direct observation. *Journal of Verbal Learning and Verbal Behavior,* 1970, *9,* 99–105.

Smith, W. R. Retention as a function of natural language mediation and of time. *Psychonomic Science,* 1969, *14,* 288–289.

Wollen, K. A., Weber, A., & Lowry, D. H. Bizarreness versus interaction of mental images as determinants of learning. *Cognitive Psychology,* 1972, *3,* 518–523.

Yates, F. A. *The art of memory.* Chicago: University of Chicago Press, 1966.

chapter 12

Verbal forgetting processes

Trace decay and interference were discussed as two theories of sensory memory in Chapter 10, and for some of the sensory traces it seemed that both theories applied. Sensory memory is precategorical memory, where the material exists as the internal persistence of a sensory event until it is processed or "read out." Once having been processed, what theory, or theories, of forgetting apply? To follow Plato's metaphor (Chapter 9), what has happened to the impression that experience has placed on the wax tablet of the mind? Has time eroded it? Do new items get written on the tablet and obscure older ones? Does the presence of other tablets make a particular tablet hard to find and identify? In more modern and less picturesque terms, we ask if the response potential has decayed with time, if the learning of other responses has interfered with the to-be-remembered response, or if the response potential is in high strength but our retrieval operations have failed to recover it. These statements represent three main theories in modern psychology about the causes of forgetting: trace decay, interference, and failure to retrieve.

We say that forgetting has occurred when a performance loss is observed after a retention interval. Keep in mind that a retention loss and a memory loss are not necessarily the same. Retention could be poor because motivation has dropped or fatigue is present. Or, an item might not have been learned, so we cannot be expected to remember something that has not entered memory in the first place. But even with such variables as motivation and fatigue held constant on the learning and the retention test, and even insuring that the item has been learned in the first place, there is no guarantee that the loss of an item on the retention test means a loss from memory storage. An item may exist in full strength in memory and yet not occur at the retention test. Assume that you once learned the name of an early American patriot who invented bifocals, but now you cannot recall it when asked. The item may have disappeared totally from memory, requiring you to learn it anew, but it also could be fully in memory but inaccessible to your recovery efforts. Suppose a friend said teasingly to you, "Of course you can remember his name! Let me give you some hints. He signed the Declaration of Independence. He was a delegate to the Constitutional Convention. He was the first secretary of the American Philosophical Society." Then you say, "I've got it! Thomas Jefferson!" Your friend replies, "No! I'll give you one more hint. He invented the lightning rod." And you say, "*Now* I've got it! Benjamin Franklin!" The item was in your memory store all of the time but it took some jogging to arouse it. Subjectively, you had a strong feeling of knowing the answer. William James, founder of the first psychological laboratory in the United States, captured the feeling of retrieval very nicely:

> Suppose we try to recall a forgotten name. The state of our consciousness is peculiar. There is a gap therein; but no mere gap. It is a gap that is intensively active. A sort of wraith of the name is in it, beckoning us in a given direction, making us at moments tingle with the sense of our closeness, and then letting us sink back without the longed-for term. (James, 1890, p. 251)

Memory recovery mechanisms come under the heading of *retrieval from memory*. Having an item in memory and being able to use it are two different things. Tulving and Pearlstone (1966) distinguished between an item that is *available* in memory but not necessarily *accessible*. A book may be available in the library but if the card is missing from the catalog it may not be accessible to you.

The means by which we can access items that are full-strength in memory is a rather new research interest in psychology, and today we are less inclined to equate retention loss with memory loss. There are those who believe that once information is processed in memory it is permanently available, and remembering is entirely a matter of retrieval; everything is remembered indefinitely and in principle can be retrieved. Evidence for this strong assertion would be techniques that would allow us to remember anything we had ever learned. The abolition of forgetting would be an enormous achievement (and a mixed blessing), but there is no indication that it is attainable. The evidence at present supports an intermediate position. Feats of retrieval are certainly possible because daily we experience instances like the Benjamin Franklin example, and retrieval has been amply demonstrated in the laboratory, but there is no evidence that all forgetting is nothing more than a failure to retrieve.

Interference, trace decay, and retrieval will be developed in detail in the sections that follow. Interference and trace decay will be discussed in the same section because interference and trace decay have been played off against one another in the same experiments.

INTERFERENCE AND TRACE DECAY

The *interference theory of forgetting* is an active theory because it contends that events within time, not time itself, cause forgetting. Forgetting may or may not occur over the retention interval, depending upon the nature and frequency of interfering events. So many things are forgotten so often that some feel a need for an inevitable forgetting process independent of experience like trace decay, but interference theorists say that widespread forgetting occurs because active organisms have a high likelihood of encountering events that will interfere.

Experimental psychologists have been vigorous in their conduct of laboratory experiments on interference. Much of the research on interference has the implicit assumption that the laws that are found will explain forgetting because the interference theory of forgetting says that the laws of interference and the laws of forgetting are the same. First let us examine representative laboratory research on the laws of interference, and then examine their value as an explanation of forgetting.

Design of experiments for interference

Interference is produced by two basic kinds of experimental designs, and we refer to the retroactive interference and proactive interference that is found with the two designs.

Retroactive interference is defined as decrement in recall produced by events between learning and recall. The experimental design for retroactive interference is:

	Learning	Retention interval	Recall
Experimental group.	Learn A	Learn B	Test A
Control group	Learn A	—	Test A

If activity B causes a decrement in the test of activity A for the experimental group, relative to the test of activity A for the control group, then retroactive interference has occurred. Activity B may not always interfere; it can be neutral or even transfer positively to A on the test.

Proactive interference is defined as a decrement in recall of a criterion activity produced by events that occurred before learning of the criterion activity. The experimental design for proactive interference is:

	Prior learning	*Learning*	*Retention interval*	*Recall*
Experimental group.	Learn B	Learn A	—	Test A
Control group	—	Learn A	—	Test A

If the prior learning of activity B causes a decrement in Test A for the experimental group when compared to Test A for the control group, then proactive interference has occurred.

Most research on interference has been with lists of verbal paired associates. A standard laboratory arrangement for interference with paired-associates is to have companion pairs in the two lists A and B whose stimuli are the same and whose responses are different. For example, for retroactive interference, a pair of criterion List A could be HOUSE-TRACTOR, and its learning could be followed by the learning of an interfering List B which has the pair HOUSE-TREE. Recall of criterion List A would then follow. In the case of proactive interference, the interfering List B with HOUSE-TREE would be learned before learning and recall of criterion List A with the companion pair HOUSE-TRACTOR.

Representative data on retroactive interference

An experiment by Briggs (1957) nicely presents fundamental facts about retroactive interference. Briggs investigated amount of practice on each of the two lists, which were comprised of paired adjectives whose stimulus terms were the same and whose response terms were different. The criterion list was given 2, 5, 10, or 20 trials, and the interfering list was given either 0 (control), 2, 5, 10, or 20 trials. Recall on the criterion list followed. The amount of retroactive interference for the various conditions was measured by a formula which Briggs called Relative Retroactive Interference:

$$100 \times \frac{\text{Control group score} - \text{Experimental group score}}{\text{Control group score}}$$

The formula tells us how much an interfering list reduced recall of the criterion list below that of the control group which had only learn and recall of the criterion list. Consider an example from Briggs' own data. A control group with 20 trials on the criterion list (and no trials on the interfering list) had 9.44 responses correct on the recall test. An experimental group with 20 trials on the criterion list (and 20 trials on the interfering list) had 4.38 responses correct on the recall test. Thus,

$$100 \times \frac{9.44 - 4.38}{9.44} = 54\% \text{ Relative Retroactive Interference}$$

Brigg's results, in terms of Relative Retroactive Interference, are shown in Figure 12–1. Interference is related positively to amount of practice on the interfering list, and inversely to amount of practice on the criterion list.

FIGURE 12–1

Retroactive interference in paired associates as a function of amount of practice on the criterion list to be recalled and the interfering list.

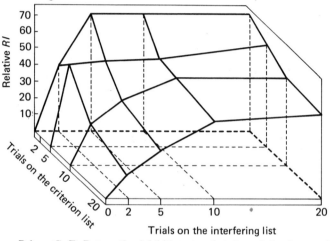

Trials on the interfering list

Briggs, G. E. Retroactive inhibition as a function of the degree of original and interpolated learning. *Journal of Experimental Psychology,* 1957, *53,* 60–67. Reprinted by permission of the American Psychological Association.

Representative data on proactive interference

Amount of prior interfering activity and length of the retention interval are two main variables for proactive interference. Data on effects of amount of prior activity are given in a study by Archer (reported in Underwood, 1957), and they are shown in Figure 12–2. Using serial learning, Archer's subjects learned lists of 12 adjectives. Each list was learned to a criterion of 1 perfect trial and recalled 24 hours later. Immediately after recall the next list was learned to criterion, then recalled 24 hours later, and so on, for 9 lists. Percent recall declined steadily from 71 percent for the first list to 27 percent for the ninth list.

An experiment by Greenberg and Underwood (1950) demonstrates the effects of both number of lists and length of the retention interval on proactive interference. There were three groups of subjects, where each group successively learned and recalled four lists of ten paired

FIGURE 12–2
Proactive interference steadily increases as a function of the number of prior lists learned and recalled.

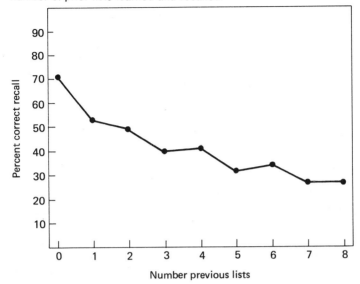

Number previous lists

Underwood, B. J. Interference and forgetting. *Psychological Review*, 1957, *64*, 49–60. Reprinted by permission of the American Psychological Association.

adjectives. The retention interval between learning and recall was the same throughout for a group, but was different for each group—10 minutes, 5 hours, and 48 hours. One group learned List 1, rested ten minutes, recalled List 1, learned List 2, rested ten minutes, recalled List 2, and so on for four lists. Other groups did the same but each with a different retention interval. The results are shown in Figure 12–3. Retention is unaffected by number of prior lists when the retention interval is brief, but sizable effects are obtained as the retention interval increases. Archer, in the experiment cited above, used a 24-hour interval, and we can see from the Greenberg and Underwood data that the interval was properly chosen to give a substantial proactive interference effect.

Single verbal items in the paradigm for short-term retention (e.g., Peterson & Peterson, 1959) exert proactive interference effects just as verbal lists do. Figure 12–4 are data from Wickens (1970), and they show increasing decrement in recall as successive items are learned and recalled. The three curves are for different classes of verbal materials: three consonants, three numbers, or three words. The retention interval was 20 seconds throughout for the words, and 10 seconds for the other two kinds of material. Regardless of kind of material, there is a buildup

FIGURE 12-3

Proactive interference as a function of number of prior lists learned and recalled, and length of time interval between learning and recall of a list (shown as curve parameter).

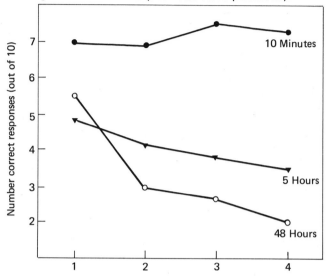

Number of lists learned and recalled

Greenberg, R., & Underwood, B. J. Retention as a function of stage of practice. *Journal of Experimental Psychology,* 1950, *40,* 452–457. Reprinted by permission of the American Psychological Association.

of interference, shown by the progressive decline in recall over trials. The buildup is rather rapid, leveling off after the initial items.

Wickens' data in Figure 12–4 show high retention for the first item and less thereafter, suggesting that there would be little short-term forgetting without prior items and the interference they produce. This possibility was thoroughly explored, and supported, in experiments by Keppel and Underwood (1962). They used trigram consonant syllables (e.g., QXF) as their verbal materials, and in one of their experiments they manipulated both the number of items learned and recalled, as well as the retention interval. Their results are shown in Figure 12–5. Retention was perfect for one item learned and recalled, where there were no prior items to exert proactive interference. But, when two or three items were learned and recalled, there is proactive interference and the rapid forgetting that we identify with short-term retention. The Keppel and Underwood study gave encouragement to the view that the short-term forgetting which Peterson and Peterson (1959), and Brown (1958), obtained was a consequence of interference.

FIGURE 12–4

Proactive interference in short-term retention as a function of the number of single items learned and recalled. Curves for three types of verbal material are shown.

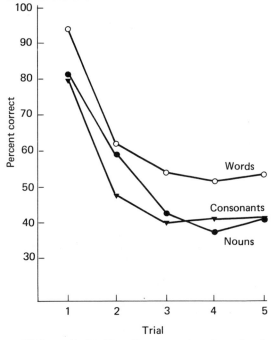

Wickens, D. D. Encoding categories of words: An empirical approach to meaning. *Psychological Review,* 1970, *77,* 1–15. Reprinted by permission of the American Psychological Association.

Theories of interference

The independence hypothesis. The first viable theory of verbal interference was McGeoch's *independence hypothesis* (McGeoch and Irion, 1952) which held that interfering responses compete at recall and the strongest one in the competition is the one that occurs. The retroactive interference data of Briggs (1957) in Figure 12–1 would be explained by the relative strengths of the responses and the dominance that they might or might not have in the competition. The greater the number of trials on List 1 the stronger the responses and the more dominance they have at recall. The greater the number of trials on interfering List 2 the greater the dominance of interfering responses and the lower the recall of List 1 which now tends to lose out in the competition.

The unlearning hypothesis. Melton and Irwin (1940) challenged the independence hypothesis and provided the germ of the new hypothesis

FIGURE 12–5

Proactive interference as a function of retention interval and number of prior items learned and recalled. Short-term forgetting is absent for one item where the conditions of proactive interference are absent.

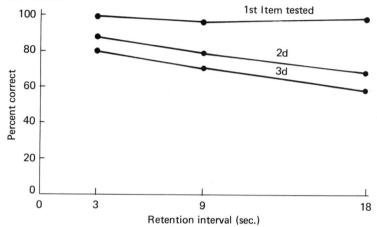

Keppel, G., & Underwood, B. J. Proactive inhibition in short-term retention of single items. *Journal of Verbal Learning and Verbal Behavior,* 1962, *1,* 153–161. Reprinted by permission of Academic Press, Inc.

of *unlearning*. Theirs was a study of retroactive interference with nonsense syllables, with amount of practice given List 2, the interfering list, as the experimental variable. List 1 decrement was directly related to the amount of List 2 learning (similar to the findings in Figure 12–1), but they found that intrusion errors, the occurrence of List 2 items during List 1 recall, accounted for only a small part of the total decrement. The rest of the response failures were omissions. With a strict competition theory like the independence hypothesis, the expectation would be for most or all failures of List 1 responses to be accounted for by occurrence of List 2 responses that have become dominant in the competition. The failure for this effect to appear caused Melton and Irwin to suggest that some of the decrement is attributable to unlearning, or a kind of permanent weakening of List 1 responses.

Underwood (1948a, 1948b), borrowing from principles of animal learning and conditioning, gave the unlearning idea researchable content by turning it toward extinction (Chapter 2). The 1940 statement of unlearning by Melton and Irwin was important for its challenge to the independence hypothesis, but Underwood gave the idea substance by identifying it with extinction and saying that the phenomena of extinction, such as spontaneous recovery, should be an outcome of the interference process also. Unlearning, as an extinction process, goes like this: In a retroactive interference paradigm an interfering List 2 is interpolated between the learning and recall of a criterion List 1. On the assumption that verbal learning involves a kind of "reinforcement" process, and the withdrawal of the reinforcement an "extinction" process, the learning of List 2 brings a strengthening of its responses and the extinction of List 1 responses which also occur in the situation but which are not reinforced. If time is interpolated between the end of List 2 learning and List 1 recall, spontaneous recovery of the extinguished List 1 responses should occur. Figure 12–6 shows the learning and extinc-

FIGURE 12–6
Idealized performance curves for the unlearning explanation of retroactive interference.

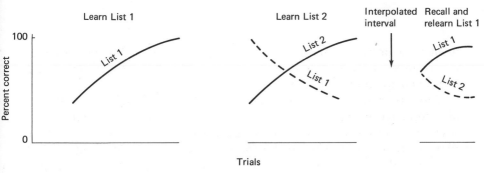

tion processes in a retroactive interference paradigm. Figure 12–6 shows that the learning of List 2 brings the extinction of List 1. At recall, where List 1 is tested, the responses of List 1 that have not been extinguished and List 2 compete for occurrence. Extinction and competition cause the decrement in List 1 recall that represents retroactive interference. List 1 is being reinforced in the test trials, however, and it rapidly becomes dominant over List 2 as its relearning progresses. The longer the time interval between the end of List 2 learning and the test of List 1, the greater the spontaneous recovery, up to a point, and the less the interference decrement.

Proactive interference has the same logic (Figure 12–7), but here the paradigm has the interfering List 2 learned first, followed by the learn and recall of List 1 after an interval. The learning of List 1 brings the extinction of List 2, and List 2 experiences spontaneous recovery in the interpolated time interval. Lists 1 and 2 compete at recall, causing a decrement in List 1 recall and the decrement that represents proactive interference. The longer the time interval the greater the recovery (up to a point) of List 2 and the greater the List 1 decrement because List 2 will carry greater weight in the response competition at the test. Notice that response competition carries the entire burden of the decre-

FIGURE 12–7
Idealized performance curves for the unlearning explanation of proactive interference.

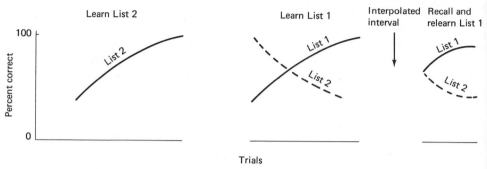

ment in a proactive interference paradigm. List 1, whose performance is measured at the test, has undergone no extinction; its only decrement is from competition with List 2.

The strongest evidence for the unlearning hypothesis was in studies of retroactive interferences which showed that decrement decreased as amount of original learning on List 1 increased (increased resistance to extinction), and that decrement increased as the learning of List 2 increased (increased extinction of List 1) (e.g., Briggs, 1957—see Figure 12–1; Barnes and Underwood, 1959).

The bright days for the unlearning hypothesis began to dim when investigators had trouble documenting spontaneous recovery, which was so basic to the unlearning hypothesis. Evidence was found for recovery in some studies but not others. The second area of trouble came with the notion that the learning of List 2 in a retroactive interference paradigm brought about the extinction of List 1. One approach to this topic reasoned, and correctly, that a hastening of unreinforced elicitation of List 1 responses during the learning of List 2 should hasten the extinction of List 1 and increase List 1 decrement at recall. Several approaches were tried, and in general the outcome was a failure to affect amount of decrement. One approach was to use instructions to encourage a relaxed attitude toward the occurrence of List 1 responses during the learning of List 2, with the assumption being that the greater the number of unreinforced List 1 responses the greater the List 1 extinction (Keppel and Rauch, 1966; Houston and Johnson, 1967). The instructions worked to increase the number of List 1 responses during List 2 learning, as the investigators wanted, but the decrement in List 1 recall was unaffected. Studies on this theme undermined the use of extinction as a mechanism in the interference situation which, in turn, undermined the unlearning hypothesis.

Lastly, a source of difficulty for the unlearning hypothesis was a failure to find evidence for competition. Under paced recall, where there is a time limit for responding (often two seconds was used), there should be a heightening of the competitive relationship between List 1 and List 2 responses. Subjectively, in a competitive situation of this sort, the subject is trying to decide which response to give and, while trying to decide, time runs out and an omission error is recorded. Under unpaced recall, however, where time is virtually unlimited, decrement should be less because the subject has time to resolve the response conflict. A major prediction is that proactive interference, which relies entirely on competition, should be eliminated with unpaced recall. Comparisons of paced and unpaced recall, however, found no appreciable effect on the amount of decrement in the retroactive interference paradigm (Houston, 1969; Howe, 1967; Keppel and Zavortink, 1968), or proactive interference paradigms (Houston, 1967; Koppenaal, 1963; Postman, Stark, and Fraser, 1968; Wipf and Webb, 1962).

The differentiation hypothesis. The *differentiation hypothesis* asserts that when two lists are learned in an interference paradigm their recallability depends on the discriminability, or differentiation, of the lists. During learning, verbal items become organized into one or more sets in terms of their perceived dimensions, and this structure is a determiner of behavior. The list might be a set, for example, and subjects learn to differentiate the responses of the different lists that have been learned. When differentiation has occurred subjects "know" the appropriateness of a response that they are about to give for the set that is required. Decrement at recall in an interference paradigm occurs because responses are not sufficiently differentiated or because responses cannot be judged as appropriate for the required set in the time that is available (perhaps because differentiation is poor). Thune and Underwood (1943) first hinted at the differentiation hypothesis, and shortly thereafter Underwood (1945) made a major statement of it.

Consider the retroactive interference paradigm to illustrate a recent version of the differentiation hypothesis (Postman, Stark, and Fraser, 1968). The learning of List 1 brings a capability for knowing that the items belong to the set called List 1. As this capability for identifying List 1 responses develops, the subject uses the capability to discriminate List 1 responses from preexperimental responses and gives only the List 1 responses. Similarly, knowledge of the permissible List 2 responses develops and the subject comes to inhibit the List 1 responses which are now inappropriate. At List 1 recall the assumption is made that the set to give List 2 responses is dominant and prevents the subject from immediately switching on the set of List 1 responses and giving them. The result is decrement in List 1 recall. However, the inertial tendency to persist with List 2 responses decreases because the differentiation of List 1 and List 2 decreases with time. The need for this assumption comes from studies of spontaneous recovery and of output priority where the tendency to give List 2 responses before List 1 responses at recall decreases in the time interval between the end of List 2 learning and List 1 recall. Postman, Stark, and Fraser (1968) regard the dominance of the most recently learned items as short-lived and a matter of minutes, but changes in List 2 dominance have been observed for up to two days (Adams, 1962; Silverstein, 1967). Notice that the specific associative weakening effects of List 2 responses on their sister responses in List 1, which is the heart of the unlearning hypothesis, is not required by the differentiation hypothesis.

Positive evidence for the differentiation hypothesis can be found in Figure 12–1 which shows that retroactive interference decreases with practice on List 1 and increases with practice on List 2. A well-practiced List 1 is clearly differentiated from List 2, and so its responses can be readily identified and given at recall. A well-practiced List 2 increases the difficulty of identifying responses from the List 1 set at recall, and so decrement is substantial. While wholly consistent with the differentiation hypothesis, this line of evidence does not discriminate the differentiation hypothesis and the unlearning hypothesis. The effects of amount of List 1 and List 2 practice on interference decrement is also consistent with the unlearning hypothesis, as we have seen.

From the differentiation hypothesis we would expect decrement in retroactive interference experiments to be related positively to the similarity of the two lists because as similarity increases the items of the lists should be increasingly difficult to differentiate. Studies of retroactive interference and free recall, where the items of List 1 and List 2 were in the same or different conceptual categories (e.g., both lists had items representing fish, birds, cars, and flowers, or they did not), found greater decrement when conceptual categories were the same (Shuell, 1968; Strand, 1971; Watts and Anderson, 1969; Wood, 1970).

The proactive interference paradigm also plays a part in support of the differentiation hypothesis. Using paired associates, Underwood and Ekstrand (1967) and Underwood and Freund (1968) employed the method of repeated pairs as a way of affecting list differentiation. When the two lists have pairs in common, they should be more difficult to discriminate, according to the differentiation hypothesis, and this is what Underwood and his associates found. Common pairs increased the amount of proactive interference.

Proactive interference in short-term retention situations, requiring learn and recall of single verbal items, has also produced evidence for the differentiation hypothesis. Figure 12–4 shows a progressive buildup of proactive interference, and this finding is comfortable with the differentiation hypothesis because as more items are stored in memory, the greater the difficulty of discriminating a particular item for recall. A variation in this kind of study has given us the phenomenon of *PI release*, and it has been studied extensively in recent years; it bears on the differentiation hypothesis also. In a series of learn-recall trials all of the items on all of the trials but the last will be the same class (e.g., all numbers) in a *PI* release experiment. Proactive interference steadily builds as long as the item class remains the same, but when it is shifted on the last trial (e.g., letters) the amount of proactive interference decreases, sometimes dramatically. In explanation, as more and more items of the same class are learned they become increasingly difficult to differentiate, and so recall is less and less successful. But, when the type of item is changed, its comparative uniqueness makes it easily differentiable and recall level increases. Wickens (1973) reports a *PI* release experiment where four learn-recall trials were given. The fourth trial was the shift trial on which all subjects learned and recalled words which were the names of fruits. Wickens' groups differed in the material learned over the first three trials. One group learned items that were names of vegetables, a second group names of flowers, a third group names of meats, and a fourth group names of professions. The idea of the experiment was that *PI* release should be directly related to the similarity of attributes between the items of the first three trials and the fruit items which all subjects learned and recalled on Trial 4. The results appear in Figure 12–8. Vegetables and fruits both grow in the ground and both can be eaten. They have two attributes in common and so they have the most decrement of all; they are difficult to differentiate. Meat and fruit have one attribute in common—both can be eaten, and their decrement is less. Flowers and fruit also have one attribute in common—they both grow in the ground, and they have about the same level of recall as meat. Fruit has no attributes in common with professions, and so recall is high because differentiation is easy.

All things considered, the differentiation hypothesis has an edge over the unlearning hypothesis as an explanation of interference. The weakness of the unlearning hypothesis is that its principles were drawn from animal learning and conditioning, and these principles probably have little to do with verbal learning and retention. Any scientific law has its limits (Chapter 6), and it appears that the unlearning hypothesis overextended the principles of animal learning and conditioning.

How good is the interference theory of forgetting?

Interference is easily obtained in the laboratory, but this does not prove that forgetting is caused by interference. How do we test the interference theory of forgetting? Because the interference theory of forgetting is an active theory that depends upon the occurrence of events

FIGURE 12–8
Effects on proactive interference of shifting to a common category, fruits, as a function of category on the first three trials (shown as the curve parameter).

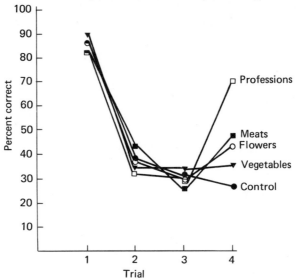

Wickens, D. D. Some characteristics of word encoding. *Memory & Cognition,* 1973, *1,* 485–490. Reprinted by permission of The Psychonomic Society, Inc.

to interfere with the ones stored in memory and being remembered, a straightforward test would be to eliminate the interfering events. If the theory is true, elimination of interfering events should eliminate forgetting. There have been two approaches to this issue. One approach has been to have subjects sleep during the retention interval on the assumption that sleep insulates the subject from incoming stimuli, some of which can interfere. Comparisons are with subjects who have been awake during the retention interval. The other approach has been to compare implications of the interference and trace decay theories of forgetting in the same experiment to see whether time or events in time is the variable for forgetting. Pitting rival hypotheses against one another in an experiment is a standard approach in science.

The sleep studies. The implications of sleep during the retention interval for the interference theory of forgetting was seen over 50 years ago by Jenkins and Dallenbach (1924), and they performed a classic experiment. Two subjects were used, and they had serial learning of many lists of nonsense syllables over many sessions as they participated in all experimental conditions. The variables of the experiment were retention intervals of one, two, four, and eight hours, and whether the

interval was spent asleep or awake. The results are presented in Figure
12–9. Over twice as many items were recalled after sleeping than after
being awake. Sleep did not totally eliminate forgetting, but it was effective enough to be in comfortable agreement with the interference theory

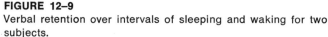

FIGURE 12–9
Verbal retention over intervals of sleeping and waking for two
subjects.

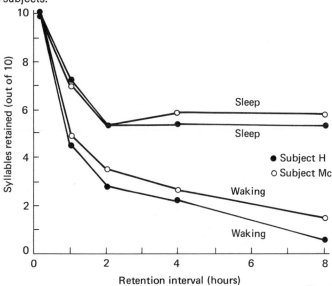

Jenkins, J. G., & Dallenbach, K. M. Obliviscence during sleep
and waking. *American Journal of Psychology*, 1924, *35*, 605–612.
Reprinted by permission of the University of Illinois Press.

of forgetting. The investigators conclude that ". . . forgetting is not
so much a matter of the decay of old impressions and associations as
it is a matter of the interference, inhibition, or obliteration of the old
by the new" (Jenkins and Dallenbach, 1924, p. 612). Subsequent experiments (Ekstrand, 1967, 1972; Barrett and Ekstrand, 1972; Spight, 1928;
Van Ormer, 1932) also found the superiority of sleeping over waking
for retention, and so the original Jenkins-Dallenbach finding is a secure
one in psychology.

An example of the more modern work that is consistent with Jenkins
and Dallenbach is a study by Ekstrand (1967). His subjects learned
a list of verbal paired associates and recalled them after eight hours.
One group of subjects slept during the retention interval and the other
was awake. The awake subjects had 73.3 percent correctly recalled,
while the sleep subjects had 84.6 percent correct. This is not a large

difference, but it is significant and in the same direction as the one that Jenkins and Dallenbach found. The same finding of a small but significant difference in favor of subjects who slept was found in another study by Ekstrand (1972) also.

If the interference theory of forgetting is empirically true, and if sleep is a mechanism that denies registry of incoming stimuli, then there should be no forgetting whatsoever for subjects who sleep in the retention interval. This was not so however, because all of the studies found some forgetting for sleeping subjects, although not much forgetting in some cases. These findings could mean several things:

1.   Interference theory is not the sole explanation of forgetting. Some forgetting occurs even with sleep controlling all of the interference, so some other factor must contribute to the forgetting.

2.   The sleep experiments conform to a retroactive interference paradigm where the interfering material, presumably controlled by sleep, occurs between the original learning and recall of the criterion material. The sleep experiments, however, do not control for proactive interference from prior learned material and it could be the cause of decrement for the sleeping subjects. The Jenkins and Dallenbach study is particularly vulnerable to this criticism because the two subjects learned and recalled many lists, and so most lists had the learn and recall of other lists preceding them. The Ekstrand experiments were better in this respect. Ekstrand had his subjects learn and recall only one list, and the forgetting was considerably less as a result. Nevertheless, some forgetting was found.

3.   Sleep is an imperfect mechanism for controlling potentially interfering events; it is not the control that investigators think it is. The brain is a mass of electrical activity, and one way to monitor it is with the electroencephalogram (the EEG) which is a record of the brain's electrical activity obtained from electrodes pasted on the skull (the EEG was discussed in Chapter 4 under biofeedback). For our purposes here the EEG is informative about levels of sleep and wakefulness. Figure 12–10 shows the different kinds of EEG records that are obtained for the awake-sleep continuum, and during a night's sleep we fluctuate in and out of these levels. Simon and Emmons (1956), in an experiment on learning while asleep, presented their sleeping subjects with questions and answers at five-minute intervals while simultaneously recording the EEG to determine the level of sleep at the time the item was presented. An example question was: "In what kind of store did Ulysses S. Grant work before the war?" and its answer was: "Before the war, Ulysses S. Grant worked in a hardware store." Upon waking the questions were presented again and the recall of answers was attempted. Recall was about 80 percent correct for state *a* (Figure 12–10), about 50 percent correct for state *b*, about 5 percent correct for state *c*, and

FIGURE 12–10

The EEG function is related to depth of sleep. The function was used in an experiment that related verbal learning and recall to depth of sleep.

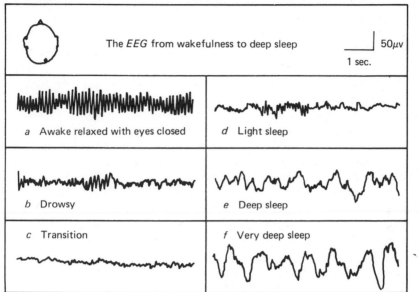

The EEG from wakefulness to deep sleep   50μv
1 sec.

a   Awake relaxed with eyes closed

d   Light sleep

b   Drowsy

e   Deep sleep

c   Transition

f   Very deep sleep

Simon, C. W., & Emmons, W. H. Responses to material presented during various levels of sleep. *Journal of Experimental Psychology,* 1956, *51,* 89–97. Reprinted by permission of the American Psychological Association.

essentially zero-level recall thereafter. For their purposes, Simon and Emmons saw the data as denying the popular thesis that learning can occur while asleep because they found no learning in states *d, e* and *f* where sleep was genuinely present. For the purpose of analyzing sleep and memory experiments, their data emphasize that sleep is imperfect for insulating subjects from potentially interfering stimuli because subjects sometimes fluctuate into semi-awake states that allow stimuli to be received and responses to be learned.

Interference versus trace decay. Interference has received the bulk of the research effort, but the trace decay theory of forgetting has had intuitive appeal for psychologists and it is common to find it assumed in their theorizing. Empirical tests of the trace decay theory of forgetting have been few in the history of experimental psychology, however, and for good reason. One reason is that a strict test of the theory requires empty time in which the memory trace can spontaneously decay, and this is very difficult to achieve. An organism has experiences in time, and the experiences could be the cause of forgetting rather than time itself, which is support for the interference theory of forgetting. Another reason is that humans deliberately offset verbal forgetting processes with self-generated rehearsal in the supposedly empty retention interval. Only a very few experimental studies have faced trace decay head-on.

Waugh and Norman (1965) did an experiment that compared trace decay and interference as explanations of short-term retention, and trace decay fared poorly in the comparison. An item for the subject was auditory presentation of a list of 16 digits, with the last digit called the probe digit, accompanied by a tone. The probe digit had occurred only once before in the list, and the subject's task was to give the digit that immediately followed it in the series. The experimental variables were presentation rate and amount of retroactive interference. Presentation rates were one digit per second and four digits per second. Interference was defined by the number of digits between first occurrence of the probe digit in the list and its second occurrence as the signal for recall. The critical comparison between trace decay and interference theories was this: If trace decay accounts for forgetting in the time between a digit's presentation and its recall, then time, as defined by presentation rate, should be the controlling variable, but if interference is the primary determiner of forgetting then the number of intervening digits should be the determining factor. The results are shown in Figure 12–11. There

FIGURE 12–11

Short-term retention as a function of number of interfering items between learning and recall and item presentation rate. Only number of interfering items affected recall, which supports the interference theory of forgetting.

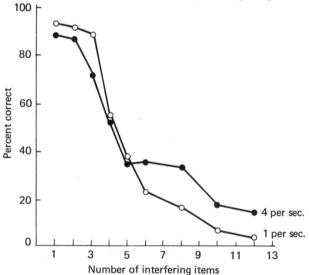

Waugh, N. C., & Norman, D. A. Primary memory. *Psychological Review*, 1965, *72*, 89–104. Reprinted by permission of the American Psychological Association.

are no differences between the rates of presentation; only number of intervening digits controls performance at recall. Events in time, not time itself, control the amount forgotten.

One potential problem for the Waugh and Norman experiment is that rehearsal is uncontrolled and could be a variable to conceal evidence of trace decay. If trace decay is true, then the rate of one digit per second should produce more forgetting than the four-per-second rate. But, the rate of one digit per second also allowed more time between digits for rehearsal, which would offset the greater amount of forgetting that was expected. There was no evidence for or against rehearsal, however. Only four experienced, sophisticated subjects were used over and over again in the various experimental conditions, and this weighs against the rehearsal argument because the subjects undoubtedly were informed about rehearsal and its upsetting effects for the issues at hand. An experimental design that used many naive subjects would have run a greater risk of contamination from rehearsal.

Reitman (1971) undertook the difficult assignment of defining procedures for empty time to test for trace decay theory. In addition, in other conditions of the same experiment, she had filled time for an evaluation of the interference theory of forgetting. A short-term retention paradigm was used. The task was 3 words presented visually, and their recall was solicited after a 15-second retention interval. The procedure for creating empty time over the retention interval was based on a study by Johnston et al. (1970) who found that the storage, rehearsal, and recalling of words during the concurrent performance of a motor task caused a worsening of motor performance. Reitman reasoned that if a difficult discrimination task filled the retention interval there should be a drop in its performance relative to a control condition if verbal rehearsal occurred, and so she filled the inverval with a tonal detection task where a brief 1,000-cycle tone occurred in a background of white noise. The subject had to press a key every time the tone was heard. A control condition had the same task requirement except that the words did not have to be recalled and so there was no incentive to rehearse. A comparison of the experimental and control conditions on the tonal detection task failed to turn up evidence of rehearsal. Post-experimental interviews with the subjects also failed to find evidences of rehearsal. Reitman had some of the retention intervals without any tones for detection whatsoever so, if there was no rehearsal and no tones in the interval, then a state of empty time existed and trace decay theory could be legitimately tested. She found retention to be 93 percent over the empty retention interval, which is very high. Thirteen of her 18 subjects had 100 percent correct. Reitman properly accepted her findings as evidence against trace decay theory because there was almost no forgetting over empty time. In other conditions Reitman had verbal interference in the retention interval, where the discrimination task was detection of the syllable "toh" in a tape recording among a background series of "doh." Sometimes the subjects had to report the detection by pressing a key, as in the tonal detection task, and sometimes the reporting was saying "toh" aloud. The percent correct recall for silent and vocal syllabic detection tasks was, respectively 77 percent and 70 percent. Reitman concluded in behalf of the interference theory of forgetting and against trace decay theory. Interpolated verbal events degraded verbal recall, so events that fill time, not time alone, causes forgetting.

Constructive criticism of research by peers commonly occurs in a science, but constructive self-criticism is the best of all. Reitman (1974) conducted a second series of experiments where she raised two questions about her 1971 work. One question concerned a ceiling effect. The three words could have been learned so well that the forgetting was not sufficient to cause much incorrect responding. In her 1974 study Reitman had the learning of five words rather than three, and it was expected that the increased difficulty of the task would increase the chances of errors due to forgetting. The second question dealt with undetected rehearsal. Reitman had technical objections to her method of detecting rehearsal, and in the 1974 study she introduced improvements. The results were that she found evidence for *both* trace decay and interference. In the absence of rehearsal there was significant forgetting over time, which is evidence for trace decay. And, as in the 1971 study, there was interference from the interpolation of simple verbal materials in the retention interval.

RETRIEVAL FROM MEMORY

Retrieval from memory can occur in the absence of any apparent stimulus, as when we sit alone in a room and try to recall the name of Socrates' wife. Virtually all of psychological research on retrieval, however, has used a stimulus at recall as means of arousing forgotten responses to recall. This approach is called *prompting*, and the reminder stimulus is called the *prompter*. We all know that a prompter can be stimulating for forgotten responses. Recalling the name of the invincible character of movies and television who sheds his ordinary identity and clothing in a phone booth is helped if we know that his name begins with S. Recalling is helped even more if we know that awe-struck people look into the sky and say. "It's a plane, it's a bird, it's S_____!" Recall is cue-dependent in the prompting situation, and undoubtedly psychologists are attracted to prompting for the study of retrieval because prompters can be systematically manipulated and related to the efficacy of recall.

Representative studies of prompting

The study that stimulated the interest in retrieval mechanisms in recent years was by Tulving and Pearlstone (1966). They presented their subjects with lists of nouns that were blocked according to conceptual categories and accompanied by the category name in each case. For example, during presentation the category word WEAPONS would be followed by the words BOMB and CANNON, and the category word PROFESSIONS would be followed by ENGINEER and LAWYER. Only instance words like BOMB, CANNON, ENGINEER, and LAWYER needed to be learned and remembered; the subjects were instructed not to learn the category words. Free recall was used, and it was either cued with the category names present as prompters, or noncued. Prompting produced superior recall.

A well-known study on prompting is by Bahrick (1969), and it is a good example of the systematic manipulation of the characteristics of prompters. Bahrick had his subjects learn a list of 20 paired associates (Table 12–1), most of them simple nouns, to a criterion of six correct anticipations. One experimental variable was retention intervals of zero (immediate test), two hours, two days, or two weeks. The retention test had unprompted recall followed by prompted recall. Unprompted recall was a version of standard recall for paired associate learning—the subjects were given a written list of the stimulus terms and were asked to recall as many of the response terms as they could. Prompted recall followed, to see how many of the items that were forgotten on the unprompted test could be stimulated by prompters. The stimulus term for each missed item was presented again and, while the subject looked at it and tried to recall the response again, the experimenter spoke a prompter word. The main experimental variable was the associative relationship between the response terms and the prompters. Table 12–1 illustrates. The prompter probability levels in the table represent the probability that the response term will be elicited by the prompter in a free association test. In a free association test the prompter is presented as a stimulus and a subject gives the first response that comes to mind. For example, in Table 12–1, the word VELVET elicits the response BLUE 3 percent of the time in a free association test. The word SKY, on the other hand, elicits BLUE 66 percent of the time. Bahrick presumed, and correctly, that the probability relationship between the prompters and the response terms of the list would be an effective variable for retrieval. His results are shown in Table 12–2. Notice how the percentage of correct recall for the responses that had been forgotten in the unprompted test increases steadily as a function of prompter level. Prompter Level 5 has a high associative relationship between the

TABLE 12-1

The paired-associate list and the five levels of prompters in the Bahrick study.

Paired-associate list		Prompter probability levels									
		1 (.01-.08)		2 (.09-.21)		3 (.23-.36)		4 (.38-.59)		5 (.61-.86)	
Stimulus	Response										
Time	Blue	Velvet	.03	Grey	.10	Green	.28	Azure	.58	Sky	.66
Shoe	Book	Print	.02	Comic	.15	Read	.35	Chapter	.59	Author	.65
Top	Chair	Leg	.02	Cushion	.09	Upholstery	.36	Furniture	.48	Table	.74
Went	Telephone	Pole	.04	Extension	.17	Communication	.33	Dial	.59	Operator	.75
Tile	Girl	Child	.03	Cute	.18	Feminine	.26	Coed	.54	Boy	.86
Party	Water	Desert	.05	Drink	.12	Swim	.23	Fountain	.44	Faucet	.68
Abrupt	Flower	Tree	.03	Fragrant	.15	Pollen	.35	Rose	.54	Blossom	.82
Effect	Car	Journey	.01	Travel	.15	Gas	.23	Truck	.56	Trolley	.80
Sign	Cold	Weather	.05	Winter	.15	Cough	.25	Ice	.56	Hot	.83
Sorry	Fast	Scurry	.03	Haste	.10	Accelerate	.24	Rapid	.40	Slow	.80
Wing	Sleep	Trance	.05	Retire	.14	Pillow	.30	Dream	.47	Doze	.81
Fail	Horse	Pasture	.03	Chariot	.20	Ranch	.30	Gallop	.58	Saddle	.79
Bitter	Light	Sun	.04	Electric	.16	Switch	.34	Dark	.54	Illuminate	.71
Marble	Flag	Parade	.04	Patriotism	.18	Salute	.23	Allegiance	.38	Banner	.65
Business	Short	Small	.02	Stocky	.10	Stubby	.34	Tall	.52	Long	.77
Sack	Fire	Forest	.04	Smoke	.14	Burn	.27	Extinguish	.50	Blaze	.64
Rope	School	Teacher	.08	Institute	.15	Academy	.32	Elementary	.55	Prep	.75
Door	Talk	Pep	.06	Whisper	.13	Speech	.26	Chatter	.51	Converse	.83
Stop	Apple	Banana	.07	Pie	.12	Fruit	.30	Orchard	.56	Cider	.61
Window	Doctor	Hospital	.08	Prescription	.21	Medicine	.36	Nurse	.53	Physician	.71
	Average		.041		.141		.295		.521		.743

Bahrick, H. P. Measurement of memory by prompted recall. *Journal of Experimental Psychology*, 1969, 79, 213–219. Reprinted by permission of the American Psychological Association.

TABLE 12-2

Percent of correct recall on the prompted recall test as a function of the time interval between training and testing.

Prompter level	Retention interval				Overall average
	0	2 hours	2 days	2 weeks	
1	18	16	13	14	15
2	48	43	42	27	40
3	49	55	58	50	53
4	79	72	62	63	69
5	86	80	70	80	79
Overall average	56	53	49	47	

Bahrick, H. P. Measurement of memory by prompted recall. *Journal of Experimental Psychology*, 1969, *79*, 213–219. Reprinted by permission of the American Psychological Association.

prompters and the responses, and the subjects recover an impressive 70–86 percent of their forgotten responses.

The experiment by Tulving and Pearlstone (1966) had the prompter presented along with its corresponding items to be remembered during learning so they can be encoded together. There is currently a controversy about the importance of this operation. Certainly the Bahrick (1969) study has strong evidence for retrieval when prompters are presented only at the retention test. How necessary is it to encode the to-be-remembered item with respect to its prompter at the time of storage (learning)? The controversy on this topic was highlighted in an experiment by Tulving and Osler (1968).

The Tulving and Osler study either had prompters present at both learning and recall, absent at learning and recall, or present at learning or recall. The method was free recall, and the to-be-remembered items was a list of 24 simple words. The words were presented visually with a slide projector. A to-be-remembered item was in capital letters and a prompter item was shown along with it in lower case letters when the experimental condition required it. The prompters were low associates of the to-be-remembered words in a free association test. Recall was in writing, and in a prompting condition the prompters were written on the page. The results are shown in Table 12–3. There is a very considerable benefit that results when the prompter is present at both learning and recall, but not otherwise.

It is not easy to reconcile the Tulving and Osler experiment with the experiment by Bahrick (1969), which was discussed above. Bahrick had his prompters, which were effective, present only at recall, not learning. One possibility for reconciliation, which is far-fetched, is that the prompters in the Bahrick study were *really* present during learning be-

TABLE 12–3
Effect on recall of the presence or absence of a prompter at learning and/or recall. Entry is percent correct for a list of 24 words.

| | *Learning condition* | |
Recall condition	Prompter absent	Prompter present
Prompter absent.	44	36
Prompter present	35	62

Tulving, E., & Osler, S. Effectiveness of retrieval cues in memory for words. *Journal of Experimental Psychology,* 1968, *77,* 593–601. Reprinted by permission of the American Psychological Association.

cause the subjects thought of associations of a to-be-remembered item when it was presented and the prompter, being an associate of the item, had a chance of being among them.

Theories of prompting

The study of retrieval in general, and prompting in particular, is a comparatively new undertaking in experimental psychology, and it is not surprising that theories abound and that there is little basis for choosing among them at the present time. Mainly, there are three theories that are attractive to psychologists today. They are mental search, generation-recognition, and encoding specificity.

A cognitive view of memory places considerable stock in *mental searching* as a retrieval process for recovering the item that is recalled. Earlier it was discussed how failure of recall does not necessarily mean that an item is lost from memory but rather that it could be viewed as a failure to find the item in memory. Now mental searching should not be conceived as an exhaustive search of all possible responses that are stored in memory because, undoubtedly, there must be millions of them (depending on how one defines a response). Mental searching, then, is among a finite set of responses. One way to view a prompter is that it controls the response set to be searched, and the reason a prompter is effective is that it narrows the response set and makes the search efficient. The better the prompter the smaller the set and the more readily the response is recovered.

Another explanatory possibility is *generation-recognition theory.* The gist of generation-recognition theory is that the prompter is a stimulus for generating responses, and if the to-be-remembered response is among them the subject will recognize it and recall it. The better the prompter the closer its relationship to the to-be-remembered response and the greater the chances of generating the to-be-remembered response. In more detail, Bahrick (1969) describes this theory in explanation of his own data:

> It is assumed that a prompter is likely to produce a hierarchy of responses as a result of past learning, and that one of these responses is likely to be the training response. The subject is thus unburdened of the search strategy involved in unaided recall tasks. He continues to produce responses associated with the prompter until he can identify one of them as the response presented during training. This portion of the prompted recall task functionally approximates a recognition task.[1]

Notice that response generation and recognition are the core of this theory, and that the theory explicitly denies mental searching as a retrieval mechanism.

The third visible theory of prompting is the *encoding specificity hypothesis* (Thomson and Tulving, 1970; Tulving and Thomson, 1973). This hypothesis says that no prompter, no matter how strongly associated with the to-be-remembered word, will be effective unless it is encoded along with the to-be-remembered word at the time of learning. The basis of this hypothesis, and its empirical strength, lies in the study by Tulving and Osler (1968), which was reviewed above, and a follow-up study by Thomson and Tulving (1970). A difficulty with the hypothesis is that it cannot gracefully account for the findings of Bahrick (1969) where prompters were present only at recall and were very effective. The encoding specificity hypothesis emphasizes events at the time of learning, but Bahrick's data seem best explained by the generation-recognition hypothesis which has the retrieval mechanism operating at the time of recall.

Concluding remarks on theories of forgetting

Theories of forgetting have been under scrutiny since ancient times, and we still have a long way to go. Thousands of experiments on memory have been conducted, and they document many determinants of retention, but rather few studies bear incisively on why forgetting occurs. This chapter has documented difficult problems involved in testing theories of forgetting, and so it is not surprising that the topic is unresolved.

What is the status of the three basic theories of forgetting? There is no doubt that interference is a factor in forgetting. Interference is an empirical fact, and when it occurs in the retention interval it can

---

[1] *Journal of Experimental Psychology*, 1969, 79, 217. Reprinted by permission of the American Psychological Association.

be a force for decrement. Similarly, there is no doubt that failure to retrieve is a factor in forgetting. Material can lie in memory in full strength but be impotent until the proper conditions of retrieval occur. Trace decay has the flimsiest support of all, but the recent studies of Reitman have given it more credibility than ever before. Future research will have to establish more explicitly whether Reitman's domain was pre-categorical sensory memory as was discussed in Chapter 10, or deeper levels of memory.

The three theories of forgetting are discussed as if they are independent, and we act as if our scientific assignment is the choosing of one of them as a single, powerful cause of all forgetting. The thinking of the past has definitely been of this sort, but today it seems as if all of the three theories have some truth. If so, then we are faced with a new question of dependence among the three processes. Does interference cause the irreversible weakening, and thus a kind of decay, of the stored information? This would be a version of the unlearning hypothesis of interference if true. Does interference increase the difficulty of retrieval? Does trace decay increase the difficulty of retrieval? It may turn out that retrieval is a secondary process, derivable from interference and decay. An understanding of trace decay, interference, and retrieval as separate processes has not been easy, and an understanding of their interactions will be formidable.

SUMMARY

What are the theories to account for the forgetting of material that has passed through sensory memory and into more stable memory beyond? Three theories of forgetting prevail today: interference, trace decay, and failure to retrieve.

The interference theory of forgetting says that events which occur between the learning of material and its recall, or before the learning of material and its recall, can interfere with the material and induce decrement in its recall. Interference is an active theory of forgetting—without interfering events there is no forgetting.

Trace decay theory says that the trace of the material stored in memory spontaneously decays with time, like the spontaneous disintegration of radioactive materials. Trace decay is a passive theory—forgetting occurs regardless of the subject's experience. Experimental comparisons of trace decay and interference theories weigh toward interference, although there is evidence that trace decay and interference are both valid.

The notion of retrieval says that the material resides at full strength in memory, and that a recovery operation is required for recall. Failure to retrieve as a theory of forgetting says that the material exists at full strength in memory but that we cannot find it and so cannot recall it.

The common method of studying retrieval is prompting, where a cue is presented at recall in an effort to stimulate otherwise unavailable material. Experiments generously support the concept of retrieval.

It would be scientifically elegant if one of the three theories accounted for all of the circumstances of forgetting that we know, with the other two failing to qualify. Unfortunately, elegance does not prevail—there is evidence for all three theories. Interference theory and failure to retrieve are both sound explanations of forgetting. Trace decay has the weakest direct support of all, but some support for it does exist.

REFERENCES

Adams, S.　Temporal changes in the strength of competing verbal associates. Unpublished doctoral dissertation, University of California, Berkeley, 1962.

Bahrick, H. P.　Measurement of memory by prompted recall. *Journal of Experimental Psychology*, 1969, 79, 213–219.

Barnes, J. M., & Underwood, B. J.　"Fate" of first-list associations in transfer theory. *Journal of Experimental Psychology*, 1959, 58, 97–105.

Barrett, T. R., & Ekstrand, B. R.　Effect of sleep on memory: III. Controlling for time-of-day effects. *Journal of Experimental Psychology*, 1972, 96, 321–327.

Briggs, G. E.　Retroactive inhibition as a function of the degree of original and interpolated learning. *Journal of Experimental Psychology*, 1957, 53, 60–67.

Brown, J.　Some tests of the decay theory of immediate memory. *Quarterly Journal of Experimental Psychology*, 1958, 10, 12–21.

Ekstrand, B. R.　Effect of sleep on memory. *Journal of Experimental Psychology*, 1967, 75, 64–72.

Ekstrand, B. R.　To sleep, perchance to dream (about why we forget). In C. P. Duncan, L. Sechrest, & A. W. Melton (Eds.), *Human memory: Festschrift in honor of Benton J. Underwood*. New York: Appleton-Century-Crofts, 1972, pp. 59–82.

Emmons, W. H., & Simon, C. W.　The non-recall of material presented during sleep. *American Journal of Psychology*, 1956, 69, 76–81.

Greenberg, R., & Underwood, B. J.　Retention as a function of stage of practice. *Journal of Experimental Psychology*, 1950, 40, 452–457.

Houston, J. P.　Proactive inhibition and competition at recall. *Journal of Experimental Psychology*, 1967, 75, 118–121.

Houston, J. P.　Paced vs. unpaced paired-associate recall. *Psychonomic Science*, 1969, 17, 235–236.

Houston, J. P., & Johnson, O.　Unlearning and the unreinforced evocation of first-list responses. *Journal of Verbal Learning and Verbal Behavior*, 1967, 6, 451–453.

Howe, T. S. Unlearning and competition in List-1 recall. *Journal of Experimental Psychology,* 1967, 75, 559–565.

James, W. *Principles of psychology* (Vol. 1). New York: Holt, 1890.

Jenkins, J. G., & Dallenbach, K. M. Obliviscence during sleep and waking. *American Journal of Psychology,* 1924, 35, 605–612.

Johnston, W. A., Greenberg, S. N., Fisher, R. P., & Martin, D. W. Divided attention: A vehicle for monitoring memory processes. *Journal of Experimental Psychology,* 1970, 83, 164–171.

Keppel, G., & Rauch, D. S. Unlearning as a function of second-list error instructions. *Journal of Verbal Learning and Verbal Behavior,* 1966, 5, 50–58.

Keppel, G., & Underwood, B. J. Proactive inhibition in short-term retention of single items. *Journal of Verbal Learning and Verbal Behavior,* 1962, 1, 153–161.

Keppel, G., & Zavortink, B. Unlearning and competition in serial learning. *Journal of Verbal Learning and Verbal Behavior,* 1968, 7, 142–147.

Koppenaal, R. J. Time changes in the strengths of A-B, A-C lists; Spontaneous recovery? *Journal of Verbal Learning and Verbal Behavior,* 1963, 2, 310–319.

McGeoch, J. A., & Irion, A. L. *The psychology of human learning.* 2nd ed. New York: Longmans, Green, 1952.

Melton, A. W., & Irwin, J. M. The influence of degree of interpolated learning on retroactive inhibition and the overt transfer of specific responses. *American Journal of Psychology,* 1940, 53, 173–203.

Peterson, L. R., & Peterson, M. J. Short-term retention of individual verbal items. *Journal of Experimental Psychology,* 1959, 58, 193–198.

Postman, L., Stark, K., & Fraser, J. Temporal changes in interference. *Journal of Verbal Learning and Verbal Behavior,* 1968, 7, 672–694.

Reitman, J. S. Mechanisms of forgetting in short-term memory. *Cognitive Psychology,* 1971, 2, 185–195.

Reitman, J. S. Without surreptitious rehearsal, information in short-term memory decays. *Journal of Verbal Learning and Verbal Behavior,* 1974, 13, 365–377.

Shuell, T. J. Retroactive inhibition in free-recall learning of categorized lists. *Journal of Verbal Learning and Verbal Behavior,* 1968, 7, 797–805.

Silverstein, A. Unlearning, spontaneous recovery, and the partial-reinforcement effect in paired-associate learning. *Journal of Experimental Psychology,* 1967, 73, 15–21.

Simon, C. W., & Emmons, W. H. Responses to material presented during various levels of sleep. *Journal of Experimental Psychology,* 1956, 51, 89–97.

Spight, J. B. Day and night intervals and the distribution of practice. *Journal of Experimental Psychology,* 1928, 11, 397–398.

Strand, B. Z. Further investigation of retroactive inhibition in categorized free recall. *Journal of Experimental Psychology,* 1971, 87, 198–201.

Thomson, D. M., & Tulving E. Associative encoding and retrieval: Weak and strong cues. *Journal of Experimental Psychology,* 1970, *86,* 255–262.

Thune, L. E., & Underwood, B. J. Retroactive inhibition as a function of degree of interpolated learning. *Journal of Experimental Psychology,* 1943, *32,* 185–200.

Tulving, E., Osler, S. Effectiveness of retrieval cues in memory for words, *Journal of Experimental Psychology,* 1968, 77, 593–601.

Tulving, E., & Pearlstone, Z. Availability versus accessibility of information in memory for words. *Journal of Verbal Learning and Varbal Behavior,* 1966, *5,* 381–391.

Tulving, E., & Thomson, D. M. Encoding specificity and retrieval processes in episodic memory. *Psychological Review,* 1973, *80, 352–373.

Underwood, B. J. The effect of successive interpolations on retroactive and proactive inhibition. *Psychological Monographs,* 1945, *59,* (3, Whole No. 273).

Underwood, B. J. Retroactive and proactive inhibition after five and forty-eight hours. *Journal of Experimental Psychology,* 1948, *38,* 29–38. (a)

Underwood, B. J. 'Spontaneous recovery' of verbal associations. *Journal of Experimental Psychology,* 1948, *38,* 429–439. (b)

Underwood, B. J. Interference and forgetting. *Psychological Review,* 1957, *64,* 49–60.

Underwood, B. J., & Ekstrand, B. R. Studies of distributed practice: XXIV. Differentiation and proactive inhibition. *Journal of Experimental Psychology,* 1967, *74,* 574–580.

Underwood, B. J., & Freund, J. S. Effect of temporal separation of two tasks on proactive inhibition. *Journal of Experimental Psychology,* 1968, *78,* 50–54.

Van Ormer, E. B. Retention after intervals of sleep and waking. *Archives of Psychology,* 1932, No. 137.

Watts, G. H., & Anderson, R. C. Retroactive inhibition in free recall as a function of first- and second-list organization. *Journal of Experimental Psychology,* 1969, *81,* 595–597.

Waugh, N. C., & Norman, D. A. Primary memory. *Psychological Review,* 1965, *72,* 89–104.

Wickens, D. D. Encoding categories of words: An empirical approach to meaning. *Psychological Review,* 1970, 77, 1–15.

Wickens, D. D. Some characteristics of word encoding. *Memory and Cognition,* 1973, *1,* 485–490.

Wipf, J. L., & Webb, W. B. Supplementary report: Proactive inhibition as a function of the method of reproduction. *Journal of Experimental Psychology,* 1962, *64,* 121.

Wood, G. Organization, retroactive inhibition, and free-recall learning. *Journal of Verbal Learning and Verbal Behavior,* 1970, 9, 327–333.

chapter 13

Recognition

Recognizing a face that you saw yesterday or a tune that you heard last week is not a matter of recalling and repeating a response that has been reinforced or rehearsed before. Recall is the production of a response, but *recognition* is deciding that a stimulus has been experienced before. Recognition is sometimes used to mean the correct naming of a stimulus, like saying "Mona Lisa" when shown the painting. This latter kind of "recognition" is of no concern here (perhaps it is better called "identification").

METHODS FOR STUDYING RECOGNITION

Two basic methods are used for studying recognition behavior in the laboratory, and both have their parallels in everyday life. One is called the method of single stimuli and the other is called the forced-choice method. Both methods first expose the subject to stimuli, and then in a later recognition test they require the subject to identify the old stimuli from among new ones that have not been presented before. The two methods differ in the conduct of the recognition test.

Method of single stimuli

The *method of single stimuli* has the old and new stimuli mixed and presented one at a time at the test, with the subject judging each one "old" or "new." The difficulty with this procedure is response bias where, in the extreme case, a subject can identify all of the old stimuli correctly or fail to identify any of them. With an indifferent attitude the subject can designate all of the stimuli as "old." All old stimuli will be correctly classified, and 100 percent recognition will be scored. All new stimuli will be falsely classified, however. Or, the subject can be very conservative and designate all stimuli as "new" because she is not absolutely sure that she has experienced the old stimuli before. All new stimuli will be correctly classified, but all old stimuli will be falsely classified and the percent recognition score will be zero. For these reasons percent correctly recognized is an inadequate measure for the method of single stimuli. The percent correct measure assumes that an item is either recognized or not, or that we guess at it. By using a statistical correction for guessing we get a "true" measure of recognition but in failing to consider response bias the percent correct measure fails to account for a subject's motivation to respond with laxness or strictness. Commonly, the motivation level which the subject adopts is called her *criterion*. An approach which abandons the percent correct measure and its assumptions, and which takes criterion into account, is the *Theory of Signal Detection*.

Psychologists first applied the Theory of Signal Detection to psychophysics, which is the study of sensory behavior. Suppose that a subject is asked to detect a weak tone whenever it occurs. For a long time percent of tones detected was the measure of sensory capability used. However, the measure has the same problem as in a recognition memory experiment: It reflects the sensory capabilities of the auditory system, as the users believed, but it also reflects response bias, which was not considered. The subject may adopt a strict criterion and respond only when she is absolutely sure that a tone has occurred, or she may adopt a lax criterion and respond almost with indifference to the presence of a tone.

The application of the Theory of Signal Detection to recognition memory assumes that items are arranged on a psychological continuum of familiarity, and the subject sets a criterion along the continuum and uses it at the recognition test to make a decision about an item's familiarity. If the feeling of familiarity is greater than the criterion the item will be judged "old" but, if it is less, the judgment is "new."

The essence of the Theory of Signal Detection is that the subject is in a decision situation. A stimulus on the recognition test is either old or new, and the subject must decide "old" or "new" for each stimulus on the basis of her criterion. In the Theory of Signal Detection the percentage of "old" responses to old stimuli are called "hits," and the percentage of "old" responses to new stimuli are called "false alarms." With the level of familarity fixed, these two measures will covary as a subject varies her criterion. If a subject has a conservative criterion she will be very sure of herself before she says "old," so she will have a low hit rate and a low false alarm rate. As the criterion relaxes, both the hit rate and the false alarm rate will increase.

The valuable feature of the Theory of Signal Detection is that it separates the sensory-perceptual aspect of the situation from the criterion, and provides a separate measure of each. The index of sensory-perceptual discrimination is called d' (d prime), and the index of the criterion is called β (beta). These are easily calculated (Hochhaus, 1972; Theodor, 1972). For a more complete discussion of Signal Detection Theory and recognition memory, see Parks (1966), Banks (1970), and Lockhart and Murdock (1970).

Forced-choice method

The *forced-choice method* is a method of multiple stimuli, where a test item is an old stimulus presented along with one or more alternative new stimuli and the subject must discriminate the old one from the new ones. Here the response bias problem does not apply because the subject is forced to discriminate the features of the several stimuli of the test and declare one as "old." Percent correct is a valid measure of recognition when the forced-choice method is used. One would think that the forced-choice method gives a "true" measure of recognition, but this is not so because different ways of defining the test will give different recognition levels. Both the similarity and the number of alternative stimuli affect recognition accuracy.

It is an intuitive expectation that the more similar the alternatives the lower the level of recognition because the similarity makes it more difficult to discriminate an old item from the alternatives. This intuitive expectation has been borne out in several experiments (Bahrick & Bahrick, 1964; Bruce & Cofer, 1965; Klein & Arbuckle, 1970). Moreover, the greater the number of alternatives in the forced-choice test the lower the recognition level (Bruce & Cofer, 1967; Underwood, 1972). From his data on the recognition of words, Underwood (1972) estimated that each alternative in the forced-choice test adds 6 percent to recognition error. Measurement problems such as these would seem an uncomfortable handicap for research on recognition, but they are not. Even though a measure is not a "true" one it can be used for relative comparisons. Thus, we can study the recognition of stimuli over different retention intervals just so long as all subjects use, say, the forced-choice method where each test item has four stimuli.

RECOGNITION OF COMPLEX STIMULI

Visual stimuli

A truly remarkable feature of human memory is the excellence of recognition. You see a Rembrandt painting and know that you have seen it before (your teacher in second grade had it above her desk). As a child you ride on a train pulled by a steam locomotive, and 20 years later you recognize the chug and wheeze of the engine when you hear it on a radio program. All of us are convinced of our great powers of recognition when we reflect on incidents such as these, but more convincing than informal recollection is psychological research which shows that everything we ever suspected about our powers of recognition can be true. .

Research on the recognition of complex visual stimuli like pictures has been going on for a long time in psychology (e.g., Strong, 1912, 1913), but none of the early investigators seemed particularly aware of the high capacity which the human has for visual recognition. Recent investigators, however, have become sensitive to the human power of recognition and have pursued it in their experiments. Shepard (1967) allowed his subjects one chance to study at their own pace 612 pictures of common scenes (they averaged 6 seconds per picture), and then gave them an immediate recognition test. They averaged 97 percent correct. Nine out of 35 subjects had 100 percent correct. An even more remarkable demonstration is by Standing, Conezio, and Haber (1970). They had their subjects study 2,560 slides of common scenes for 10 seconds each over 2 to 4 days. In an immediate retention test the group averaged 90 percent correct, with one subject having a score of 95 percent correct. The poorest subject, if he can be called that, correctly recognized 85 percent of the pictures.

All of this is very impressive, and conforms to a great deal of our everyday experience, but Goldstein and Chance (1970) remind us that these studies used dissimilar pictures culled from popular periodicals, and that this is only one kind of everyday recognition experience. Often we must recognize a complex visual stimulus from highly similar ones, like recognizing our child from among many classmates or recognizing our car among 500 others in a parking lot. To balance our understanding, they used similar faces, ink blots, and photographs of snow crystals as stimuli in their experiments. Each stimulus was presented for 2–3 seconds. Faces were best recognized, with 71 percent correct. Ink blots had 46 percent correct, and snow crystals had 33 percent correct. These values are not as high as Shepard (1967) and Standing, Conezio, and Haber (1970) found for dissimilar stimuli.

Visual recognition is not immune to the forces of forgetting. Using meaningless forms, Clark (1965) found no forgetting over intervals of 5–20 minutes, and Arnoult (1956) found no decline in recognition accuracy over 5 hours, but longer intervals are different. Shepard (1967) had retention intervals up to 4 months among his experiments, and the recognition accuracy for pictures presented only once was 97 percent in an immediate test and 58 percent after 4 months. Nickerson (1968), whose subjects viewed ordinary photographs that had been presented once for five seconds, had a retention interval of one year. Eighty percent of the pictures were correctly identified after 1 day, but the value dropped to about 35 percent after 1 year. These findings on forgetting make us temper sentiments about humans and their high powers of recognition somewhat, but nevertheless recognition can be extremely good under some circumstances.

Auditory stimuli

The history of recognition memory is almost entirely one of visual recognition. Recently, however, as part of the modern interest in memory, there has been research on the recognition of complex auditory stimuli that has run parallel to the research on complex visual stimuli, and with similar results. Heterogeneous, dissimilar auditory stimuli have been found to have the same high level of recognition as dissimilar visual stimuli.

Lawrence and Banks (1973) had their subjects listen to a tape with such diverse sounds as machinery, laughing, sneezing, horses neighing, tap-dance routines, and thunder. The tape had 194 different sounds, and each one was presented for 30 seconds. The test tape followed after a five-minute break, where the subjects had to discriminate the old sounds from new ones. The level of recognition was very high, ranging from 85–89 percent for the different types of stimuli. As with visual stimuli, the recognition level for highly similar sounds should be decidedly lower.

VARIABLES FOR RECOGNITION

We saw in previous chapters that recall is a function of many variables, and no less can be said for recognition. Familiarity and verbal mediation are two prominent variables that have been given thorough study.

Familiarity

Exposure time. The basic operation for recognition is sensory experience, and it is common to refer to it as the familiarity variable. Potter and Levy (1969), in their study of recognition and exposure time, show how recognition is positively related to the amount of sensory experience.

Potter and Levy devised 8 short films, where each film was a sequence of 16 color photographs. Each film was projected at a different rate, and it was followed by a recognition test where the projected pictures were mounted on cardboard and had to be selected from among new pictures. Seven different exposure rates were used, ranging from ⅛ second (125 milliseconds) to 2 seconds (2,000 milliseconds) per picture. One group of subjects was given the shorter intervals and another group the longer intervals. Figure 13–1 has the data of the experiment. One hundred twenty-five milliseconds per picture gives a trivial level of

FIGURE 13–1

Recognition accuracy for pictures as a function of exposure duration. The break in the curves represents two groups of subjects, one which had short exposures and one which had the longer exposures. The upper function is for the correct recognition of old stimuli, and the lower function is for incorrectly identifying new stimuli as old (false alarms).

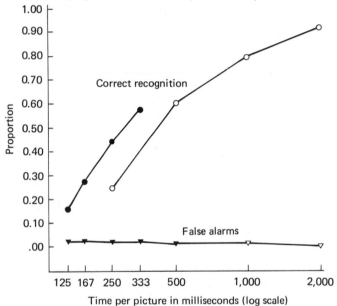

Potter, M. C., & Levy, E. I. Recognition memory for a rapid sequence of pictures. *Journal of Experimental Psychology*, 1969, *81,* 10–15. Reprinted by permission of the American Psychological Association.

recognition, but the trend is a steadily increasing one, and by the time the rate has increased to two seconds the subjects are recognizing almost all of the pictures correctly. Findings like these help us understand in part the very high level of recognition obtained by Shepard (1967) and Standing, Conezio, and Haber (1970). Shepard used self-paced presentation which averaged six seconds per picture, and Standing et al. allowed ten seconds per picture. While six to ten seconds is not long to gaze at a picture, the Potter-Levy data tell us that it is more than enough to guarantee a high level of recognition.

The perception and registration of visual detail. From reading the familiarity literature there is no reason to doubt that the form which is experienced by one (or sometimes more) of the senses is not registered in memory, completely, in all of its detail. Rock, Halper, and Clayton (1972) challenged this thesis that memory for form is like a photographic record.

Their approach was to present a form visually for five seconds under incidental learning conditions, where the subjects thought that they were looking at it for the purposes of forming an after-image, and then to test ten seconds later for recognition. The forms used were meaningless nonsense forms, and the ones presented for study in the various experimental conditions are shown in Figure 13–2. The *A* form was the basic

FIGURE 13–2

The forms used by Rock, Halper, and Clayton (1972) in their experiments on how much of a complex form is stored and enters into subsequent recognition. Forms *B* and *C* are the outer and inner components of Form *A*.

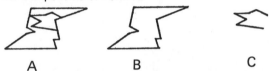

A   B   C

Rock, I., Halper, F., & Clayton, T. The perception and recognition of complex figures. *Cognitive Psychology,* 1972, *3,* 655–673. Reprinted by permission of Academic Press, Inc.

complex form, where the contour enclosed an inner configuration of detail. The *B* form and the *C* form represent a separate display of the contour and the inner configuration, respectively. Figure 13–3 has the items of the recognition tests that were used in the various experimental conditions. A ten-alternative test item was used, as shown.

FIGURE 13–3

The recognition tests used by Rock, Halper, and Clayton (1972).

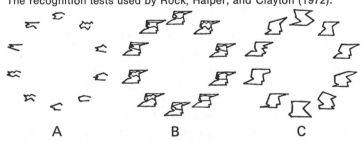

A   B   C

Rock, I., Halper, F., & Clayton, T. The perception and recognition of complex figures. *Cognitive Psychology,* 1972, *3,* 655–673. Reprinted by permission of Academic Press, Inc.

Rock and his associates had several conditions in their main experiment, and the conditions are described along with the results for them in Table 13–1. In Condition 1 the basic complex form (Figure 13–2A) was presented for study and then tested only for the recognition of

TABLE 13–1
Percent of forms correctly recognized for the various presentation and test conditions in the study by Rock, Halper, and Clayton.

Condition	Form exposed	Form tested	Percent correctly recognized
1	Complex (Figure 13-2A)	Inner configuration (Figure 13-3A)	11
2	Complex (Figure 13-2A)	Inner configuration in context (Figure 13-3B)	0
3	Complex (Figure 13-2A)	Outer contour (Figure 13-3C)	56
4	Outer contour (Figure 13-2B)	Outer contour (Figure 13-3C)	69
5	Inner configuration (Figure 13-2C)	Inner configuration (Figure 13-3A)	83

Rock, I., Halper, F., & Clayton, T. The perception and recognition of complex figures. *Cognitive Psychology*, 1972, *3*, 655–673. Reprinted by permission of Academic Press, Inc.

the inner configuration (Figure 13–3A). With guessing level at 10 percent, the 11 percent that was correctly recognized is equivalent to no recognition at all. Condition 2 asked if the poor level of performance in Condition 1 was because of a lack of context in the test, so Condition 1 was repeated except that the recognition test had the ten inner patterns enclosed in a common contour (Figure 13–3B). This time the inner configuration of the study figure was not recognized at all. Condition 3 tested for recognition of only the contour (Figure 13–3C) after study of the whole complex figure (Figure 13–2A), and the recognition level was fairly good although not as good as in Condition 4 where the outer contour was both studied and tested. Condition 5 was the same as Condition 4 except that the inner configuration was both studied and tested, and here the recognition level was quite good. The purpose of the separate assessment of the contour and the inner configuration in Conditions 4 and 5 was to see if there was something about these elements of the complex form that made them inherently difficult to recognize. The inner configuration is an easy pattern to recognize when studied in isolation (Condition 5), but when it is studied in the context of the complex figure it can be recognized hardly at all (Conditions 1 and 2). Then, to secure the matter, Rock et al. repeated all of the conditions of the experiment using curvilinear figures rather than rectilinear ones. The results were about the same.

In another experiment Rock et al. varied the exposure time for the complex figure from 2–15 seconds, and the recognition of the inner configuration was affected little or not at all. In still another experiment the question was asked whether the inner configuration had actually been received in memory but had been forgotten very rapidly and was no longer available ten seconds later at the recognition test. Retention intervals of 200 milliseconds and 10 seconds were compared, and no appreciable difference was found. It was concluded that the problem was failure in perception of the inner configuration in the first place, not in memory, and that much of what impinges on the sense receptors in daily life does not necessarily enter memory. Rock et al. remind us of the difficulties we have of discriminating the faces of people of other races; the details for making these discriminations do not readily enter memory. Although the data of Rock et al. do not show it, we can expect the detail to become recognizable eventually. The details of forms undoubtedly become articulated with enough experience.

Eye fixations and recognition.   Rock et al. have shown that the failure to recognize detail is a matter of perception—some elements of the visual scene are not received in the first place. Why is this so? Why do some things enter memory and some not? One possibility is attention as a central mechanism, where some elements of impinging stimuli are preordained for registration because of their importance for the subject. Without denying the importance of attention, it is likely that the explanation of selective perception in Rock's subjects is in terms of eye fixations. The eye is a highly selective, directional sensor of the visual environment; it is not a passive element like a camera lens. The center of the visual field, called the fovea, is acutely sensitive to color, form, and detail, and through eye movements the subject actively directs the foveal region of the eye to extract key features of the visual scene. One might presume that the simple figures which Rock et al. used in their experiments had compelling outer contours which the subjects saw as informative and which commanded their eye fixations, so the outer contours were the elements that were primarily perceived rather than the inner contours.

But what is the evidence that eye fixations are fundamental in forming the representation in memory that is the basis of visual recognition? The importance of eye fixations for visual recognition has been demonstrated in an excellent experiment by Loftus (1972). He presented pairs of color photographs for various viewing times, and recorded eye fixations throughout the presentation. His results were unequivocal: Recognition is determined by number of eye fixations, not by viewing time itself. Viewing time was a variable for recognition only insofar as it determined the number of fixations. With viewing time held constant, correct recognition was directly related to the number of fixations (Figure 13–4).

In using pairs of pictures, Loftus was able to examine the question of whether recognition is possible for a picture that was in peripheral

FIGURE 13–4
Recognition accuracy for photographs as a function of number of eye fixations.

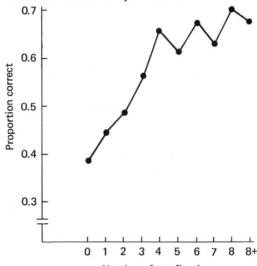

Loftus, G. R. Eye fixations and recognition memory for pictures. *Cognitive Psychology*, 1972, *3*, 525–551. Reprinted by permission of Academic Press, Inc.

vision and had received no eye fixations. The answer is no. Recognition occurred only when the picture had been fixated, and the more fixations the better the recognition. The failure of recognition to occur in peripheral vision is consistent with a hypothesis by Trevarthen (1968). Reasoning from physiological evidence mostly, he contends that there are two mechanisms of vision in primates. Peripheral vision is crude and provides general alerting information about the environment; it distinguishes gross objects, intensity changes, movement, and the like. On the basis of undifferentiated information from the periphery the organism decides whether an eye movement should be made to fixate the event with the precision of focal vision. The learned behavior that we call recognition occurs for the events that strike the fovea.

We can now reconcile the familiarity variable with the studies by

Rock et al. and by Loftus, and to say what it all means for visual recognition. The study by Rock et al. showed that the perception of visual form was imperfect, and that only aspects of it are entered into memory and are available for recognition. The Loftus study demonstrated that only that which is visually fixated can be recognized. By inference, the imperfect perception found in the Rock et al. study could be because eye fixations imperfectly scan the visual scene and enter only parts of the scene into memory.

Remember that all of these data and conclusions apply only to visual recognition, which receives most of the experimental and theoretical effort. What of the other sense modalities? What determines the representation in memory that controls recognition by touch? Smell? Hearing? We know nothing about the mechanisms that control the fidelity of memory's representation for the nonvisual modalities. You do not have to be blind to be convinced of the overwhelming importance of vision for human functioning, and so psychology's emphasis on visual recognition is understandable. Notwithstanding, people do not live by vision alone, and our understanding of memory will be vastly increased when we also ask how other sensory events are encoded in memory.

Verbal factors

The standard literature on familiarity and recognition says that the representation of sensory experience that is laid down in memory is related positively to exposure time, and the generalization has validity. What is left unsaid is that processes can occur in the exposure time. We have seen that eye fixation is one of the processes, and for humans another likely process is verbal labeling and description. Rather than simply sensing a stimulus and judging whether it has been experienced before, a subject may also recall verbal labels and descriptions that were generated when the stimulus was presented before. The issue is whether this verbal recalling is a variable for recognition.

We are all aware of verbal codes that can occur for form stimuli. Some are obvious, like the association *A* when the form *a* is presented. Other associations are not so obvious, like a billowy cloud reminding us of Santa Claus. We have complex, diverse associations to the random shapes that are inkblots, and some psychologists and psychiatrists think that these responses to inkblots in the Rorschach Test have diagnostic value for mental disorders. For our purposes here, verbal responses will sometimes play a positive role in form recognition.

Scientists always strive for control and quantification of their subject matter, and the topic of verbal factors and recognition is no exception. One cannot study verbal factors and recognition with stimuli representing common objects like houses, trees, and dogs because they all elicit elaborate verbal descriptions from human subjects; all subjects have the full value of the verbal variable all of the time. To get around this problem, investigators generated random, or nonsense, shapes of different complexities according to specified rules (Attneave, 1957; Attneave and Arnoult, 1956), and then scaled them for their power to arouse verbal associations. Adapting methods that have been used for the scaling of verbal material (see Underwood and Schulz, 1960, Chapter 2), Vanderplas and Garvin (1959a) scaled random shapes of several complexity levels that have come to be used frequently in research on form recognition. They presented random forms one at a time and asked the subjects if the form reminded them of anything or not. The associative value for a form was the proportion of subjects who had an association for it. The tendency was for simple forms with 4–6 sides to have more associations than complex forms with 16–24 sides. Nonsense shapes of intermediate complexity with twelve sides are shown in Figure 13–5, to illustrate the general kind of form that was used.

FIGURE 13–5

Examples of random shapes which were scaled for association value by Vanderplas and Garvin (1959a).

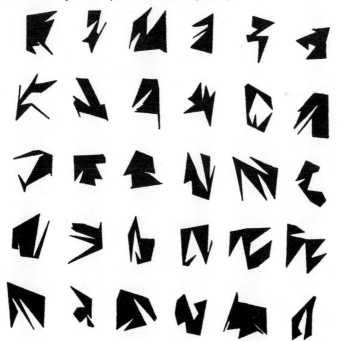

Vanderplas, J. M., & Garvin, E. A. The association value of random shapes. *Journal of Experimental Psychology*, 1959, *57*, 147–154. Reprinted by permission of the American Psychological Association.

A vexing problem with research on verbal factors and form recognition is that the results of experiments are mixed, with some investigators showing positive results and others not (for a review, see Paivio, 1971, pp. 184–192). The Vanderplas and Garvin (1959a) scaling study was part of their larger research program on recognition, and in a subsequent recognition experiment (Vanderplas and Garvin, 1959b) they had three different association values for shapes of three complexity levels as primary variables. The verbal factor is inherent in the association value of the forms, but Vanderplas and Garvin also deliberately trained a verbal factor by preceding the recognition test with paired associate training where low association value nonsense syllables were associated with the shapes. Each subject learned a list of eight pairs. The strength of the verbal association was manipulated by giving different groups of subjects either 2, 4, 8, or 16 practice trials. The outcome of the study was that the simple forms with the fewer sides were recognized better than the complex forms, but with no effect of association value or amount of practice. Certainly the negative finding for association value must have been discouraging for a research team whose theoretical thrust was verbal factors in form recognition.

The intent of the paired-associate training was to increase the verbalness of the form in pursuit of positive evidence for verbal factors in recognition, but maybe the approach chosen by Vanderplas and Garvin might have worked against their hypothesis. Adult subjects would often have their own verbal associations for the shapes that were used, and to have them also associate nonsense syllables with the shapes would place the nonsense syllables in conflict with the natural language associations. The artificiality of the nonsense syllables assigned to the forms in the Vanderplas and Garvin experiment may have upset the subjects' verbal processing of the form, thus preventing a role for the verbal variable. One way to avoid this problem would be to use verbal labels that are not arbitrary like nonsense syllables but are meaningful verbal descriptors of the forms. Ellis (1968) helped clarify this issue by manipulating the relevance and meaningfulness of verbal labels.

Ellis' labels were either meaningful and relevant for the forms, meaningful and irrelevant, or indifferent. Meaningful and relevant labels were the most typical ones given by subjects in another experiment (Ellis and Muller, 1964), and so they had a good chance of being the labels that any one might associate with the forms. For example, a form might have an oval center and two long projections from the top, and a meaningful, relevant label might be "steer." A meaningful but irrelevant label that might be assigned to this form would be "book." The indifferent labels were nonsense syllables. Paired associate training of the labels and forms preceded the recognition test, and Ellis found a positive effect for verbal factors in recognition, with relevant labels producing the primary benefit. The meaningful and relevant labels gave better recognition performance than either irrelevant or indifferent labels, which had about the same level of recognition performance. Verbal factors are beneficial for form recognition as long as the form and the verbal label stand in a meaningful, relevant relationship to one another.

How do verbal associations work to benefit recognition? Ellis (1973) believes that a verbal label operates at the time of input when the subject is studying the form. Through the verbal labeling process the subject directs attention to prominent parts of the visual form, and these prominent parts become more noticeable to her at the recognition test and she has a greater chance of correctly recognizing the form. If the form vaguely resembles a steer's head, and the subject labels it "steer" to herself, she is likely to pay more attention to the projections that resemble the horns than she would without the label. In effect, Ellis is saying that the verbal label shapes the visual representation of the form that is stored in memory. An alternate hypothesis is by Adams and Bray (1970). They contend that the verbal factors operate at the time of the recognition test, not at the time of input. Adams and Bray found that correct recall of responses at the recognition test that had been associated with stimuli increased the probability of stimulus recognition and the subject's confidence in the recognition. They reasoned that the availability of the correct response at the test gives the subject a feeling of confidence about the stimulus and increases the chances that he will recognize it. Santa and Ranken (1972) also provided evidence that verbal factors operate after the input stage, as Adams and Bray contend. They used counting backwards during the retention interval as a verbal interfering activity, and it lowered the level of recognition. Presumably the interference degraded the verbal label of the stimulus being remembered and decreased its effectiveness at the recognition test. A more direct comparison of these two hypotheses someday might come from the study of eye movements and the recognition process. If verbal labeling directs where the subject looks during input then there should be a relationship between the content of the verbal label and eye movements. If this correlation is low then the Adams and Bray output hypothesis is likely to be true.

With evidence on the positive role of verbal factors for visual recognition we might think that recognition and recall of verbal responses are one and the same, and that recognition is no more than retrieval of the verbal associate. This is not so. Keep in mind that visual recognition is fundamentally based on a sensory code, and that the verbal code is only a supplement to it. It is the code from sensory experience that is basic, not the verbal code, and there are several lines of evidence to support the preeminence of the sensory code:

1. Recognition occurs even though the verbal label has been forgot-

ten (Ellis and Daniel, 1971). Something else besides the verbal label must be operating.

2. The capacity for storing visual stimuli for later recognition is enormous, as we saw earlier in this chapter. Hundreds, indeed thousands, of stimuli can be stored after only a brief exposure. Verbal recall has no such capacity.

3. We recognize far more detail than is in a verbal code. The verbal code is gross. We can identify one hat from among many others that differ by very slight details. The verbal label would be "hat" in all instances and could not be the basis of the discriminations.

4. Pictures are recognized better than the names of the same objects (Jenkins, Neale, and Deno, 1967; Kaplan, Kaplan and Sampson, 1968; Paivio and Csapo, 1969). If the presentation time is long enough, the picture can have a verbal label *plus* a visual sensory code, which gives it an edge over words that are only verbal.

5. Abstract forms that defy verbal labeling in most subjects can be easily recognized. This effect is present in any experiment that uses abstract visual forms of low association value (e.g., Clark, 1965).

THEORIES OF FORM RECOGNITION

How is sensory information stored in memory so that recognition is possible? Psychologists are always challenged by the determinants of behavior that are hidden from them in the dark folds of the brain, and much of psychological theorizing is about the nature of these unseeable events. There are three theories of recognition behavior: template matching, feature matching, and schema matching. Like in so much of psychology, recognition has multiple theories. Any science can have competing theories for a subject matter, but the competition often has more entries in psychology, which is a young science. Theories are resolved by empirical data, and a young science often lacks enough of it to decide among the competing theories.

A word of caution: None of the three theories have a place for verbal factors. As important as verbal factors are for recognition, the three theories are concerned only with the subjects internal representation of the environmental stimulus and how it determines recognition. Furthermore, all of the theories focus on visual recognition; none of them face the mechanisms of recognition for other sense modalities.

Template matching

Template matching theory has sensory experience lay down a direct representation of itself (the template) and, at the recognition test, when the stimulus is experienced again, the incoming stimulus is compared with the template. If they correspond and a match occurs, the subject says that the stimulus is familiar and that he recognizes it. If the match fails, however, the stimulus will seem unfamiliar and the subject will have little confidence that it has been experienced before.

Template matching is a theory of recognition that is about as old as recorded history. Plato (translated edition, 1892) wrote about it. Speaking through Socrates, he said:

> . . . when knowing you and Theodorus, and having on the waxen block the impression of both of you given as by a seal, but seeing you imperfectly and at a distance, I try to assign the right impression of memory to the right visual impression, and to fit this into its own print: If I succeed, recognition will take place. . . . (p. 257)

Recall from Chapter 9 that Plato, perhaps metaphorically, saw memory as a wax tablet on which experience imprints its seal. In more modern times the image has filled the role of a template. In Chapters 7 and 11 we were concerned with the use of an existing image which the subject has aroused in the situation and uses as mediator in the learning and retention of verbal items. Template theory, however, is concerned with a laying down of the image by experience in the first place.

The strength of the image template in recognition is a function of experience with the stimulus; the more the stimulus is experienced the more familiar it becomes and the more accurate the recognition. As we have seen, a function of visual experience is to increase the opportunities for eye movements to scan the stimulus (Loftus, 1972), presumably enriching the template.

Problems for template matching. The notion of an image template as a direct (although not necessarily high fidelity) representation of sensory experience is an appealing one, and not without scientific merit. Certain classical findings of perception do not fit an image explanation of recognition very well, however. One kind of data that fails a bit is our ability to recognize a form when it undergoes changes in size. How can a sensory input with an altered size on the retina match the image from earlier experience? The image notion carries with it, implicitly, an assumption of one-to-one mapping of the stimulus input and the image, and the easy recognition of a stimulus of altered size violates this assumption.

The same criticism applies when we recognize a form whose orientation has been changed. Tilt a triangle in the recognition test and we all will recognize the triangle, nevertheless. There are limits, of course, to the recognition of forms when their orientation is changed because the change can drastically alter some forms, as the rotation of a square converts to a diamond. Notwithstanding, our very considerable capabilities for recognizing forms when their orientation has been changed is a violation of the one-to-one mapping assumption and so can be taken as evidence against template matching.

Perhaps the greatest difficulty for the image template is findings for cross-modal transfer—the discrimination of stimuli in one sense modality and the transfer of the discrimination capability to another sense modality. Given the visual presentation of a triangle, would you be able to recognize it if it were presented to you in the dark for tactual discrimination? "Yes!" you would reply, but this simple experiment does not prove anything because the verbally clever human would label the triangle during the study period and use the label rather than the brain's sensory systems to mediate recognition. Whether verbal behavior can mediate visual-tactual transfer is not the issue. The issue is whether the transfer can be mediated by sensory mechanisms alone. If the mediation is wholly sensory, then the image can exist in modalities which did not share in the sensory experience that created the image. The image is ordinarily assumed to be a specific product of the sensory channels that participated in the sensory experience with the stimulus.

The challenge of cross-modality transfer to template theory is weakened somewhat by the mix of positive and negative findings for cross-modality transfer (for reviews, see Ettlinger, 1967; von Wright, 1970) that we have today. One might think that the use of nonverbal animal subjects would be the way to avoid language mediators which can contaminate an experiment with human subjects, and yet the animal findings turn out to be less than decisive for cross-modality transfer (Ettlinger 1967; von Wright, 1970). The best positive evidence comes from medical case histories of patients who have had their sight restored with surgery after long-term blindness. The person who has endured long-term blindness necessarily comes to place an enormous reliance on the tactual modality as a source of information. When sight is restored, the issue is: Will tactual experience benefit the newly-endowed visual behavior? Recent investigation into the post-operative visual behavior of the newly sighted has answered this question in the affirmative (Gregory and Wallace, 1963; Valvo, 1971).

Gregory and Wallace (1963) studied the single case of a man who had been blind in both eyes from the age of 10 months, and who received corneal graftings and sight at the age of 52 years. (All cases of this sort deal with surgical correction of the eye's front surface, where the retina has remained healthy and intact.) They found that the patient had immediate visual comprehension of upper-case letters which he had learned by touch, and that he was unable to read lower-case letters which had not been learned by touch. Valvo (1971) found the same evidence for cross-modal transfer by observing competence in the visual processing of uppercase letters that had earlier been learned by touch and an inability to read lower case letters.

Each card of the Ishihara Color Vision Test has dots of one color that form a numeral and are on a background of dots of another color. Normally it is used to assess color vision, as the name of the test implies; a subject who is color blind will, depending upon the colors, be unable to discriminate the numeral from the background. Gregory and Wallace found that their subject read every numeral perfectly. The normalcy of color vision after a lifetime of visual inactivity is a worthy finding, but for our purposes here we once again find positive cross-modal transfer because the subject had visual competence in a skill that was acquired by touch. Scientists are polite, persistent critics of one another, and a critic could point out that the subject might really have been making unobtrusive motor movements during the test which were informative of the numeral, and that he might not have been visually reading at all. Granting that the subject could discriminate the colors, he might have used his finger to trace out the pattern in the palm of his hand covertly. Or, maybe his eye movements traced the pattern and were informative about the numeral. Gregory and Wallace countered both of these arguments by watching for finger movements during the test (there were none) and by observing eye movements. The eye movements were gross and jerky and could not have informed about much of anything.

Feature matching

A feature is a dimension of difference which allows stimuli to be distinguished from one another. The feature matching theory of recognition holds that distinctive features of the stimulus, not an image representation, is stored in memory. For example, the distinctive features for the upper-case letter D might be a straight line and a curved line that connects with its ends. An upper-case E might be expressed as three equally spaced lines of approximately equal length at right angles to a fourth line. At the time of stimulus input the subject does not process the entire stimulus as is done in the case of template matching theory. Instead, distinctive features of the input are selectively processed. For visual inputs the stored features could be primarily due to the selectivity of eye fixations (Loftus, 1972). Eye fixations are localized points on the scene being scanned, and they could be the basis of the features that are stored. The more exposure to the stimulus (familiarity) the greater the number of key features stored and the more accurate the recognition.

Feature matching has an advantage over template matching because it circumvents the problems that template matching has with size and form orientation. Regardless of size or orientation of the form, as long as the features are present in the stimulus and match those that have been stored, the stimulus will be recognized. Feature matching has been used with some success by scientists trying to engineer machines for pattern recognition, and this is another, and weaker, reason for some to favor feature matching. That a machine uses a particular process in simulating a human function does not mean that the human system uses the same process for the function.

Problems for feature matching.   It is not at all clear that the findings on cross-modal matching are embarrassing for feature matching theory, as they are for template matching theory. Template matching is based on the image which arises out of explicit sensory experiences. Feature matching, being a newer theory, is less clear in its defining principles. Most advocates of feature matching seem to imply that the features are extracted from the impinging stimuli, just as the image derives from impinging stimuli, and so they can be defined only by the modality of the sensory experience. If so, cross-modal matching is the same embarrassment for feature matching as it is for template matching.

Schema matching

A face in the crowd momentarily catches our eye and tomorrow we recognize it when we see it again. Both template matching and feature matching theory can explain this act of recognition because both are concerned with the perceptual learning and recognition of a single form. But not all perceptual learning and recognition is of a single form. A goodly amount of our perceptual behavior is with respect to stimulus classes and is closely akin to concept behavior. Concept behavior is a matter of classification and abstraction for the instances of a class of stimuli, and our perceptual processing of a class of stimuli is the same in principle. If we had a high pile of pictures, half of them pictures of various cats and half not, we would most certainly be able to recognize cats and sort cat pictures in one pile and non-cat pictures in another. We seem to have a mental representation of cats as a class, and we are able to recognize all instances of the class, whether we have experienced them before or not. Even if the high pile of pictures contained a remote jungle cat that a sorter had never seen before, the chances are high that its picture would be tossed into the cat pile. Thus, the human memory is capable of abstractions, and of classifying stimuli with respect to the abstractions. In the realm of perception these abstractions are called prototypes or *schemata*. In recognition by schema matching, it is assumed that a stimulus is compared against the schema for the stimulus class and a decision made about its class membership.

The notion of schema primarily comes to us from Bartlett (1932) who was impatient with the position that memory is a composite of traces, one for every little thing we think and do. In more recent times, in perception, schema was revived as a research topic by Attneave (1957). Today, cognitive psychology, in its concern with higher mental functioning, has a lively interest in the schema. Our research literature is currently debating the conditions under which a schema is formed, and an example of a present-day experiment is by Peterson, Meagher, Chait, and Gillie (1973, their Experiment I).

The general plan of the Peterson et al. experiment was to train subjects on specified kinds of stimulus instances of a form, and then test for recognition on the same and different kinds of stimulus instances of the form. Peterson et al. used four different prototype forms defined by dot patterns: a triangle, the letter *F*, and two random patterns. Each form class was systematically distorted to provide various instances of it, and the method of distortion was a technique developed by Posner, Goldsmith, and Welton (1967). An example of the triangle prototype and four levels of distortion are shown in Figure 13–6. The Posner et al. technique is a probabilistic one, so a level of distortion

FIGURE 13–6

Five levels of distortion of a triangle. The distortion is by a probabilistic technique.

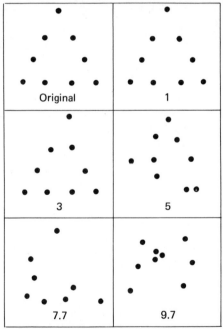

Posner, M. I., Goldsmith, R., & Welton, K. E., Jr. Perceived distance and the classification of distorted patterns. *Journal of Experimental Psychology*, 1967, *73*, 28–38. Reprinted by permission of the American Psychological Association.

in Figure 13–6 represents the kind of figure that is typical of an indefinite number of figures that could be generated with the same degree of distortion.

There were three groups. A group was trained on instances of the four patterns, with either distortion level 1, 5, or 7.7, as illustrated in Figure 13–6 for the triangle (the extreme distortion, level 9.7, was not used). The stimuli were on slides, and the subject responded with four telegraph keys, one for each stimulus class. The subject had to classify each slide as one of the four stimulus classes by pressing a key. After pressing the key, a reinforcement lamp signalled the correct key to the subject. Training continued until 24 consecutive slides were classified correctly. In the recognition test series, with the reinforcement light removed, each group had to classify new slides which were instances of the old training stimuli, the prototype stimuli, and new stimuli for the prototypes with distortion levels 1, 3, 5, and 7.7. Notice that each group had to classify instances of stimuli that had not been experienced before.

TABLE 13–2
Average errors (out of three instances of a category on transfer test.) The meaningful stimuli in training were a triangle and the letter *F*; the random stimuli were meaningless patterns.

Training condition	Old training stimuli	Proto-type pattern	*Test stimuli*			
			1	*3*	*5*	*7.7*
Group 1						
Meaningful.	.04	.08	.09	.31	.98	2.40
Random	.38	.48	.34	.47	.86	1.58
Average	.21	.28	.22	.39	.92	1.99
Group 5						
Meaningful.	.84	.80	.96	1.18	1.88	1.76
Random	.78	1.04	1.44	1.36	1.33	1.89
Average	.82	.92	1.20	1.27	1.60	1.83
Group 7.7						
Meaningful.	1.04	1.75	1.67	1.76	1.61	1.86
Random	1.08	1.72	1.61	1.73	2.05	2.28
Average	1.06	1.73	1.64	1.75	1.83	2.07

Peterson, M. J., Meagher, R. B., Jr., Chait, H., & Gillie, S. The abstraction and generalization of dot patterns. *Cognitive Psychology*, 1973, *4*, 378–398. Reprinted by permission of Academic Press, Inc.

The results are shown in Table 13–2. Performance on the old training stimuli is the baseline against which performance on the new instances of the stimuli should be compared. Notice that the formation of abstractions, or the capability for classifying novel instances of stimuli, is facilitated by training on low levels of distortion. Group 1, which trained on level 1 distortion, had the best performance of all. Not only was the accuracy of identifying the prototypes greater when training was on patterns with low levels of distortion, but more distorted stimuli were correctly classified.

Problems for schema matching. Not a problem in a theoretical sense, but it pays to keep in mind that schema matching cannot be a general theory of recognition because it does not account for the power of recognition that develops from a single, brief sensory experience. It is remotely conceivable that a schema could be formed in one experience, but it is generally believed that multiple experiences are required. Whether varied instances of the stimulus class are required for schema learning is another matter. Varied instances are certainly one condition for the acquisition of a schema, as the Peterson et al. experiment testifies, but it may be only one way to do it. Charness and Bregman (1973) report some proficiency with novel instances of a stimulus class when training was only on the prototype stimulus. Intuitively, it would seem that training with the prototype alone would be ideal for deriving the core essentials of the stimulus class. Maybe so, but it is well to keep in mind that intuition is an unreliable companion on scientific campaigns.

All of the theories of form recognition neglect verbal factors, and this neglect seems to be particularly damaging for schema matching because verbal factors could easily give the appearance of schema formation. In the Peterson et al. experiment, some of the subjects certainly must have seen that some of the stimuli were meaningful (triangle, the letter *F*), verbally labeled them, and then used recall of the label as a basis for the key-pressing classification response. Random shapes were also used but, as we saw in our earlier discussion of the Vanderplas and Garvin (1959a) experiment, random shapes do not necessarily eliminate verbal associations. That verbal labeling might have been present in the Peterson et al. experiment does not undermine it. Rather, the implication is that there is another variable to be understood for the concept of schema, and that we should consider broadening the concept to include verbal factors. At present, schema is defined wholly on the perceptual side as a function of sensory experience, and this is a good conception, as far as it goes. It is necessary for us to know if abstractions can be formed solely on the sensory-perceptual side, but we must inquire further and ask if verbal factors contribute to the schema also.

The general sense of the schema concept, as it has evolved by its protagonists (Attneave, 1957), is that it is a genuine abstraction on the sensory-perceptual side, a transcendent entity that embodies all of the essentials of the stimulus instances of the class without embodying the stimulus particulars of any of them. That it is a true abstraction makes schema matching different from template matching and feature matching which entail the storage of particular aspects of each stimulus. A moment's reflection tells us that a true abstraction is not the only possibility for a schema, however. There is no reason why *each* stimulus could not be stored, either in terms of an image or features, and why the successive stimuli could not build a composite or average that is the schema or "abstraction." If this latter possibility turns out to be so it will reduce schema matching to either template matching or feature matching and also will be an enriching of them. As presently conceived, template matching and feature matching do not gracefully accommodate the human capability for perceptual abstraction.

SEARCH AND RETRIEVAL FACTORS IN RECOGNITION

All of the theories of recognition have the assumption that recognition will occur if the second presentation of the stimulus on the test "matches" the traces of the stimulus in memory that were laid down on the first presentation. But is matching all there is to it? In the last chapter we saw search and retrieval as processes of recall. Do search and retrieval processes operate for recognition also? Subjectively it is apparent that we search our memory at recall, but it is not subjectively obvious that search and retrieval operate for recognition. Our thinking about this was changed when Sternberg (1966, 1969) developed data and theoretical reasoning that caused us to consider search and retrieval as factors in recognition. Sternberg's work is in the modern manner of information processing (Chapter 9).

The Sternberg theory

One of the attractions of Sternberg's work was the classic simplicity of his approach. The use of reaction time to infer about mental processes is one of the oldest approaches in psychology, and Sternberg used it to infer about mental search time. Sternberg (1966) used the ten digits as stimuli. On each trial the subject saw a random series of 1 to 6 different digits presented singly at a fixed locus for 1.2 seconds each. Then followed a two-second delay, a warning signal, and a test digit. The test digit was a recognition test and the subject had to decide whether it was a member of the set that was just shown. If the subject decided "Yes" one lever was pulled, and if "No" another was pulled. The measure of performance was reaction time, or time between onset of the test stimulus and occurrence of the response. If the test digit was a member of the set it was called a positive set, and if not it was a negative set. Sternberg found that reaction time was a linear increasing function of set size, and it is an effect that is easily obtained. Representative data are shown in Figure 13–7, which is a recent replica-

FIGURE 13–7
Recognition reaction time as a function of stimulus set size.

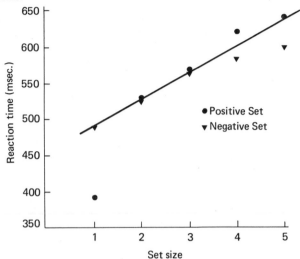

Theios, J., Smith, P. G., Haviland, S. E. Traupmann, J., & Moy, M. C. Memory scanning as a serial self-terminating process. *Journal of Experimental Psychology,* 1973, *97,* 323–336. Reprinted by permission of the American Psychological Association.

tion by Theios et al. (1973). Notice that the functions for positive and negative sets are the same. Sternberg's interpretation of data such as these is that recognition is a serial scanning process, where the test digit is compared successively with the digits stored in memory, and the larger the set the longer the search time. That the functions for the positive and negative sets are about the same has the interesting implication that the scanning is exhaustive; even when a match occurs the scanning continues through the entire set. The logic of the argument is that the reaction time to the positive set would be less than to the negative set if the search terminated when a match occurred. Only about half of the items on the average must be searched for a match to occur in a positive set, but all of the items must be examined before the subject can say whether an item is missing and is a member of the negative set. Serial scanning of this sort is contrasted to parallel scanning, as another theoretical possibility, where all items of the set would be searched simultaneously. One implication of a parallel scanning model is that reaction time would be a horizontal function of set size, where all set sizes have the same reaction time because all items were tested simultaneously.

The linear relationship between reaction time and set size is a well-established finding in modern experimental psychology, and one would think that Sternberg's interpretation of retrieval processes in recognition would be beyond challenge, but not so. One line of challenge has been to study reaction time values to the digits within a set. If search is exhaustive, as Sternberg contends, then reaction time should be the same for all digits of a set because all are scanned before the reaction time response occurs. The study of items as a function of their position in the set is the study of the serial position curve, a phenomenon which we encountered in Chapter 9 within the context of verbal recall, and Morin, DeRosa, and Stultz (1967), and Corballis (1967), appear to have been the first to show that reaction time is dependent on serial position. A good demonstration of the serial position effect in the Stern- berg's situation is an experiment by Corballis, Kirby, and Miller (1972) which used experimental procedures similar to Sternberg's. Positive sets of one, two, three, four, or six items were used, and a plot of reaction time as a function of serial position for each of the lists is given in Figure 13–8. The serial position effects are sharply defined for the longer

FIGURE 13–8

Reaction time as a function of number of items in the set and serial position in the set.

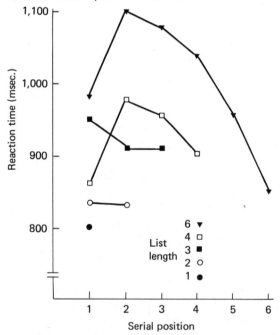

Corballis, M. C., Kirby, J., & Miller, A. Access to elements of a memorized list. *Journal of Experimental Psychology,* 1972, *94,* 185–190. Reprinted by permission of the American Psychological Association.

lists. Serial position effects are well documented by now. Kennedy and Hamilton (1969) report data very similar to those in Figure 13–8. Forrin and Cunningham (1973), and Aubé and Murdock (1974), also report serial position effects for the Sternberg recognition task.

Another challenge to Sternberg's theory is stimulus probability effects. The evidence has been long standing that the more frequent the occurrence of a stimulus event in a session the faster the reaction time (Hyman, 1953), but recently there has been a revival of interest and more data on the topic (Krueger, 1970; Theios et al., 1973; Theios and Walter, 1974) within the context of Sternberg's theory. If the subject responds fast to a frequently presented stimulus and slow to an infrequent one, then he is not exhaustively scanning the set because, as we noted above, exhaustive scanning requires the same reaction time for all items of a set. Better recognition (faster reaction time) for the stimulus which has been experienced most often are data consistent with the discussion on familiarity and recognition earlier in this chapter; primarily, a notion of trace strength can explain data like these. Not all believe that the findings on stimulus probability threaten Sternberg's position. Sternberg (1969) contends that the search stage is preceded by a stimulus encoding stage, where the stimulus is converted into a representation in memory. Miller and Pachella (1973) believe that the effect of stimulus probability is on the encoding stage. The more familiar the stimulus the faster the encoding and the faster the reaction time.

SUMMARY

Recognition is deciding that a stimulus has been experienced before. Recognition accuracy can be very high. Exposure to hundreds, indeed, thousands of pictures, usually can produce a recognition level of 90 percent correct, or more. High similarity of the stimuli can reduce this value, however.

The basic operation for recognition is sensory experience, and the duration of the experience is called the familiarity variable. Recognition accuracy is positively related to exposure time in most experiments. Recent research has shown that eye fixations are a more fundamental determiner of visual recognition than exposure time, and that exposure time is a variable only insofar as it determines number of eye fixations. Verbal factors, as a supplement to a sensory code, are also a variable for recognition. The human subject has a rich propensity for verbal labeling and description, and the labels and descriptions that are hung on a stimulus benefit its recognition.

There are three theories of recognition: template matching, feature matching, and schema matching. Template matching is an image theory, where the stimulus lays down a rather direct representation of itself. At the recognition test an incoming stimulus is compared with the template, and if a match occurs a sense of familiarity is present and the subject declares that he has experienced the stimulus before. Feature matching is similar to template matching except that only critical features of the stimulus are stored, not an explicit image. Feature matching gives greater versatility in recognition because only critical features of the stimulus need be recognized, not the detailed stimulus. Schema matching is recognition of the members of a stimulus class. Schema matching theory contends that an abstract representation of the members of a stimulus class is stored, and an item is recognized when it is compared against the schema and judged to be a member of the class.

REFERENCES

Adams, J. A., & Bray, N. W.   A closed-loop theory of paired-associate verbal learning. *Psychological Review*, 1970, 77, 385–405.

Arnoult, M. D.   Familiarity and recognition of nonsense shapes. *Journal of Experimental Psychology*, 1956, *51*, 269–276.

Attneave, F.   Transfer of experience with a class-schema to identification-learning of patterns and shapes. *Journal of Experimental Psychology*, 1957, *54*, 81–88.

Attneave, F., & Arnoult, M. D.   The quantitative study of shape and pattern perception. *Psychological Bulletin*, 1956, 53, 452–471.

Aubé, M., & Murdock, B.   Sensory stores and high-speed scanning. *Memory and Cognition*, 1974, *2*, 27–33.

Bahrick, H. P., & Bahrick, P. O.   A re-examination of the interrelations among measures of retention. *Quarterly Journal of Experimental Psychology*, 1964, *16*, 318–324.

Banks, W. P.   Signal detection theory and human memory. *Psychological Bulletin*, 1970, 74, 81–99.

Bartlett, F. C.   *Remembering: A study in experimental and social psychology.* Cambridge: University of Cambridge Press, 1932.

Bruce, D., & Cofer, C. N.   A comparison of recognition and recall in short-term memory. *Proceedings 73rd Annual Convention of the American Psychological Association*, 1965, pp. 81–82.

Bruce, D., & Cofer, C. N.   An examination of recognition and free recall as measures of acquisition and long-term retention. *Journal of Experimental Psychology*, 1967, 75, 283–289.

Charness, N., & Bregman, A. S.   Transformations in the recognition of visual forms. *Canadian Journal of Psychology*, 1973, 27, 367–380.

Clark, H. J.   Recognition memory for random shapes as a function of complexity, association value, and delay. *Journal of Experimental Psychology*, 1965, *69*, 590–595.

Corballis, M. C.   Serial order in recognition and recall. *Journal of Experimental Psychology*, 1967, 74, 99–105.

Corballis, M. C., Kirby, J., & Miller, A.   Access to elements of a memorized list. *Journal of Experimental Psychology*, 1972, *94*, 185–190.

Ellis, H. C.   Transfer of stimulus predifferentiation to shape recognition and identification learning: Role of properties of verbal labels. *Journal of Experimental Psychology*, 1968, *78*, 401–409.

Ellis, H. C.   Stimulus encoding processes in human learning and memory. In G. H. Bower (Ed.), *The psychology of learning and motivation*. (Vol. 7). New York; Academic Press, 1973, pp. 123–182.

Ellis, H. C., & Daniel, T. C.   Verbal processes in long-term stimulus-recognition memory. *Journal of Experimental Psychology*, 1971, *90*, 18–26.

Ellis, H. C., & Muller, D. G.   Transfer in perceptual learning following stimulus predifferentiation. *Journal of Experimental Psychology*, 1964, *68*, 388–395.

Ettlinger, G.   Analysis of cross-modal effects and their relationship to language. In F. L. Darley (Ed.), *Brain mechanisms underlying speech and language*. New York: Grune & Stratton, 1967, pp. 53–60.

Forrin, B., & Cunningham, K.   Recognition time and serial position of probed item in short-term memory. *Journal of Experimental Psychology*, 1973, *99*, 272–279.

Goldstein, A. G., & Chance, J. E.   Visual recognition memory for complex configurations. *Perception and Psychophysics*, 1970, *9*, 237–241.

Gregory, R. L., and Wallace, J. G.   *Recovery from early blindness: A case study*. Cambridge: Heffers, 1963.

Hochhaus, L.   A table for the calculation of d' and β. *Psychological Bulletin*, 1972, *77*, 375–376.

Hyman, R.   Stimulus information as a determinant of reaction time. *Journal of Experimental Psychology*, 1953, *45*, 188–196.

Jenkins, J. R., Neale, D. C., & Deno, S. L.   Differential memory for picture and word stimuli. *Journal of Educational Psychology*, 1967, *58*, 303–307.

Kaplan, S., Kaplan, R., & Sampson, J. R.   Encoding and arousal factors in free recall of verbal and visual material. *Psychonomic Science*, 1968, *12*, 73–74.

Kennedy, R. A., & Hamilton, D.   Time to locate probe items in short lists of digits. *American Journal of Psychology*, 1969, *82*, 272–275.

Klein, L. S., & Arbuckle, T. Y.   Response latency and task difficulty in recognition memory. *Journal of Verbal Learning and Verbal Behavior*, 1970, *9*, 467–472.

Krueger, L. E.   Effect of stimulus probability on two-choice reaction time. *Journal of Experimental Psychology*, 1970, *84*, 377–379.

Lawrence, D. M., & Banks, W. P.   Accuracy of recognition memory for common sounds. *Bulletin of the Psychonomic Society*, 1973, *1*, 298–300.

Lockhart, R. S., & Murdock, B. B., Jr.   Memory and the theory of signal detection. *Psychological Bulletin*, 1970, *74*, 100–109.

Loftus, G. R.   Eye fixations and recognition memory for pictures. *Cognitive Psychology*, 1972, *3*, 525–551.

Miller, J. O., & Pachella, R. G. Locus of the stimulus probability effect. *Journal of Experimental Psychology,* 1973, *101,* 227–231.

Morin, R. E., DeRosa, D. V., & Stultz, V. Recognition memory and reaction time. *Acta Psychologica,* 1967, *27,* 298–305.

Nickerson, R. S. A note on long-term recognition memory for pictorial material. *Psychonomic Science,* 1968, *11,* 58.

Paivio, A. *Imagery and verbal processes.* New York: Holt, Rinehart and Winston, 1971.

Paivio, A., & Csapo, K. Concrete image and verbal memory codes. *Journal of Experimental Psychology,* 1969, *80,* 279–285.

Parks, T. E. Signal-detectability theory of recognition-memory performance. *Psychological Review,* 1966, *73,* 44–58.

Peterson, M. J., Meagher, R. B., Jr., Chait, H., & Gillie S. The abstraction and generalization of dot patterns. *Cognitive Psychology,* 1973, *4,* 378–398.

Plato. *The dialogues of Plato* (Vol. 4) (3rd ed.). (B. Jowett trans.). Oxford: Clarendon Press, 1892.

Posner, M. I., Goldsmith, R., & Welton, K. E., Jr. Perceived distance and the classification of distorted patterns. *Journal of Experimental Psychology,* 1967, *73,* 28–38.

Potter, M. C., & Levy, E. I. Recognition memory for a rapid sequence of pictures. *Journal of Experimental Psychology,* 1969, *81,* 10–15.

Rock, I., Halper, F., & Clayton, T. The perception and recognition of complex figures. *Cognitive Psychology,* 1972, *3,* 655–673.

Santa, J. L., & Ranken, H. B. Effects of verbal coding on recognition memory. *Journal of Experimental Psychology,* 1972, *93,* 268–278.

Shepard, R. N. Recognition memory for words, sentences, and pictures. *Journal of Verbal Learning and Verbal Behavior,* 1967, *6,* 156–163.

Standing, L., Conezio, J., & Haber, R. N. Perception and memory for pictures: Single-trial learning of 2500 visual stimuli. *Psychonomic Science,* 1970, *19,* 73–74.

Sternberg, S. High-speed scanning in human memory. *Science,* 1966, *153,* 652–654.

Sternberg, S. Memory-Scanning: Mental processes revealed by reaction-time experiments. *American Scientist,* 1969, *57,* 421–457.

Strong, E. K., Jr. The effect of length of series upon recognition memory. *Psychological Review,* 1912, *19,* 447–462.

Strong, E. K., Jr. The effect of time-interval upon recognition memory. *Psychological Review,* 1913, *20,* 339–372.

Theios, J., Smith, P. G., Haviland, S. E., Traupmann, J., & Moy, M. C. Memory scanning as a serial self-terminating process. *Journal of Experimental Psychology,* 1973, *97,* 323–336.

Theios, J., & Walter, D. G. Stimulus and response frequency and sequential effects in memory scanning reaction times. *Journal of Experimental Psychology,* 1974, *102,* 1092–1099.

Theodor, L. H.   A neglected parameter: Some comments on "A table for the calculation of d' and β." *Psychological Bulletin,* 1972, *78,* 260–261.

Trevarthen, C. B.   Two mechanisms of vision in primates. *Psychologische Forschung,* 1968, *31,* 299–337.

Underwood, B. J.   Word recognition memory and frequency information. *Journal of Experimental Psychology,* 1972, *94,* 276–283.

Underwood, B. J., and Schulz, R. W.   *Meaningfulness and verbal learning.* New York: Lippincott, 1960.

Valvo, A.   *Sight restoration after long-term blindness: The problems and behavior patterns of visual rehabilitation.* New York: American Foundation for the Blind, 1971.

Vanderplas, J. M., & Garvin, E. A.   The association value of random shapes. *Journal of Experimental Psychology,* 1959, *57,* 147–154. (a)

Vanderplas, J. M., & Garvin, E. A.   Complexity, association value, and practice as factors in shape recognition following paired-associates training. *Journal of Experimental Psychology,* 1959, *57,* 155–163. (b)

von Wright, J. M.   Cross-modal transfer and sensory equivalence—a review. *Scandinavian Journal of Psychology,* 1970, *11,* 21–30.

chapter 14

Memory for sentences and prose

PSYCHOLOGY has had an upsurge in research on language in recent years, and it is different than the study of verbal learning and memory which has been covered throughout this book so far. The study of verbal learning and memory, which has been with us since psychology's earliest days as an experimental science, did not represent an interest in verbal behavior for its own sake. Rather, verbal behavior was studied as a route to the understanding of more general processes and laws, just as any other response class might be studied. In Chapter 6 we saw that for a long time psychology had a philosophy of science which believed in general laws, and with this philosophy the study of one response class is as good as another. With general processes and laws being sought, there was no motivation for studying verbal units that are realistic in the natural language.

Investigators of language today have their interests strongly focused on the natural language with its units of phrases, sentences, and prose, and frequently they reject study of the isolated verbal unit that has been the style of the past. There is no doubt that the tradition of isolated units made a receptive bed for the study of larger, more realistic verbal units, and given the receptive bed, events of the present moved psychologists in new directions, primarily toward developments in linguistics by Chomsky (1957, 1965). Studies of sentences and prose can be found along psychology's research routes of the past, but they were never accompanied by ideas that drove scientists to vigorous research action. Chomsky's ideas had this power, and they are embodied in his development of *generative theory*, or transformational grammar as it is often called. The unit of study is the sentence.

GENERATIVE THEORY AND THE RETENTION OF SENTENCES

Generative theory is a cognitive theory that opposes an associationist view of language. Cognitive theory, with its emphasis on the organizing powers of the mind, has been a long-standing opponent of associationism, and behaviorism with its focus on the learning of responses to stimuli. The modern bout between behaviorists and cognitive psychology in the arena of language began with a paper by Mowrer (1954). Mowrer said that "the sentence is, preeminently, a *conditioning device,* and that its chief effect is to produce new associations, new learning, just as any other paired presentation of stimuli may do." Communication is a transfer of meaning from sign to sign, so that the listener associates one word of the sentence with another and acquires its meaning by virtue of the association. Mowrer's example is John telling Charles that "Tom is a thief," and the assumption is that Charles already has meaning attached to the words "Tom" and "thief." What, then, is the function of the sentence? The sentence is fundamentally a classical conditioning paradigm (Chapter 4), where "Tom" is a conditioned stimulus and "thief" is an unconditioned stimulus, and by association "Tom" comes to elicit some of the reaction evoked by "thief." For Charles, by the principles of conditioning, "Tom" comes to mean an untrustworthy person who steals, and the next time Charles meets Tom he reacts to him as if he is a thief. Mowrer went on to derive various other characteristics of language behavior from the principles of learning, and they were all well-reasoned, ingenious derivations. In 1957, Skinner published a book *Verbal Behavior,* which also derived language behavior from the behaviorist's point of view (Skinner, 1957). Both Mowrer and Skinner saw language behavior as instances of general laws of learning. The basic determination of the laws has often been with animals or simple human learning situations, and the use of these laws to explain language is the application of them to new situations. General scientific laws have such power.

Chomsky (1959) unleashed a cognitive counterattack in his review of Skinner's 1957 book. Chomsky held that the application of the laws of learning, derived as they were from simple situations, to the complexities of language, was gross and superficial. In other words, the general laws were not as general as Mowrer and Skinner believed them to be. When it comes to the learning of language there is no meaningful identification of stimulus, response, or reinforcement, which are the essential ingredients of the behaviorist's laws, Chomsky argued. And, if learning is so fundamental, how is it that we can speak sentences that we have never spoken before or understand sentences that we have never heard before? Given a knowledge of grammar, the rules of which can generate all the permissable sentences in the language and exclude all those that are not permissable, we seem capable of seemingly infinite variety in language, and it is very difficult to see the conditions of its learning. Miller (1965) estimated that there are 10^{20} sentences 20 words long, and it would take a child 1,000 times the age of the earth just to listen to them.

Chomsky's more substantive reply to the associationists was his theory of linguistics (1957, 1965). Much of linguistics is descriptive and of passing interest to the psychologist, but Chomsky's generative theory is different because aspects of it have implications for language as behavior, which is the field of psychology called psycholinguistics. As behavior theory, generative theory is idealized because it deals with an ideal speak-listener who has a complete knowledge of the language without the imperfections of lapses of memory, slips of the tongue, instances of bad grammar, etc. It is commonly said that Chomsky's theory is one of *competence,* which is the idealized potential of the speaker-listener, rather than one of *performance,* which is the imperfect, less-than-ideal behavior that we observe. Linguistics as a science is competence oriented, and psycholinguistics is performance oriented. Idealized theory implies that the variables which produce everyday performance have been left out, but this does not prevent the meaningful study of variables that have been included.

Of most interest to psychologists was Chomsky's distinction between surface structure, deep structure, and transformational rules. *Surface structure* is a physical form of the sentence as it is observed, *deep structure* contains the abstract, fundamental meaning of the sentence and the grammar functions that relate to meaning, and *transformational rules* relate surface structure to deep structure. The importance of the distinction between deep structure and surface structure can be appreciated when it is noted that different deep structures can have the same surface structure, and different surface structures can have the same deep structure. The ambiguous sentence "They are cooking apples" is an example of how different deep structures can have the same surface structure. It can mean that someone is cooking apples, or that the apples are for cooking. The sentence "The bird ate the seed" and the sentence "The seed was eaten by the bird" is an example of different surface structures but identical deep structure—both sentences have the same meaning. The simple, active, declarative expression of the idea in deep structure is called the *kernel sentence,* and if it is not exactly the same as the idea in deep structure it is the simplest transformation of it that occurs at the surface. Other syntactical forms of the idea are more complex transformations. Consider the kernel sentence "The bird ate the seed." By transformation rules the kernel sentence can be transformed into a passive, a negative, or a question form, or any combination of the three. "The seed was eaten by the bird" (passive), "The bird did not eat the seed" (negative), or "Did the bird eat the seed?" (question). There can be all combinations of these, like passive + negative, "The seed was not eaten by the bird."

What kind of research themes for learning and memory do psychologists see in Chomsky's generative theory? One theme lies in surface structure. Different surface structures can express the same meaning and have the same deep structure. Is learning and memory influenced by surface structure or the underlying meaning? Another research theme concerns transformation rules. Miller (1962), working from Chomsky's generative theory, assumed that the number of transformations was important for sentence memory. Do the transformations that lie between deep structure and surface structure make a difference for the retention of sentences?

Effects of surface structure

The study of the surface structure of a sentence is the study of syntax, and it can be separated from semantics for analysis. *Syntax* is a study of the ordering of words or morphemes (the morpheme is the smallest unit of the language that conveys meaning) to form larger language units like phrases and sentences. *Semantics,* as another fundamental characteristic of sentences, is the study of meaning. The syntactical and semantical structure of sentences can have some independence (Miller & Isard, 1963). A sentence can be syntactically and grammatically correct: "A witness signed the official legal document." A sentence can be syntactically correct but semantically meaningless, or "semantically anamolous" as it is often called: "A witness appraised the shocking company dragon." Or, a sentence can be syntactically and semantically meaningless: "A diamond shocking the prevented dragon witness." It is in ways like this that syntax can be studied independently of other sentence properties.

The research on syntax had its beginning in an experiment in the psychology of language by Miller and Selfridge (1950). They studied free recall as a joint function of length of passage and eight orders of approximation to the statistical structure of the English language. The "statistical structure" of a language is the relative frequency with which words, phrases, and even higher units occur in use of the language. No one has ever established the statistical structure of the English language, but it can be estimated and that is what Miller and Selfridge did. Zero-order approximation to English was a random sample of words, unrelated to usage practices. First-order approximation drew a random sample of single words from printed texts, which represented the relative frequencies of words in the language. For approximation orders two through seven, human subjects were used for estimates. Progressively higher orders of approximation have increasing sequential dependencies, like the probability of any word following another, any two words following a word, any three words following a word, any word following any two preceding words, etc. Perhaps someday when machines can read a computer of prodigious capacity will compile the statistical structure of the language, but in the meantime we must use adult humans to estimate because they have the sequential dependencies of the language residing in them. To give an idea of the procedure which Miller and Selfridge used to generate orders two through seven, here in their own words is an example of the procedure they followed to generate the second order:

> At the second order, for example, a common word, such as *he, it,* or *the* is presented to a person who is instructed to use the word in a sentence. The word he uses directly after the one given him is then noted and later presented to another person who has not heard the sentence given by the first person, and he, in turn, is asked to use that word in a sentence. The word he uses directly after the one given him is then noted and later given to yet another person. This procedure is repeated until the total sequence of words is of the desired length. Each successive pair of words could go together in a sentence. Each word is determined in the context of only one preceding word. (Miller & Selfridge, 1960, p. 180).

For approximation order three through seven (order six was omitted), the subject saw a sequence of two or more words each time and used them in a sentence. The highest order was written language text taken from fiction and biography. Lists of 10, 20, 30, and 50 words were devised in this fashion.

Here are examples of the ten-word passages that were generated:

Zero order: Byway consequence handsomely financier bent flux cavalry swiftness weather-beaten extent

First order: Abilities with that beside I for waltz you the sewing

Second order: Was he went to the newspaper is in deep and

Third order: Tall and thin boy is a biped is the beat

Fourth order: Saw the football game will end at midnight on January

Fifth order: They saw the play Saturday and sat down beside him

Seventh order: Recognize her abilities in music after he scolded him before

Text: The history of California is largely that of a railroad

Each passage was presented once orally, with immediate recall. The subject was instructed to recall the passage in order, but was scored number of words correct regardless of order. The results are shown in Figure 14–1. Retention is positively related to order of approximation and inversely to length of passage. The reliability of the findings is

FIGURE 14–1

Recall of prose passages as a function of length of passage and approximation of the passage to the structure of the English language.

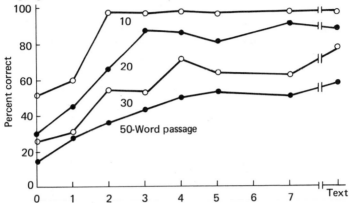

Order of approximation to statistical structure of English

Miller, G. A., & Selfridge, J. A. Verbal context and the recall of meaningful material. *American Journal of Psychology,* 1950, *63,* 176–185. Reprinted by permission of the University of Illinois Press.

shown in their replicability by others (Sharp, 1958; Richardson & Voss, 1960). Hanawalt and Diepenbrock (1965) asked if the Miller-Selfridge finding might not be a short-term retention effect that would change or even disappear with longer retention intervals. They used a 24-hour retention interval and found the same trend for order of approximation and length of passage as Miller and Selfridge found.

The Miller and Selfridge experiment is presented in considerable detail because it was the stimulus for the work on syntax and retention that followed. A problem with the Miller-Selfridge experiment for understanding the role of syntactical structure for retention is that it confounds syntactical and semantical structure—the higher the order of approximation the better the syntax and the greater the meaning. Epstein (1961) unscrambled the confounding by working with syntax alone, with meaning omitted. He used nonsense strings of syllables and words.

Table 14–1 has the categories of sentences that Epstein used. Category I was sentences made up of nonsense syllables, but with the addition of function words like articles, prepositions, and conjunctions. Grammatical tags, such as *ed* for past tense and *s* for plural, were also added. Category II was the same but without the grammatical tags. Category III was the same as Category I but with the items arranged in random order. Category IV was the same as Category I except the appended grammatical endings were shifted around in a manner inconsistent with

TABLE 14–1

Six categories of sentences used by Epstein (1961) in his study of the syntactical structure of sentences.

Category	Sentence	Mean trials to learn
I	A vapy koobs desaked the citar molently um glox nerfs.	5.8
II	a vap kook desak the citar molent um glox nerf	7.6
III	koobs vapy the um glox citar nerfs a molently	8.1
IV	A vapy koobed desaks the citar molents um glox nerfly.	6.9
V	Cruel tables sang falling circles to empty bitter pencils.	3.5
VI	sang tables bitter empty cruel to circles pencils falling	5.9

Epstein, W. The influence of syntactical structure on learning. *American Journal of Psychology*, 1961, 74, 80–85. Reprinted by permission of the University of Illinois Press.

English usage. Categories V and VI used meaningful words but were meaningless sentences. Category V, however, had word series with syntactical structure that were sentence-like, but Category VI did not.

Epstein had the sentence presented on a card for 7 seconds of study, and the subject was then given 30 seconds for recall in writing. The study–test procedure continued until the criterion of one perfect reproduction of the sentence was met. Presenting the sentence on a card for study is the *method of whole presentation,* and it is to be contrasted with serial presentation which some have used. In serial anticipation the items of the sentence are presented one at a time, in order, as with a memory drum.

Epstein's results are also shown in Table 14–1. First consider Categories I–IV with the nonsense syllables. Only Category I had sentences with syntactical structure commensurate with the English language, and they required the fewest trials to learn. Next, consider Categories V and VI. Category V had nonsensical sentences but with structure, and they were easier to learn than Category VI sentences, which did not. Epstein (1962, Experiment I) replicated the essentials of his 1961 experiment, as have others (see O'Connell, 1970, for a review).

Epstein demonstrated that syntax was a variable for sentence learning and recall, and Marks and Miller (1964) brought a measure of closure to the topic by showing the influences of both syntactic and semantic factors. Four kinds of word strings were used. *Normal sentences* were used, with proper syntax and meaning ("Pink bouquets emit fragrant odors"). A second kind of sentence was *semantically anamolous,* where the syntactic structure was the same as the normal sentences but it was meaningless ("Pink accidents cause sleeping storms"). Two nonsense strings of words were also formed as the other two kinds of word strings, and they were control conditions. One kind, called *anagram strings*, was a random rearrangement of the words of normal sentences ("Bouquets pink odors fragrant emit."). The other kind, called *word lists*, was a random rearrangement of the words of anamolous sentences ("Accidents pink storms sleeping cause."). Five trials were given, using aural presentation. Recall was immediate and in writing, by the method of free recall.

Figure 14–2 has the results in terms of complete word strings correctly recalled. The normal sentences with good syntax and meaning are recalled

FIGURE 14–2

Findings of an experiment which separate the influences of syntax and meaning on the recall of sentences.

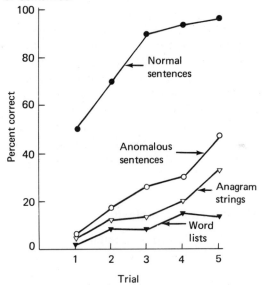

Marks, L. E., & Miller, G. A. The role of semantic and syntactic constraints in the memorization of English sentences. *Journal of Verbal Learning and Verbal Behavior,* 1964, *3*, 1–5. Reprinted by permission of Academic Press, Inc.

best of all. Next are anamolous sentences which are meaningless but have good syntax, and the two random strings without syntactical or semantical structure are the poorest of all. Both syntax and meaning are variables for the learning and recall of sentences. Slamecka (1969) obtained the same results as Marks and Miller by the method of recognition.

Strategies of learning.   Epstein (1961, p. 84) suggested that the syntactical organization of the material may affect the strategy of learning which, in turn, is a strong variable for retention (Chapters 7 and 11). Syntactically organized elements of a sentence group themselves into subsets, and grouping is a variable that is positively related to verbal retention (Bower, 1970). Low syntactic structure, on the other hand, could be inefficient grouping, and poorer learning and retention is the result.

There is indirect evidence for this strategy of learning hypothesis. Epstein (1962, Experiment II), in continuation of his work on syntactical structure, presented the elements of his nonsense strings one at a time, on a memory drum, for serial anticipation learning. In contrast to his earlier study (Epstein, 1961), which was reviewed above, no effects of syntactical structure on recall were found. An interpretation of this finding is that the element-by-element presentation on the memory drum broke up the beneficial groupings that syntactical structure provides, thus forcing a poorer strategy of learning and poorer recall. In indirect support of this hypothesis, O'Connell, Turner, and Onuska (1968) used auditory presentation and found that nonsense strings were recalled well when the intonational pattern of syntactically structured, normal English was used by the speaker. Strings spoken in a monotone were recalled less well, and the investigators hypothesize that intonation provides groupings of the elements beneficial for learning and recall. Speaking in a monotone destroyed the beneficial groupings in the same way that serial learning on the memory drum destroyed beneficial visual groupings in Epstein's study.

Effects of transformational complexity

Generative theory holds that the essential idea of the sentence resides in deep structure, and the surface structure of the sentence can reflect the basic meaning of the sentence rather directly or be one or more transformations of it. Miller (1962) took this assumption and turned it into a hypothesis about memory for sentences. He said that the learning of any sentence involves a recoding of it as a kernel sentence, and what is carried in memory is the kernel sentence plus a "footnote" about syntactic structure. If the sentence for remembering is: "The small boy wasn't liked by Joe," the subject would recode it as the kernel "Joe liked the small boy" plus a tag that it is a passive-negative transformation and is two transformations of the kernel. The semantic and the syntactic properties of a sentence are stored separately according to this hypothesis, and presumably can be forgotten independently. The subject might forget the transformations and remember the kernel, and so recall only the simple form of a complex sentence.

Mehler (1963) tested Miller's hypothesis, and the logic of his experiment is shown in Figure 14–3. A kernel sentence (K) can be transformed

FIGURE 14–3
Representation of the eight types of sentences that were used in the Mehler experiment. Seven transformations of a basic kernel sentence *(K)* were used. See text for explanation.

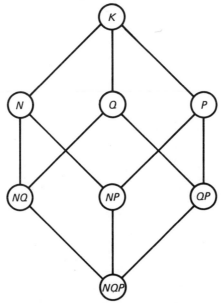

Mehler, J. Some effects of grammatical transformations on the recall of English sentences. *Journal of Verbal Learning and Verbal Behavior,* 1963, 2, 346–351. Reprinted by permission of Academic Press, Inc.

into passive (P), negative (N), interrogative (Q) form, or any combination of the three. The kernel sentence "The boy hit the ball" would have the negative form "The boy hasn't hit the ball." The passive form would be "The ball has been hit by the boy," and the interrogative form is "Has the ball been hit by the boy?" An example of a combination of the three basic transformations is the passive-negative-interrogative form "Hasn't the ball been hit by the boy?" Mehler used 8 kernel sentences and 7 transformations of each, and the 64 sentences were organized as 8 lists of 8 sentences, where no sentence or its transformation was represented more than once in a list. Presentation was auditory,

and five trials were administered. Recall after each trial was immediate
and in writing.

Mehler's results are shown in Figure 14–4, presented in terms of sentences correctly recalled. Retention differs for kernel sentences and their

FIGURE 14–4

Results of the Mehler experiment.

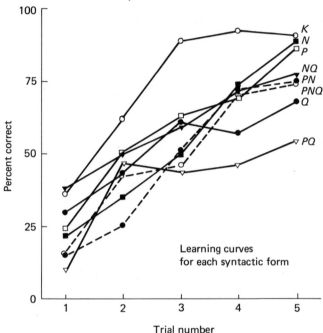

Mehler, J. Some effects of grammatical transformations on the
recall of English sentences. *Journal of Verbal Learning and Verbal
Behavior*, 1963, *2*, 346–351. Reprinted by permission of Academic
Press, Inc.

syntactical forms, as the hypothesis says. Kernel sentences are remembered the best of all, and the various transformations less well. The
data are not clear on how number and type of transformations are related
to retention.

Martin and Roberts (1966) ran an experiment similar to Mehler's
in design and purpose. They studied the immediate recall of kernel
sentences and five transformations of them, and they found that kernel
sentences were recalled the *poorest* of all. Similarly, Roberts (1968)
found passive sentences better retained than active (kernel) ones.

Another line of negative evidence was the pattern of errors which
Martin and Roberts (1966) found. They found that the most frequent
type of error was a sentence of the same kind as the sentence presented.

This should not be if sentence memory consists of a kernel sentence plus transformational tags. If one or more of the transformational tags were forgotten the remembered sentence should not be of the same form as originally learned, but it often was.

But why did Mehler (1963) find the best retention of kernel sentences and Martin and Roberts find the poorest retention of kernels? Martin and Roberts (1967) suggest it was because Mehler did not control for sentence length. Kernel sentences tended to have fewer words in the Mehler study, and as a consequence they were recalled better. To make this point, Martin and Roberts (1967) report an experiment where sentence length was the variable. Their sentences were either five, seven, or nine words in length, and they found the shorter the sentence the better the recall. Mehler's findings may be accounted for by sentence length.

Conclusion and critique. There is no evidence that Miller's hypothesis about sentence memory, derived from generative theory, is valid. This does not mean that sentence form is not a variable for the retention of sentences, but rather that the particular hypothesis about sentence form and memory derived from generative theory is invalid. One of the problems with the hypothesis is that the basic notion is wrong. The kernel sentence is supposed to represent the basic idea in deep structure, and syntactical transformations retain the idea but with change at the surface. This may not be so for all transformations. The kernel sentence "Joe liked the small boy" has the negative transformation "Joe didn't like the small boy." These two sentences connote entirely different behavior on the part of Joe, and so different ideas are represented in deep structure; they are not two reflections of the same idea. And this neglected logical difficulty is only one problem which generative theory has, even though it has been a stimulus for research in psychology. Generative theory may have a short theoretical life in psychology because it is not a psychological theory, despite psychological implications. Generative theory is a theory of grammar for an ideal speaker-listener, and as such it says little or nothing about the important kinds of behavioral topics that make psychology the challenge that it is—how meaning and syntax are learned, storage in memory, retrieval from memory, and so on. These criticisms notwithstanding, generative theory has done an important thing for psychology by reminding us that sentences can be novel. A main criticism of a behavioristic view of language, that used basic learning paradigms to explain sentence learning, is that it cannot account for sentence novelty. This is a good criticism. Standard learning paradigms require the repetition of events in experience, and a novel sentence has not had them. Perhaps learning psychologists have not worried enough about novel behavior, and yet does not concept behavior contain the power for novel responding?

The concept of triangularity gives us the power to recognize a version of a triangle that we have never experienced before, and the concept of twoness would give an astronaut the power to recognize two Martians that he has never encountered before. That a particular meaning can have many sentences representing it is, in principle, concept behavior. In effect, this position says that Chomsky's deep structure is a network of concepts, and they can be manifest in behavior in an enormous number of ways. Several analysts of generative theory have made this point (Broadbent, 1970; Black, 1970, p. 458; Bourne, Ekstrand, & Dominowski, 1970, p. 327; Siegel, 1973; Weimer, 1973). To say that creativity in language is a property which language has in common with concept behavior does not mean that language is the same as concept behavior. Nor is the converse that concept behavior is the same as language, necessarily true. In fact, it can be argued reasonably that a prelanguage child first acquires the meaning and relations of the world in her cognitive structure, and language is worked out in relation to it (MacNamara, 1972). Once language develops it can be an agent of thinking, but it is possible that the primary agents of thought are nonverbal. Paivio (1971, Chapter 13) argues that the image is this deep-lying, nonverbal agent.

On the empirical side, new methods are needed to investigate the strategies that are used in learning the sentence. The customary experimental procedure is to present the sentence as a whole for learning, and this gives the resourceful subject options in how to distribute study. If, say, the subject focuses primarily on the subject, verb, and object of the sentence, which a lifetime of verbal experience has taught conveys a lion's share of the information, then it is not surprising that a kernel sentence like "The boy hit the ball" is remembered better than the transform "Wasn't the ball hit by the boy?" The kernel sentence is a clean presentation of informational essentials, and to know them is to almost insure its high recall. A transformed sentence is different because it requires attention to informational essentials and to other sentence elements as well. How a subject will distribute attention and study of a relatively complex, transformed sentence is unknown, and we may not come to understand memory for sentences until the strategies of learning, as one determinant of sentence retention, are appreciated, investigated, and understood. The experiment on visual recognition by Loftus (1972) was discussed in Chapter 13, and it demonstrated that accuracy of recognition is positively related to number of eye fixations. Presumably, eye fixations mostly determine the regions of the visual scene which are registered in memory. There is no reason why the same should not be expected of a sentence or a prose passage. Words that are not fixated may be barely registered in memory. There is a substantial research literature on eye movements and reading, but the investigations were not motivated by memory theory and have not contributed to it. Some relevant work is beginning, however (Mehler, Bever, & Carey, 1967).

THE RETENTION OF INFERENCE

The studies that have been reviewed so far in this chapter have in common their concern with memory for the form and meaning of an individual sentence. Beyond the individual sentence is the processing of multiple sentences, which typically come to us in the form of prose. We can have the literal, exact learning of a prose passage (e.g., Cofer, 1941), but there is little modern-day interest in the rote learning of prose because prose is rarely processed that way. True, the rote memorization of lines is required of an actor, but our usual processing of prose is inferences about ideas, with little literal recollection. You read a novel and can give a summary of the plot, but the chances are high that you cannot remember a single sentence exactly.

The study of memory for prose dates to the 1890s and it has been investigated ever since. The best known of the older studies was by Bartlett (1932), who had his subjects study a folk tale and repeatedly recall it at irregular intervals. He had the theory that one remembers an abstraction or schema about the prose selections, and at recall will reconstruct the essentials of the story from the schema. Memory for prose is abstract, not the literal storage of information, according to Bartlett (for a contemporary position on schema, see Cofer, 1973; Flores D'Arcais, 1974). Welborn and English (1937) have a review of this early literature, and they refer to "logical memory," by which they mean "memory for connected material measured in terms of the 'substance' remembered." They place "logical memory" on one end of a continuum and "rote memory" for the isolated verbal unit on the other. The term "logical" has implications that go beyond memory, so in discussing these matters it is better to use *inferential memory*, which describes in a clearer way the process of inferring ideas from text.

The Bransford and Franks experiment

The modern revival of interest in memory, coupled with the renewal of psycholinguistics, has created thrusts which have brought new research to bear on inferential memory. Not all recent research has been done on prose, in the sense of several sentences comprising a passage. Instead, some of it has been done with complex sentences which have several components that express a complex idea, just as a prose passage. An experiment by Bransford and Franks (1971) exemplifies this approach.

The Bransford and Franks experiment is about idea acquisition, or inference, where the idea is embodied in a complex sentence like, "The ants in the kitchen ate the sweet jelly which was on the table." During the acquisition phase, where sentence material was presented for study, the subjects were never presented with the complex sentence, only lesser sentences which were presented nonconsecutively and which contained component ideas of the complex idea to be acquired. Instead of remembering the sentences that were presented in acquisition, the subject had to infer the complex idea from the component ideas. On the retention test, which was a recognition test, subjects were presented with OLD and NEW sentences, where OLD sentences had been presented in acquistion and NEW sentences had never been seen before but contained different amounts of the complex idea. Subjects should be able to recognize the NEW sentences which embody aspects of the complex idea if they had been assembling the meaning of the complex idea during acquisition. Irrelevant sentences, called NONCASE, were presented also as a baseline control condition. Table 14–2 is an example of sentences

TABLE 14–2
Sentences representing various degrees of the meaning in complex sentence "four."

FOUR:	The ants in the kitchen ate the sweet jelly which was on the table. (on recognition only)
THREES:	The ants ate the sweet jelly which was on the table. (on acquisition only)
	The ants in the kitchen ate the jelly which was on the table. (on acquisition only)
	The ants in the kitchen ate the sweet jelly. (on recognition only)
TWOS:	The ants in the kitchen ate the jelly. (on acquisition only)
	The ants ate the sweet jelly (on both acquisition and recognition)
	The sweet jelly was on the table. (on recognition only)
	The ants ate the jelly which was on the table. (on recognition only)
ONES:	The ants were in the kitchen. (on acquisition only)
	The jelly was on the table. (on acquisition only)
	The jelly was sweet. (on recognition only)
	The ants ate the jelly. (on recognition only)

Bransford, J. D., & Franks, J. J. The abstraction of linguistic ideas. *Cognitive Psychology,* 1971, *2*, 331–350. Reprinted by permission of Academic Press, Inc.

that were used in acquisition and recognition testing for one complex idea. A FOUR was the complex sentence which provided the complex idea. The ONES were simple declarative sentences drawn from FOUR. The TWOS were an embedding of two ONES, and THREES were an embedding of three ONES.

Bransford and Franks have their data in the form of a confidence rating in the recognition judgment. A +5 was a very high confidence that the sentence had been heard before, and a +1 was very low confidence. Similarly, —5 is very high confidence that the sentence had not been heard before, and —1 is very low confidence. Figure 14–5 shows

FIGURE 14–5
Rated on a ten-point scale, confidence in having experienced sentences that have various amounts of the ideas of a complex sentence (FOURS).

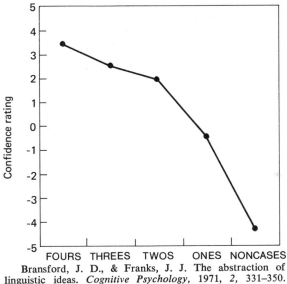

Bransford, J. D., & Franks, J. J. The abstraction of linguistic ideas. *Cognitive Psychology,* 1971, *2,* 331–350. Reprinted by permission of Academic Press, Inc.

the results in terms of these confidence ratings. Notice that there is no recognition of the irrelevant NONCASE sentences, which is expected, and that the more elaborate the sentence and the more components of the complex idea that are present the better the recognition. Many NEW sentences received positive ratings, indicating that subjects thought they had heard the sentences during acquisition. Actually, whether a sentence was OLD or NEW made little difference in the rating. The memory storage was in terms of ideas, not representations of particular sentences. These findings speak for an active mind that

is receiving and organizing the language information into an idea structure which is later used to judge new information.

Relative importance of different ideas

The foregoing experiments by Bransford and Franks dealt with component ideas of a whole idea, and did not treat the differential weighting
of component ideas. Do subjects judge some ideas more important than
others and process them more thoroughly? Johnson (1970) had his
subjects learn prose passages which independent raters had categorized into linguistic "units" of seven to eight words between which
the reader might pause to catch a breath, give emphasis to the story,
or enhance meaning. Other raters then classified the importance of these
units for the theme of the passage into six categories. Acquisition was
reading the story twice, and recall was in writing after retention intervals
of 15 minutes, 7 days, 21 days, or 63 days. The results of one of his
experiments are shown in Figure 14–6, with the recall protocol scored
in terms of the linguistic units and their importance. Recall declined
with length of the retention interval, which is a routine finding, but
recall was positively related to the importance of the unit, which is
a new finding.

FIGURE 14–6

Recall as a function of importance of the ideas in a prose passage.
The curve parameter is retention interval.

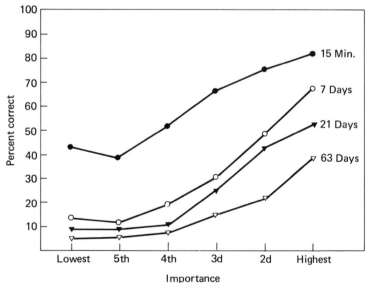

Johnson, R. E. Recall of prose as a function of the structural importance
of the linguistic units. *Journal of Verbal Learning and Verbal Behavior,*
1970, *9,* 12–20. Reprinted by permission of Academic Press, Inc.

An obvious explanation for this finding of Johnson's is that subjects were spending more study time on the important units. If so, this would reduce the significance of the findings because it would mean that retention is a positive function of study time, a generalization which has been with us since Ebbinghaus. To control for study time, Johnson performed another experiment where presentation of the linguistic units was with a slide projector and controlled. Recall was immediate or after 21 days, and the results are presented in Figure 14–7. Even with presenta-

FIGURE 14–7
Immediate and delayed recall (21 days) as a function of importance of the ideas in a prose passage. The study time for the words of the passage that contained each idea was controlled.

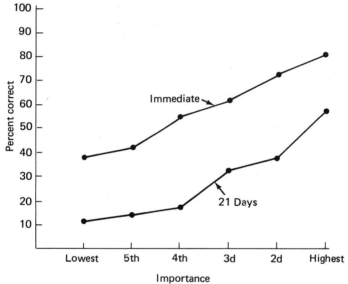

Johnson R. E. Recall of prose as a function of the structural importance of the linguistic units. *Journal of Verbal Learning and Verbal Behavior,* 1970, *9,* 12–20. Reprinted by permission of Academic Press, Inc.

tion time controlled, importance is a variable. In a manner unknown, the human weighs the relative importance of ideas while reading a prose passage, and the processing which he gives them on the basis of his weighting is a variable for retention.

RETRIEVAL FROM SEMANTIC MEMORY

Psychologists of today are less inclined to talk about short-term and long-term memory than they were a few years ago, but if they had the inclination they would classify the study of sentences and prose as mostly the study of long-term verbal memory (Chapter 9). Instead of long-term verbal memory, however, the talk is often about *semantic memory*. In terms of the levels of processing point of view discussed in Chapter 9, semantic memory is memory's deepest level. Investigators of semantic memory are little concerned with learning, it seems. The material in semantic memory is accepted as the fully learned product of life's verbal experiences, and the concern is with its organization, its retrieval, and its use. As the name implies, semantic memory is concerned with the organization of words and their meanings.

Cognitive viewpoint

Retrieval time has been a primary way of studying the organization of semantic memory, and its first major use was in test of a model by Collins and Quillian (1969). Retrieval time is the reaction time used by a subject to ascertain the truth or falsity of a sentence, such as A CANARY CAN FLY. If the subject believed the sentence to be true, she would press a button with one hand, and if she thought it to be false she would press a second button with the other hand. The model that was tested is shown in Figure 14–8. The model is a hierarchical or network model which assumes that the descriptive concrete properties of CANARY are stored immediately along with it, and that more abstract

FIGURE 14–8
A network model of semantic memory. It is assumed that longer processing times are associated with higher positions in the hierarchy.

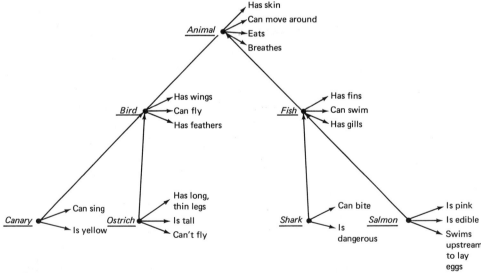

Collins, A. M., and Quillian, M. R. Retrieval time from semantic memory. *Journal of Learning and Verbal Behavior*, 1969, *8*, 240–247. Reprinted by permission of Academic Press, Inc.

properties are stored more remotely. The higher the position in the hierarchy the longer the reaction time to decide about the truth of a sentence. Following Figure 14–8, the sentence A CANARY CAN SING should have the fastest reaction time of all, A CANARY CAN FLY should have a somewhat slower reaction time because flying is a more general property associated with all birds, and A CANARY HAS SKIN should have the slowest time because it requires the abstract knowledge that a canary is an animal and that all animals have skin. All of this seems like an orderly dictionary rather than human memory, which can be anything but orderly, but this should not altogether upset testing of the hierarchical arrangement of knowledge, which is the model's main property. That the model has some justification is found in the positive results which Collins and Quillian obtained. The sentence A CANARY CAN SING had the fastest reaction time, with A CANARY CAN FLY being about 75 milliseconds slower, and A CANARY HAS SKIN being about 75 milliseconds slower still. A false sentence like A CANARY HAS GILLS had a relatively slow reaction time, about the same as A CANARY HAS SKIN. Collins and Quillian surmised that a decision about a false sentence requires the search through several levels in an attempt to verify the assertion and, when verification fails, a false response is reported. Searching through several levels takes more time in the model, and so false sentences have longer reaction times.

Rips, Shoben, and Smith (1973) were not content with the network model of Collins and Quillian because of its rationality where "memory structure mirrors logical structure, and logically valid relations can be read directly from the structure of stored semantic information" (p. 3). They wanted a model that was more psychological, without a dictionary-like quality, and their solution was the concept of *semantic distance*. What they call the "semantic distance effect" is that verification time increases as a function of the relatedness of the two main words in a sentence like A CANARY IS A BIRD. The sentence A CANARY IS A BIRD would be expected to have a faster reaction time than A CANARY IS AN ANIMAL because CANARY-BIRD are more related than CANARY-ANIMAL. Determining relatedness or semantic distance, is a matter of having subjects scale various word pairs, which Rips et al. did, and they found that reaction time was related to semantic distance, as they had hypothesized. In a subsequent paper (Smith, Shoben, and Rips, 1974) the position was taken that the semantic distance of word pairs is more fundamentally a function of the *semantic features* which the words have in common. Semantic features are all of the defining characteristics of a word, and some are more salient than others in a hierarchy of features that define the word, according to Smith et al. The reason that CANARY-BIRD has less semantic distance than CANARY-ANIMAL is that CANARY and BIRD have more features in common than CANARY and ANIMAL and so, for the same reason, the reaction time in verifying A CANARY IS A BIRD is faster than that for A CANARY IS AN ANIMAL. Semantic features have their problems, not the least being that they can have the rational dictionary as their source and not be empirically determined by the direct observation of imperfect human behavior. Semantic distance is an attempted escape from the dictionary of the Collins and Quillian network model, but the use of hierarchies of semantic features to explain semantic distance risks a turn toward the dictionary again. Empirical methods for determining features are under development, however (Perfetti, 1972).

Associative viewpoint

Semantic memory and retrieval from it is in the cognitive tradition, but a worthwhile question is to ask what the older associative view, with its emphasis on isolated verbal units, has to offer. We saw in Chapter 7 that association had its origins in antiquity, flowered as a theory of thought under British Associationism in the 17th–19th centuries, and was the goad for so much of the work on verbal associative learning that has been done. It is good science to ask what the associative view has to say about the kinds of data which are in evidence of retrieval from semantic memory. The pitting of rival viewpoints against one another always produces greater scientific advance than asserting one view or the other and doing experiments about it. So far, associative and cognitive views of verbal thought processes have confronted each other little in the laboratory. Clustering in free recall is often given a cognitive interpretation in terms of the organizing powers of the mind, and in Chapter 7 we saw experimental efforts, of some success, to explain clustering in terms of associations. Confrontation research of this sort is interesting and atypical.

Rips, Shoben, and Smith (1973) scaled word pairs for "relatedness," using a four-point rating scale, and the rating values were correlated with reaction time measures and became the basis of semantic distance, and more fundamentally semantic features, as theory. But the words of a pair can be associates of one another or have associations in common, so the question is: Are semantic features or associations the fundamental explanation? One way to look at semantic features is that they are the associations which two words have in common. The word pair CANARY-BIRD have the feature wings in common, but if we asked subjects to give words in free association to CANARY and BIRD it is likely that WINGS would be among them.

Cofer (1957) was the first to show that rated similarity of word pairs and number of associations which the pairs held in common were highly correlated, and he observed that the study "should help to determine to what extent the association-oriented and the meaning-oriented investigators are talking about the same thing" (p. 603). Cofer's study does not stand alone. Garskof and Houston (1963; 1965) also found high relationships between rated similarity and number of associations which the two words had in common. While it is true that Rips, Shoben, and Smith (1973) had their subjects rate pairs for "relatedness" rather than "similarity," it is likely that subjects would rate pairs for relatedness and similarity in about the same way. Underwood and Schulz (1960, Chapter 2) summarize the evidence which shows that the seemingly different ways of scaling verbal materials can be highly correlated. The implication is that the scaled relatedness of word pairs, which is the empirical index of semantic distance and number of semantic features, is highly correlated with the number of associations which word pairs have in common, and so the cognitive and the associative viewpoints are tangled.

Another line of evidence which the advocates of semantic memory should face is associative reaction time, or the time taken to give a word in free association to a verbal stimulus. The research on retrieval from semantic memory is mostly founded on simple sentences like A CANARY IS A BIRD. If the mental process of verifying the truth of this sentence is a subject's testing to see if BIRD is an associate of CANARY, then the reaction time data in semantic memory experiments have association as the primary cause. The sentence A CANARY IS A BIRD has a faster reaction time than A CANARY IS AN ANIMAL, but Marbe's Law could account for this finding. Marbe's Law is an old relationship in psychology (Woodworth, 1938, p. 360), and it says that the more frequently a response is given by subjects in a free association test the faster its associative reaction time. BIRD would certainly be a more common associate of the stimulus CANARY than ANIMAL, and so its reaction time would be faster, according to Marbe's Law.

SUMMARY

There is a lively interest in memory for conventional units of the natural language, with the sentence and the prose passage being the elements of study. Because of the concern with natural language, contemporary research is closely in touch with developments in linguistics and psycholinguistics. There is a strong interest in Chomsky's generative theory. Learning psychologists have theorized that the sentence is a learned chaining of verbal response elements, but generative theory rejects this position because it fails to account for the obvious fact that we can speak sentences that have never been spoken before. How could they have been learned? Generative theory expresses the versatility and complexity of a sentence in terms of deep structure, surface structure, and transformational rules. Deep structure is the fundamental meaning of a sentence; surface structure is the particular form that the sentence takes when it is physically expressed; and transformational rules express the relationship between deep structure and surface structure. Experimental tests of generative theory have not always been confirming, but it has been a stimulus for psychological research on language and has pressed psychologists to consider new topics. Other developments in the psychology of language are the retention of inferences from sentences rather than the literal retention of sentences, and conceptions of semantic memory which ask how verbal events, concepts, and thoughts are organized.

REFERENCES

Bartlett, F. C.   *Remembering: A study in experimental and social psychology.* Cambridge: Cambridge University Press, 1932.

Black, M.   Comment on "Problems of Explanation in Linguistics" by N. Chomsky. In R. Borger & F. Cioffi (Eds.), *Explanation in the behavioural sciences.* London: Cambridge University Press, 1970, pp. 452–461.

Bourne, L. E., Ekstrand, B. R., & Dominowski, R. L.   *The psychology of thinking.* Englewood Cliffs: Prentice-Hall, 1971.

Bower, G. A.   Organization factors in memory. *Cognitive psychology,* 1970, *1,* 18–46.

Bransford, J. D., & Franks, J. J.   The abstraction of linguistic ideas. *Cognitive Psychology,* 1971, *2,* 331–350.

Broadbent, D. E.   In defence of empirical psychology. *Bulletin of the British Psychological Society,* 1970, *23,* 87–96.

Chomsky, N.   *Syntactic structures.* The Hague: Mouton, 1957.

Chomsky, N.   Verbal behavior (a review). *Language,* 1959, *35,* 26–58.

Chomsky, N.   *Aspects of the theory of syntax.* Cambridge: M. I. T. Press, 1965.

Cofer, C. N.   A comparison of logical and verbatim learning of prose passages of different lengths. *American Journal of Psychology,* 1941, *54,* 1–20.

Cofer, C. N.   Associative commonality and rated similarity of certain words from Haagen's list. *Psychological Reports,* 1957, *3,* 603–606.

Cofer, C. N.   Constructive processes in memory. *American Scientist,* 1973, *61,* 537–543.

Collins, A. M., & Quillian, M. R.   Retrieval time from semantic memory. *Journal of Verbal Learning and Verbal Behavior,* 1969, *8,* 240–247.

Epstein, W.   The influence of syntactical structure on learning. *American Journal of Psychology,* 1961, *74,* 80–85.

Epstein, W.   A further study of the influence of syntactical structure on learning. *American Journal of Psychology,* 1962, *75,* 121–126.

Flores D'Arcais, G. B.   Is there memory for sentences? *Acta Psychologica,* 1974, *38,* 33–58.

Garskof, B. E., & Houston, J. P. Measurement of verbal relatedness: An idiographic approach. *Psychological Review,* 1963, *70,* 277–288.

Garskof, B. E., & Houston, J. P. The relationship between judged meaning similarity, associative probability, and associative overlap. *Psychological Reports,* 1965, *16,* 220–222.

Hanawalt, N. G., & Diepenbrock, E. C. Verbal context and meaning in immediate and delayed recall. *Journal of General Psychology,* 1965, *73,* 125–135.

Johnson, R. E. Recall of prose as a function of the structural importance of the linguistic units. *Journal of Verbal Learning and Verbal Behavior,* 1970, *9,* 12–20.

Loftus, G. R. Eye fixations and recognition memory for pictures. *Cognitive psychology,* 1972, *3,* 525–551.

MacNamara, J. Cognitive basis of language learning in infants. *Psychological Review,* 1972, *79,* 1–13.

Marks, L. E., & Miller, G. A. The role of semantic and syntactic constraints in the memorization of English sentences. *Journal of Verbal Learning and Verbal Behavior,* 1964, *3,* 1–5.

Martin, E., & Roberts, K. H. Grammatical factors in sentence retention. *Journal of Verbal Learning and Verbal Behavior,* 1966, *5,* 211–218.

Martin, E., & Roberts, K. H. Sentence length and sentence retention in the free-learning situation. *Psychonomic Science,* 1967, *8,* 535–536.

Mehler, J. Some effects of grammatical transformations on the recall of English sentences. *Journal of Verbal Learning and Verbal Behavior,* 1963, *2,* 346–351.

Mehler, J., Bever, T. G., & Carey, P. What we look at when we read. *Perception & Psychophysics,* 1967, *2,* 213–218.

Miller, G. A. Some psychological studies of grammar. *American Psychologist,* 1962, *17,* 748–762.

Miller, G. A. Some preliminaries to psycholinguistics. *American Psychologist,* 1965, *20,* 15–20.

Miller, G. A., & Isard, S. Some perceptual consequences of linguistic rules. *Journal of Verbal Learning and Verbal Behavior,* 1963, *2,* 217–228.

Miller, G. A., & Selfridge, J. A. Verbal context and the recall of meaningful material. *American Journal of Psychology,* 1950, *63,* 176–185.

Mowrer, O. H. The psychologist looks at language. *American Psychologist,* 1954, *9,* 660–694.

O'Connell, D. C. Facilitation of recall by linguistic structure in nonsense strings. *Psychological Bulletin,* 1970, *74,* 441–452.

O'Connell, D. C., Turner, E. A., & Onuska, L. A. Intonation, grammatical structure, and contextual association in immediate recall. *Journal of Verbal Learning and Verbal Behavior,* 1968, *7,* 110–116.

Paivio, A. *Imagery and verbal processes.* New York: Holt, Rinehart and Winston, 1971.

Perfetti, C. A.   Psychosemantics: Some cognitive aspects of structural meaning. *Psychological Bulletin,* 1972, *78,* 241–259.

Richardson, P., & Voss, J. F.   Replication report: Verbal context and the recall of meaningful material. *Journal of Experimental Psychology,* 1960, *60,* 417–418.

Rips, L. J., Shoben, E. J., & Smith, E. E.   Semantic distance and the verification of semantic relations. *Journal of Verbal Learning and Verbal Behavior,* 1973, *12,* 1–20.

Roberts, K. H.   Grammatical and associative constraints in sentence retention. *Journal of Verbal Learning and Verbal Behavior,* 1968, 7, 1072–1076.

Sharp, H. C.   Effect of contextual constraint upon recall of verbal passages. *American Journal of Psychology,* 1958, *71,* 568–572.

Siegel, L. S.   The relationship of language and thought in the young child: The case of quantity concepts. Paper presented at 1973 meeting of The Psychonomic Society, St. Louis, Missouri.

Skinner, B. F.   *Verbal behavior.* New York: Appleton-Century-Crofts, 1957.

Slamecka, N. J.   Recognition of word strings as a function of linguistic violations. *Journal of Experimental Psychology,* 1969, 79, 377–378.

Smith, E. E., Shoben, E. J., & Rips, L. J.   Structure and process in semantic memory: A featural model for semantic decisions. *Psychological Review,* 1974, *81,* 214–241.

Underwood, B. J., and Schulz, R. W.   *Meaningfulness and verbal learning.* New York: Lippincott, 1960.

Weimer, W. B.   Psycholinguistics and Plato's paradoxes of the *Meno. American Psychologist,* 1973, *28,* 15–34.

Welborn, E. L., & English, H.   Logical learning and retention: A general review of experiments with meaningful verbal materials. *Psychological Bulletin,* 1937, *34,* 1–20.

Woodworth, R. S.   *Experimental psychology,* New York: Holt, 1938.

Indexes

Author Index

Blodgett, H. C., 65–66, 86
Bobrow, S. A., 182, 188, 194, 238, 240
Boice, R., 158, 168
Boies, S. J., 244, 263
Bolles, R. C., 61, 86, 155, 158, 168
Boren, J. J., 26–27, 48
Boucher, J.-L., 208–9, 217
Bourne, L. E., 208, 217, 356, 366
Bousfield, W. A., 189, 194
Bower, G. H., 182, 187–88, 194, 238
    240, 276, 279–82, 352, 366
Bowman, J. P., 215, 217–18
Bransford, J. D., 357–60, 366
Bray, N. W., 205, 217, 327, 340
Bregman, A. S., 355, 340
Breland, K., 154, 168
Breland, M., 154, 168
Briggs, G. E., 287–88, 291, 294, 311
Broadbent, D. E., 356, 366
Brogden, W. J., 123–24, 147
Brower, J. V. Z., 158, 168
Brower, L. P., 158, 168
Brown, J., 226, 228, 240, 267–68, 282,
    290, 311
Brown, J. S., 82, 86, 126–27, 147
Brown, T., 171
Brownstein, J. A., 73, 87
Bruce, D., 316, 340
Bruce, D. R., 190, 194
Brush, E. S., 157, 169
Bryden, M. P., 248, 263
Buell, J. S., 38–39, 49
Bugelski, B. R., 54, 60, 86, 279, 282
Bunderson, C. V., 208, 217
Burnand, G., 111, 115
Burns, V. D., 250, 262
Burwitz, L., 256, 261
Butler, R. A., 79–84, 86

C

Calkins, M. W., 174, 194
Campbell, C. B. G., 152, 155, 163, 168
Capaldi, E. G., 31–32, 48
Carey, P., 357, 367
Carmon, A., 258–59, 261
Carmona, A., 106–7, 117
Cason, H., 197–99, 207, 219
Chait, H., 333–35, 342
Chance, J. E., 317, 341
Charness, N., 335, 340
Chase, W. G., 244, 262
Chhina, G. S., 113, 115
Cho, C., 157, 168
Chomsky, N., 344–47, 356, 366
Church, R. M., 121–22, 147
Cicero, 274–76, 283
Cieutat, V. J., 176–77, 194

Clark, H. J., 317, 328, 340
Clayton, T., 320–22, 324, 342
Cofer, C. N., 190–92, 194, 316, 340, 357,
    364–66
Cohen, B., 215, 218
Cohen, B. D., 69–71, 73, 86
Cohen, B. H., 189, 194
Cohen, E., 69–71, 73, 86
Collins, A. M., 362–63, 366
Collins, J. F., 246–47, 262
Combs, C. M., 215, 217–18
Conezio, J., 317, 319, 342
Conrad, R., 231, 240, 250–51, 254, 261
Coquery, J.-M., 259, 261
Corballis, M. C., 338, 340–41
Coriell, A. S., 228, 240, 243–49, 261
Cowen, G. N., Jr., 253, 262
Cowles, J. T., 54, 87
Craig, H. B., 40, 48
Craik, F. I. M., 234, 236–40, 251–52, 261,
    267–68, 283
Croll, W. L., 208, 218
Crowder, R. G., 237, 240, 249, 253–55,
    262
Csapo, K., 328, 342
Culler, E., 123–24, 147
Cunitz, A. R., 232–34, 240
Cunningham, K., 339, 341

D

Dallenbach, K. M., 298–300, 312
Daly, H. B., 57, 87
D'Amato, M. R., 158, 168
Daniel, T. C., 328, 341
Darwin, C. R., 152–53, 162
Davis, J. N., 216, 219
Dember, W. N., 84, 87
DeNike, L. D., 71–73, 87, 89
Deno, S. L., 328, 341
Denny, M. R., 77, 89
DeRosa, D. V., 338, 342
DiCara, L. V., 107–10, 116–17
Diepenbrock, E. C., 349, 367
Dijkstra, S., 259–57, 261
Dittmer, D. G., 103, 116
Dodd, D. H., 208, 217
Dominowski, R. L., 356, 366
Drabman, R., 43, 50
Dragoin, W. B., 157, 169
Dworkin, B. R., 110, 117
Dyal, J. A., 25, 48

E

Ebbinghaus, H., 171–73, 194, 196,
    225–26, 240, 361
Egger, M. D., 59, 87, 137, 148

Subject index

*This book has been set in 10 and 9 point
Caledonia, leaded 2 points. Part and chapter
numbers are 24 point Helvetica (large) and
30 point Helvetica. Part titles are 24 point
Helvetica (large) and chapter titles are 24
point Helvetica (small). The size of the type
page is 27 × 45½ picas.*